SOLA · PROBA · QUÆ · HONESTA

Julius Arthur Sheffield Neave

A SENSE *of* SECURITY:
150 YEARS *of* PRUDENTIAL

———

A SENSE *of* SECURITY:
150 YEARS *of*
PRUDENTIAL

Laurie Dennett

Now, if as I believe to be indisputable, a sense of security
is one of the very first requisites both for material improvement and
mental development, whatever creates or strengthens that sense of
security is an important element of human progress.

Lord Derby

GRANTA EDITIONS

Published by Granta Editions
25–27 High Street, Chesterton, Cambridge CB4 1ND,
United Kingdom.

Granta Editions is a wholly owned imprint of Book Production Consultants plc

First published in 1998
© Prudential Corporation plc, 1998
142 Holborn Bars, London EC1N 2NH, United Kingdom.

A CIP catalogue record for this book is available from the British Library.

ISBN 1 85757 060 X

Edited by Alison Leach.
Designed by Peter Dolton.
Design, editorial and production in association with
Book Production Consultants plc, 25–27 High Street, Chesterton,
Cambridge CB4 1ND, United Kingdom.
Reprographics in Great Britain by Z2, Thetford, Norfolk, United Kingdom.
Printed in Great Britain by Jarrold Book Printers, Thetford, Norfolk, United Kingdom.

Contents

Foreword

In commissioning *A Sense of Security* we were anxious to produce a book which was objective, informative and, perhaps most difficult of all, interesting to a wide audience that has known the Prudential over the years – as customers, employees, policy makers and decision takers. The reason for such concern is that Prudential is demonstrably more than just another company.

For much of its 150 years Prudential has been a national institution. Most people share the collective memory of 'The Man from the Pru' and the Company has, in a unique way, mirrored the development of welfare and savings provision in the United Kingdom.

This corporate history is therefore of greater interest than most and, in Laurie Dennett's research and writing, I believe we have secured the definitive account of the first 150 years of one of Britain's best known companies – and of the evolution of the life assurance industry here and in those other markets where Prudential has been present.

One of the Company's enduring strengths is its ability to adapt to change and indeed, in many instances, to pre-empt it. Even as this book is being published, the United Kingdom and the European Union are considering how best to restructure both pensions and long-term savings to take account of the changing patterns of employment, demography and the realities of a global market place.

Prudential remains close to these debates and continues to play an active role in proposing how we might anticipate and adjust to such developments in a way which benefits all. Prudential's recent acquisition of Scottish Amicable and its growth in the UK and Asian markets are other indications that the

Company recognises that it needs continually to adapt and grow, sometimes organically, sometimes by acquisition and, particularly in Asian markets, by a strategic combination of the two.

A Sense of Security is a book which I believe will endure as an historical statement and as an absorbing account of a great company which, despite the many changes it has faced, retains its distinctive identity to take it forward into the next millennium.

Sir Peter Davis
Group Chief Executive

May 1998

Acknowledgements

Many people and institutions have contributed to the information gathered together in this book, and were I to acknowledge them all the list would run to several pages. Some, nonetheless, deserve special mention. Chief among them are the long-serving former members of management who, at my request, read the successive chapters as they appeared: Sir Brian Corby, Ron Artus, Ronald Skerman and Derek Fellows. With characteristic generosity, Derek Fellows answered many queries on actuarial matters and read the final text, besides producing the account of Group Pensions that forms Chapter Nineteen. Mick Newmarch, Peter Rawson, Gwes Lloyd and Jeremy Wyatt commented on parts of the draft, while Damian Leeson's help during the production stage was invaluable. The Prudential's former Archivist, Peter Traynor, offered much helpful comment on the text, based on his wide knowledge of the Prudential. To Jennie Campbell, who took over as Archivist in October 1995, and her assistant, Victoria Killick, thanks are due for facilitating my research in specific areas and helping with the illustrations. I should especially like to acknowledge the more than 75 retired Prudential staff who granted me interviews, and so helped to bring alive the period between 1925 and the present. Grateful thanks are also due to Stephanie Zarach, Jo Potier, Sue Gray and Peter Dolton of Book Production Consultants, and to Alison Leach as editor.

The Prudential Archives are voluminous, but far from complete. Outside the Company, the assistance of the following in filling some of the gaps was greatly appreciated: Birkbeck College; the University of Birmingham Archives; the British Library; Cambridge University Library; the Local Studies Collection of Camden Public Library, Swiss Cottage; the Carpenters' Company; the Library of the Chartered Insurance Institute; the Clothworkers' Company; the Fawcett Library; the Genealogical Society; the Greater London Record Office; Guildhall Library; the House of Lords Record Office; the Institute of Actuaries; the Archives of King's College, University of London; the National Union of Insurance Workers (especially Michael McLoughlin); the *Post Magazine*; the Library of the Royal Institute of British Architects; the Archives of St Mary's Hospital, Paddington; the Library of the United Grand Lodge of England; the Central Reference Library, Westminster Public Library; the West Sussex Record Office.

Laurie Dennett

May 1998

SECTION ONE

——

The Early Years

A Background Sketch

I T is self-evident that all things great must once have been small. In the case of a company regarded as a national institution for two-thirds of its 150-year existence, the discovery of just how small it once was may be as surprising as the facts of its present immensity. The company known worldwide as 'the Prudential' – or in the United Kingdom, where at one time every third household was insured with it, as 'the Pru' – began with less capital than optimism, after a false start, at a less than auspicious time and in an insignificant place. Today it is one of the world's largest and strongest financial services groups, for much of this century Britain's biggest institutional investor, and its major provider of life assurance, pensions and allied financial services. Describing how those obscure and tentative beginnings led, over the course of a century and a half, to the colossal corporation of today, is the business of this book.

The England which formed the backdrop for the creation of the Prudential was the most prosperous nation in the world. An economy based on agriculture was still undergoing the process of transformation to one based on industry that had been gaining momentum since the eighteenth century. The expansion of the iron and textile industries and the construction of a vast railway network were changing the face of the country and the habits of the people, at the same time as they generated wealth at home and abroad.[1] The pace of change was rapid, and its impact felt most forcibly by people adapting to life in the burgeoning industrial towns of the North and the Midlands, having abandoned or lost their livelihoods on the land. By the middle of the nineteenth century, for the first time, more people were living in urban areas than rural – a condition no other nation would achieve until after 1900.[2]

There was probably no aspect of life that during the period from the 1830s to the 1870s was unaffected by the march of industrial change. Social mobility, patterns and causes of mortality, transport and leisure, manufacturing, working conditions, public health and in due course education and culture – all were profoundly altered. Since change, innovation and expansion usually involve a degree of risk, it is hardly surprising that this period also witnessed the development of the means for the management of risk: the proliferation of insurance, in other words, of all types – marine, fire and life. It is life assurance and, in particular, what came to be called industrial life assurance, that is most significant in the early history of the Prudential.

The effects of industrialisation were accompanied by economic fluctuations and, inevitably, social tensions. By the end of the 1840s, an increasingly prosperous and self-confident middle class had exerted sufficient organised pressure to obtain the vote, and to establish free trade, with the signal victory of Corn Law repeal, as the creed that would dominate economic thought to the end of the century. Belief in progress, based on the evidence of practical improvements in many areas of life and in their own resulting comfort, was central to the outlook of most middle-class people. Though generalisations are dangerous, it might safely be said that the masses enjoyed little of the confidence, in either their material circumstances or their outlook, of the socially and economically better off. Politically they were voteless, but their aspirations found expression

Town and country, 1840: a pastoral idyll threatened by the march of industrialisation.

in early attempts at collective bargaining and, on a larger and more organised scale, in Chartism. The depression of the early 1840s and the internal disunity of labouring-class movements combined to defuse popular discontent, but could not disguise the fact that the working classes had benefited from industrial expansion to a very limited extent.[3]

The quality of working-class lives depended only in part on whether people were skilled or not, on their particular trade, or on where they lived. In contrast, sudden changes of circumstance over which they had no control could herald economic disaster: poor harvests that sent the price of bread skyrocketing, as in 1842, or the sudden loss of employment.[4] People who had difficulty even making ends meet had nothing to put aside to tide them over a lean time. The illness or death of the breadwinner was often the first step in a family's descent into the abyss of poverty. In times of destitution, as in infirmity and old age, there was one final, dreaded recourse: the workhouse, and relief under the hated Poor Law of 1834. Worse than the shame of the workhouse was the shame – should someone die with no-one to bury him – of the 'pauper funeral', or 'being buried on the parish'.

The dread of the pauper funeral – the ultimate social disgrace – haunted working people and ran very deep. It had its roots in the basic human instinct to honour the dead, but among the poor, this frequently took the form of a show of mourning far grander than any celebration the departed had enjoyed in life. Not only did they wish to provide grave-clothes, a coffin and a funeral that fitly expressed devotion, but mourning clothes for the grieving family and a funeral feast for friends and neighbours. The cost of all this was a considerable sacrifice even for those employed in some stable trade. For families whose collective income barely assured subsistence, there was no alternative but to sell their few possessions or send a loved one to a common grave.

Earlier, when most labour was still agricultural, local co-operative societies of working men had formed to provide mutual help with funeral expenses and sometimes a grant to a stricken family. In the case of these 'burial clubs', small weekly (or at least regular) contributions were paid into a common fund, which was drawn upon when a member or one of his dependants died. The funding of communal self-help and educational initiatives by penny-a-week contributions was a working-class tradition. While the 'burial clubs' only provided a sum to cover funeral expenses, the so-called 'friendly societies' might in addition promise regular payments during a time of sickness, or in old age. Such societies were permitted as long as they did not attempt any collective betterment of the working conditions of their members. Until 1824, when certain laws were repealed, self-help could not extend to 'combination' – the ancestor of modern trade unionism.[5]

This simple, age-old system, like so much else that was traditional, broke down under relentless industrialisation. Once, a rural labourer might have spent his entire life in the locality where he was born, his work varying with the seasons, and have been buried in the parish churchyard, as was his right. As mills and factories sprang up to enlarge the industrial towns, he and his family might move to one of them, where the clock and the factory whistle governed the day. The attraction of regular work outweighed the crowded conditions, dangerous machinery, noise, heat and dirt of the factory or the mill. One of the benefits forfeited in the move to the factory town would have been the contributions made to the local burial club or friendly society. If a man joined a burial club in his new locality, he might have to face a waiting period of a year before any claim would be accepted. The fear of dying without the means to ensure a proper funeral was as much a feature of his new life as of the old. In an environment where there might well be a higher risk of illness or accident, he was less protected than ever.

Fear of the workhouse and being buried 'on the parish' fostered the rise of 'burial clubs' promising the poor a sum sufficient for a decent funeral in exchange for a small weekly premium.

There thus evolved, in the period from about 1815 to the 1830s, the federated friendly societies with branches dotted all over one area of the country, or with a country-wide network of branches. They arose first in the areas where the impact of industrialisation had been felt earliest, such as Lancashire and the West Riding of Yorkshire.[6] They allowed for the movement of labour and provided a mechanism for working men to build up savings during the whole of their active lives. Their branches, or 'lodges', increased greatly in number between 1835 and 1845, a particularly difficult period for working people, especially in industrial districts.[7] There were still plenty of the older, local burial clubs and friendly societies to rival them, however, and the problems inherent in both types of organisation often continued to provide one more element of uncertainty in the lives of labouring people. Both kinds of organisation – and there were many sub-types within each category – were expressions of the far larger working-class culture whose ideals were communal and resolutely independent of outside influences. As such, they were preferred (despite the frequency with which they foundered) to well-meant efforts on the part of the rural gentry, clergymen or middle-class philanthropists to improve or replace them.[8]

The burial clubs, which employed men to go from door to door collecting the members' contributions, restricted themselves to assuring the modest sums necessary to cover funeral expenses.[9] All members, whatever their age and state of health at the time of joining, paid the same subscription. The difficulties came when members advanced in years began to die off. Since accumulated funds were not invested and consisted solely of the total of small contributions, a run of lump-sum funeral payments could bankrupt a fund, robbing the younger members – those of 40 or 50 – of their savings. Many clubs collapsed in this way after long periods of apparent stability. With no likelihood that their own funerals would be paid for, the remaining members would drift away and the clubs dissolve. Sometimes the originators of these clubs absconded with the contributions. Evidence given before the Select Committee on Assurance Associations in 1853 asserted that 'as many as 60 out of 120 aged paupers in the Birmingham workhouse had been members of Clubs that had broken up for want of funds'.[10]

Much the same fate was frequently in store for subscribers to local friendly societies. These combined insurance against sickness with convivial 'feasts' and day-outings for the members – often paid for out of the funds! – and until mid-century remained largely uncontrolled despite legislation. The first Friendly Societies Act 1793 had made it possible for such societies to protect their contributions from theft by their officers, but many societies remained unregistered through the inertia of their officers, or their hostility to authority. In an era before the skilled calculation of mortality, the use of faulty tables and flat-rate systems often led to collapse. In other instances, contribution money was used to pay management expenses, with disastrous results. The problem of what later came to be called 'lapses' was a perpetual one. There was no provision for the return of accumulated contributions if a family fell on hard times and could no longer keep up its payments, so that whatever money had been paid in was irrevocably lost.

An official attempt to prevent abuse came in 1819, when Justices of the Peace were made responsible for seeing that the tables used by friendly societies were approved by two actuaries – members of a relatively new calling that would develop into a recognised profession as the century wore on. A barrister was appointed by the Government in 1828 to keep a register of friendly societies, and a year later was given the task of certifying their rules. (The holder of this position was taken under the wing of the Treasury and given the title of 'Registrar of Friendly Societies' in 1846.) In 1829 a consolidating Act removed stamp duty from the policies issued by friendly societies. Those that registered were allowed to insure any amount, and to invest their funds with the National Commissioners of Debt at an advantageous rate, but these privileges were removed in 1841 from any society assuring more than £200 at death to a single individual and in 1850 from those assuring more than £100. By 1853, no friendly society could be established that assured more than £100 at death, or paid an annuity of more than £30 a year, or sickness payments of more than £1 a week.[11] Generally speaking, those that registered tended to be the larger, federated societies, and appealed to a higher stratum of the working population than the smaller, local societies. Artisans, tradesmen, domestic servants and others with fairly steady incomes tended to prefer the former, and to disdain the 'club nights' that offered those lower down a distraction from repetitive, exhausting and meaningless work.

Legislation went some way to making it advantageous for friendly societies to operate efficiently, but it did not eliminate collapses, or the scandals that resulted when societies became the tools of the unscrupulous. What it did do by limiting the amount insurable, was ensure that the friendly societies continued to be resorted to by the working classes, and life assurance companies, which were not limited in the amount of assurance they could offer, by the better-off. In the 1840s life assurance companies were being founded in great numbers, along with many other kinds of enterprise, as part of a boom in company promotions. This surge in commercial activity was one more expression of the middle-class prosperity referred to earlier, and the great increase in the life assurance ventures marked a change in 'the use and distribution, as well as the amount, of personal incomes'.[12] Life assurance, usually for sums of £100 or more, was mainly purchased to guarantee the security of one's family or business, and paid for by monthly, quarterly or biannual premiums. It was thus only likely to be undertaken by those who already enjoyed a comfortable standard of living.

But among the life assurance companies, too, the scope for instability and dishonesty was wide, and regulation scanty. Before 1844, joint stock companies could be established only by the slow and expensive mechanisms of Royal Charter, private Act of Parliament or letters patent administered from 1825 onwards by the Board of Trade. The Joint Stock Companies Registration and Regulation Act 1844 was, despite its name, 'a device for registration rather than regulation', and was therefore a convenient and popular means of forming new companies.[13] Every new company with transferable shares and more than 25 shareholders was now bound to register with the Registrar of Joint Stock Companies before it could be publicly promoted. Banks came under a separate Act of the same year that demanded more detailed information. In order to obtain a full registration the company had to provide basic information about its purposes, constitution, capital and directors. Once operational, it had to keep accounts, a register of shareholders and directors, and minute books. A 'full and fair' balance sheet was to be compiled yearly, made available to the shareholders and lodged with the Registrar of Joint Stock Companies.

This legislation made the formation of unlimited liability joint stock companies easier and cheaper, but as the emphasis was on facilitating, rather than controlling, left ample loopholes for the continuing formation of unsound companies. In the field of life assurance these seemed to succeed one another with exceptional rapidity. The *Post Magazine and Insurance Monitor* (referred to from now on as the *Post Magazine*), a weekly paper founded in 1840 to act as a reporter on the assurance industry and exposer of its abuses, certainly found numerous subjects for dissection.[14] So did a host of letter-writers to its columns until well into the 1860s, signing themselves 'Amicus Populi', 'Ex Fumo Dare Lucem', 'One of the Duped' and the like. The fraudulent schemes uncovered by the *Post Magazine* were many and its reportage of them merciless. The editor on one occasion referred to an entity 'brought into existence under the facilities for forming such companies by the Registration Act ... whose robberies amounted to £60,000', another 'composed of a low set of vagabonds, whose signatures as shareholders were procured at a pot-house for pints of beer', and finally, one which 'at the end of three years, had only £14,512 left in every shape and form out of £45,081 received in solid cash ...'.[15] Charles Dickens' 'Anglo-Bengalee Disinterested Loan and Life Insurance Company' had plenty of prototypes in life, as did its dissolute President, Tigg Montague, alias Montague Tigg.

Fictitious names on the Deed of Settlement, almost no subscribed capital, and directors on the run from the law – these were common enough revelations. Far from having curbed the number of ill-founded companies, the 1844 Act was felt by some to have achieved nothing, and by others almost to have encouraged the process. 'The law,' wrote John Francis in 1853, 'since 1845, any more than prior to it, has not been effective, and ... it is as easy to establish fraudulent companies now as it was before the passing of the act.' The *Post Magazine*'s sister publication, the *Post Magazine Almanack*, annually compiled a list of 'Projected Assurance Associations'; in 1847 it included one called the 'Defender Fire and Life' whose promoters were listed as '32 Pawnbrokers', and another that was the latest venture of a notorious swindler, Augustus Collingridge, who gave his occupation – *caveat emptor*! – as 'None'.[16] Querying whether Sisyphus or the editor of the *Post Magazine* had the more difficult task, an editorial of August 1853 suggested that the mythical character had 'but one rolling stone to deal with. We, on the contrary, as soon as we have disposed of a rascal, have only to cast our eye downwards and we are sure to see some scheming vagabond waiting at the bottom of the hill for his turn to come'.[17]

The intention to defraud was, however, only one factor in the brief duration of so many of these life assurance entities. For those charging uniform contributions regardless of age or state of health, insolvency was only a matter of time. The fundamental problem was the general lack of reliable statistics on which to base premium or contribution rates.

It was almost mid-century before enough information about rates of illness and mortality was available to calculate probabilities and liabilities with much accuracy.[18] When in 1819 friendly societies seeking to register were required to submit their tables and rules for approval by 'two persons at the least, known to be professional actuaries or persons skilled in calculation' nominated by local Justices of the Peace, it was found that such persons were not so numerous as had been supposed. The Justices were often 'satisfied with the signatures of petty schoolmasters and accountants, whose opinion upon the probability of sickness, and the duration of life, is not to be depended upon'.[19]

There was thus a shortage both of information and of those trained to evaluate it. The great reformer Edwin Chadwick argued in 1828 that one of Government's most important duties was to collect and publish information on mortality and sickness in the form of tables for insurance purposes. At that time many insurance companies were still using the Northamptonshire Life Tables, which were known to be inadequate. They had been calculated by Dr Richard Price from the mortality records of the parish of All Saints, Northampton, between 1735 and 1780. The Carlisle Life Tables, set out by an actuary called Joseph Milne from figures collected by a Dr Heysham between 1779 and 1787 in Carlisle, were based on a sample of only 1,149 deaths.[20] Both tables were still widely used by companies calculating insurance for middle- and upper-class proposals in the 1840s.

Chadwick also felt that social class must be taken into account. This was particularly important with regard to the working classes, whose 'provident institutions', the local burial clubs and friendly societies, could then be based on sound knowledge.[21] As it was, they often relied on amateur actuaries to draw up tables for them. Even in the late 1850s Charles Hardwick, an authority on working-class financial institutions and Grand Master of the Manchester Unity of Oddfellows, thought it 'lamentable to find that so many Clubs yet construct their financial laws on old hypotheses and imperfect data, whose worthlessness has long since been fully demonstrated'.[22] Hardwick also pointed out the variation in calculations of sickness among even recognised actuaries: Dr Price's figures allowed for three weeks' sickness annually at age 70; the experience of the Manchester Unity of Oddfellows, the largest of the federated friendly societies, was ten weeks.[23]

The earliest attempts to rectify this deficiency of information also came from the federated societies. The probabilities of sickness and mortality across a wide spectrum of the labouring population had never been rigorously studied until the new mobility of the workforce, and the rise of the federated societies in response to this, made such study essential on the one hand, and possible on the other.[24] The Manchester Unity was one of several societies responsible for collecting and evaluating the data upon which a great deal of actuarial assessment came to be based. Once such data was available, actuarial tables that were based on sound information rather than conjecture could be compiled. The tables elaborated for the Manchester Unity by its actuary, Henry Ratcliffe, for example, expressed 'not merely opinions entertained by him, but facts disclosed by the past action of the laws of sickness and mortality upon the members themselves'.[25]

The evolution of the profession of actuary, which took place during the first half of the nineteenth century in parallel to the developments mentioned above, was an essential part of the process by which stable insurance institutions were created. Earlier on it was found that there was 'no body of actuaries ready and waiting in the counties of England to calculate suitable tables for all the local clubs or to check the tables in use' under the regulations of 1819. By the 1830s there was some feeling among the actuaries of the established insurance companies that a professional association ought to be founded, to formulate standards and provide a forum. Various factors combined to retard the formation of such a body until 1848. John Finlaison, the Government Actuary and the first President of the Institute of Actuaries (founded out of an informal association called the Actuaries' Club on 8 July 1848), claimed when he was elected that he had foreseen the need for such an institute for the previous 20 years.[26]

The final factor which should be kept in mind in considering the evolution of life assurance was the high, fluctuating and unpredictable level of sickness and mortality that characterised the age, and, especially, the process of industrialisation. It was accepted that the death rate was lower than at the time the Northamptonshire Table was compiled, but it was some time before it was recognised that rates of sickness and death were higher in the large industrial cities than in county towns or in the countryside, and that different occupations carried varying rates of illness.[27] Public health, promoted by Edwin Chadwick and other reformers, was as yet in its infancy. Lack of pure water and sanitation,

Sir Luke Fildes' *The Doctor* captures the anguish of parents keeping vigil beside a sick child. The Victorian era's high mortality rate among young children resulted from widespread poverty and disease.

foul air, the presence of 'nuisances' such as abattoirs and dunghills in the midst of human habitation, overcrowded slums – all of these went hand in hand with the burgeoning growth of urban populations, and predisposed them to disease. Together with the widespread adulteration of food, and ignorance of elementary hygiene, they were evils that in one way or another affected the whole of society, but most directly the poor. An added feature of this unwholesome panorama were the epidemic diseases – cholera, typhoid, scarlet fever and influenza – that periodically swept the country.

Child mortality was particularly horrifying: one child in five in the 1840s died before its first birthday. Statistics that appeared in the *Post Magazine* in 1858 reported that 'nervous disorders' (meaning those such as convulsions and meningitis) had killed an average of 37,000 children a year between 1848 and 1856, at a rate twice as high in the north-west of England as in the south-east. Respiratory infections such as bronchitis and croup had killed 28,700 in 1856 alone. Dysentery and similar bacterial illnesses annually killed almost 11,000 children under five years old.

While such visitations also struck at the better-off and the rural poor, the greatest decimation of lives took place in the cramped courtyards of the industrial cities, in areas where the ill-nourished poor were crowded together in dank cellars and tenements; where water supplies were polluted with sewage and the air laden with industrial effluvia. What all this meant in assurance terms was that the people most likely to need the help it could offer were the least able to afford it; what it meant in actuarial terms was that they were also the worst risks. The Manchester Unity was typical of the federated societies in selecting lives, and in having a long list of exclusions, from consumption to gout, hernia to old age, and those employed in trades that involved health risks. The calculations that held good for the artisan and the tradesman could not be applied to those lower down the social scale, the conditions of whose lives promoted disease and early death. The labouring poor, so often the victims of the industrialising process and all its attendant ills, were also and all too frequently preyed upon by clubs and societies that promised them the small security of a decent burial or relief from want in old age, and failed them utterly. The idea that the features of the burial club and friendly society that were suited to their circumstances (the door-to-door collection of a small weekly premium to secure a modest sum) could be based on tables devised to reflect the realities of their lives and offering the same security as the assurance available to the better-off, seems, as late as mid-century, to have occurred to no-one. It would not be long before it did.

In an Office in Hatton Garden

I N 1848, Queen Victoria had been on the throne for just over a decade. The nation, taking its cue from the domestic life of the royal family, had come to prize 'respectability' above all other social virtues. The ethos that would characterise Victoria's reign for future generations was gradually taking shape: a blend of self-reliance, a positive attitude to work, thrift and *laissez-faire* in matters economical; earnestness, propriety and sobriety in matters social; and in intellectual life, a wide-ranging fascination with technology, invention and exploration that owed something to the Prince Consort's promotion of them, but more to a prevailing sense that through advances in transport, manufacturing and medicine the world could be brought under control.

Britain had enjoyed peace since 1815. Unlike some of her European neighbours, she also enjoyed an enviable degree of political stability. Nevertheless, the 1840s in Britain were an uncomfortable decade, beginning with depression, widespread unemployment and unrest in the textile districts of the north, and a succession of bad harvests. The middle years saw the beginning of recovery with the boom in company formations already referred to, of which the so-called 'railway mania' was but a part. But the year 1845 also saw the onset of the Irish famine, with its appalling distress and resulting mass emigration, much of it to the industrial cities of Liverpool and Manchester. Chartism, given fresh impetus by the influx of disaffected Irish, flared up again in 1848. In England, coinciding with the series of uprisings in Europe – France, Prussia, Hungary, Austria and Italy all suffered political upheavals of one sort or another – there was widely felt apprehension at the possibility that domestic unrest might take a similar turn, mingled with confidence, thanks to a sound constitution and a reviving economy, that it would do no such thing.

Upon this background, the formation of the Prudential made not a ripple. It was one of several dozen assurance companies founded in that momentous 'year of revolutions', 1848. Most of the men associated with its earliest phase left few traces, and had the enterprise not survived, they would no doubt have vanished like autumn leaves into oblivion. Such evidence as there is to explain how and why they came together points to one Captain Charles Hanslip, 'attorney, solicitor and parliamentary agent', as having been the originator and promoter of the idea of forming an assurance company. Many solicitors involved themselves in company promotions, ideally placed as they were to bring together men of means and influence. They also dealt with the array of human affairs likely to give rise to the need for assurance – partnerships, mortgages and loans, wills and trusts. Hanslip, in partnership with William Manning and Job Conworth, practised at No. 12 Hatton Garden, just inside the City of London boundary, on the edge of the legal district centred on the Inns of Court. His professional and business connections were wide. He was solicitor to at least two railway companies by the early 1850s. His other clients ranged from members of the traditional professions – clergymen, naval, military and medical men – through the newer ones such as engineering and surveying, to tradesmen, proprietors of small businesses and prosperous artisans. Hanslip himself came from Huntingdonshire, with strong Norfolk connections through both marriage and business. In 1848 he was 36 years old, living with his wife and three small children at No. 13 Hatton Garden next to the practice.

The Prudential was not the first assurance company that Hanslip tried to form. His claim to have brought together its first Board in 1848 rests on the fact that seven members of it had been associated with him a year earlier in a less fortunate venture called the General Investment, Loan, and Endowment Association (GILEA). There is no doubt that Hanslip was the originator of the GILEA, whose Directors were drawn from his clients and business connections. This short-lived entity, provisionally registered on 16 February 1847, is only worth examining because it was the Prudential's predecessor. As the documents issued by both Companies reveal, those involved with the GILEA who went on to become shareholders and Directors of the Prudential learned from their experience.[1]

The GILEA, as its name suggests, was basically an investment and loan company, whose shareholders, in purchasing their shares by instalments, could build up a sum of capital for themselves or secure a sum for their dependants should they die before purchase was completed. They could also obtain an advance against the value of their shares. The Company's nominal capital was an ambitious £500,000, in 10,000 shares of £50, with provision for increasing this to £2,000,000 by creating additional shares.

Its stated objects were firstly, 'To enable Members to Purchase Real, or other Property', then 'To grant Loans or purchase Annuities on Real or Personal Security', 'To provide for Families or Assigns of Members Dying within stated periods', 'And to create an Accumulating Fund distributable amongst the Members according to the number of Shares'. Through judicious investment it was calculated that 'the Funds will so accumulate, that at the termination of the Association there will be a large Surplus Capital to be distributed amongst the Shareholders, and that each

Share will amount to upwards of £120'. This dissolution was to take place at the end of 21 years, when the Association's property 'of every description, will be converted into money, and divided ratably among the Shareholders'.[2]

All this was clear and attractive enough. The appeal of the Company was explained as somewhat novel: the Association aimed 'to benefit the Industrial Classes and Persons of Limited Capital and Income' in a new way. The last paragraph of the GILEA's prospectus refers to the plethora of building societies that had sprung up since the passing of the Building Societies Act 1833. These provided a useful, but limited, function: the better course was said to be the purchase of the goodwill of a business or other commercial investment. The GILEA had been established for this purpose, as well as for the objects mentioned above, and looked forward to a time when the advantages it offered would obtain the widespread support they deserved. The Company claimed that it would bring together 'for one common object the Capitalists and the Industrial Classes, by making it as much in the Interest of the latter to borrow as of the former to lend', and to give 'peculiar advantages in obtaining Capital for any useful object, with the protection from the extortion to which the needy are generally exposed'.

Whatever the motives of the GILEA's Directors, the sudden souring of the financial climate during 1847 curdled any hopes of prosperity, of benefiting the 'Industrial Classes', or even of putting the Company on a firm footing. The early months of the year brought signs that all was not well with the national economy. Capital was flowing out of the country in the form of large shipments of gold to the United States to pay for corn and cotton, there was increasing distress in Ireland, and the absorption of funds by calls payable on railway shares exceeded £6,000,000. Bullion stocks held by the Bank of England dropped from £14,900,000 in January to £11,000,000 at the end of March. From then on, the country, and especially the City of London, was in the grip of what came to be called 'the financial panic'. Some commentators believed it to have arisen 'more from groundless fear and distrust than any other cause', but the summer brought a series of bankruptcies, mainly of overseas trading companies and provincial banks.[3] September saw 20 'firms of rank' fall, among them Cockerell, Larpent and Co., one of whose proprietors, Sir George Larpent, appears on a list of persons that the GILEA intended to approach as potential trustees.[4]

This was hardly a propitious atmosphere into which to launch a business, and by the middle of the year the promoters of the GILEA must have realised as much. The date of the first minuted meeting, at which officers were elected and procedures decided upon, was 21 April 1847. A week later – meetings were held in the evenings at No. 12 Hatton Garden – advertisements were prepared for insertion in the press:

Agents wanted in London and its vicinity and also in Populous Provincial Districts to receive the Monthly Payments from Subscribers to a Joint Stock Association. A

Commission will be allowed. This Agency will only suit Persons who have an extensive general connection — no Person need apply who cannot produce the most satisfactory references for character and respectability. Security will be required.[5]

On 5 May it was decided to print 100 copies of the 'long form of Prospectus' and 500 copies of the share application, and on 25 June, 500 more copies of the prospectus. The Directors had by then appointed two trustees: Swynfen Jervis, Chairman of the Freemasons and General Assurance Company, of whom little else is known, and Charles Purton Cooper, a lawyer, antiquary and prospective parliamentary candidate — a man of some influence who may well have been instrumental in bringing others into the Prudential on its formation in the following year.

The Directors themselves were a mixed collection of professionals and tradesmen. Charles Eden Wagstaff was a partner in the firm of Jago and Wagstaff, agents to the Phoenix Office, but whether to the life company or the fire office is unknown. Charles Wilson Macbryde, whose wine and spirits import house stood in Watling Street in the City, and George Swaby, a Lieutenant in the Irish Regiment of Foot, are equally shadowy figures. Three others — Major Hawkes, James Harris and Joseph Levy — have proved impossible to trace.

Of the rest, Christopher Adcock was a doctor, a general practitioner from Cambridge who also appears on the provisional prospectus as one of the GILEA's consulting surgeons. He was almost certainly a connection of Charles Hanslip. So too were the Sers brothers, Peter and William, brothers-in-law to Hanslip, having married two of his sisters in 1832. James Allanson, variously listed in directories and census returns as a leather merchant and bootmaker, would eventually become a Director of the Prudential as well as serving as one of its auditors until 1890.

Alan Chambre was the most exotic of this disparate group. He was the son of a judge and came of a landed Kendal family. In 1847 he was a Major in the Royal Lancashire Militia, having served in Gibraltar, Canada, Jamaica, India and France. Clearly he did not count his foray into the world of investments and loans as one of his more interesting experiences, as it is not even mentioned among the events recounted in his *Recollections of West-End Life, with Sketches of Society in Paris, India etc*, published in 1858. More energetic in his commitment was the man whose services the GILEA acquired as its Consulting Physician, Dr Patrick Fraser, known to have been a client of Hanslip. As Actuary, there was W.S. Barker Woolhouse, Fellow of the Royal Astronomical Society, Actuary of the National Loan Fund and founder member of the Institute of Actuaries, which would be established in the following year.

Alas, once the initial setting-up was done, the GILEA never seems to have got off the ground. The Directors postponed electing a Chairman for the year and instead chose one of their number — often Chambre, the most senior in years at

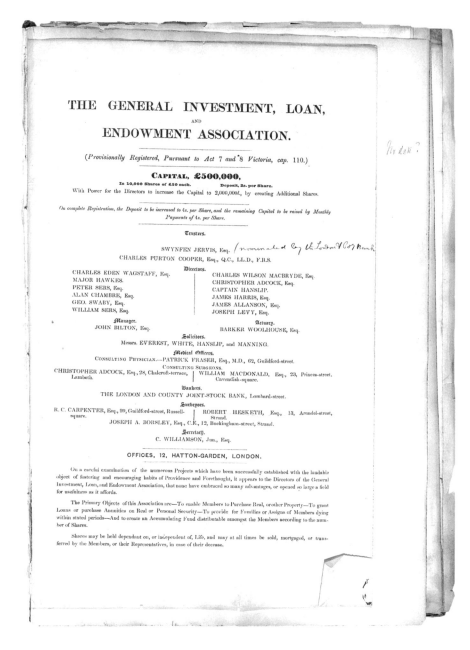

51 – to take the chair at each meeting. In June we find them dithering over altering the Company's name – possibly to reflect a change in its objects in reaction to the adverse financial conditions by then prevailing. The press advertising does not appear to have resulted either in the sale of shares or in the appointment of agents. In mid-October 'an Analysis of the Deed of Settlement was laid on the table and read'. After October, coinciding with the time when the 'panic' reached a high point and then eased, silence fell until the following May. No records survive to throw light on this six-month period of suspended animation.

Edgar Horne, one of the promoters of the Prudential Investment, Loan, and Assurance Association, founded on 30 May 1848, and Chairman of the Prudential Assurance Company from 1877 to 1905.

On 30 May 1848 another meeting was held at No. 12 Hatton Garden. Present were Hanslip, three other members of the GILEA Board, Alan Chambre, James Allanson and Dr Patrick Fraser, and several men new to the undertaking. It was 'Resolved – that this Association be dissolved', and that a new company, to be called 'The Prudential Investment, Loan, and Assurance Association' (PILAA), be established.

Silence reigns again until 5 August, when the new company's Provisional Deed of Settlement was produced. This document indicates that seven of those who had been Directors or officials of the GILEA, together with Hanslip, were now associated with the Prudential in some capacity. These included Jervis and Purton Cooper, who were now joined as trustees by the Reverend James Worthington, Rector of Holy Trinity Church, Gray's Inn Road, and a prolific editor, writer and lecturer. Dr Fraser, Alan Chambre, the Sers brothers and James Allanson also crossed from one association to the other.

Of the new men, three signed themselves as promoters: Edgar Horne, George Steet and William Croggan. Edgar Horne was the man destined to play the largest part in the Prudential's affairs, serving as a Director, and later as Chairman, until his death in 1905. He was a partner in Eversfield and Horne, Auctioneers and Appraisers, which occupied premises in Westminster, close to the Houses of Parliament. His roots, however, were in the City, and more specifically at Bankside, where his family – originally Quaker – had been coal merchants since the seventeenth century. At the time the PILAA was formed, Dr George Steet was Surgeon to Queen Adelaide's Lying-in Hospital and had already served for several years in the same capacity at the Royal Maternity Charity. Like so many of his colleagues, Steet was young – not yet 30. He was appointed one of the Company's two Medical Officers. William Croggan was older, at 42, and like Horne, was an auctioneer and surveyor.

The most important of the remaining newcomers were George Harrison Rogers Harrison and his brother Charles. The former was the most socially elevated of the active Directors, a member of a gentry family closely connected with the College of Arms. He served as Blue Mantle Pursuivant and after 1849, as Windsor Herald and was presumably chosen as Chairman of the PILAA on account of the influence he could bring to the position. Charles Rogers Harrison was one of the first medical men to obtain a Fellowship of the Royal College of Surgeons, in 1843. Specialising in diseases of the spine and chest, he went into private practice; presumably this was what he was doing at the time the Prudential was formed, when he became both a Director and Medical Officer. Slightly later in his appointment than the other medical men was Dr Robert Barnes, one of the most eminent obstetricians of the nineteenth century. Barnes is one of the few Directors (though he shortly resigned, retaining his position as a Medical Officer) about whom there exists sufficient information to convey a firm idea of his character and accomplishments. He too was a physician to the London Hospital, and was probably brought into the Prudential by his colleague Dr Patrick Fraser; like him, he would remain associated with the Prudential until almost the end of the century.

There were four Directors of whom little is known. Thomas Gay, a Norfolk-born law stationer operating from premises in Southampton Buildings, Chancery Lane, was almost certainly a contact of Hanslip. The others – William Chambers, William Tringham and Henry Payne Gallwey, RN – had no apparent links either to Hanslip – although they may have been clients – or to any other Director. David Jones, who replaced Barker Woolhouse as Actuary, was already acting for several other insurance companies including the Universal Building Society. Within a month of the Prudential's formation he too would help found the Institute of Actuaries, and in a few years would enhance his reputation by the publication of a monograph on annuities. Finally, there was the Secretary, John Shillinglaw, a former Assistant Secretary to the Royal Geographical Society, and probably a nominee of the Reverend James Worthington.

All of these men committed themselves to purchasing shares in the PILAA; each Director's requirement was five shares – presumably fully paid. Although some of them had insurance experience with other institutions, the majority did not. George Harrison, Chambers and Tringham were the Directors who committed themselves most heavily, with 150 shares each. Of the three promoters, Horne initially took 25 shares, Croggan 90 and Steet only 5, though he would soon purchase 80 more; the other Directors took varying numbers. Oddly enough, the largest commitment of all was that of the Secretary, Shillinglaw, who paid the deposit on 250 shares.

There is no clue as to who exercised the tempering influence that established the PILAA on a more modest scale than the GILEA. Its nominal capital was £100,000 (a fifth of the amount envisaged for the GILEA) and the price of

George Harrison Rogers Harrison, Windsor Herald of the College of Arms, and Chairman of the Prudential from May 1848 until May 1849.

the shares a more manageable £20. Its objects, in so far as they related to loans, were identical, with the addition of a provision for securing payment to a surety on the death of a borrower. When in September 1848 it was decided to alter the Company's name to 'The Prudential Mutual Assurance, Investment, and Loan Association' (PMAILA), its aims were expanded to include 'important New Features and Advantages in Life Assurance ... earnestly impressed on the attention of the Public, particularly of the Industrial Classes'.[6]

The alteration of the Company's name barely a few months after its formation is interesting. Initially, the Directors seem to have anticipated that for the PILAA, as for the GILEA, loan and investment business was to be the Company's primary activity, with assurance being mainly a safeguard for loans. But within a matter of weeks they re-thought this, altering the orientation of the Company in favour of placing more emphasis on insuring lives and providing a means of saving. Purchasers of the £20 shares, 'by small monthly or quarterly instalments', could 'securely invest their savings and participate in the whole amount of profits', the shares to be secured to their dependants in case of death. There were also offered, 'Life Assurance on a reduced scale for the whole of life, or term of years, on Lives, Joint-Lives and Survivorship' and 'Security in the event of death ... for payment of Shares in Building Societies'.

The GILEA's flat-rate payments table was replaced in the Prudential by more sophisticated tables in which the sum assured (a multiple of the £20 shares) was determined at the outset, and the monthly or quarterly premiums calculated to reflect both the sum and the medical referee's expectation of life of the purchaser. Other tables set out the rates for assuring the sum of £100 on lives, joint lives and the last of two lives, and for securing building society shares to a representative on death. The tables illustrating these options were based on those used by the Universal Life Assurance Association which David Jones, Actuary to the Universal as well as to the Prudential, proposed early on that the latter adopt.[7]

As might be expected, considerable space was devoted in the PMAILA's earliest prospectus to a discussion of life assurance as 'a medium by which ... important advantages are conferred on society'. The assured bought peace of mind and security for his dependants in the event of his death. Those 'whose

Dr Robert Barnes, an early Medical Officer of the Prudential and a Director from 1848 to 1849 and from 1884 until his death in 1907, was a pioneer in the field of gynaecology and obstetrics.

means of support are derived from their own personal exertions' were bound to appreciate this. But there were a host of other situations where assurance could make a difference, 'conferring a stability on transactions which would otherwise be precarious and uncertain', and making it possible for:

The Young to make provision for themselves in the decline of life, and Parents to secure endowments for their children by Deferred Annuities

Possessors of entailed estates to provide for the younger members of their family

Creditors to obtain ultimate payment of debts

Borrowers to secure a fund to provide for their engagements

Parties in marriage contracts to secure the terms of settlement

Expectants to secure Property in Reversion against every contingency

Purchasers of Annuities on the lives of others to secure the return of the capital invested

The list ended with an appeal to 'All who have a pecuniary interest contingent on the life of another' to recognise that 'Life Assurance affords a certain means of providing for the loss which must otherwise arise on death'.[8]

So long as a company was well run, the purchase of shares dependent on life was an attractive investment for people looking for an effective, protected means of saving. A man aged 30, for instance, who wanted to insure for himself or his dependants the sum of £100 at the end of ten years or on his death, would pay 18s 9d monthly, (£10 5s yearly, or £102 10s over the ten-year period); for this he would obtain, in addition to the peace of mind much emphasised in the Association's literature, a share in its profits during the ten-year term.

Despite the prospectus's mention of 'the Industrial Classes', the advantages it held out were only accessible to the better-off – tradesmen, professional men, businessmen, the clergy, and landed proprietors. The word 'Industrial' (which would within a very few years be applied to insurance designed specifically for the working classes) seems to have been used at this time, and in this instance, somewhat differently, to indicate people whose *industry* had won for them their place in the world: *industrious* but undoubtedly prosperous people, whose assets were sufficient to allow them the luxury of choice. By the time the Company was fully registered on 4 December 1848 the list of those who had bought shares included, in addition to the Directors and their connections, solicitors and barristers, doctors, grocers, a tobacconist and a wine merchant, printers, builders, clerks, a farmer, and the inevitable collection of those signing themselves 'Gentleman'. Altogether such persons accounted for the first 1,530 shares in the Prudential Association, and having paid the 2s deposit on each, enriched it by £153. In the first year of operation, which ran from

4 December 1848 to 19 December 1849, a further 455 shares were sold, to persons of similar status. This brought the subscribed capital to £45,524, though in terms of deposits received the sum was modest indeed.

Predictably, some of the names appearing on the list of early share-holders were obvious or likely connections of Hanslip – those with addresses in East Anglian localities such as Holbeach, Gedney, Wisbech and St Ives, and those residing in the legal district around Holborn and the Inns of Court. Hanslip must have been an energetic and persuasive, perhaps very sociable, individual. That he used his influence in the Association's interest is certain. As well as providing it with Directors and office holders, he continued to supply it with shareholders from the ranks of his personal and business acquaintances. The Association met at No. 12 Hatton Garden for the first several months of its life (there is an engaging minute voting thanks to Mrs Hanslip for providing supper for the Board when it met in the evenings; later, for providing tea). Hanslip and his partner William Manning – who also served as a Director for a time – carried out all of the legal work attendant on the provisional and full registration of the Association during the second half of 1848. In lieu of fees to cover their bill of costs, the solicitors took 100 shares with £1 paid up, but later loaned the Association £300; Hanslip attended board meetings without fee for the first year. He appears to have been a tireless and determined shepherd, though his reasoning, in the absence of any account of why he thought the fledgling Association (in such a climate, and following the GILEA's demise) was worth so much of his professional effort, must remain a matter for speculation.

Tentative Beginnings

BY the beginning of January 1849 the Prudential Mutual Assurance, Investment, and Loan Association was fully registered, and theoretically, at least, in a position to undertake the business for which it had been formed. Practically speaking, however, there were matters such as equipping the premises, making the Association known and acquiring a corps of agents that were still to be settled. All this occupied the first few months of the year, by which time there were external challenges to face.

Having spent six weeks seeking offices situated 'between Temple and Cornhill', the Association had moved into premises of its own at No. 14 Chatham Place, Blackfriars, early in November 1848. A minute book entry for 2 November relates that £90 per annum was to be paid as rent to a gentleman named Randall, and that the premises consisted of '1 room on Ground Floor, 3 rooms on the First Floor, & closet; and Strong Room and coal cellar underneath the Ground Floor'.[1]

The row of buildings known as Chatham Place was knocked down in 1862 when the Embankment was constructed, but formerly it ran off New Bridge Street, and No. 14, the last house, stood close to the river, just below where Unilever House stands today. There exist several representations of it: one in *Tallis's London Street Views*, and two belonging to Guildhall Library. It was a severe-looking building of five storeys, with a bow window, its sole decoration, providing a vantage point over the Thames from the first and second floors. According to an earlier history of the Prudential, the house opposite on the east side of Chatham Place was occupied by the Humane Society's first-aid station, where people recovered from the heavily polluted river were taken to be revived.[2] The area around New Bridge Street was full of insurance companies, and in Chatham Place itself there were several, together with the six-month-old Institute of Actuaries, which occupied No. 11.[3] There is no indication of the state of the premises at No. 14, only that they were unfurnished. The Association proposed to hire furniture, but gratefully accepted the loan of a writing desk from Hanslip, to be bought after three months 'at a value to be fixed by the Surveyor'. Funds were carefully dispensed: in January a carpet was bought for the board room and the waiting room, but the 12 cane chairs ordered for the latter by the Surveyor (Croggan) from Charles Harrison were countermanded, to the apparent irritation of both men. Two tons of coal were bought from Edgar Horne's family connection, 'Messrs. W. & J. Horne of Bankside, coal merchants',

The Prudential's first office, No. 14 Chatham Place, appears at the far left of this view of the City. It was pulled down in 1862 during the construction of the Embankment.

and a housekeeper engaged at 3s per week, to clean and make up the fires. The Association was not the building's only occupant: part of it was tenanted by the Lord's Day Observance Society, whose signboard overhung the Association's windows. In April 1849 an appeal to the landlord compelled the Society to move its sign.

Gradually, procedure was agreed: board meetings were to be held twice weekly, on Mondays and Thursdays. Formality was the keynote of meetings. Promptly at 3.00 p.m. when they began, the Chairman was to draw a line under the last of the signatures of those in attendance: this was the origin of a Prudential custom that many staff in more recent times will recognise. Anyone addressing the chair was to stand. George Harrison designed a seal showing the figure of Prudence, and a Mr West was engaged to draw her on wood, to head the prospectus and other documents the company might issue. Both images were adapted from the *Prudentia* painted on glass by Sir Joshua Reynolds for the chapel of New College, Oxford. The female figure is shown with her convex mirror, representing sincerity in self-examination, and a resulting humility. Her other attributes are a visual play on the name of the virtue: a serpent, emblem of wisdom, twines its way around an arrow, representing purpose or direction, to suggest wisdom-in-action: prudence, in other words.

Well before the Company was fully registered, the Board had begun its search for agents, and had appointed a subcommittee comprising Steet, Croggan and Shillinglaw to deal with applications. Late in September 1848 advertisements had been placed in *The Times* and the *Daily News*. A few replies were received from these and another series of advertisements in October, with the result that some agents were engaged. On life assurance policies they were to receive a commission of 10% on the first year's premium and 5% on those of subsequent years. Like most new offices, the Company paid 10% in an effort to attract good men; the older offices and the Scottish offices usually paid 5%.

At a meeting on 5 February 1849, the Reverend James Worthington, one of the Association's trustees, announced that he proposed to introduce 'some influential Merchants' to the Board and six of his nominees duly purchased the requisite 20 shares.[4] One of them, George Clark, later served as an auditor until his death in 1878. The Board now comprised some 18 individuals. The resolution was passed on 7 May that those who held paid offices as well as directorships should resign one or the other. Charles Harrison, Steet, Croggan and Barnes promptly resigned as Directors but retained their paid positions. No doubt everyone was pleased that Worthington could summon up men who were prepared to invest in the fledgling Association, but there are hints that this repositioning did not take place without a degree of friction. Tringham and Gay left the Board altogether, Allanson threatened to do so, and George Harrison stepped down as Chairman to make way for Worthington, who was elected on 10 May.[5]

The Company seal bearing an early image of the cardinal virtue of Prudence.

Under Worthington, its second Chairman, the Association stood to become known among the literati and the clergy as well as men of means. He was recognised in literary circles as a lecturer, translator and editor. The variety of his interests led one acquaintance to refer to him as 'that prodigy of scientific and classical lore' and made Worthington a man whose connections were potentially advantageous. In his younger days his ambitions had been somewhat hampered by the needs of his large family – after ten years of marriage to his

Italian-American wife he had seven children – but the inability or disinclination to live within his clerical means seems still to have been a besetting fault in 1849. It was probably no coincidence that his drive to provide the Prudential with shareholders – and himself with the chairmanship – followed hard on his failure to obtain the post of Assistant Secretary to the Royal Geographical Society.[6]

The bare facts of Worthington's life suggest that he was a forceful and confident man. The board minutes offer the only reflection of his tenure as Chairman – no correspondence survives. Nowhere is it indicated which of the Directors initiated a particular course of action, but it is clear that some at least harboured doubts about the way the Association had been operating under Harrison. A three-man Finance Committee was appointed on 31 May to review the Company's accounts.

Keeping control of such funds as there were was a primary aim during the next few months: the Association was incurring expenses but as yet no money was coming in. Rent, the printing of a prospectus, the hire of a clerk, Goodman Jenkyn, at £50 a year, in addition to the Secretary's £200 and the Actuary's £50, the ever-growing debt for legal work to Hanslip and Manning (not to mention a further £800 loan from the law firm), the £150 in fees to the medical officers for 'services rendered', though as yet no lives had been accepted – taken together these must have seemed a daunting sum. In July 1849 the Association borrowed £1,000 from its bankers, Messrs. Barnard and Dimsdale, and soon after, another £1,000 from Robert Mossop, a fellow-solicitor and friend of Hanslip. Those who neglected to pay the quarterly call on their shares were deprived of them; this eliminated both the Company's Auditors from the shareholders' list and led to sharp advice from the Board to Croggan, to the effect that 'if he wished to be relieved of the responsibility of his shares it can be done by relinquishing his office as Surveyor'. What Croggan decided to do was never recorded: he died of cholera on 22 July at the height of one of the worst epidemics of the century.[7] His wife received the Board's condolences, but finances being as tight as they were, not the donation that she requested.

With a view to drumming up business by circulating the prospectus to a preferential type of client, a copy of the clergy list was ordered. The summer of 1849, however, was almost as unfortunate a time to be promoting assurance as that of 1847. The cholera epidemic that raged from June to the autumn carried off an average of over 1,500 people a week in London alone, reaching its height in early September when more than 2,000 died in seven days. Since the illness was commonly believed to spread through contact with infected persons, many Londoners left the city. The Board reduced its meetings from twice weekly to once, and ordered a case of cognac – a supposed prophylactic against cholera – to sip on these occasions.[8] In January of the following year it was revealed that the epidemic had made it impossible to issue policies on lives from May onwards.

Although conditions were so inauspicious, a very few policies continued

to be purchased by persons close to the Association. One of these, only the twentieth to be issued, was on the life of Edgar Horne: a policy of £399 taken out by
Mrs Maria Eversfield (shortly to become Horne's wife) which would remain in
force until his death in 1905. The other was a £300 policy on the life of one Henry
Harben – the Prudential's first link with the man who would shape its destiny.
Prospects were otherwise so scarce that by early September the Directors had
passed a resolution binding on themselves, requiring each of them to subscribe
for a policy or policies, either personally or by bringing in a friend, to the amount
of £500 before 29 September, the date of the Company's financial year end.

      This manoeuvre appears to have brought in enough funds to carry on with,
but no sooner was it effected than the Committee deputised to report on the
Company's finances set off a small bombshell. Its findings, submitted on 4
October, laid bare 'a great want of system and much irregularity in the accounts',
and several other disagreeable facts relating to the 'late Chairman and Treasurer'
George Harrison. Foremost of these was that he had never possessed the Director's
share qualification as set out in the Deed of Settlement, having paid only £3 10s,
though he had signed the Deed for 150 shares. He was alleged also to have set a
payment from a shareholder against the amount owing on his own shares, to have
run up a tavern bill of £24 10s and misappropriated the Association's funds
to settle it, and to have been responsible for 'a Multiplicity of both debits and
credits which are wholly fictitious ...' in the accounts. The sum of all this was 'so
manifestly improper and so likely at some future time to operate injuriously to
the interests of the Association' that the Committee recommended opening a new
set of books and calling upon Harrison to repay the funds.[9]

      There are several aspects of this affair that are less than clear. Why, after
his displacement by Worthington, and when it must have been obvious that his
manipulation of funds would come to light, did Harrison remain on the Board?
His financial stake was negligible; the risk of humiliation large. Existing records
cannot answer this, nor suggest why a man otherwise so esteemed – Harrison
was appointed Windsor Herald in July 1849, a position his uncle had held before
him – should indulge in such chicanery.

      Much as the Finance Committee's Report must have dismayed Harrison's
colleagues, they could scarcely have been less scandalised by a further discovery.
Sometime in 1849, Harrison had become Chairman of an even younger insurance venture than their own: the Kent Mutual Life Office. This was an offshoot
of a fire office of the same name, and was based at Rochester in Kent. Since their
meetings frequently ended with a reminder to use their best efforts in the interests of the Association, the Directors of the Prudential might well have felt that
in dividing his allegiance Harrison was *not* using his influence for the best. At
the Prudential's first Annual General Meeting on 1 January 1850 he was
proposed as Shareholders' Auditor by two of the medical men, Steet and Barnes
– another puzzling occurrence, suggesting that opinion was divided as to his

value to the Association. Only seven hands from among the 27 persons present were held up in his favour. With this, the Prudential's first Chairman disappears from its records, leaving behind him a number of unanswered and unanswerable questions.[10]

The Association had survived its first full year, though the point was made that its activities so far in fact covered about 18 months. The Report delivered at the first Annual General Meeting was intended to instil confidence in the shareholders and no doubt did so, though it conveys an unmistakable impression of 'whistling in the dark'. The Directors' exertions, it was claimed, had been 'crowned with a success beyond their warmest expectations', and had it not been for the cholera epidemic, the business effected would have been 'still more amply augmented'. Despite this, the road was said to be open 'to secure before long a clear income of some thousands per annum, unaccompanied by any perilous risk', with nearly every board meeting adding 'extensively to the list of Proprietary, and to the income of the Society'. As the board minutes reveal, this was far from having been the case. As for the accounting, the assets shown in the balance sheet included £45,524 of capital subscribed, but there is no indication of how much of this was paid up. On the liabilities side sums assured, amounting to £13,963, were shown, though there is no reference to an actuary's valuation; and, after allowing for other items, the balance brought down was quoted as £33,303. How this latter sum was arrived at is not clear, but it nevertheless implies that capital was in fact being absorbed quite heavily in the development of the business.[11]

The Report is helpful, though, in redefining in simple terms the Association's areas of activity, and its intended clientele. The services it provided were said to be two: loans and life assurance. Those who would find such loans useful might include 'the Clergyman who requires advances for the erection of a Parsonage, &c.,' and who fell outside the provisions of Queen Anne's Bounty, 'the Barrister who seeks to pay his entrance fees, the Officer the price of his commission, or the Tradesman means to increase his working capital ...'.[12] As to life assurance, 'its practical influence is unfelt by three-fourths of the community', but once 'introduced among Working Mechanics and Small Tradesmen, must prove an immense benefit when fully known'.

This untouched 'three-fourths of the community' meant the more prosperous community, not the wage-receiving and poorer classes. As yet, none but the most enlightened members of the vast working population would have been expected to recognise the benefits of life assurance: the burial club and the friendly society, despite their defects, were the 'natural' savings vehicles for the lower orders. Certainly within the Association there was at this point little idea of catering for those farther down the social scale.[13] It was appealing to 'men of large fortune and means', 'such opulent parties as should be fully competent when called on, to answer any demand made on the Association', which meant, by definition, the man with money to invest. The second Annual Report in January 1851 reported that prudence was indeed the Directors' watchword: 'In the selection of lives they have carefully avoided every probability of an early claim,' and in the following year they were equally careful to emphasise that they had not, for the sake of business-getting, 'sought out the dangerous facilities easily attainable among the lower orders. A greater amount of transactions, accompanied with larger risks from the character of the lives, would not be so desirable as to command a quiet business of the best description'.[14]

This proviso, then, underlay the concerted effort to enlarge the business that began in earnest early in 1850, with the Harrison affair and the first Annual General Meeting over and the way ahead more clearly marked. Henry Gallwey, posted to France, had resigned and a new Director, the Reverend John Harvey Ashworth, purchaser of 100 shares and lender of £1,000, had joined the Board. He, Worthington and Jones, the Actuary, revised the tables and the prospectus. The revised versions were sent to all the clergy during the spring, in the form of a small pamphlet describing the Company's advantages. There seems to have been some debate over whether those engaged as agents should put up a surety and receive a commission, or be paid a salary and expenses; the Association tried both courses perhaps, depending on the references of the respective agents. More advertisements were inserted in newspapers ranging from *The Times* to local ones as far away as Inverness. There was now an agent in Dover, and the end of the year would find others at work in East Grinstead, Brighton and East Retford.

How the Reverend James Gillman came to join the Board is not documented anywhere – he may have been an acquaintance of Worthington or Purton Cooper, or he may simply have replied to the newspaper appeal for backers. He was to play an important role in the Company's affairs for the next 27 years, for 25 of them as Chairman. On purchasing his shares in May 1850, he too loaned the Association £1,000, renewable as long as he was a Director. Another such loan was received from Henry Crawter, who filled the vacant post of Surveyor from June onwards.

These and other loans, together with additional stop-gap funds put up by the Directors themselves and by the Association's bankers, Barnard and

The Reverend James Gillman, Chairman of the Prudential from 1852 to 1877.

Dimsdale, were essential during this formative period.[15] What emerges from surviving records is the degree of faith in its eventual prosperity the Association's promoters had, or had come to have. The amount of its business may have been small – only 62 policies were sold in its first year and 194 in its second, bringing the amount assured to £39,798 and premium income to just over £2,250 – but as most of these were taken by persons known to the Directors, they could truthfully say that it was select. Their faith was partly reflected in their resistance to overtures from other companies. The Association appears to have attracted at least one offer of amalgamation early on. At the second Annual General Meeting in January 1851 the Directors reported how they had 'refused to treat on any other basis, than that of complete independence for the PRUDENTIAL' and went on to reiterate that 'Satisfied with their own position, requiring no aid ..., either for support or continuance, this Institution is only prepared to deal ... on terms advantageous to itself'.[16]

Growing confidence was also expressed in the hiring of further permanent staff – including Alexander Munro, taken on as a clerk in 1852 and destined to stay on until 1872 – and finally, in December 1851, after much searching and ordering of surveys, in the move to larger offices at No. 35 Ludgate Hill, on which a 21-year lease at £300 a year was taken. Ludgate Hill was the main thoroughfare through a warren of courts and alleys. Access to No. 35 from the rear was via the picturesquely named Belle Sauvage Yard, where there had once been a galleried playhouse.[17] An early account mentions that the Prudential preserved an ancient right of way by requiring the staff to use this entrance, usually locked, four times a year. The lease included the use of a separate building behind the main one, the so-called 'Back House', to which a bridge was built when the offices were enlarged a few years later. In trading windows overlooking the Thames for a view of Ludgate Hill, the Company exchanged the laden barges and sailing boats of the port for the wheeled traffic of London's commercial heart and the occasional event of national importance. When the Duke of Wellington died in 1852, the staff were allowed to watch from the upper windows as the funeral procession filed past on its way to St Paul's.

No sooner was the move accomplished than the Association lost – or ousted – its second Chairman. This followed closely on the resignation of John Shillinglaw as Secretary. As the cause of the disagreement between Worthington and his colleagues is nowhere recorded, it is impossible to know whether the two incidents were related. Speculation as to why Worthington suddenly fell from favour must necessarily be very tentative. It is possible, considering the composition of the Board, that the issue was entirely personal. Worthington had published two abrasively anti-Roman Catholic works in the previous 18 months; the second, directed against the re-establishment of the Roman Catholic hierarchy in England, was addressed to Cardinal Wiseman and entitled *Romish*

Usurpation. By any standards it was an impudent and discourteous piece; to colleagues who counted among their number at least one Roman Catholic (James Allanson) and various others of dissenting sympathies – a Quaker, a Unitarian – the Chairman's stance may have been personally offensive.[18] But this is a long shot.

There is no doubt, however, about the chilliness with which any subsequent approach from Worthington to the Board was greeted. After his non-election at the Annual General Meeting in January 1852 – when he was replaced by James Gillman as Chairman and lost his directorship on a show of hands – his name was removed from the list of trustees, and his £100 endowment deposit and a promissory note returned. The Board 'declined to enter into any further negotiation on the subject' of commission on the shares of Directors and others he had introduced, and other letters from him were deliberately left unanswered.[19] This may point to the row having been focused on his shareholding, or perhaps on the suspicions – later confirmed – that had arisen about the conduct of John Shillinglaw.

In January 1852, in the aftermath of these two departures, it looked very much as though the Association had been defrauded for the second time, though the facts would not be set down as a special report to the Board until 11 March 1853, more than a year later. By then, the truth had emerged about the extent of Shillinglaw's liability. It amounted to some £526 11s 7d, composed of an unpaid call on his shares, a 'deficiency in Policy Stamps entrusted to his care', and sums 'received but not accounted for'. The writers of the report – the Company's Auditors – wasted no words: 'The existence of these circumstances implies a want of care on the part of the Directors which we trust will never be permitted to occur again'. Rather than attach their comments to the formal audit, which 'would lead to the injury of the Company a result we are anxious to avoid', they were content to insert them in the board minutes, 'Knowing as we do that the Directors now exercise due vigilance over the financial affairs of the Company we are persuaded that a repeat of such irregularities is next to impossible ...'. This report, delivered at a Special General Meeting of the shareholders, provoked an explanatory statement from the current Directors, respectfully pointing out that at the time the peculations were taking place 'the Court of Directors as at present constituted can hardly be said to have been in existence ...'. 'Notwithstanding the salvo ...' at the end of the auditors' report, the Directors considered the latter 'liable to misconception as regards themselves ...' and placed their rejoinder, signed by Gillman as Chairman, immediately below it in the Minute Book.[20]

The Association was never again to be in as shaky a financial condition as at this point. Only 139 policies had been sold during 1851, bringing in premiums of £1,837, and the number of shares sold, after three years, totalled just 3,207. The best that could be said of the previous 12 months was that there had

FACING PAGE

**Henry Harben as a young
man.**

been no death claims, a singularly fortunate circumstance unlikely to continue very long. Gillman's election marked a minor watershed for the Association. He seems to have been able to prevent disillusion setting in, as well it might have, and instead to put in place some practical measures that revived the Board's belief in the Association. His first act was to appoint a committee to report in detail on the accounts, and thereafter to inspect them weekly. The resulting conclusions were high on the agenda at board meetings thereafter.

The departure of Shillinglaw had left the position of Secretary vacant, and in so doing, had brought into the Company the 28-year-old Henry Harben, unquestionably the most significant figure in its nineteenth-century history. His immediate connection with the Association probably arose through his friendship, and a possible professional relationship, with Henry Crawter and his nephew Thomas, whose firm had been appointed Surveyor a year earlier, although one of Harben's grandsons would report a century later that Harben had met Gillman at the home of a mutual friend.[21] No details survive of his education and his career up to this point is difficult to trace. It would appear, however, to have included a seven-year stint in the wholesale dry-goods firm run by his uncle, and an apprenticeship as a surveyor – possibly to Crawter.

His appointment was in any case to be a false start: his own account of how he started off in the Company he would shape so profoundly is worth quoting here, as it throws an interesting light on the expectations of all concerned and the way in which the situation was handled. Some months after Shillinglaw's departure, the Directors

> *… sought for a Secretary among their friends and connexions* [sic]*, two of the applicants for the post being Mr. Harben and Mr. Barfoot. On the day fixed for the election, Mr. Harben attended the Board, but Mr. Barfoot was absent, and his friends therefore wished the election to be deferred. It appeared, however, that Mr. Harben had made application for the Secretaryship of another Life Company, the election for which post was to take place on the same day as that proposed for the election in this Company. He had attended this meeting in preference to the other, in consequence of his application having been made here first; and it was represented that if the election were deferred, he would be certain to lose the position in the other Company, and might not be elected in this. It was accordingly resolved to proceed to the election, and Mr. Harben was unanimously appointed to the vacant post.*

> *The friends of Mr. Barfoot subsequently stated that it was purely a mistake that he had not attended the Board at the appointed time; and as it was stated he would be able to introduce large capital and influential connexions to the Company, an appeal was made to Mr. Harben not to stand in the way of the best interests of the Institution, and at the following Board Meeting he resigned his position as Secretary, but received the appointment of Accountant.*[22]

The respective terms that he and Barfoot were offered indicate that there must have been high hopes indeed for the quantity of business the latter could introduce. Barfoot's annual salary as Secretary was £200 to the £100 offered to Harben; he was to get an additional £50 if premiums passed the £2,000 mark, and £50 more for each additional £1,000 in premiums. Harben, in his acceptance of the post of Accountant, was paid £100 a year, with the usual agency commissions on introductions and the promise of 5% of new business if his tables were used by the Association.

Harben was as capable of one job as of the other, and offered to the Association on his joining it a set of mortality tables of his own devising. As the future would reveal, he was an astute judge of a project's – or a person's – inherent strengths and weaknesses. He seems to have set about trying to rectify the Association's administrative deficiencies almost as soon as he arrived, clearly with the Board's blessing. He was fanatically industrious, and quickly got himself appointed 'receiver' as well as Accountant. This meant that he chased any debts owed to the company, obtaining a commission of 7½% on those he ran to ground. One wonders whether, in July 1852, it was he who advised Barfoot, and through him the Board, that 'the late Secretary Shillinglaw intended to leave England for Australia' on the following day with his debts unpaid. Hanslip and Manning recommended taking out a *capias*, or arrest writ, and apprehending the fugitive at Gravesend. Barfoot apparently hurried to the quay and was able to report on 15 July that he had 'taken such measures as to prevent Shillinglaw sailing with his family in the *Agnetu*, and the solicitors were negotiating with his friends for the discharge of his liabilities'.[23]

The first year of Gillman's chairmanship witnessed a good deal of consolidation and reorganisation. A further prospectus, supposedly to include new tables, was ordered, but David Jones, the Actuary, procrastinated over the preparation of these to such lengths that he was given £25 and dismissed. (There was clearly a decision not to use Harben's tables, perhaps because the Board felt it advantageous to have them produced by an actuary whose name carried more weight.) Jones's replacement was Edward Ryley, consultant actuary to several insurance companies, including the British Industry, founded in this very year and shortly to have an important part in the Prudential's history.[24] Limits were placed on the amount that could be assured (£600) or loaned on personal security (£500). A fresh loan of £3,000 was obtained at a rate of 5% from the Commercial Bank in Lothbury, to which the Association transferred its account. (The sum transferred from Dimsdales was a modest £837 4s 8d.) In September, the Deed of Settlement

An early advertisement for the Prudential in the *Illustrated London News* of February 1853.

was altered so as to establish the date of the Annual General Meeting as the first Tuesday in April, and the financial year end as 31 December instead of 29 September.

By the end of 1852 the Association had engaged more agents, notably in Ramsgate, Hastings, Edinburgh, Birmingham and Warwick. Those who were appointed had responded to the Company's notices in the press and had convinced the Board that they possessed a degree of influence in their native towns. The Directors had also begun to receive enquiries from persons wishing to set up agencies abroad. The idea of agencies in Calais, Paris and Dublin was rejected. Policyholders, too, sought permission to travel or live elsewhere. There were strict regulations about this: the risks attendant on changed circumstances had to be recalculated to produce an additional premium when someone wanted to make a tour of the United States, live in France or go off to the gold diggings in Australia. (In the case of the last-mentioned, policies were declared invalid; the voyage to Australia was judged to be risky enough, but its dangers were nothing compared to the violence of life in the mining towns of New South Wales.)

Very gradually, the number of proposals that came before the Board began to increase. Many of those to do with life assurance were temporarily deferred while medical reports were obtained. The normal 'Court of Directors', as board meetings were called, dealt with each instance individually, as well as with applications from prospective agents, arrears and extensions on loan repayments, and the drawing of cheques. No aspect of the Company's affairs was left out of the Board's scrutiny. Perhaps it was the result of having been twice bitten that lay behind having the whole Board, rather than individuals or subcommittees, deal with even the minutiae of the Association's day-to-day workings. Gillman may have insisted on such close attention.

For Harben, the commitment to strengthen the Association became almost a crusade: his success in pursuing defaulters to obtain what was owed to the Association emerges clearly from surviving records. He was virtually given a free hand, and had little hesitation in activating the solicitors or running the late payer to earth. One E. Mills, repeatedly chased for being behind with loan repayments, was tartly reminded that '... punctuality in payment, as well as Security, is expected in all Transactions with this Office'.

By 1853 tighter controls and a modicum of expansion in the form of new agencies had enabled the Association at least to hold its own. The first valuation revealed that as yet there were no divisible profits, and no possibility of a dividend to the shareholders. In April changes were made to the Deed of Settlement. Shares issued now stood at about 3,500. The original 5,000 £20 shares at £1 were split, so that there were now 10,000 £10 shares at 10s. The clauses which made it difficult to allocate a dividend to shareholders before a bonus was given to with-profits policyholders were rescinded. They were replaced by a measure that gave 5% interest to shareholders and provided for periodic valuations at which four-fifths of the new profits were to be distributed as bonus, and the remaining one-fifth to the shareholders in accordance with their holdings. These changes may be read as further signs of the faith in the Association's eventual prosperity that had so far sustained everyone connected with it. Events would shortly challenge them to seek that prosperity in a change of direction.

Firmer Ground

IT is not known who opened the door of the Prudential's offices at No. 35 Ludgate Hill one morning early in June 1852 to find, waiting to be admitted, a group of men dressed in the regulation overalls of factory operatives. Was it the young Alexander Munro who asked them their business and invited them to step inside? Or was it, perhaps, the recently appointed Henry Harben who showed them into the Secretary's room and lingered to hear their proposal? No-one realised that this seemingly insignificant occasion was the harbinger of a momentous decision. The only physical record of the visit appears among the minutes of the next board meeting: a note to the effect that 'a deputation of operatives had visited the office to find out if it were disposed to grant them small policies varying from £20 upwards premiums to be paid weekly or in monthly instalments as adopted by Friendly Societies, promising to introduce a very large amount of such business.'

Barfoot had already consulted Edward Ryley about the viability of the proposal. Ryley's view was that 'tables might be calculated to make it a safe and remunerative business', and he was thus instructed to prepare these, 'provided he is of the opinion it may be safely and profitably carried out'.[1]

Ryley prepared the tables, but the Association did not at once proceed. The operatives' suggestion in the summer of 1852 came exactly at the point where James Gillman, Henry Harben and Henry Barfoot were trying to stabilise the Association's finances: they were just about to seek the £3,000 loan mentioned previously. Not until nearly a year later was the idea suddenly seen in a more positive light.

The increase in the number of life assurance companies during the late 1840s and early 1850s had brought mixed benefits. Between 1844, the year of the Joint Stock Companies' Act, and 1853, 311 assurance companies were provisionally registered and 140 completely registered, though only 96 of these survived at the latter date.[2] By late 1852, after the public had been treated to a protracted dispute in the press among representatives of the older assurance houses and their younger rivals, there were enough official doubts about the way some institutions came into being and how they functioned – or didn't – to prompt the creation of a House of Commons Select Committee on Assurance Associations, which delivered its *Report* in April 1853.[3]

It was generally accepted that sound life assurance served the public well: James Wilson, Secretary to the Treasury, in his speech before the House of Commons had expressed the view, regarding insurance offices, that he knew of '... nothing in the history of modern inventions, or in the progress of modern ingenuity which, in a social point of view, was of greater importance than the establishment of these offices'.[4] While others in the House might not have been quite so fulsome in their praise, it was on the whole agreed, despite the frauds and collapses attendant on the nascent industry, that the growth of life assurance was a beneficial development.

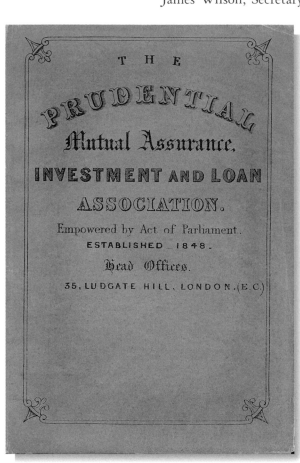

The prospectus of The Prudential Mutual Assurance, Investment and Loan Association, 1852–60.

Among the topics covered by the Select Committee's *Report* was the purported existence of 'a sort of intermediate business, something between the great majority of life assurance offices and the friendly societies', which was supplying assurance for small sums. F.G.P. Neison, Actuary to the Medical and Invalid Life Office, testified before the Select Committee that in his opinion such business was on the rise. He was then questioned:

Q. 2347. It consists of life policies effected by persons of a lower station in society than those who assure in the other life offices, and for smaller sums?
A. Yes, by careful working men and small tradesmen.
Q. 2348. Do you consider that that is a sort of business which, on public grounds, should be encouraged?
A. Undoubtedly, because it reaches the people themselves, the bulk of the community.[5]

One of the Select Committee's conclusions developed the point:

... the ground hitherto occupied by these useful institutions has been comparatively limited, and their application is capable of great extension, not only in the higher and middle classes of society, but also among the humbler classes, to whom it has been recently very considerably applied; it is, therefore, very important that no check or impediment should be placed in the way of further extension of this enterprise not absolutely necessary for the security of the public.[6]

When the Select Committee referred to this kind of business having recently been 'very considerably applied' among the 'humbler classes', it may well have been singling out a company known as 'The British Industry Life Assurance Company and Family Friendly Society'. This entity (registered under both the Companies' Act 1844 and the Friendly Societies' Act 1829 so that purchasers of policies could avoid stamp duty) came into being in 1852, apparently as an offshoot of one called the Industrial and General which had operated from Waterloo Place since 1849.[7] The British Industry claimed, via its 'Industrial Provident Branch', to be the first to have 'adopted a machinery likely, in reality, to reach the masses who have hitherto been overlooked' by combining the friendly society and burial club practice of small weekly premiums with the insurance companies' provision of varying the amount assured according to the age and state of health of the proposer. This was put forward as the solution to the problem of eventual insolvency resulting from the levying of uniform payments, regardless of age at entry. That this problem was real enough we have already seen. Whether the British Industry would live up to its claims was, in the spring of 1853, impossible to tell. On paper, at least, it appeared to be thriving. A prospectus issued by it in 1853 contained a page describing the 'Progress of the Institution', which showed that 12,837 policies had been issued in the company's first six months of life, assuring some £173,199.[8]

The Directors of the Prudential, meanwhile, were sufficiently intrigued by the findings of the Select Committee to be making enquiries into the existing state of insurance for the labouring classes. As they knew, the middle classes were the ones who insured their lives with assurance companies; the burial club or friendly society was the usual facility for the less well off, and in these, 'the grossest mismanagement almost universally prevailed ... the subscriptions were in almost every instance totally inadequate to meet the benefits promised'. With respect to the burial clubs:

> *The collectors ... belonged, as a rule, to a class who preferred preying upon their neighbours to earning an honest livelihood in their own calling; the committees perpetrated the most serious frauds upon the public; the funds were recklessly squandered; and the benefits were only paid so long as it was profitable to do so, and when it ceased to be profitable, the committee had no hesitation about breaking up the Club and transferring their services to some other town or neighbourhood.[9]*

It was clear that there was a pressing need for an alternative to the existing system, and – if the evidence given to the Select Committee, and the operatives' deputation the previous year were anything to go by – a demand for it from working people themselves. In the example of the few insurance companies which had been bold enough to step into the breach, there were grounds for optimism. The Prudential's enquiries revealed that the 'special working-class section' of the Industrial and General had already transacted 'a fair amount of business', and that the British Industry had also 'commenced Industrial business, and had issued a very large number of policies'.[10] Edward Ryley was probably the source of this information, as he of all people would have known whether the British Industry's success was well founded and possible to emulate.[11]

Not to be outdone, and somewhat more confident of the Association's future in the light of 1852's improved results, the Directors of the Prudential decided to set up an industrial section of their own, to commence business in 1854. They were not deterred by the fact that 1853 did not bear out the promise of 1852; as a result of the recent alteration in the Deed of Settlement the shareholders received their first dividend, of 5%, on 18 April 1854, and this must have struck an optimistic note.[12] If the unsettled situation abroad that in March had become the Crimean War worried the Directors, there is no trace of it in surviving documents. The 'Industrial Department' was established on 14 September 1854 (the day of the Battle of Inkermann), under John Clark and his brother Thomas, who were each given the title of Superintendent of Agents.[13] The first agents were engaged on 28 September.

The Industrial Department used Ryley's tables, and offered somewhat lower rates assured for 1d per week than those being used by the British Industry.[14] There were eight tables or plans, six of which offered the possibility of withdrawal, whereby the policyholder, once two years' premiums were paid, could surrender the policy for half the premiums paid or take a loan of that amount at 5%. The oldest age assured was 60 and the youngest, 10. The proposer had to pay a deposit of 1s entrance fee and 6d for a policy stamp (the duty which the British Industry, with its dual registration, had managed to evade). The premium receipt book in which payments were to be recorded every seven days cost a penny. The acceptance of a proposal, then, cost the client, in all, 1s 7d, which was not an inconsiderable sum to be paid all at once compared with the penny a week needed to keep the policy in force.

Considering the Association's precarious existence so far, the decision to go ahead with industrial insurance may be regarded as an attempt on the part of the Directors to catch hold of the coat-tails of opportunity. Their habitual caution, however, was very much in evidence in the regulations governing the Industrial Department. The British Industry apparently operated special insurance plans for high-risk groups of workers, such as miners. Such persons could obtain policies that would assure them of £25 on death by accident, for the sum of 3s 6d in advance, payable annually, or 'to suit the pay table of the miner', 2d per fortnight or 1d per week.[15] This was possibly seen as less than prudent by the Directors of the Prudential, since mining accidents, like shipwrecks, railway disasters and explosions, usually took a multiple toll of lives.[16] Applicants for Prudential industrial policies who were employed as 'Soldier, Sailor, Policeman, Waterman, Lighterman, Miner or Railway Servant' had to pay a higher than normal premium. Moreover, no-one already insured was to take up one of these occupations without permission, and must then 'submit to such increase in the amount of the Premium ... or such reduction in the amount of the Sum Assured as the Directors shall in each case decide upon'.[17] Another area where the Directors decided to exercise caution was in the assurance of the lives of children. Infant and child mortality was so high that the Prudential initially chose not to insure children younger than ten years old. There was also the wish to avoid even the shadow of any involvement in the periodic debate about whether the assurance of young children contributed to infanticide.[18] This was not, however, a position that it was possible to maintain for very long in the field of industrial assurance, as the first few years of the Industrial Department would reveal.

The Directors did not wish to reduce the criteria for 'quality' lives that applied in its usual business, nor to incur the cost of early claims. Medical examinations were therefore required for all prospective policyholders, though the Association paid the cost of these. Not for the Prudential was the claim made by the Chairman of the British Industry (which demanded no medical test) to the effect that 'Their agents were a body of intelligent men, and from the experience they had now acquired, they were able to judge as to the eligibility of candidates, as well as any doctor'.[19] This assertion was made during a public meeting, and quickly countered by an accountant who questioned whether agents, intelligent or not, '... could go out in the evening and by some intuitive faculty determine subjects which a life of long devotion to medical science could not do more than making [*sic*] them competent to decide'.

Whatever attributes the Board of the Prudential expected from those it engaged as agents, acting as judges of fitness was not one of them. They were not to pronounce on individuals, beyond using their eyes and common sense to avoid sending people who were obviously sickly for examination by local doctors, who were paid a fee for acting as medical referees. Even the burial clubs forbade those employed in particularly unhealthy trades, such as lead mining or milling, from becoming members, and demanded that six or twelve months' contributions be received before any claim was made.

But even if 'quality' lives were felt to be a priority for the Industrial Department as for ordinary business, it was clear that the same methods were not suitable for both. Making inroads in the uninsured working population demanded that the people be reached directly, in their own homes; they had no time to visit distant offices. Advertising, the usual means of appealing to the artisan and middle classes, was wasted on the illiterate poor. Agents who could go from house to house, as the collectors of the burial clubs and friendly societies did, were the answer, but in far greater numbers than for ordinary business. That industrial business required different tactics was recognised by leading actuaries such as F.G.P. Neison, who asserted that to tap the great reservoir of the uninsured,

'... you must saturate the country with a number of agents who are active in making the institution known, and the advantage which it is capable of conferring ...'.[20] What it came down to was competing with the burial clubs and friendly societies on their own ground: using their collecting methods, while ensuring that the administration and actuarial basis of the business were sound.

An early dilemma was how, in the effort to 'saturate the country' with agents, it was possible to avoid taking on examples of what Henry Harben would

The slums of Seven Dials, in what is now London's Covent Garden, were a notorious breeding ground for vice and disease.

later describe as 'a class of men who might be called, without harshness, the veriest scum of England'. Initially, it was not completely possible. Many who offered themselves for employment as agents were products – even promoters – of those same burial clubs, seeking work because the institutions in question had ceased to exist. There were a number of excellent men among the Association's first intake of agents, among them John Peel, or Pell, who retired from his Stockport agency a prosperous man in 1875. Some like Pell, John Tongue and William Chadwick, embarked at this time on careers as Prudential agents and superintendents that would last for a quarter of a century or more. Their professional success raises the question of what, exactly, made a good agent. Though the overall description from which the following lines are taken relates to the position of superintendent, the qualities identified are those that would also have fitted a man for agency work. Such a task required

*... a knowledge of men, knowledge of the practical working, and the scientific appli-
cation of Life Assurance to every man's wants – a ready reply to every objection, ...
and above all, a peculiar tact that cannot be described, but which is thoroughly
marked and recognised in a few individuals.*

*A man to represent a respectable Office, should likewise have the education of a
gentleman, to enable him to mix in any society, and yet without any pride that
should prevent him being "Hail fellow, well met" with a cobbler.*[21]

That an agent be literate and numerate, not an evident sufferer from any vice,
possessed of sufficient personal contacts in his own neighbourhood to get off to
a good start, the initiative and persistence to expand this circle, and enough
sturdy independence to organise his day unsupervised – these were the essential
requirements. Of these, persistence had a special importance. Competition for
'good lives' was fierce in many industrial towns as the burial clubs fought back
against the companies seeking to enter the market for industrial insurance.[22]
(The companies simply engaged more agents.) Life assurance was not initially
easy to sell or to explain at their level. The appeal to scripture – 'But if any provide not for his own, and especially for those of his own house, he hath denied
the faith and is worse than an infidel' – was a commonplace, but even where this
struck a chord, there were practical obstacles. Even simple tables, presented to
illiterate labouring folk, often produced confusion. Industrial assurance had
no equivalent to the payments in sickness and old age promised by friendly
societies. No amount of talk about the peace of mind of providing for one's
dependants could make the Prudential's compulsory medical examination more
appealing. Finally, there was most people's inherent dislike of commitment.[23]
These attitudes would be altered within a reasonably short space of years, but
not without effort.

The Prudential's Industrial Department, having come into being in
September 1854 and having established the ground rules for agents and policyholders in October, proceeded to sell its first policies and appoint its first clerk,
G.J.K. Gillespie, in November. By the end of the year 126 policies had been
sold. The first industrial claim, for £30 6s, came in January 1855 and was the
result of a railway accident.

Initially, the Association resisted the idea of 'saturating' populous industrial cities with agents, mainly on the grounds of expense, but also because
men of character to occupy supervisory positions were few. It was thought that
branch offices where premiums could be paid would be more economical.
Manchester, Birmingham and Liverpool were the areas chosen, and a Mr Neal
joined the brothers Clark as a Superintendent, to be based in Manchester with
responsibility for the new offices. Neal was an energetic individual who saw
the need to adapt methods to circumstances. He was the originator of the
idea of publishing a testimonial signed by 'Clergy, Ministers, Magistrates,

Municipal Authorities and Gentlemen' of the industrial cities, to the effect that, in their opinion,

the benefits and advantages arising from Life Assurance are calculated to promote provident habits and social economy amongst the "Industrial Population", and that its more general adoption would be the means of averting much destitution and distress by securing a competency for the Widows and Orphans as well as a degree of independence to families of working men generally, and we have consented to our names being published with a view to lending our sanction and aid to the furtherance of this most desirable object, as promoted by Mr Neal.

One of his first ideas – an astonishing one for the time, and the fact that the Prudential accepted it even more so – was to engage married women as canvassers. 'Canvassing' really meant drumming up business – identifying and interesting likely proposals, then passing them on to the local agent. (Perhaps in Manchester where the idea was tried, it meant encouraging people to visit the branch office.) Since in working-class homes the wives usually controlled the purse strings, it may have been felt that women canvassers had a natural advantage in talking to housewives about life assurance, particularly about how the weekly penny premium was to be found. There is no indication how many women were employed, but their agreement stipulated that they should be allowed the 1s entrance fee on all business introduced by them. They were not to work on Saturday afternoons – presumably because working men would be at home then, or perhaps because the canvassers' own husbands would be.

It was one thing to engage staff and another to keep them. Previous accounts of the Company's early years mention the existence of a rival called the Safety Life Assurance Company, similarly seeking industrial business and directed, among others, by politicians Richard Cobden and John Bright. This company was swallowed up by another in 1859 after only a few years, but its formation is said to have involved John and Thomas Clark, who left the Prudential after a short time.[24] Neal's career was also brief: in September 1855 he had to confess to the Board that his clerk 'had committed defalcations' and was told that he had not exercised proper caution in appointing the man. Offended, he left shortly afterwards with a £25 settlement. Interest in a proposed 'Ladies Life Office' which was being discussed at this time – was it his idea? – evaporated.[25]

There is no way of knowing quite what was spent in setting up the Industrial Department, but the inference must be that expenses were high. Premium income in 1855 from this source exceeded £2,000 (1,937 policies were sold), but by the spring of 1856 the Directors were deeply concerned about the Company's indebtedness, which mainly derived from the new additional costs. Henry Harben later wrote that the branch offices were expensive, and that neither they nor the testimonials referred to above brought in any business to speak of. On 20 May the Board decided to look hard at the workings of the Industrial Department.

There were two questions for which it sought answers: whether the amount of new business since the beginning of the year justified continuing for the rest of it, and whether the general level of expenditure was warranted by the amount of business obtained. The answer to the first emerged as a resounding negative; the answer to the second was less easy to determine. It was clear that expenses were unwarrantably high, but while some of the Directors felt that industrial assurance ought to be abandoned, others were unwilling to let what had been spent so far go for naught. On the other hand, what had begun as an experiment could not be allowed to imperil the Prudential's future.

The measures taken between May and July 1856 determined the survival of the Industrial Department and, in the longer term, the orientation of the Prudential. Paid-up capital at this point amounted to only about £2,750. A call of £1 was made on the shares, but brought in little; it was then that, in Harben's words, 'The bold step was therefore adopted of declaring forfeited all the shares upon which the calls had not been paid', so as to avoid the need for compulsion against the non-payers and the possibility of their forming a nucleus of future discontent. The amount of nominal capital disposed of by this means was £34,120, though it represented only about £1,000 paid-up.[26] At the same time the Directors had a final, concerted round of borrowing and raised £35,000 from friends and from their own resources.

Stringent economies were also introduced, and though it can be assumed that these were generally applied, the only individual whom they are known to have affected was Henry Barfoot. His £200-a-year salary remained untouched, but premium income now had to surpass £5,000 before he got his additional £50, and his commission on the business he introduced disappeared. He was also asked to undertake the supervision of agents, to save the cost of engaging another superintendent. This and other measures seem hard – perhaps Barfoot was not popular, though the meticulousness of the minutes and the tasks delegated to him suggest that he served the Company well.[27] When he protested, he was 'invited' to tender his resignation, did so, and left the Company's employ with a £300 payment. His departure left the way open for Henry Harben.

The background of the man who now moved to a central position at a crucial point in the Prudential's affairs is worth examining. The circumstances of Harben's early life are tantalisingly difficult to discern. Later, when he was wealthy and respected, he avoided ever revealing anything about his past. His education and professional training, for example, were areas that appear to have been kept deliberately well hidden. He was born on 23 August 1823, the fourth but second surviving child of Henry Harben, a wholesale provisioner of Whitechapel High Street, and Sarah Da Costa Andrade, who came from a

FACING PAGE

A simplified genealogy of the Harben family.

Portuguese Jewish family. His father was one of 18 children and traced the family's ancestry to Lewes in Sussex, where clock-making and banking had made it prosperous. Its wealth had dwindled by the time Harben senior was born, although it was still comfortably off. (One of his many sisters, Caroline Harben, married Joseph Chamberlain, a Unitarian and a partner in a family ironmongery business in Milk Street in the City of London. Their eldest child, also called Joseph Chamberlain, became the famous politician, and was thus the younger Henry Harben's first cousin.)

Between 1824 and 1830 five more children were born to Henry Harben and Sarah Da Costa Andrade. Then, according to a Chamberlain family pedigree, when the young Henry was just eight years old, his father 'deserted his wife ... and lived with Mary Anne Roberts ...' by whom he had two more children. There are no clues about how Sarah managed, financially or emotionally, to bring up her young family. She was one of seven children herself, left well-off through a bequest from her father, a merchant who owned numerous properties in the East End of London, but in marrying outside her religion, she had placed herself far from the usual avenues of support. Her brother-in-law Charles Harben, who took over the Whitechapel business after the death of his father in 1831, maintained a kindly interest, and, as an adolescent, the young Henry went to work in what was now his uncle's store. But Charles Harben was no businessman, and had five children of his own. When in short succession both he and his errant brother Henry went bankrupt, the outlook for the two families must indeed have been bleak. To add to Sarah's heartbreak, two of her small daughters died, possibly in the cholera epidemic of 1832. The five remaining children – Henry, his brother Benjamin, and sisters Sarah, Julia and Emily – grew up on the fringes of an extended clan centred on the Chamberlain household, first in Camberwell Grove, then in Islington.[28] Their array of cousins included the Nettlefolds, the Baileys and the dauntingly clever Martineaus. There is nothing to suggest that the Harben children and their mother suffered from the stigma of desertion and the elder Harben's bankruptcy. It is possible, however, that Sarah's inheritance had been squandered by her wayward husband, and that the children's education was paid for by their uncle-by-marriage, Joseph Chamberlain senior.[29]

The young Henry Harben, then, had experienced sufficient insecurity in the first decade of his life to leave a mark on any child. He grew up a strong-willed survivor for whom the narrowness of the line between comfort and want, between 'respectability' and its opposite, was never forgotten. For a boy in such an ambiguous situation as his, life was a stark contrast between the sunny drawing room in Camberwell Grove where his aunt Caroline allowed the group of young cousins to mount theatricals, and the squalor of the teeming streets around the Whitechapel store. So much responsibility early in life made him conscientious; fortunately, he was endowed with robust health, and the combination produced driving ambition and seemingly limitless energy.

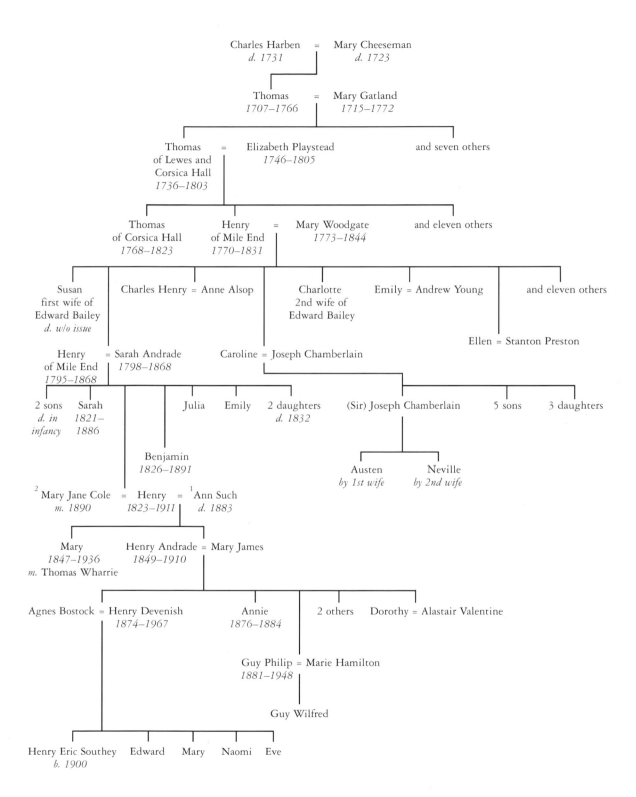

It cannot have been accidental that he so clearly saw life assurance as a weapon against insecurity and poverty. Harben was well acquainted with the artisan and tradesman class, whose economic independence rested on the determined application of skills. He knew at first hand how easily the scaffolding of such lives could be destroyed by accident, illness or death. He also must have seen the conditions – the crowding, the ignorance and disease – which dogged the lives of the multitude of people below that stratum. This was the milieu into which he and his brother and sisters, had they been less fortunate in their connections, might easily have fallen. To claim for him a sense of mission is not an overstatement. He was a married man with two small children when he came to the Prudential.[30] By his own account he was imbued with the same faith in industrial assurance as the Directors of the Prudential had shown all along, but with the difference of having seen some of the conditions mentioned in the prospectus at close quarters.[31]

Reducing expenditure and increasing efficiency were the first priorities in his reorganisation. The branch offices, envisaged as just as effective and cheaper than collectors, had attracted little business and proved almost as costly. It would have been easy – and probably fatal at this point – to abandon the branch offices, hastily hire dozens of agents and attempt to compete at once with the burial clubs. Instead, it was decided to alter the system gradually. Those in charge of these offices (others must have been engaged after the first three left) and the leading agents were called to London to discuss the particular needs of their areas. Two innovations resulted from these conversations. With the aim of investigating where efforts might best be concentrated, Henry Harben was deputised to spend at least half his time travelling: visiting the industrial centres where the branch offices were, together with likely new areas where in due course agents might be appointed. He would spend the next dozen years like this, moving from one great city to another, from urban centre to county town, on three days of each week, keeping an unfaltering eye on expenses.[32]

The other new departure was the decision to insure very young children. This came about through the discovery that the agent for the Potteries, a man called Bell, was alone among the agents summoned to London in having obtained a great deal of industrial business. He had found the Prudential's lack of provision for children under the age of 10 a barrier to selling policies to parents. Working people were 'anxious to insure their children, as in the event of death they found the funeral expenses press very hard upon them, and gladly welcomed the aid which a Society afforded'. Mr Bell had given them the 'Society' they wanted by starting one himself, accepting premiums on their children's lives and paying any claims out of his own pocket. The possibility of insuring the whole family had increased the number of his adult policyholders accordingly. Contrary to prevailing opinion, the mortality rate on the children so insured had not proved high.

Harben promptly devised a children's table to add to the Prudential's tables, taking into account the mortality risk involved, the expenses to be incurred, and the likely interest that could be gained on the monies paid in. Under this scheme children as young as three months could be insured. The premiums were deliberately kept as low as possible. The policy had to have been in force for at least three months before a claim could be made, but for 1d a week a child could be insured for up to £10, depending on its age. The amount payable on the deaths of children under five was deliberately kept small to eliminate 'the temptation to infanticide', and achieved a maximum only at the age when a child could begin to earn. The Association was still wary of this type of insurance and at first confined it to the area of the Potteries, buying Mr Bell's 'Child's Society' in December 1856.[33] During the next two years it became apparent that insuring children was one means of extending industrial business rapidly; indeed, it was not really possible to resist the demand for it – or the demand for assurances on old people – and succeed. As to the infanticide question, Harben reflected more than 20 years later that:

> ... while the numbers of lives admitted are counted by millions, the experience of the Company completely negatives the idea that malfeasance generally is practised, for, in the twenty years during which the practice of infantile assurance has been carried on, no such case has been known to have occurred, and only two in which the circumstances were of a distinctly suspicious character.[34]

During the several years following the decision to persevere with industrial assurance, Henry Harben saw the immense possibilities for the growth of this business at first hand. In his travels around the country he found employers in the great manufacturing cities receptive to the idea of insurance, and was often permitted to address the men right in the factories. In smaller centres meetings were held in schoolrooms, though Harben suspected that linking them so visibly with authority may have kept some people away.

Coming face-to-face with the Company's representatives was a salutary experience, in the light of what has been said above about the quality of many of them. Harben himself engaged many agents and superintendents, personally interviewing those who applied by letter for positions. Some of these would disappoint him: he carried back to the Board in London his decisions about those who misappropriated funds, allowed their collections to get into arrears, kept illegible accounts or brought the Company's name into disrepute. If the number of dismissals recorded in the Company minutes are anything to go by, he had by now inspired in the Board great confidence in his judgment, as his suggested course of action was never refused.[35] He had no hesitation in prosecuting a really dishonest man. One such individual, a collector working out of the Birmingham branch office, forged an industrial policy and was sentenced to four years' penal servitude. On more than one occasion Harben and Dr Patrick Fraser visited Millbank Prison or some other gaol to identify men who had attempted to defraud the Company.

His motive for being so intransigent, wholly supported by the Directors, was to ensure that by being seen to put its own house in order, the Prudential would achieve a reputation for fair dealing that would lift it above its rivals. The way forward was not simply to be larger, but to be larger and universally trusted. Harben saw that there were virtually no limits to the growth that popular recognition of the Prudential's honesty might generate. For this reason he was just as forceful in prosecuting ex-agents who libelled the Company in the press after being discharged as those who damaged it from within. There were a number of instances in the late 1850s when disgruntled agents – or rival companies – published comment that reflected badly upon the Association and were threatened by Harben with prosecution; a retraction was the usual means of ending the incident.

But the emphasis must have been on finding the right men rather than on weeding out the unsuitable ones, for the number of agents appointed spiralled ever upward. In 1857, the first year that Harben carried out his investigations, more than 100 were appointed; in 1858, 237, and in the following year, 437. The number of industrial policies rose correspondingly, from 3,050 in 1856 to 6,842 in 1857, 12,435 in 1858 and 18,123 in 1859 – a six-fold increase in less than four years.[36] Other factors may have contributed to this, such as a further wave of epidemics during these years: cholera, typhus and the newly arrived 'Boulogne Disease', or diphtheria. The real reasons, however, were probably the following. The first was the suitability of the agency system to the clientele the company sought to win. The lacklustre performance of the branch offices suggested that if the Association were going to compete effectively with the burial clubs and friendly societies, it could no longer resist adopting wholeheartedly the direct methods used by them: door-to-door collections. The large-scale creation of agencies after 1856 took the product to the customer in the way most convenient to him. Payments collected weekly at the policyholder's own door avoided the further investment of time or money needed to visit an office. Neither was there any substitute for the agent's direct explanation of the advantages of a life policy.

The second reason was the Company's adoption of certain principles that enhanced the reputation for fair dealing referred to above, and its success in making this known. One of these principles was the exceedingly simple one of paying claims as quickly as possible. A working-class household usually had no finances in reserve to meet immediate costs when misfortune struck. To the poorer classes, as James Gillman commented at the Annual General Meeting in April 1857,

... an immediate payment of a £5 or a £10 note is of the very greatest service when death visits their dwellings, as it enables them to pay a doctor's bill or the funeral expenses attendant upon the decease of their departed relative or friend. I hold in my hand a letter ... written by a poor man ... fervently thanking us for the assistance which has been so timely rendered to him, and promising to do all he can to make known among his neighbours the blessings of this society. We have many similar letters ... .

Industrial claims were as yet very few (amounting to only £467 in 1857), a circumstance Gillman credited to Dr Fraser and to the 'country' medical officers engaged to examine proposals. There is no doubt that in industrial business, as in ordinary business (the assurance for the middle and upper classes originally undertaken by the Association), care was taken in the selection of lives. In contrast to the practice of some companies which did not demand a medical examination, the Prudential accepted proposals on the assumption that if a medical investigation had already been carried out, the Company could respond quickly when a claim was made, confident that it was genuine.

Another such principle, and one for which Henry Harben was able to gain public approval for the Prudential, was in the matter of 'days of grace'. This concerned a lawsuit in the Court of Common Pleas early in 1858, revolving around the death of a policyholder within the allowed period of 30 days' grace, the premium having been submitted within the period but after the death of the policyholder. The verdict for the defendants, the Merchant's and Tradesman's Life, touched off a debate in the pages of the *Post Magazine* that ran for weeks.

Harben's letter of 27 February to the Editor clarified a point of law and contested the verdict. In its conclusion he requested that the Prudential's name be added to the list of companies '*bound* to pay if a claim arises during the days of grace' and pointing out that it had already paid one such claim, when the premium was not tendered until the last day. 'Moreover,' he pointed out, 'we were the first Company to enter our indignant protest against the monstrous decision of the Common Pleas.'[37] This referred to the notice issued by the Directors immediately after the court decision: 'That payment in their Office within the days of grace will be considered valid, and that all claims arising within that time will be admitted in the same manner as if the premiums had been absolutely paid'. The *Post Magazine* considered its list of companies pledging themselves to do the same 'so important that it will be kept standing in its present place, so long as we are enabled to make additions to it', and within a few weeks the list grew to a full column of names.

By 1858 the beneficial results of the measures taken two years earlier were becoming visible as increased premium income – at £7,382, nearly double that of the year before – and reduced expenses. Of this, some £5,743 derived from new business, up considerably over the £3,997 of 1857 and the £2,042 of 1856

– and this in a year of economic disruption 'characterised by some of the leading journals as one of the worst insurance years on record'. Some insurance companies had foundered or been taken over during a commercial crisis similar to that of 1847. The Prudential, however, weathered this storm and in 1859 could report a further rise in premium income, to £10,909. The exceptionally rapid expansion of the Industrial Department in the previous two years acted as a brake on the Directors' wish to declare a bonus; as usual, caution prevailed, as they had heard that 'some offices had materially affected their prospects in the anxiety to divide profits at too early a period'.[38]

One incident which reveals that, although cautious, the Board was willing to take a chance in singular circumstances was that of the Leeds Burial Club. The manager of this, it seems, had utilised the premiums he had received for his own purposes, leaving nothing for the payment of claims that might arise. He possessed sufficient vestiges of a conscience – or regard for his own reputation – to seek a way out of the inevitable embarrassment and distress his dishonesty was likely to cause, and approached the Prudential with a view to transferring the membership. The Company baulked temporarily, as some of the persons assured were not in sufficiently good health to pass the required medical examination. The probability of a rapid increase of business as a result of this transaction swung the balance, however, and the unfit were accepted along with the healthy, as a consideration for goodwill. The former manager was even taken on as an agent – and proved, according to Harben's account of things, one of the most successful. Leeds and other nearby towns, to which this episode provided an introduction, became in time one of the Prudential's key areas.

The successful reorientation of the Industrial Department after 1856 showed also in the growth of the staff. Some of those who joined the Company in these years eventually came to hold high office, and founded family connections that lasted until well into the twentieth century. Such were Thomas Dewey and William Lancaster, appointed as clerks at the age of 16. R.T. Pugh, Thomas Bulman Cole and Thomas Reid became Directors.[39] They, together with Gillman (who seems to have been a popular Chairman), Edgar Horne, James Allanson, Peter Sers and George Clark, with Dr Fraser and Dr Barnes as medical advisors, directed the Company. It was not, as Gillman once put it, 'a Board of great names, yet we have been a working industrious Board, and we have endeavoured, as far as we could conscientiously, to discharge those duties which we have undertaken ...'.[40]

A most satisfying duty it must have been to approve, on 1 November 1860, the 'offer from another Company to transfer their business to this Association' placed before the Board by Henry Harben. The 'other Company' was the Prudential's only real rival, the British Industry. Harben himself is the only first-hand source for the background to how this came about. Late in 1859, he was apparently travelling more than he normally did. On a journey to Liverpool he met John Plumb, the Managing Director of the rival firm, who 'hinted' that an offer to take over its business might be favourably received. Harben promptly made one. In the autumn of the following year Plumb called at Ludgate Hill to ask whether the offer had been serious: if so, the British Industry was prepared to accept. Its Chairman since 1852, Dr Jonathon Elmore, had died on 26 August and the rest of its Board were also elderly. An agreement was signed a few days later.[41]

The legal steps needed to effect the move went on through November and December 1860.[42] Because the Prudential's original deed of settlement contained no provision for taking such a step, a new deed was prepared, and executed on 17 January 1861. The Association was thus dissolved, and under this document a new company was registered as the British Prudential Assurance Company. The shares were again divided, this time into shares of £5 with 10s paid, and the shareholders (to whom was payable a 5% dividend in the five-yearly valuation) were given the right to participate in the profits along with the policyholders.

The British Industry was the larger and richer company, with assets of £18,000, a premium income for 1860 of £25,000 of which £6,000 was new business, and more than 200,000 industrial policies in force. The Prudential's premium income of £18,000, of which £12,000 was new, indicates that its growth rate was the healthier; indeed, the figures suggest, as does reading between the lines of Harben's narrative of these years, that the British Industry's new business was falling off badly, possibly because of the Prudential's level of activity.[43] This may have been particularly true in the British Industry's traditional strongholds in the north of England, where, as reports of Henry Harben's journeys indicate, great emphasis was being placed by the Prudential. Apart from the purchase price of £29,928, details of this important merger are disappointingly scarce.[44]

'The advantages to the shareholders are obvious,' Harben had written in his letter to them dated 19 November 1860, 'for, with the same amount of capital employed, the income will be more than doubled, and the per centage of expenses considerably reduced.' Whether he was right, the next few years would tell. Posterity and previous histories of the Company have tended to see the merger as a turning point for the Prudential, the point at which the struggling Association began to look like living. This was far from having been the case, as its progress following the reorganisation of the Industrial Department in 1856 should indicate. However great was the boost given to the Prudential by the events of 1860, the evidence suggests that the Company had already shifted into a higher gear. Henry Harben was quite rightly given credit for the amalgamation; his more profound achievement was to have salvaged and shaped the Association in the years preceding it.

By his colleagues, Harben was seen as the man of the hour. After only four years as Secretary he had become indispensable. He was given a rise in salary and £50 to buy 'a watch and appendages'. The Directors also offered him a choice of three gifts: a £500 debenture payable in two years' time; a whole-life policy for £1,000, or an endowment policy for £700 payable when he became 50 years old. He chose the third but, in thanking the Board, asked that the sum be reduced to £500, 'from a conviction that in the present juncture of our affairs we must all exercise self-denial and must show others that in the first flood of prosperity we can keep our judgments cool and remember the vicissitudes through which we have passed'.

SECTION TWO

Growing into Greatness

Confronting Mr Gladstone

W ITH the acquisition of its only rival in the field of industrial assurance, the British Prudential began the steady climb that in little more than a decade would make it the largest assurance company in the United Kingdom. In 1861 new income exceeded the anticipated £18,000 by a comfortable margin to reach £19,370. The results of the third valuation, in the autumn of 1861, prompted the declaration of the Company's first bonus: 10%, or 10s, added to the shares, and an average bonus of 25% or 25s, to non-industrial life policies that predated the merger.

The new business figures were especially pleasing because the economic slump that affected agriculture, commerce and manufacturing at the turn of the decade had worsened with the outbreak of the American Civil War in April 1861. By the following winter the blockade imposed by the North on Confederate goods was creating real distress in the Lancashire cotton districts. As the supply of raw cotton dried up, men were thrown out of work in their thousands. The British Prudential's Report for 1862 referred to the 'unparalleled stagnation of trade caused by the cotton famine', and certainly the northwest of England, the former stronghold of the British Industry, must have produced little in the way of new business while the adverse conditions lasted. It did, however, produce men who became Prudential agents when their work in the cotton mills so abruptly came to an end. Company tradition has it that John Moon, who had come into the Company through the British Industry, enlisted George (later Sir George) Green, George Twyford and others from this area. Moon's own two sons, John and James, also became agents. All of these put in long days building up debits, against strong opposition from other agents. They also found time to recruit more men of the same type: self-educated, usually teetotal, non-conformist, and well acquainted with the habits of the working class through their own experience in the textile and other industries.

The 'cotton famine' had one other consequence that is of interest with reference to the Company, in that it inspired Henry Harben to try to devise a substitute for the cotton plant! In his tours of the cotton districts, the suffering of the factory people impressed him deeply. He had little time to spare, but what he had he spent in his laboratory, where he carried out scientific and photographic experiments.[1] His attempts to produce a viable substitute for cotton fibre using the marine plant *Zostera marina*, and a machine that would extract the fibre from the plant, resulted in two patents, but cost prevented the process from being developed commercially.[2]

Shortly after the takeover of the British Industry, the Ludgate Hill premises were rebuilt to accommodate the business resulting from the amalgamation.[3] The British Prudential's offices, 'though large, were inconveniently arranged', and the best course seemed to be to pull them down and rebuild on the site, on which an extension of the lease had been obtained. The Company moved into temporary premises at No. 6 John Street, Bedford Row, while the rebuilding was going on. The Annual General Meeting held on 8 May 1863 found the British Prudential back at Ludgate Hill. The new building was built in an 'Anglo-Greek' style, and had a modest redbrick frontage 20 feet wide; the *Building News* commented that while it enjoyed a modicum of decoration, it 'kept to that *juste milieu* which does what is required and no more', in a truly 'prudential' fashion.[4]

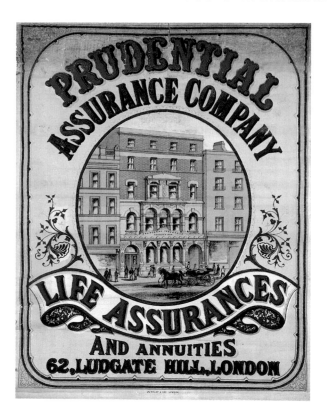

The British Prudential's new offices in Ludgate Hill, 1863.

At every Annual General Meeting, much emphasis was placed on the Directors' commitment to rigorous financial control. It was this that would enable the Company to settle claims immediately and keep expenses down.[5] It was clearly wise for the British Prudential to distance itself from competitors by acquiring a reputation for financial soundness and efficiency in its dealings. The effort was worthwhile. In September 1863, the Registrar of Friendly Societies – John Tidd Pratt – published his Report, which drew attention to the numerous failures of friendly societies during the previous year, and itemised some of the complaints about the way they functioned. There was a protracted public discussion of the subject in the national press. The upshot was that W.E. Gladstone, the Chancellor of the Exchequer and the outstanding figure in the Liberal Government then in office, took up the question.

Gladstone's aim was to provide a secure alternative source of assurance for the labouring classes. On 11 February 1864 he introduced a Bill in the House of Commons to amend the law relating to the purchase of Government annuities through the medium of the Post Office Savings Banks. Under legislation of

1853, the Government could grant assurance up to the amount of £100, with the proviso that purchasers had to buy a deferred annuity at the same time as the assurance.[6] By removing this restriction and making it possible for people to purchase assurance or annuities by small deposits through the Savings Banks, the Chancellor sought '... to offer facilities for the increase and extension of frugal habits among the industrious classes'.[7]

As Gladstone asserted three weeks later when the Bill went to debate, it was not aimed primarily at the assurance companies, but at the friendly societies and, at 'the wholesale error, deception, fraud and swindling, which are perpetrated upon the most helpless portion of the community, who find themselves without defence'.[8]

Nonetheless, the prospect of direct competition from the Government was most unwelcome to the companies undertaking industrial assurance. When in subsequent debate they were lumped together with the friendly societies, their managements felt that their particular contribution to working-class thrift was being unfairly tarred. On behalf of the British Prudential, Henry Harben wrote to Gladstone on 13 February, putting the case against removing the limit on Government assurances.[9] As the 'pioneers of a new system', the Prudential had 170,000 policyholders, 'of whom no less that 68,363' had joined during 1863, and whose numbers were still being swelled by an average of 1,500 per week, 'notwithstanding the dulness [*sic*] of the time and the depth of winter'. Harben's company could compete fairly with the Government under the existing limits, but the view was very forcefully expressed that 'if the restriction be removed it will be utterly useless for this Company to continue its operations ... and the proposed Bill would therefore be a most injurious interference with the business of this office'.[10]

After the Bill's second reading on 15 February, Harben wrote again to protest more vigorously. It was, he agreed, the duty of Government to remove abuses, but not to set itself up in trade ('... the evils attendant upon the employment of children in the factories were not alleviated by Government becoming cotton spinners ...').[11] The Chancellor had been misinformed, he claimed, as to the number of institutions that already transacted small assurance policies: no less than three-quarters of them now granted policies of £100, £50 and £25, and hence would suffer by direct competition from the Government if the provision regarding annuities were rescinded.

While he felt that the British Prudential's pioneering venture was under threat, Harben could not rest. James Gillman, Edgar Horne and the rest of the Board had already endorsed his letters to Gladstone; once again they gave him the authority to protect the Company's interests.[12] Harben recognised that the best defence lay in numbers. He quickly prepared a circular to other assurance companies and the most reputable friendly societies. This was followed by a letter to *The Times*, and by a petition under seal to be allowed by Counsel to appear against the Bill.

Harben was not alone in finding Government intervention in economic and commercial affairs distasteful. He was merely voicing the prevailing doctrine of *laissez-faire* in pointing out, through his various missives, the unfairness of Government 'entering into competition with a large body of its subjects'. The *Post Magazine* voiced its disapproval on 20 February, in a ten-point manifesto entitled 'Why the Bill is Objectionable': most of the points rested on the complaint that the Government's efforts to rectify abuses would end in the creation of a monopoly. Its lack of experience in the selection of lives was also held to be dangerous.[13]

These were among the arguments put to Gladstone when he received a deputation of actuaries and secretaries from the life offices, Harben among them, on the afternoon of 27 February 1864. The petition they presented was intended to forestall direct competition from the Government. It was signed by the representatives of some 70 companies, and requested the elimination of a clause in the Bill proposing to do away with the need to purchase an annuity in conjunction with Government assurance. The companies feared that what they had sown by investing in an agency force, the Government would eventually reap because the absolute security it offered would attract much business that would otherwise have come to the companies. The job of convincing working-class people of the value of insurance was not easy, and the companies held that it was their investment and labour that had accomplished it. (Harben suggested in one of his contributions to the discussion that 'if Government is to reap the fruits from the seed these agents have sown, they ought to buy up the existing institutions in some way or other' but the idea – not surprisingly – was not taken up by the Chancellor.) The questions arising from the discussion ranged widely over topics such as whether the companies published their accounts (the Prudential did but the practice was far from universal) but the most important fact to emerge was that the Chancellor neither believed in, nor felt the Government could afford, the large-scale agency force that the companies assured him was essential.[14]

If he had not already been so convinced of the need for the Bill, his meeting with the life offices deputation should have persuaded Gladstone of the inherent difficulties in mounting a Government scheme. He discounted what he was told about the need for an army of agents to sell policies and collect premiums, the cost of the mechanisms for record-keeping, and the great questions of lapses and company solvency relating to the security of working-class peoples' funds. Neither did he accept, in his determination to challenge the companies, that the habits and needs of working-class people were a basic factor in the viability of any scheme.

These were topics that would occupy the critics of industrial assurance for the next hundred years. Their first and most passionate airing came when the Government Annuities Bill went to Committee on 7 March. There were few speakers in Parliament who could match Gladstone for crusading moral fervour. On this occasion, as an observer related,

> *Mr Gladstone held the House for two hours enchained by his defence of a measure which avowedly will not benefit the class from which members are selected; which involve [sic] not only a "wilderness of figures", but calculations of a kind as intelligible to most men as equations to London cabdrivers; and which, though it might and would interest the nation, would never in the nature of things be made a hustings cry.*[15]

Gladstone first dispatched charges of Government interference, and considered the positive attitude to the Bill expressed by the larger ordinary life offices (which might well have been pleased to see harm done to the offices transacting both ordinary and industrial business). Then he turned his attention to the industrial assurers, en route to his assault on lax and inefficient friendly societies.

His complaints about the companies were the unscrupulousness of agents, lapses, the policyholder's helplessness in the face of amalgamations, and the dubious financial position of some companies, contrary to what they published in their accounts. The companies, he asserted, were

> *everywhere soliciting the people, not merely by placards on the wall, not merely by institutions in the towns and villages, but employing agents, whom I cannot call by any other name than preachers and denominational missionaries, who, animated by the golden vision of 25 per cent on the premiums paid, find their way into every cottage in the country and become eloquent and learned in praise of the institutions to which they belong.*[16]

The Rt. Hon. William Ewart Gladstone.

If – on principle – the Government would not employ 'these touting agents' who saved the working man the trouble of visiting an assurance office, it could still offer the attractions of security, more favourable terms in the case of missed payments, and greater convenience to those who frequently moved in search of work. Dealing with the problem of 'the fugitive nature' of some of these institutions occupied him longer. A table published in the previous year's *Post Magazine Almanack* was referred to as a summary of what had happened to the 596 insurance companies projected between 1844 and 1862: '... founded, 276;

ceased to exist, 259; amalgamations, 12; ... Transfers of business, 161; ... winding up in Chancery, 57'.

The last was 'a subject which has both a comic and a tragic side', but not wishing merely to entertain the House with the adventures of certain individuals, 'some of them with "Reverend" affixed to their names', Gladstone confined himself to the sobering facts. In the case of companies winding up in Chancery,

> *the policy holder has no remedy when a company is mismanaged ... until he dies he has no claim that can be enforced ... directly a man hears that a company in which he is assured has gone into Chancery, he feels naturally scrupulous about what is commonly called throwing good money after bad. Practically, the policy holder ceases to pay any more premiums, and, therefore, he loses his claim to that which he has already paid.*

Nor had the policyholder any control over what happened to his policy when it was passed from hand to hand in the course of a merger. He gave as his example a company named the 'Professional', which had amalgamated with the 'European', at great disadvantage to its policyholders. The result was

> *... an illustration of what you will probably say is no better than wholesale robbery. Nay, more, I will go a step further, and say that a great many of those proceedings are worse than wholesale robbery, and there are many persons who have never seen the inside of a gaol, and yet who had fitter be there than many a rogue that has been convicted ten times over at the Old Bailey.* [17]

This was uttered with true Gladstonian fire, before the Chancellor turned to the reliability of published accounts, and fixed his attention upon the British Prudential in a long discourse on its 'remarkable' condition. The Company, he said,

> *... is conducted by Mr Harben, a gentleman of great energy, and it is owing to Mr Harben, I understand, that there is an organised opposition to this Bill ... Mr Harben waited upon me some ten days ago, as one of a deputation on the subject of this measure. I inquired of him whether the society to which he belonged had any objection to the publication of their accounts. His reply was "Oh dear no. I am extremely anxious for their publication". Subsequently when sending the accounts, he said, "These are to be for private use". I replied I did not need them for private but for public use; and then Mr Harben said, "If all the others publish I have no objection. But as all the others do not publish, I would rather not, inasmuch as I think the facts I have given you might be the subject of unfavourable comment, of course owing to defective knowledge". I can only refer them to the balance sheet of the British Prudential for 1861, which has been published ...*

As it stands it presents a balance of £41,000 in favour of the society; but it has been examined by actuaries, and those gentlemen, proceeding upon principles which are no more open to question than a proposition of Euclid, say, that instead of a balance of £41,000 in favour of, there is one of £30,000 against the society. There was, it is true, a capital of £45,000 not paid up, and which if paid up would undoubtedly more than liquidate this balance; but all I can say is, that in 1861, when its balance sheet was published, it did not appear to be in contemplation to demand that it should be paid up, and the accounts stood as I have said. I am not going to push this further than to say, that it is not just that societies in this condition should come forward and say, "We admit that the great Assurance Offices do not do the business that the Friendly Societies do, nor do it in a satisfactory way, but leave it to us and we shall do it." I decline to accede to that proposition. I demur to it. I do not feel satisfied as to the business the "British Prudential" is doing.[18]

The British Prudential's balance sheet for 1861 was attached as an appendix to the debate.

These insinuations were bad enough, but Gladstone then went on to consider, still under the broad heading of industrial assurance companies, the affairs of a dishonestly administered venture with an unfortunately similar name, the British Provident, that had ended up in Chancery in 1862. He then passed directly to an indictment of the friendly societies, about a hundred of which failed every year. The Chancellor wanted it understood that he was not making an attack on all of them: 'Nothing is more satisfactory or congenial; nothing more harmonises with the best English ideas than to see men of the labouring classes associating together in the true and real spirit of self-government for the purpose of providing against the contingencies of old age, sickness, and death ...' but there were many societies in which the labouring man, after a lifetime of regular payments on a life policy, missed a few through sickness and lost all that he had paid. There were many in which the costs of collecting premiums and administering the business were so disproportionate as to arouse disbelief. Then there was the question of lapses. The Royal Liver Society was singled out as having issued 135,000 policies in the previous year and having had 70,000 lapses in the same period; its £77,000 premium income apparently cost £36,000 to collect and manage. The Chancellor went on to explain that the state could not assume the onerous actuarial responsibility of directing and regulating these societies. Offering an alternative to them was 'the most prudent, the safest and the most satisfactory mode of proceeding that can be adopted' and one on which he appealed to all parties to agree.[19]

Gladstone's lengthy speech appeared in *The Times* and other dailies the following day, 8 March. That the British Prudential should be so castigated, and in such a context, aroused Harben's deepest indignation. Knowing Gladstone's calculations to be based on an erroneous reading of the accounts, and no doubt smarting at the reference to his own part in opposing the Bill, he wrote personally to the Chancellor on 9 March, requesting an interview. On the same day a letter from Harben appeared in *The Times*:

GOVERNMENT ANNUITIES BILL
To the Editor:
Sir, – In his speech last night Mr Gladstone animadverted on our balance-sheet for the year 1861, and stated upon the opinion of an Actuary, that the balance of £41,000 in favour of the Company should in reality be reversed, and a liability of £30,000 be shown against the Company.

I am quite at a loss to understand how any actuary could form an opinion without being supplied with all the necessary data, as so much depends on the age of the lives insured and the duration of the policies, and other attendant circumstances; but I am prepared to maintain the substantial accuracy of the balance sheet in question, and to state that the valuation of the policies was conducted by a competent actuary, and the principle upon which it was based was confirmed by one of the first actuaries of the day.

Furthermore, Mr Gladstone had in his possession, at the time he made that statement, figures respecting the present position of this Company, and which figures had been supplied to him in answer to questions put to me when I attended with the deputation, and subsequently by letter.

The results of these figures showed, on data admitted at the meeting, that the Company had, at the present time, invested assets exceeding 33 per cent of the sums received upon all policies actually in force, while the tables upon which the great bulk of our business had been effected only required 25 per cent to be reserved.

As, by the forms of the House, I could not there reply to Mr Gladstone's injurious statement, I appeal to your sense of justice to give publicity to this answer.

I am, Sir, your obedient servant,
HENRY HARBEN
Secretary
British Prudential Assurance Company,
35, Ludgate Hill, March 8th

Gladstone's remarks had been based upon 'the opinion of certain Actuaries who were not acquainted with our business', and the effect, as Harben put it in yet another letter, was damaging and misleading:

It is a most difficult matter ... to make people believe that we are right and that so high a functionary as the Chancellor of the Exchequer should have been misinformed. They naturally say that information of the best and soundest character must be in his possession otherwise he would not make the assertions alluded to.

We do not belong to that class which would use hard words or impute improper motives to any one who happens to differ from us, still less would we do so in the present case, but nevertheless our valuation was based upon facts absolutely true while the opinion of the Actuaries consulted by you was upon an assumption based upon data applicable to Offices of a very different character and even upon other Offices they could not arrive at a correct decision. [20]

On 17 March the Bill came up again for debate in the Commons and it became clear that the British Prudential was not the only company to feel itself maligned by the Chancellor's previous speech. Gladstone, in at length agreeing to the adjournment of the debate, made a statement that went a little way in the direction Harben had requested when he said:

I wish the House to very clearly understand the position in which I stand in reference to existing Societies. I quoted the cases of various Societies, and of those which I cited, I think there were four which I mentioned only for the purpose of commendation. I quoted several other Societies, the British Prudential among others; but I did not presume to take upon myself to say that they were insolvent societies. I pointed out facts connected with their balance sheets, and merely went to the point of saying that they were not societies which carried with them sufficient evidence to guarantee the minds of the public, and entitle them to say to the Government "Don't enter upon our field, which is satisfactorily occupied already." [21]

But this softening of attitude was really very slight in relation to the injury Harben felt that the British Prudential had suffered, and he was determined to see its financial condition exonerated. By 21 March he was in touch with T.B. Sprague, the Actuary of the Equity Law and Life Association. On 1 April he wrote to him enclosing the 1861 balance sheet and the data on which it was based, together with Gladstone's statement, and requesting Sprague to clarify three points:

1st. whether at the 31st December 1861 there was anything to cause alarm to the Policy Holders of the Company
2ndly. whether upon the facts submitted there was any apprehension of the Shareholders being required to pay a call
3rdly. whether the Company was in a position to meet its existing liabilities or not. [22]

Sprague's Report of 7 April 1864 calmed the situation by clarifying the basis of misunderstanding on both sides. The Chancellor had indeed mistaken the Company's situation, but this was hardly surprising, since the balance sheet for 1861 had been drawn up on a premise that on the face of it seemed right, but was in fact fundamentally incorrect. Sprague suggested that in future, instead of appearing as assets, policies and annuity bonds should be treated as liabilities, 'for the simple reason that every policy is liable to be discontinued at the option of the holder; and if any policy has been treated as an asset instead of a liability, its discontinuance will cause an immediate loss to the Company, whereas it should rather be reckoned as a gain, because a liability has been cancelled'.[23]

He was then able to turn to the charge of unsoundness. The Chancellor's calculation that there was a balance of £30,000 against the Company, rather than one of £41,000 in its favour, he traced to 'an apparently trifling cause', the proportion of the value of the premiums payable, which is 'deducted for future bonuses and expenses'. The Company, in preparing the balance sheet, had deducted 24%; the Chancellor's actuarial advisors, using a rule of thumb, had deducted 33%. Sprague was 'decidedly of the opinion that that proportion is not the correct one, but is too large, and is unfair towards the Company'.

Demonstrating the effect of utilising various proportions on the figures, he expressed the view that

> *... the proper proportion is not to be arrived at by any rough rule, such as that adopted by the Chancellor of the Exchequer, who has taken off exactly one-third of the value of the premiums. The proper proportion can only be ascertained by laborious calculations, when the particulars of all the policies are given. It is, therefore, impossible for me, or for any actuary, to determine, from the imperfect data furnished me, what is the correct proportion to deduct. It is, however, not difficult to make an approximate estimate, so as to be in a position to speak confidently as to the solvency of the Society, when an explanation is given of the exact processes by which the figures set out in the balance sheet are arrived at.*

Sprague then proceeded to do exactly that. No previous account of the matter has reproduced his explanation for the way the 1861 balance sheet was compiled, so it is worth doing here for the light it casts on the thinking within the Company. He revealed that the British Prudential's Actuary had deliberately calculated that all policyholders were five years older than in fact they were, as a precautionary measure, but one which had led to the deduction of a smaller proportion of the value of the premiums, in this case, 22%. (The valuation had been done, as usual, on the basis of the Carlisle 3% Life Tables.) The Directors had then added the 'empirical amount' of £20,147 to the Actuary's valuation, as a further precautionary measure, but one which served another purpose: 'to prevent the publication of an unduly favourable Statement of Accounts', and by doing this, Sprague admitted, 'It may be said that the Directors have invited unfriendly criticism.' This information had not been passed to Gladstone's actuaries, but Sprague was sure that '... when this explanation is communicated to them, it cannot fail to induce them to modify their opinion most materially'. Without elaborating much further on this Sprague proceeded to his conclusion, and the statement that he was

... of the opinion that the Chancellor of the Exchequer was erroneously advised in reference to the balance sheet of the British Prudential Company, and that there is no ground whatever for his Statement that there was a balance of £30,000 against the Company on 31 December 1861.

... I have no hesitation in saying that the British Prudential Company was perfectly solvent on the 31 Dec'r 1861; and that there was no cause for alarm on the part either of the shareholders or of the policy holders. ... in my opinion the amount of the available assets at that date was sufficient to enable the Company to meet all its engagements honourably. [24]

Sprague's Report was taken as a vindication by the British Prudential, but in addition the Company put the same questions to the actuary whom it had previously engaged to value its non-industrial business, S.L. Laundy. Though recognising the compensatory element inherent in using the Carlisle 3% Tables and the prudence of the actuary making the calculations as he had, Laundy recommended to the Board that 'In future ... your valuations be conducted on the basis of the Table from which your premiums are derived'.

But he was firmly of the opinion that the amount set aside was 'quite ample to establish the perfect solvency of the Company at the date of the balance sheet in question' and fully concurred in Sprague's view that the figures contained nothing that should give anyone cause for alarm. [25]

Laundy's Report is dated 11 April. There can be little doubt that the two independent opinions were swiftly communicated to Gladstone, for on 12 April in the House of Commons he issued a guarded qualification of his earlier remarks that at last pacified Harben:

I have not a word of reproach to say to any society or public company; but I wish to define the precise extent to which I meant to carry my remarks in respect of living societies: I do not mean dead societies, of which I introduced examples, but such societies as the ... British Prudential, and other societies. I did not presume to attach, nor do I think I should be justified in attaching, to any of these societies a fraudulent character.

He had merely wished to challenge what seemed to him an overweening confidence. Those friendly societies that were guilty of malpractice were his real target, '... but when I used language which, I regret to say, I am not prepared to retract, respecting the heartless iniquity that had been at work, I did not mean it to be understood that any such language was applicable to existing societies'. [26]

This was accepted as a sufficient disclaimer of the charge of financial instability, and there the matter was allowed to rest. The British Prudential made no further protest to the Bill. Under the Act that followed, the

Government offered sums assured of no less than £20 and no more than £100, and annuities were limited to between £4 and £50 a year. The business was to be handled by certain Post Offices scattered about the country and the premiums to be invested in Government securities. The first Government policies were sold in April 1865.

As for the British Prudential, after initial fears about the effect of all the publicity cast on the Company's reputation, Harben and the Directors were elated to find that, on the contrary, the result was a wave of new proposals. At the Annual General Meeting in May, James Gillman, in the course of a lengthy account of the year, remarked that since Gladstone's famous speech in the House of Commons, the Company had done more business than ever. For the ten weeks up to March 1863, the business done was at a rate of £3,715, and in the corresponding period of 1864 it was £6,158; for the six weeks ending 20 April 1863, it was £2,202, while for the six weeks ending 18 April 1864 it was £4,280. Those figures were proof that the speech of the Chancellor of the Exchequer had done them no harm.

When Harben got to his feet to speak, he expressed much the same view. Some were of the opinion '... that the opposition had done harm, but it was not so. The wind could only do harm to the little sapling, it did not affect the old trees; the storm had passed over. The wind had its proper functions, and those trees that had no roots and could not stand had much better be dug up.'

Harben 'firmly and conscientiously' believed the Company to be in a perfectly solvent condition, without any reservation, 'as he had sworn but a short time ago in a court of justice'. Within two years he expected the income to reach £100,000.

His prediction proved to be quite justified: annual premium income two years later in 1866 topped £154,000, a considerable jump from the £92,417 of 1864. Gillman had summed up the situation when he said he believed that 'so far as they were concerned, the Bill would be comparatively harmless'. It turned out, in fact, to be a positive help. Fortunately for the British Prudential, and unfortunately for the Government, Gillman's other prediction, lost in the earlier stages of his speech at the Annual General Meeting, would also come true: that 'if the Government persevered in their object they would sustain a loss without any great gain'. The disastrous object lesson of the Government-sponsored assurance scheme would be worked out over the next 65 years. Within the next ten, on the other hand, the British Prudential would be the country's largest assurance company.

Acquisitions and Foundations

THE 1860s might well be called the British Prudential's 'decade of acquisitions': ten years in which a number of small friendly societies or other assurance companies were absorbed one after another. As the period that witnessed the vigorous expansion of the Company's industrial business, it was the bridge between the early years of struggle and the triumphant 1870s when, with a newly stream-lined name, the Prudential Assurance Company emerged as the front runner in a crowded field. It was the time, too, when experimental forays into other types of assurance came to an end, and effort was concentrated on life business and, particularly, on industrial assurance.

While the British Prudential's rate of growth was exceptional, the fact that it took over other companies on its upward course was typical of a period in which amalgamations were a commonplace of the assurance industry. While many occurred between companies seeking to complement their respective strengths, many also served to counterbalance the unsoundness of ventures founded during the late 1840s boom and floundering a decade later. There were also plenty of predators. The process whereby a small company feeling the chill wind of competition crept under the cloak of a larger one, only to find its erstwhile protector taken over by a third, was a theme about which the *Post Magazine* regularly had much to say.

Having absorbed its only real rival in industrial assurance, the British Prudential was now sufficiently well established to be a potential safe haven for smaller institutions. The Hollingworth Society, a small Birmingham-based friendly society, requested to transfer its business to the British Prudential in January 1861. Six months later, on 6 June, the Eagle Insurance Company of New Bridge Street, London, did the same. No figures were recorded, but the businesses were accepted 'with medical test'.

There was then a pause. The slackening off of new life business during the cotton famine of 1862 had the interesting result of prompting the Company to try something different, and it begin transacting fire insurance through the Prince Fire Insurance Company, which it set up in 1862.[1] Henry Harben's prodigious energy was temporarily channelled in other directions. The winter of 1863 found him lecturing on his patented cotton substitute to the British Institute for the Advancement of Science. In 1864 he was elected a Fellow of the Institute of Actuaries, by which body he would in due course be invited to explain the theory and workings of industrial assurance. Meanwhile his Fellowship brought him into contact with the best minds and practice in the actuarial profession.

No amalgamations took place while the Government assurance affair occupied Harben's attention. Once this was over, buoyed up by the confidence created by the resulting influx of new business, the Company embarked on a succession of acquisitions in the second half of the decade. The Temperance and Integrity Friendly Society was taken over in January 1865, and the London and Westminster Assurance Corporation in March. Little is known about either of these, or about the Finsbury Mutual Life Assurance Association taken over early in 1866. It would appear that all of them made overtures to the British Prudential and not vice versa. From the latter's perspective, taking on their policyholders gave the British Prudential a base in some well-defined geographical area which agents could be appointed to enlarge.

The British Prudential's amalgamation with the Consolidated Assurance Company in October 1865, on the other hand, was the first significant merger since that with the British Industry five years earlier. The Consolidated dated from 1846 and was solely dedicated to loans and ordinary life business, rather as the British Prudential itself had been before it embarked on industrial assurance. Its income for the year running up to 30 September 1864, arising mainly from premiums and investments in stocks, was about one-third of the British Prudential's £76,000.

The management of the Consolidated was cautious: before the amalgamation, its Board asked A.H. Bailey, Actuary of the London Assurance and later President of the Institute of Actuaries, for his views on the soundness of the British Prudential. His Report shows the degree to which, since the merger with the British Industry in 1860, the British Prudential's sales of industrial policies had outstripped sales of ordinary policies:

> *In the year 1864 there were issued 109,907 Policies ... and on 31 December 1864 there were in force 219,821 Policies for £1,824,980 paying weekly premiums of £1,524. In addition to these there were in force at the same date of the "General" class 3,563 Policies for £394,750 producing in annual premiums £13,378. Up to the present time the number of both classes has much increased.*[2]

The Board of the Consolidated concluded that they need have no doubts about merging its business with that of the British Prudential, and did so in an agreement of 30 October 1865. The British Prudential paid the Consolidated £28,288 – £22,288 to the shareholders and £6,000 to the Directors for their loss of office. H.J. Gibbins, the Chairman of the newly acquired concern, was appointed to the British Prudential Board.[3] Once again the Company altered its name to accommodate the identity of its new associate, and for the next 18 months was known as the British Prudential and Consolidated Assurance Company. In April 1867, however, this rather cumbersome name gave way to the simple form that lasted until 1881 and registration as a limited company, and thereafter right up to 1976: the Prudential Assurance Company.[4]

Whereas the surviving records of the late 1850s convey little about the degree of involvement of the Company's Shareholder-Directors, by the late 1860s Harben's pre-eminence, as both navigator and captain of the barque *Prudentia* emerges quite distinctly from surviving documents. During this transitional decade, as the Prudential was becoming better known in the assurance world, he assumed the role of spokesman whenever a pronouncement or an opinion was called for. Reports such as Bailey's, above, invariably state that it was Harben who presented, explained and clarified the way the Company worked. In amalgamations it would appear that Harben alone represented the Company. At board meetings his actions were always approved – never added to, amended, questioned or contravened. In defending the Prudential, whether against the Chancellor of the Exchequer or the dismissed former agent who slandered it in a provincial newspaper, Harben now identified himself with it completely. Any attack upon it, however slight, was tantamount to a personal insult.

Harben's efforts on the Company's behalf did not go unremunerated. As on the occasion of the merger five years earlier, he was financially rewarded, this time for 'having secured to the British Prudential Coy the business of the Consolidated Coy'. On awarding him £1,500 instead of a flat 10% commission on the £26,000 at which the business was valued, a note in the board minutes from the Finance Committee recorded that 'altho' there is little doubt Mr Harben could have procured such a sum by using his influence to transfer the business ... to any other Company he was to a certain degree improving his position by bringing it to his own Company ...' which becomes somewhat clearer in the light of an agreement of 1861 which gave Harben an additional £20 a year for each £2,000 added to the Company's annual income.[5] As the Company's amalgamations continued, so did the increments Harben received. There is no hint that he was ever invited to join another company, but the Prudential Board must long since have realised how valuable he was to their own.

How quickly he won the confidence of new business associates was revealed during the next amalgamation, which took place in 1868 between the Prudential and the British Mutual Assurance Society. The British Mutual, which dated from 1851, resembled the Consolidated in that it engaged in ordinary business, but it was only about a third as large as the Prudential's ordinary side. It was suffering badly from the competition of bigger offices. Its Directors were anxious to steer it into a safe harbour and when, in September 1868, a member of its Board was introduced to Harben, an offer to take on the British Mutual's risks as of 1 October was made and accepted. Arrangements for the transfer progressed rapidly, with meetings being held every few days. The minutes of the British Mutual in its final months suggest that the confidence engendered by this rapid accord resulted in a smooth transition. This seems to have had much to do with the open way that Harben made available to the auditors of British Mutual the Prudential's figures, and a personal manner that left no-one in any doubt that the Prudential viewed its new relationship seriously and honourably.[6] The British Mutual's 500 shares in the British Mutual Investment Loan and Discount Company, incorporated in 1857, passed to the Prudential. In the following year this company was reconstituted as the British Mutual Investment Company, and Harben, Gillman and Horne joined its Board.[7]

It is interesting that the British Mutual, like the Consolidated, commissioned an investigation into the Prudential's affairs before taking the irrevocable step – a reminder that the Prudential for all its size was not yet seen by its contemporaries as invulnerable. The study was carried out by the Government Actuary, Alexander Finlaison (another who praised Harben for the help he received), and provides a convenient summary of the Prudential's condition three years on from the last such report. With reference to ordinary business, sums assured had now reached £1,100,000 and premium income £35,000; the rate of mortality, 'the usual normal amount in offices of the same standing', was 2% per annum and the Company had paid out something in the region of £23,000 in claims in each of the previous two years. The valuation of 1866 had revealed a divisible surplus of £22,846, or 37% on the premiums paid during the five years prior to the valuation.

The industrial side of the business, highly praised by Finlaison, was of course 'kept entirely separate and unmingled in any way with the ordinary general business' but his study notes that, 'The industrial risks in some respects are of a peculiar nature. They are extremely transient; and the premium being garnished with a very heavy loading, out of which no extravagant amount of commission is allowed, the two circumstances combine to render this class of operations extremely lucrative.'

Just how lucrative, considering that nearly all of the industrial business had been obtained in the previous ten years and the bulk of it in the previous five, was revealed as quite astounding: premium income was now £130,000 a year on sums assured of more than £2,250,000, but 'this liability, although seemingly extensive, is in reality, as to at least four-fifths of the risk, merely nominal' due to the very short duration of so many policies, and Finlaison's own valuation left him certain that 'the reserve or guarantees fund set apart for the security of this particular branch is more than fully sufficient'. Furthermore, he added, '... the methods pursued for the conduct and promotion of the business seem, to my judgment at least, to be thoroughly efficient, perfectly respectable, and conducive in an eminent degree to a still greater degree of success than that which has been already attained'.[8] Credit for 'the methods pursued', about which more will be said below, can be attributed to Henry Harben.

Meanwhile, there was one further amalgamation. If all the transfers so far had been virtually free of problems, that of the Hercules Assurance Company – and with it, as a result of a previous amalgamation, a subsidiary company called the International – was fraught with them. How well hidden the true state of a company's affairs could be sometimes astonished the public and the insurance industry alike. In 1869 the financial world was severely shaken by the collapse of one of the largest life offices, the Albert Life Assurance Company, which in the previous 12 years had absorbed 24 smaller offices at a cost estimated at nearly £275,000. This was the largest assurance crash to date, but what surprised contemporaries were the laudatory reports about the condition of the Albert, written a matter of months before it foundered. The reported condition of the Hercules at the time it was taken on by the Prudential proved to be similarly at variance with the true account produced by its official liquidator less than two years later.[9]

The Prudential's relationship with the Hercules – a fire and life office founded in 1863 – began late in 1868. The Hercules was one of those tiresome entities pilloried by the insurance journals, the kind that Gladstone had railed against at the time of the Government Annuities Bill. The way it was run sounds almost laughable, until one considers the human lives blighted by such dishonesty. In two years of operation its Directors squandered the whole of its £10,000 paid-up capital and its entire income from premiums. By January 1866, when it was reconstituted (ostensibly to transact marine business), 'there was not a shilling in hand or invested to meet the current risks upon existing policies'. On founding the second 'Hercules', its Directors had sought to overcome the lack of interest in its shares by shamelessly rigging the market. Then, seeking a way out of their difficulties, they effected an amalgamation with the International Life Assurance Society in May 1868. Later it was alleged that the documents were 'faulty and disadvantageous' to the shareholders of the International, an unlimited company founded as the National Loan Fund Life Assurance Society in 1838, with branch offices in New York and Paris. Unfortunately the International too was in a parlous state, and certainly a worse one than was revealed to the Directors of the Hercules.[10]

At the point when the Prudential agreed to take over the Hercules, and with it the International, the stage was set for a protracted legal wrangle between the latter two, each accusing the other of misrepresentation. An agreement made with the Hercules' liquidator in January 1869 specified that in return for a payment of £329,685, the Prudential would take on the International's policies and annuities. Given the revelations that emerged during the next six months, as the International and the Hercules were wound up, there seemed less and less likelihood that this payment would be met. In the United States the legal authorities seized the International's assets as an insolvent institution.

The ten years following the Prudential's amalgamation with the British Industry brought further acquisitions, but the name of the Company was simplified to the Prudential Assurance Company in 1867.

Henry Harben almost certainly shared with the liquidators of the two companies the authorship of the scheme designed to provide partial relief to the International's annuitants and policyholders by dividing both the payment due to the Prudential, and the Prudential's obligation to pay annuities and claims, into five parts, one for each of the following five years. In June 1869 this was announced in a circular to all concerned with the International. It looked like being a constructive solution, but it was never realised. The Prudential received only a fraction of the first tranche of the payment, and even this was subject to various applications from creditors. In February 1870 Harben sent out a second circular to the policyholders and annuitants. The Prudential proposed to take over 25% of the liability of policies and annuities at once, to alleviate the plight of those relying upon them for income, and to assume the rest over a longer period, as the payments were obtained.[11]

This was the beginning of efforts that would extend well into the 1870s to recover loans due to the International, and to raise funds by means of a call on its shares. Affidavits sworn by a number of shareholders and their heirs, some of whom found themselves liable for sums quite beyond their means to pay, testify to the hardship that resulted.[12] Harben crossed the Atlantic in August 1870 to represent the Prudential in the matter of the assumption of the International's American risks, and in the engagement of a New York company, the Empire Mutual Life Assurance Company, as reinsurer.

The Prudential's Directors, 'being of the opinion that their time is more profitably occupied in the development of their own peculiar connexion than in attending to a business many thousands of miles distant', eventually disposed of the International's interests in the United States. The legal processes arising from this amalgamation in England and France were quite complicated enough: some of the claims, counterclaims and appeals that derived from it were still being heard in Chancery in 1876.

As it happened, this was the Prudential's last amalgamation in the nine-teenth century. Widespread public feeling against such combinations had been fed by the Albert disaster, but the Prudential's Directors took a surprisingly positive view in urging that 'a judicious and well-timed transfer is the safeguard of Assurance' and – leaving aside the Hercules and its attendant problems – reiterated in their Report for 1869, that the companies '... which have been united with the Prudential all come under this category. They were transferred because their New Business and averages were not sufficiently large, and from no other inherent weakness in their business'. The premium income brought by the acquired companies amounted to about £17,000 a year, 'the remaining income being consequently the result of this Company's operations'.[13]

This period of acquisitions for the Prudential coincided with Government attempts to intervene in the provision of life assurance. In many industries legal measures introduced for the protection of the public from danger, fraud or exploitation were gradually posing a challenge to the doctrine of *laissez-faire*. Public confidence in even well-established assurance companies had been all but extinguished by the Albert crash (as the Prudential's Annual Report put it, 'the confidence which for so many years has been justly placed in the system of Life Assurance received a most violent shock'). One of the indirect results of this event was the Life Assurance Companies Act 1870, which was designed to improve the information available to prospective policyholders and ensure the security of premiums. The legislation affected the ordinary, rather than industrial life, companies, as the latter were considered closer relatives of the collecting friendly societies.

The Prudential came under the Act on account of its ordinary business, though some of the new provisions were already satisfied by procedures adopted by the Company years earlier. Other clauses applied only to companies founded after 1870. The Act covered five main areas of public concern. Foremost was the problem of insolvency. Life assurance companies established after 1870 had to deposit the sum of £20,000 with the Accountant-General of the Court of Chancery before a certificate of incorporation could be granted. This sum was returnable only when the life assurance fund deriving from premiums reached £40,000. Another clause laid down that new companies transacting different kinds of insurance had to keep premiums from life business separately from other premiums. This reserve was to comprise the life assurance fund. For existing companies, only the proceeds of life business entered into after 1870 had to be kept separately.

Further clauses in the Act concerned accounts, valuation figures and other indicators of a company's financial condition, with which the public was to be acquainted by means of statements deposited with the Board of Trade. Schedules attached to the Act set out the form of the revenue account, balance sheet and profit and loss account, which each assurance company now had to file annually. Valuation by an actuary was to take place once every ten years for existing companies, and every five years for new ones; a report was to be compiled, showing the mortality tables and rate of interest used in making the valuation, the proportion of premiums reserved and the principles of the distribution of profits, and financial statements for the whole period since the previous valuation. This report would be supplied by the Board of Trade to any shareholder or policyholder who requested it, as would copies of a company's list of shareholders and deed of settlement. The Board of Trade was to present to Parliament the financial statements and reports deposited each year. All of these measures were intended to eradicate traditional abuses while encouraging financial responsibility on the part of the public. For its part, the Prudential could claim to have followed the main provisions of the Act for most of its 22 years of existence. It had printed an annual report and accounts, kept its industrial and ordinary assurance premium income separate, conducted a valuation every five years, and set aside a sum each year against future liabilities.

Against the background of deep commercial depression that had affected the country during the late 1860s, the Prudential continued to record increasing amounts of both ordinary and industrial new business, year by year. If this surge of new business had been of brief duration, it could perhaps be explained by the degree to which the public had been made aware of the Prudential by the publicity that surrounded it in 1864. But the increase in new business was not of brief duration, and while it is clear that the Company benefited by having its stability defended by the foremost actuaries in the land, there were other factors involved in the yearly totals.[14]

Firstly, given that life assurance was coming to be seen as a normal and necessary amenity by the middle classes, the Prudential was profiting from what Henry Harben identified as the 'popularising trend' that had brought all manner of conveniences within the knowledge and reach of the mass of people farther down the social scale: 'Business of every description has of late had a tendency to appeal more and more to the multitude, and while cheap trains and popular periodicals were appealing for support to the million [*sic*], it was but natural that the same rule should be applied to the transactions of life assurance'.[15]

Working-class people were, by and large, better informed by now about life assurance than they had been a decade earlier. Though assurance had long been upheld as morally commendable on the grounds that it ensured independence, provided security and encouraged thrift, it seemed that this message was at last percolating down through the social scale to those nearer the bottom.[16] To some extent the Prudential can be said to have caught the tide of an enlightening of attitude. But it was surely the accuracy with which the Company had gauged the assurance needs of the working classes that was the overriding factor. More will be said below about the statistical study of the Prudential's mortality rates carried out during the mid-1860s, from which emerged some significant differences between industrial and ordinary business. Whereas most ordinary business was transacted by people aged between 31 and 55, 75% of industrial policies were taken out by people under 30 years of age. On an ordinary policy, the premium was calculated according to the sum assured, but on an industrial one, the sum assured was calculated according to the premium a family could afford. This matching of premiums to the amount in the working man's pocket was essential: in 1871, when a 4lb loaf of the cheapest bread cost 7d, the Prudential's cheapest industrial policy cost 1d a week; the most expensive cost 14s.[17]

Equally important was having put the product within reach, in the physical sense. For the better-off, the monthly or annual premium, paid by post or at an office of the company, was most convenient. The illiterate poor, whose scanty wage could barely be stretched to cover rent and food, had not the time or the means of saving that this presupposed. 'The wage-receiving class would not bring their premiums to an office,' Harben observed to the Institute of Actuaries in 1871, so the office went to the wage-earners. The Prudential's agency system was made to grow rapidly during the 1860s to accommodate the new nuclei of policyholders brought in by the amalgamations, as well as the immense population as yet uninsured. Within a dozen years of undertaking industrial assurance, the Company was represented by agents and medical referees in most English towns of any size. It was especially well-placed in the most densely populated areas: London, and the industrial cities of the north-west (the cotton districts and the former stronghold of the British Industry). By 1871, cities like Manchester and Liverpool might have as many as 20 or 30 Prudential agents, and in London there were 75. By the same date the Company was also well established in the major cities north of the border, and in that year began to sell industrial and ordinary assurance in Ireland, although the selling of ordinary assurance would be suspended in 1874 due to the impossibility of ensuring the quality of the business.

The revision and improvement of its conditions was the main means by which the Prudential communicated, through its agents, an understanding of working-class priorities. One example was the commitment to pay out claims not merely as quickly as possible, but within a week. Even a week was sometimes too long for a family suddenly dependent on the proceeds of an assurance policy, especially if the funds were needed for burial expenses. In 1869 the Prudential let it be known that claims of less than £100 would be paid in full by return of post. The Prudential's decision in 1866, to cease subjecting every industrial proposal to medical examination, was another such instance. The dread of being examined, and the shame felt on account of ragged and dirty clothing were sufficiently strong to keep many poor people from assuring their lives. From the Company's point of view, examining every proposal was proving expensive, equal to several weeks' premiums even though the fees paid to medical referees for such examinations were small. In any case, medical examination did not weed out all the unhealthy lives, especially in urban areas. Experimental trials in some towns preceded the blanket decision to eliminate medical tests for assurances of less than £50. Deaths within the first six months would carry no benefit, however, and full benefit would only be payable after a year. (In slum neighbourhoods, when there were outbreaks of disease, agents were forbidden to seek or accept new business. The same went for the worst overcrowded or crime-ridden areas.)

Other improvements included the reduction or elimination of penalty clauses for various classes of risks: occupations hitherto considered dangerous, such as railwayman, lighterman, fisherman and miner, 'impaired lives' (as those with some chronic condition were known) in general, and specific illnesses such as bronchitis and rheumatism in particular. Most important of all, however, was the gradual improvement of the tables pertaining to children, the insurance of whom was of such paramount importance to labouring families. Harben devised a plan whereby a uniform premium bought an increasing amount of assurance, so that there would be a financial incentive in the survival of a child. The amounts offered were originally very small, but were increased in stages of 5s as the Company's experience justified it. The result was that by 1871, in relation to the overall number of its industrial policyholders, the number of children insured by Prudential industrial policies was about 10% greater than the percentage of children in the national population.[18] 'Family Policies' were devised to meet the opportunity arising out of the Married Women's Property Act of 1870 for a married woman to effect a policy on her own life, or on her husband's.

It was during the 1860s and early 1870s, too, that the Prudential began to spread its message through advertising. It had always used the national and provincial press to advertise for agents. Extracts from the annual reports and a condensation of the proceedings at the Annual General Meetings regularly appeared in *The Times*, the insurance press and selected provincial papers. From 1863 – a year after Mr W.H. Smith opened his first railway platform kiosks – the Company began poster or showcard advertising on the railways. This was one way of appealing to the better-off and to the labouring classes at the same time. The amounts spent on advertising are itemised in the Minute Books: £4,000 was spent in 1869 to promote a new 'Absolute Security' policy. An office was opened in St James's on 1 January 1869 for the more convenient transaction of ordinary business in the smarter part of the West End, though it was abandoned after three years. The Company also produced small booklets, presumably made available to enquirers at Ludgate Hill, sent on request or given to prospective clients by agents. This kind of promotion enabled the Company to demonstrate that it offered something for everyone: by 1873 there were six tables covering different types of ordinary assurance, and 15 tables for industrial assurance.

The momentum of growth on the industrial side of the business by the early 1870s could only be sustained by rigorous supervision of every aspect of its operations. As Henry Harben explained to an audience at the Institute of Actuaries, the success of industrial assurance

... has been determined by a close attention to a variety of circumstances. In the first place a more than ordinary [sic] careful selection for outdoor work must be made, the most constant supervision must be exercised, and the closest attention to details must be used; but the chief success lies in a most stringent attention to the internal economy and to the method and regularity observed at the chief office. Without these two requisites the problem of Industrial Assurance cannot be solved; but with them

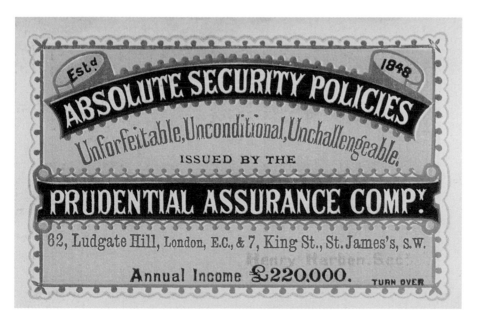

As well as industrial assurance for the working classes, the Prudential offered new kinds of ordinary policies and improved the terms of existing ones to appeal to the better-off.

the difficulty is entirely overcome, and the working man can reckon with as much certainty on the results of his frugality and prudence as his richer and more fortunate employer.[19]

Whereas between 1,500 and 1,800 industrial policies a week were being sold in 1864, by 1871 the figure sometimes exceeded 8,000 a week and by 1873, 11,000.[20] The procedures for managing a volume of business on this unprecedented scale, both in the office and out of doors, had first to be devised, and then to evolve, to match it. The office at No. 62 Ludgate Hill was soon outgrown. Several additions were made to it during the 1860s, as the Company bought up the adjacent houses to provide space for an ever-increasing number of clerical staff. One contemporary observation gives the impression of a warren, commenting that the buildings' 'irregularity of plan and other architectural features point to the fact that the company has been steadily growing', with the result that 'a severe critic might pronounce the building positively ugly'. A few years earlier, 'the whole of its operations, excepting only the board meetings, were carried on in the space now almost entirely engrossed by the cashiers' department'. By the time this comment was made, in 1873, the staff filled every cranny not occupied by the voluminous policy records.[21]

The practical running of the office does not seem to have been organised into distinct departments much before the late 1860s. Ordinary business was dealt with by one manager and 16 clerks. By comparison, industrial business required a vast administration. It is likely that the Cashiers' Department and the Audit Department – which checked the returns sent in by the agents in the field – existed earlier, though the first formal mention of the Audit Department dates from 1869. The Registration Department, which sought to trace policyholders who had moved so that their policies could be transferred to agents in their new areas, must also have been established early on. The Estates Department, which grew out of the 'Estates Account' first mentioned in 1864, came into being at about the same time to administer property investments under the supervision of Edgar Horne, who as a surveyor and valuer was best able to advise in this area. The Prudential's investments in stocks and shares were overseen by the whole Board at the weekly board meeting. Transactions – usually in Consols, colonial government stocks, municipal loan stocks or railway shares – were listed and minuted. Other departments in existence by 1873 were Claims, Lapse, Policy, Transfer and Transcript (which copied documents).

A radical departure from the routine administrative machinery was the Statistical Department, set up in May 1864 in the aftermath of the Government assurance affair. It was Harben's creation, the outgrowth of his desire that the Company should at any moment possess the statistical information to ascertain its exact position, largely to assess the development of its industrial business. Weekly, the Department recorded

... the number of policies issued and lapsed, with the annual premium of the same;
the increase in the actual premium income, and the increase in and the actual number
of policies in existence; the number of policies issued and the number of policies lapsed
in each district; the amount of premiums receivable in each superintendency; the
amount received from the agents; the amount paid in claims; the amount paid for
new business; the amount paid for superintendency; the percentage of the amount paid
for new business from the commencement of the year on the net increase of the premium
income during the same period; the percentage of claims on the net amount received
and on the gross premiums; the percentage of amount reserved ... .[22]

These returns were produced each Monday and a comparison made with the
corresponding week of previous years to give what Harben, in an image from
one of his out-of-hours pursuits, called 'a complete photographic insight' into
the Company's workings. There was a long list of additional figures drawing
upon the returns made by agents, superintendents and districts, that enlarged
the 'portrait' to reflect the state of affairs nationwide. In addition, the
Statistical Department recorded all the information sent in by agents on their
respective proposals on 'valuation cards' upon which, besides the dates when
a policy commenced and ended, the details of payments and of every incident
relating to claims were noted. As their name suggested, these cards were then
used as the basis for the quinquennial valuations. More will be said in a later
chapter about these five-yearly expositions of the Company's financial condition, out of which were decided the allocation of profits to the Prudential's
various funds, to the shareholders and to the with-profits policyholders in the
form of bonus.

Harben intended that the Prudential's industrial experience should
contribute to the wider field of actuarial knowledge, and to this end he extracted
from the figures all manner of tables and comparisons. The most useful to professional actuaries, at a time when actuarial science was still comparatively
young, was mortality experience broken down by causes of death, age groups,
geographical area and occupation. Harben published two sets of *Mortality*
Experience of the Prudential Assurance Company in the Industrial Branch, one in
1867, the second in 1871. These were ground-breaking studies in several
respects, not least because they shared the conclusions drawn from the
Prudential's data with workers in the allied fields of medicine and public
health. The two studies, each covering four years, presented the statistics both
as tables and in diagrammatic form. The analysis of deaths was made according to year, quarter and month; ages and percentages of deaths in age groups;
geographical area and cause of death. There were special tables for infant
mortality, '... records being kept of the numbers of policies issued and the
number of deaths occurring each week for each month of life from one month to
ten years of age'. These figures would prove useful when the charge relating the

assurance of children to the crime of infanticide made its periodic appearance. The statistics for men and for women were shown separately. The number of deaths under scrutiny was quite large; the 1871 study took in 17,256 male deaths and 17,655 female, and was the first attempt to show deaths arranged according to both primary and secondary causes.[23]

Statistical study was the cornerstone of industrial assurance, but essential also was what Harben had called 'a most stringent attention to the internal economy and to the method and regularity observed at the chief office'. This emphasis extended to every area of activity, from the weekly audit of the accounts conducted by the Board's Finance Committee to the more mundane clerical tasks.[24] By 1870 there were some 125 clerks employed in receiving and sorting proposals, entering their details in policy registers, keeping ledgers, checking and dealing with correspondence and processing claims, as well as auditing agents' returns and recording the details of premiums. Three years later there were 200 clerks. A rigorous system of checking every type of entry resulted in an exceptional standard of accuracy. There were years when not a single posting error was made in sending out thousands of pieces of mail. Frederick Fisher, a senior clerk in the Industrial Department who went on to become a Joint General Manager, one year made 30,000 postal entries without a mistake, and Alexander Munro, who had replaced Harben as the Company's Accountant back in 1856, is said to have spent many evenings searching out a penny lost among the figures – the only error of his 20-year career.[25]

Even at this stage, a staggering amount of paper passed through the office. The first day of each week brought some 2,000 letters and packets, with about 1,000 on the other days, delivered by a special cart from the General Post Office as the ordinary carriers could not accommodate such an avalanche.[26] Each proposal passed through a series of invariable stages – sorting, numbering, entering in the numerical life policy register and on policy forms before being filed 'so as to be capable of immediate production in the event of any question arising'.[27] From the early 1870s, the transfer of information to the policy forms was a task allocated to the Company's fifty or so female clerks. The great demand for clerical workers as businesses increased in size had led to a general lowering of standards, and a high turnover of young, untrained male staff. For the first time the option of employing women, who could be paid less and who were considered to be temperamentally better suited to routine jobs, was becoming attractive to employers, but to do so was still a novelty which only the telegraph offices had yet tried. Although the Prudential had numbered women among its collectors since the 1850s, the first female clerical workers were taken on only at the end of 1871. The decision reportedly stemmed from Harben's visit to the United States, where he had seen women employed as clerks in the Treasury in Washington. A Miss A. Wood was the first super-visor, engaged at £100 a year, and one of the first four women clerks was the daughter of Charles Hanslip, who had resigned his position as the Prudential's solicitor in the previous year.

At first the Directors had intended to engage only a handful of women, but 'as they were found to do their work satisfactorily, the business was increased also'. Harben defended them to the shareholders in 1874 as in no way rivalling the male clerks, but rather as 'doing a class of work that they could not get satisfactorily done by the male clerks'. By 1880 the Prudential had about 170 women clerks, and by 1900, 312. To be eligible, the women had to be between the ages of 18 and 25, and single; there was apparently a preference for engaging sisters, 'so that they may chaperone each other on the way to and from the office'. The women's duties required 'no special qualifications beyond an ordinary English education' and consisted 'principally in copying or writing letters from notes, so they do not even require a knowledge of bookkeeping'. A board minute of 1880, however, states that they were required to pass a simple examination.

That the company was charting a new course in engaging women was clearly recognised, and rules regarding the social standing of those engaged were strictly enforced. This confined the positions to the daughters of professional, financially secure and socially respectable men: '... officers of the army and navy, clergymen, bankers, merchants, wholesale dealers, members of the Stock Exchange, ... medical men, lawyers, architects and purely literary men, managers and secretaries of companies and chief officers of same, clerks in the Houses of Parliament, and any exceptional cases in harmony with the above principle ...'.[28]

As much as to safeguard the tone the Company was endeavouring to set, and to assure a predictable standard of education and deportment, this regulation was probably designed to reassure the parents of a well-brought up girl that she would encounter no deleterious influence under the Prudential's roof. Regulations were framed that placed the Company, quite literally, *in loco parentis* in its vigilance over the moral well-being of its female staff. As came to be customary in all offices that employed women in any numbers, the women clerks were strictly segregated from the men in the entrances, stairways and dining facilities they used, and the part of the building where they sat. 'Any attempt at flirtation' was strongly discouraged. The women's arrival and departure times were staggered so as not to coincide with those of the men, nor did their duties involve any direct contact with members of the public. This protective environment was unrepentant in its exclusivity ('It is no doubt a great advantage to the girls that they all belong to the same class as there is less likelihood of undesirable acquaintances being formed,' wrote one anonymous commentator, while another mentioned that 'There is a hard and fast barrier made at tradesmen's daughters ... by this means the class of female clerks... is kept most select'). The copying work done by the women, although repetitive and no doubt boring, required literacy and numeracy, a clear hand and good concentration. It thus offered to middle-class women the chance to earn an independent living in safe and reasonably pleasant surroundings. While it might not have been the occupation of choice for a well-read girl of superior intelligence, apart from governess positions, she had few respectable alternatives.[29]

The level of office discipline for both sexes, while exacting by modern standards, had numerous compensations. The most important was job security. As long as the rules were not persistently flouted – and the clerical departments were constantly under surveillance – the clerks enjoyed a high degree of security, although conformity was far from the only criterion for promotion or a move to another department. Until a somewhat later date, not much can be gleaned regarding the way clerks were promoted or about which duties carried higher rates of pay, but seniority must have been an important factor, presumably considered together with performance, diligence being taken for granted. At this stage Prudential clerks were not classified, apart from being assigned to either the Ordinary or the Industrial Department. The system of fourth-, third-, second-, first-class and principal clerks that lasted until well after the Second World War does not seem to have been introduced before about 1880. This was in effect the system in use in the Civil Service, but the Prudential's was more likely modelled on that of the Metropolitan Board of Works, to which Henry Harben was elected as a member for St John's Vestry, Hampstead, in 1880.[30]

In the early 1870s, male clerks' remuneration, at least until they had proved themselves, was desperately low: £15 or £20 in the first year, £20 or £25 in the second and £30 or thereabouts in the third, thereafter rising to £40 or £50 a year, the assumption being that these very young men still lived at home. After that, they tended to receive an addition to their salaries every two or three years, rising by stages of £5. There was a great disparity between the highest paid and longest serving, and the lowest paid, more recent arrivals. In 1872 the highest paid in the Industrial Department, at a level immediately below Thomas Dewey, who as Manager reported directly to Harben, were on salaries of £150 to £175, and the lowest paid, apart from the juniors, on £55 to £70. Three years later, all these salaries had risen, by £50 for the highest paid and £5 to £10 for the lowest. The same man mentioned above, Frederick Fisher, who later became the sub-manager of the Industrial Branch and eventually Joint Manager, was receiving £250 as its senior clerk in 1872 and £375 in 1875. Ordinary Department clerks were somewhat lower paid: the most senior received £150 in 1872 and £195 in 1875, and the lowest paid £60 to £70 in 1872 and £60 to £80 three years later, but the only conclusion to be drawn from the salary lists is that every man was evaluated separately.

It is interesting to observe right from 1871 that, however physically separate the women might be from the men in the office, their names are undifferentiated in the salary lists and the amounts paid seem to have been roughly equal in the junior echelons. Women clerks generally got £20 in their first year, rising by £10 in each of the second and third years. Women's pay could only rise so far, however; their salary scale seems to have had a lower ceiling, which could be attained in fewer years but which thereafter did not reflect either long service or performance.[31] The expectation was, of course, that women would be employed for fewer years and would eventually leave to get married. When they did, they had to resign their Prudential posts. There were several cases of women who were single at the time they were offered positions and married by the time they took them up; on being discovered, they were at once dismissed. Apart from the agreeable facilities at their disposal, the women received one financial perquisite which the men did not: a luncheon allowance of £12 a year if they chose not to avail themselves of the nutritious subsidised lunches provided by the Company. At this stage only the women were catered for in-house; it was considered indelicate for them to have to go outside to cafés and chophouses for their midday meal, not to mention the questionable quality of what they could afford if they did. The male clerks, on the other hand, had to go out of the office to eat, or bring food from home.

The clerks of both sexes were engaged subject to character references and a trial period of one or three months. From May 1872 onwards, new clerks were required to pass a medical examination. There are no reports this early about any tests of knowledge or ability, although by the 1890s written tests of literacy and numeracy were given. To have a relative already *in situ* was a virtual guarantee of entry; scores of cases in which the same name occurs two, three and four times in the salary lists testify to this. (Later on there would be numerous 'Prudential families' that provided the Company with generations of employees.) The system of individual annual reviews with a Manager or a Director, in which each clerk's progress – or lack of it – was assessed and his increase in salary told to him, may also derive from Harben's observation of the prevailing practice at the Metropolitan Board of Works. The Managers of the Ordinary and Industrial Departments, William Hughes and Thomas Dewey, assisted him as appropriate, forming a tribunal before whom each member of staff was obliged to pass.[32]

Another compensation for the level of concentration demanded of the clerks was a fairly gentle hand on the reins on the part of management day to day, as long as the work was done. When a shareholder put a complaint to Henry Harben at the Annual General Meeting in 1872, the latter replied: 'I fully admit that our clerks do read the papers and chatter; but I have yet to learn that human nature can go on all day long without some little relaxation.'[33] The one misdemeanour that brought serious punishment was failure to follow procedures – not double-checking entries, for example – with the result that an error was detected later on. For this kind of corner-cutting a clerk might be dismissed on being found out, or suspended without pay for a time, depending on the gravity of the offence and the degree of deviousness involved. This was dereliction of duty, and while not as serious as theft, there were few sins that ran more contrary to the prevailing moral code. Harben would tolerate neither laziness nor waste. An interchange with Thomas Dewey shows him indignant at finding the two together:

> *I have examined the sheets of the various divisions showing the overtime and am of the opinion that a large amount of overtime has been occasioned by want of diligence in the hours of ordinary business. In my constant inspections of the office I still find large numbers of clerks idling their time away and think that the chief clerks are wanting in proper supervision of their respective divisions. I do not include every division in this.*

When things did not improve to his satisfaction, Harben decided to restore discipline by cancelling the annual dinner given to the clerks by the Company. (These were occasions of limitless food and drink, speeches and musical entertainment that were much looked forward to. Harben justified his decision by saying that 'From the frequent inspections ... I was convinced that considerable laxity existed ...'.) But he clearly relented after an appeal from someone, as the clerks' dinner at the Freemasons Tavern was held as usual.[34]

The minutes record enough dismissals for such offences as pilfering, drunkenness and gambling to suggest that, as with the agents, strict supervision often found causes for correction. Mere hi-jinks, such as sliding down the banisters (by far the fastest way to descend at Ludgate Hill) usually brought a fine. A woman clerk absent from the office without permission was 'to be fined the amount of two days' pay for each day's absence', but there were male clerks who were dismissed outright for failure to give a plausible reason for absence. Timekeeping was punctiliously enforced, with the custom of drawing a line under the name of the most recent arrival at 9.30 a.m. on the dot – 10.00 a.m. for women – having made the transition from board room to general office. Lateness was punished by fines of sixpence or a shilling. Six instances of more than ten minutes' lateness in any given year brought a notice of dismissal.

But in an era when neither autocracy nor paternalism needed apologists, there was also a certain amount of rule-bending at the Directors' discretion. There evolved the tacit understanding that the Prudential cared for its own. Misfortunes such as a death in the family were mitigated by time off, and in some recorded cases of consumptive or nervous illness, by exceptional generosity in paying for a recuperative holiday. The minute books contain instances of sums of money given to clerks who had accidents, or who were the only support of aged parents who fell ill. If a clerk died while in the Company's employ, a grant of a year's salary was made to his or her parents, or wife. Staff matters such as these were dealt with at the weekly board meeting.

There was also a good deal of day-to-day socialising. The whole office could come to a halt for a really good prank, as on the occasion when one clerk pinned a festoon of coloured paper to the coat-tails of another, boxed him on the ear and fled, up Ludgate Hill, around St Paul's and back, 'to the shrieking joy of our colleagues', with his decorated victim in hot pursuit. The Prudential's managers and senior clerks do not seem to have held themselves aloof from the middling ranks, and spontaneous adjournments to nearby restaurants or to the theatre of an evening were frequent. Even in these surroundings, high spirits found their mark: in the case of one particularly excellent 'rag', the illustrious Frederick Schooling (then a sub-manager) was depicted by a delighted onlooker 'with his head on the velvet rail of the Dress Circle of the theatre ... completely and thoroughly exhausted with laughter'.[35]

The 1860s saw the beginnings of the sporting and cultural activities that came together in 1871 as the Prudential Clerks' Society, later to evolve into the singular entity known as 'The Ibis', about which more will be said in later chapters. In 1886, at one of its annual dinners, Henry Harben recalled that the Society had existed informally as long ago as 1863, and was in those days 'a learned society, too', that is, one at whose meetings papers were presented for discussion.[36] The Cricket Club was the first of the clubs, formally founded in 1870. It certainly existed earlier; as the fines imposed for misdemeanours were donated to it by the Board from 1864, it probably came into being from about the time there were enough clerks to make up teams.[37] A Prudential Clerks' Rowing Club was founded in 1870, the Ibis Literary Society in 1873, and the *Ibis Magazine* in 1878. Both the library and the choral society must have been well-established by the late 1870s, the latter with one of Harben's nephews by marriage as its director. It provided the musical interludes at the dinners held on the day of the Annual General Meeting. The custom arose – it is thought from about 1861 – of granting the clerks a half-holiday on that day.

From the clerks' point of view, subsidised cricket, rowing and reading offered better facilities than they could afford on their own. The Directors' commitment to these activities lay partly in the public school ideal of *mens sana in corpore sanum*, reinforced by Henry Harben's robustly evangelical view of sport as character-building. The sport that Harben never included among 'manly exercises', after a clerk (one W.E. Tichener, an excellent oarsman) broke his arm at it, was football, which thereafter was forbidden by his express order.[38]

Details like this give some idea of the extent of Harben's involvement, not only in the overall direction of the Company, but in the minutiae of its daily administration. It presupposed an exceptional fund of energy. William Hughes, the Manager of the Ordinary Department, once related how 'being sent on a message from the slow, old-fashioned office in which he was then engaged' (the Consolidated, pre-1865) he encountered Harben for the first time, 'in the full

FACING PAGE

The youthful triumvirate

that shared the

administration of the

Prudential with Henry

Harben: left to right,

William Hughes, William

Lancaster, Thomas Dewey.

flood of work'. On that occasion he was 'fairly frightened at the atmosphere of intense energy which pervaded the Prudential' and returned to his own establishment thankful for its slower pace. When the Consolidated was taken over and Hughes became an employee of the Prudential, he found himself motivated by the other man's dynamism, which he compared to 'the action of a steel on a rusty knife; and if he was not now the very sharpest of blades, the fault was in the material of which he was made, and not from any want of the sharpening power in the steel'.[39]

Until 1870 Harben's title was still that of Secretary; in February of that year he became Actuary as well. But he was to all intents and purposes the undisputed prime mover of the Company. By 1872, the breadth of his responsibilities demanded the devolution of some of them. First came the delegation of his actuarial role, with the appointment on 4 January of William Hughes as Actuary for Ordinary business, and Thomas Dewey as Actuary on the Industrial side. Hughes would remain with the Prudential until his retirement in 1903. He was the first man in the Prudential to become a Fellow of the Institute of Actuaries by examination. In the same year, 1870, he wrote a highly successful handbook called *Practical Information for Life Assurance Agents*, which was distributed to Prudential agents. Thomas Dewey had caught Harben's eye when he was still a junior: the minute books record that he was 'to be presented with a gold watch or a book to the value of £5 5s' for his work on the Industrial Department's accounts in 1863, and in 1870 he was given a Bible for getting the mortality returns out in good time.[40] The two were well-rewarded on their appointments: Dewey's salary was £550 and Hughes' £300.

The decision to divide Harben's duties further seems to have originated with the other Directors, though Harben readily acceded to it once they put it to him that it was not in the Prudential's interests for one man – even if he were still only 50 years old – to hold so many of the administrative reins. At a meeting in January 1873 it was suggested that '... he being possessed of the knowledge of the entire details of the Office a violent disruption might be occasioned by his sudden death or illness ...' and that it would be best

if the Directors could make an arrangement with him whereby his immediate subordinates in the Office could be entrusted with the responsibilities of the work and be inducted into the duties so as to render them fit and competent to conduct the affairs of the Company if required to do so at any time, and they suggested that they could make this communication to him from his well-known desire to benefit the Company.

A degree of self-interest was at work on both sides here: the Prudential still had only 34 shareholders, and the Directors and their families and friends, together with Harben, accounted for the majority of them. Harben for his part agreed to delegate, 'so long as his interests were properly protected'. (Presumably this

meant the right to add to his by now substantial shareholding.) Dewey and Hughes were accordingly given additional responsibilities, with no increases in the salaries they were drawing as Actuaries, when Harben finally took the title of Resident Director early in 1873. For the moment he retained his position as Secretary, but appointed William Lancaster (another highly capable manager who had come into the Prudential as a lad in 1857) as Assistant Secretary. As part of his task when he took over as Secretary from Harben in 1874, Lancaster acquired responsibility for the Company's investments from Edgar Horne.[41]

Harben preferred home-grown, hand-picked supporters, whose capabilities he knew and had nurtured. Even as he announced, in a circular to the staff, the official change in his status, he let it be known that ultimate authority continued to rest with him: Dewey, Lancaster and Hughes were now to 'take the active management of the Company, under my immediate supervision, and all communications relating to their several Departments are to be addressed to them in their official capacity only, *and not by name*'.[42]

Dewey, Lancaster and Hughes were directed to sit as a management committee to oversee the day-to-day running of the office. There was no thought of importing talent from outside. This was typical of Harben and of an age and an industry that valued continuity and stability. It was also predictable in a company whose Board contained so many of the same individuals – and all of them major shareholders – as at its formation. The Reverend James Gillman was still its Chairman, Dr Patrick Fraser, Edgar Horne, Richard Pugh, Thomas Bulman Cole and Thomas Reid its Directors, James Allanson and George Clark its Auditors. The roots of a tradition that would still be evident when the Prudential Corporation was created a hundred years later, that of 'growing one's own timber', go back this far.

Dr Patrick Fraser (known as 'The Doctor') was Medical Officer from 1848, a Director from 1852 to 1893 and an Honorary Director, a position unique to him, until his death in 1896.

Henry Harben was by now a leading figure in British assurance and actuarial circles. As a consequence of his visit in 1870 he was also recognised as an authority in the United States, where in Newark, New Jersey, the tiny Prudential Friendly Society – named in admiration of the British company by its founder and Secretary, John Dryden – was struggling for survival. Its Directors were almost ready to wind it up but, as a last resort, Dryden decided to seek Harben's advice on how to turn the Society around. He sailed for England in November 1876, arriving unannounced at Ludgate Hill.

His openness in explaining his purpose was matched, as he later reported to his Board, by Harben's generosity in offering him a virtual blueprint of how the Prudential functioned. Harben guided him around the various departments and explained the field staff system to him, supplying him with a complete set of forms and rule books. The visitor was struck by the overall simplicity of the Prudential's operations. There were salutary lessons in its early decision to abandon sickness insurance, for which his own association was experiencing high claims. Dividing the country into administrative areas also made sense, as did concentrating agents in the most densely populated centres. Dryden was given a set of Prudential life tables and mortality figures – the actuarial fruits of Harben's insistence on sound statistical research as the foundation stone of the whole industrial assurance edifice. Harben was adamant about two further points. One was that agents be allowed an unrestricted field of action (in contrast to allocating them to defined areas, as the American society did). This fostered initiative and a strong competitive spirit. The other was that money spent in the early days would be repaid in abundance once a well regulated field staff began to stir up business. In America, where booming cities were newly accessible by rail, the scope for growth was virtually unlimited.

John Dryden returned to New Jersey, and with his report of what he had learned in London, put an end to talk of dissolving the Prudential Friendly Society. Refounded as the Prudential Insurance Company of America on 15 March 1877, it revised its actuarial tables to make them suitable for industrial business, and adopted the British company's divisional structure and field staff organisation. Within three years the number of policies in force and sums assured multiplied tenfold as the company advanced into New York State and Pennsylvania. In time it would be forced to seek its own solutions to the inevitable problems of lapsing and high expense ratios, but it would survive to proclaim 'the strength of Gibraltar' as one of North America's most powerful insurance companies.

Thomas Reid, a Director from 1858 to 1885, was the first of four generations of his family to serve on the Board.

Its biggest obstacle in its early years, however, was the rival Metropolitan Life Insurance Company of New York, whose Chairman, Joseph Knapp, viewed it as an interloper in a field he was determined to secure for the Metropolitan. Acquiring a ready-made corps of agents seemed the quickest way to accomplish this. In 1878 Knapp too visited England and collected Prudential agents' materials, although there is no record of his having visited Ludgate Hill. During 1880 the Metropolitan's newspaper advertisements in the British provincial press secured the services of some 500 agents of various companies. Among them were a number of Prudential men, whose training helped their new employer to rapid dominance of the American life assurance scene, as their former one dominated the British.[43]

Holborn Bars and the Prudential Style

B Y 1873, after years of adding piecemeal to the premises at No. 62 Ludgate Hill, the Prudential had reached the point where the steady increase in Industrial Department staff and in the demands of document storage had put a severe strain on space. The freehold of No. 64 was bought as a last resort, but by 1875 more drastic measures were necessary. Other nearby properties were available, but at 'exorbitant' prices, while building upwards seemed likely to touch off an ancient lights dispute with neighbouring occupiers. Housing the Industrial and Ordinary sides of the business under separate roofs was rejected as the first step to chaos – not that (as anonymous wags on occasion suggested in the *Ibis Magazine*) No. 62 was even then altogether free of chaos. Clerks could get lost in its upper reaches, and everyone was certain that if the walls ever fell, the stacks of ledgers lining them would remain to hold up the roof and ceilings. The noise level was apparently very high. Besides, it was '... little consolation when ... the rain is pouring through the skylight, or a fearful smell pervades the office, to be told ... that the tempest pouring down upon the desk is a little unavoidable condensation, and that the odour ... cannot possibly come from the basement'.[1]

The best solution seemed to be to acquire a large new site which could be built upon as needed, in an area where land prices were still reasonable. Harben found a promising site on the borders of Holborn, less than a minute's walk away from the house in Hatton Garden where the Prudential had come into being less than 30 years before:

a plot of ground which having a good frontage and address ... ran back into a small street of poor houses & which it appeared ... might suit the Company's purposes & Mr Horne ... had at the request of Mr Harben inspected the plot ... which he considered would be a most eligible investment for the Company at the price for which he believed it could be obtained.[2]

By New Year's Day, 1876, an agreement had been signed to purchase 'Brooke House and other Freehold property in Holborn' and 'Brett's Old Furnival's Inn Hotel'.

These properties stood west of the new Holborn Viaduct over the Fleet river and Farringdon Street, just outside the City of London boundary. The viaduct, opened by the Queen in November 1869, at last linked the City and the main east–west traffic artery through the West End in one straight thoroughfare. Its construction had done away with some notorious slums and rookeries, as well as the steep hill on either side of the Fleet that had posed a hazard to goods traffic and livestock for centuries. The completion of Holborn Circus in 1874 joined the streets running southwards to Fleet Street with Smithfield and Clerkenwell to the east and north, to create a desirable area for development.

The decision to site the Prudential's new office close to the City, yet at less than a City price, was an astute one. This was the north-eastern boundary of 'legal London', close to Chancery Lane and the Inns of Court. Other monuments in the vicinity were Staple Inn, the ancient chapel of the bishops of Ely (today St Etheldreda's church), and Wren's church of St Andrew. The recorded history of

The area west of the City became more desirable with the opening of the Holborn Viaduct in 1869.

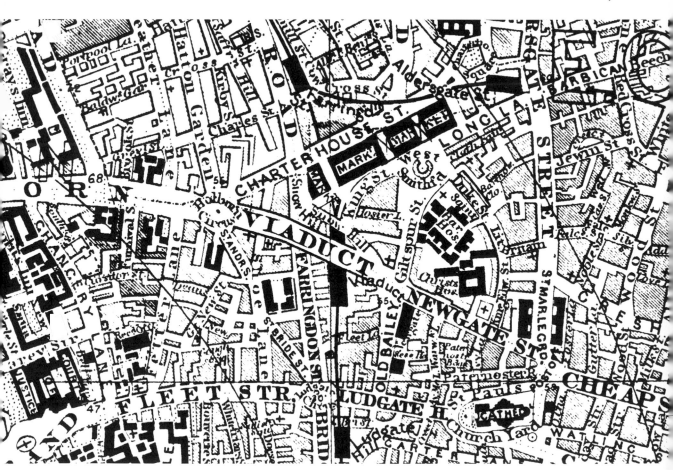

the site went back at least to the fourteenth century. Furnival's Inn, one of the medieval courts of Chancery, can be traced on it from 1385, though the sixteenth-century replacement to the original building was given a facade by Inigo Jones in the seventeenth century and by the early nineteenth had been demolished. In 1875 a more modest structure of stucco and brick housed the Old Furnival's Inn Hotel, 'for Families and Gentlemen', while Wood's Hotel stood behind it across what had once been the Inn's courtyard and gardens. Brooke House, the other major building occupying part of the site, was already several generations old when Fulke Greville, Baron Brooke and Lord Chancellor to James I, bought it as his town residence. The house where Brooke was murdered by his valet was knocked down in 1676 and rebuilt, and some of the surviving modern streets laid out: Brooke, Greville, Beauchamp and Dorrington Streets.

It was partly due to the number of sitting tenants in these somewhat insalubrious streets that the acquisition of the whole of the area today occupied by the Prudential's Holborn Bars building took more than twenty years, from 1876 to 1898. The actual construction of Chief Office took from 1876 to 1905. The section bought first was the plot occupying the corner of Brooke Street and Holborn, running north to Greville Street, with a jog to the east to go around a group of houses at the corner of Brooke and Greville Streets. This strip of land was sufficiently broad for the erection of a large new office. It consisted of Brooke House and No. 5 Brooke Street, Brett's Hotel, Old Furnival's Inn Hotel, the row of houses in Furnival's Inn Court and No. 13 Greville Street, all acquired by the end of April 1876, and Nos. 6 and 7 Brooke Street, and Nos. 15, 16 and 17 Greville Street, by the end of June, for a total price of £33,300.

It is interesting to speculate whether, had the Prudential Board been completely satisfied with the work done by its two previous architects, William Moseley and Chatfield Clarke, at Ludgate Hill, it would have engaged Alfred Waterhouse.[3] Clearly the building of a completely new office was a major under-taking, unlike the small-scale adaptations possible at Ludgate Hill. One of the conditions for the new plan was that the Ordinary and Industrial sides of the business should be kept together, which suggests that very large premises were envisaged from the beginning.[4] This was not only an opportunity to provide the Company with the kind of purpose-built, unified space it needed, but a chance to express its growing importance and its pioneering triumph. It is thus probable that once the decision to build anew was taken, it was also decided to commission a design from an architect with a wider reputation than either of the men used previously.

Whether any other architects besides Waterhouse were considered is not revealed by surviving records, nor why he was chosen over the other prominent architects of the day – Shaw, Scott, Street or Butterfield (builder of St Alban's church at the far end of Brooke Street). Two possibilities suggest themselves. One is that Henry Harben, on his travels in the north of England, could hardly have escaped seeing Waterhouse's famous Manchester Assize Courts and new Town Hall, the latter under construction in 1875. The other possible connection emerges from Waterhouse's 1870 commission for the Equity and Law Life Association in Lincoln's Inn Fields. Harben was well acquainted with T.A. Sprague, that company's Actuary, who had defended the Prudential in 1864. Harben must have known this building, a stone's throw from the Holborn property, though this is not strictly open to proof. What is certain – given that his approval was everything and his veto absolute – is that he liked Waterhouse's work, wherever he had seen it. On 9 March 1876 the Board nominated a three-man committee comprising Harben, Gillman and Horne to consult Waterhouse, who was subsequently appointed.[5]

Sir Alfred Waterhouse, at about the time he was commissioned by the Prudential to design its new Chief Office at Holborn Bars.

Alfred Waterhouse, one of the best-known of nineteenth-century architects, was at the height of his powers and reputation when he accepted the Prudential's commission in 1876. His winning entry in the competition for the Manchester Assize Courts in 1859 had made him widely admired. At the time he was engaged by the Prudential, he was working on several other major projects: besides the Manchester Town Hall, there was London's Natural History Museum, which would open in 1881. In addition, he had by this time carried out a series of commissions for Oxford and Cambridge colleges, and designed or remodelled country houses, hospitals, schools and churches. He was a most prolific and energetic architect with a highly efficient practice, and well accustomed to working with institutional clients on massive, long-running commissions.

His connection with the Prudential was indeed to be long-running: he worked directly on its projects from 1876 until his retirement at the turn of the century, and his son Paul carried out specific commissions for the Company until his own death in 1930. In the course of carrying out 27 distinct commissions, Waterhouse created a recognisable style of building for the Company. In major city centres the length and breadth of the land, these buildings came to embody the Prudential's identity in a singularly powerful way.

That his style would become such an articulate expression of the Company's presence could not have been foreseen in 1876. There is no evidence that the Prudential Board entertained any preconceived idea about the kind of building wanted; the Directors were more concerned that conditions be right for the efficient running of the business than about architectural style. Obviously the new building had to conform to certain practical criteria and these reflected the developing needs of the Company. Those needs were changing. In this the Prudential was typical: as one account puts it,

Companies no longer wanted simply an urban mansion with space for a few clerks. They needed to combine large public offices with space for substantial numbers of employees in different departments. Hierarchies of managers had to be appropriately housed; and there was usually a sumptuous boardroom to which directors would travel weekly from their country homes. Here was an architectural challenge in itself; but the increase in size meant that whole buildings could be designed, whose entire facade would express the presence and confidence of a particular company.[6]

It was no longer possible to make do with offices consisting of a biggish house (or in the case of Ludgate Hill, of houses knocked together). By the late-1870s the Prudential's Industrial Branch employed nearly 500 clerks. Supervising them was best accomplished in large halls with good lighting, with desk space for mechanical innovations such as arithmometers and the first typewriters, and in due course, dating machines and other devices.[7] As well as this kind of utilitarian space (and separate areas of it for men and women), more impressively appointed areas were needed where people seeking ordinary life assurance could come to obtain information and discuss their needs. Secure storage areas, for policy documents, share certificates, property deeds and the like, were also required, on a scale that provided for future expansion. All this, together with Board and Directors' rooms, dining facilities and a variety of other facilities for a large staff could only be contained in a large extended block. While such office blocks were not entirely new, even in London, there were few enough of them to make the Prudential Board conscious of the need and advantage of differentiating its building from others.

Alfred Waterhouse is often referred to as a pillar of the Gothic Revival, and so he was; but it is important to appreciate how originally and how freely he adapted the Gothic style – as indeed, he adapted a number of others, from Romanesque to French renaissance.[8] As a young man he had shared the contemporary interest in the picturesque and the sublime, and the artistic theories of Ruskin and Pugin. The approach summed up by Ruskin's dictum 'When we build, let us think that we build forever' is pure Waterhouse.[9] But unlike these two, Waterhouse was highly practical and did not see pure adherence to style as necessary, or as always related to the expression of an intellectual or a spiritual ideal. While Pugin, for instance, upheld the medieval style as the only one worthy of emulation because it most closely reflected man's spiritual strivings, Waterhouse believed that style should be chosen – and adapted, if need be – for its aptness for the overall task in hand: site, client, surroundings and purpose.[10]

His first sketches were submitted to the Prudential Board on 8 June 1876, and the elevations soon afterwards. He had apparently received instructions as to some of the features wanted: the building's facade was to appear 'good but not apparently costly', but he could spend more liberally on the board room and the front office, 'the only rooms that are to be costly'. The board room was to be well-lit by an oriel window. A central stairwell was to link the various floors with the secure document store provided by a muniment room, and a separate side entrance for the women clerks.[11]

These features were incorporated by Waterhouse in a design that paid his own particular homage to the Gothic Revival in its overall effect and in much of its decoration, while admirably fulfilling his own avowed belief in 'making buildings for use in the nineteenth century rather than recreating a medieval dream'.[12] The actual construction work was accomplished in a little under three years. One reason why the Prudential Board came to like and respect Waterhouse lay in his ability to keep to the agreed schedule and budget, though this project, like most, had its delays.[13] One imagines that he got on well with Harben, since his energy, professionalism and attention to the smallest details of his commissions suggest some temperamental similarities. Once the furniture and fittings

Waterhouse's first building for the Prudential: Chief Office, 1879.

(also designed by Waterhouse or his son Paul) were complete, the Company moved from Ludgate Hill.[14] The first board meeting was held in the new building on 29 May 1879.

The new building, soon known by all as 'Chief Office', was three storeys high, with its impressive public areas at the front, and access from Holborn via an ornate central portal. There was a managers' floor above, and the board room with its handsome oriel window occupied the Brooke Street corner of the second floor. Behind this and running along Brooke Street were the large, open office areas housing the clerical departments.

Above a polished granite plinth, the building's exterior was of brick ornamented with a material of which Waterhouse was a champion: terracotta. He had no intention of reproducing Dickens' Coketown ('... brick that would have been red if the smoke and ashes had allowed it'). Waterhouse held terracotta to be the material most resistant to pollution and the blackening effects of coal-smoke, capable of being washed clean by rain. Moreover, it could be easily produced in quantity and in a range of colours from an inexhaustible supply of native clay.[15] The colour selected for the Prudential's building was a deep-fired but lively red, apparently the choice of the Directors who preferred solid colour to the red ornamented with buff-coloured terracotta bricks suggested by the architect.[16] Parts of the facade were highly decorated with ornamental brickwork. The building's long roof was steep, broken by ranks of Gothicised chimneys at the front and a Germanic-style turret over the side entrance, and numerous dormer windows all the way along it. The Gothic theme was especially evident in the pointed arches used on the ground floor windows.

The Prudential calendar in the year of the move from Ludgate Hill featured the new Chief Office.

Reactions to the new premises were positive, both from inside and outside the Company. Naturally it was featured in the architectural press. The *Building News* approved of it, as a triumph for terracotta as a medium, and as aesthetically more pleasing and interesting than the other buildings as yet put up in Holborn. The review that appeared in the *Illustrated Carpenter and Builder* not only gave an impression of the building's appearance, but also an indication of some of the functions that occupied the space: 'Passing through the principal entrance from Holborn, there are to right and left of the marble mosaic floor, divided by broad mahogany counters in a high state of polish, two offices, large and handsome enough, one would think, for any commercial establishment, though in reality this part is but the entrance hall ...'

These two offices were the 'Ordinary' general office, and the paying-in office; the 'Industrial' general office lay ahead. The 'magnitude of the industrial business' was shown by the size of the rooms dedicated to it: the areas running along Brooke Street on three floors were each 300 ft long and covered an area of 12,000 sq. ft. The arrangement of Waterhouse's furniture within these areas was carried out by Harben. The first and second floors were dedicated to the Audit and Registration Departments respectively, the third and fourth to the women's clerical departments and luncheon rooms.

Predictably, the decor was more opulent at the front of the building, in the public parts and the Directors' quarters, than in the long clerical saloons, yet materials of good quality were used even there.

> *Throughout all these apartments the furnishing is of the most solid character, yet elegant in the sense of being free from meretricious show. Floors of oak, fittings, doors and windows of bright mahogany, and the walls free from plastering, finished in white glazed bricks, with dados and ornamental strings in French gray brick, testify to tasteful substantiality.*[17]

An impression of the board room, 'probably one of the most ornately finished rooms of its kind in the metropolis', comes from *The Commercial World*, whose writer described the oak linenfold panelling, the two chimney pieces with their sumptuous tooled leather friezes (one mantel held a splendid clock, the other a statue of Prudence) and other features in lingering detail. The lavish use of faience, majolica and Minton tilework and mosaic floors in the public areas at the front of the building reinforced the dignity of the spacious and richly furnished Directors' rooms. Yet to this reporter, 'Nothing is more striking in the survey of these buildings than the fact that in every particular which forethought or ingenuity could suggest, the directors have been as solicitous for the comfort of their employees as of their own', an opinion which he supported by reference to the exemplary sanitary and ventilation systems, commodious and airy clerical departments and attractive – if simpler – decor.[18]

An article in the recently founded *Ibis Magazine* claimed to reflect the feelings of the women clerks, in whom the office seems to have induced the state of mind more often inspired by a church:

> *We quite enjoy turning in from the noisy streets by the retired and select entrance in Brooke Street, to the grand and noble edifice, with feelings almost akin to awe and reverence, when we think of the many hours, days, months and years of anxious thought that must have been spent before such a magnificent building could rear itself to the admiring gaze of the passing multitude.*

The women occupied a 'spacious apartment': 'A grand room it is, having plenty of light and air, two of the greatest essentials towards health, and every possible convenience necessary in the way of drawers and cupboards ...'. The luncheon room reminded the writer of 'the saloon of a fine steamer, with its leaning side windows, through which may be observed the palisading of the roof like the upper deck' and gave onto an open-air terrace on the roof, which the women could use for healthful exercise in fine weather.[19]

The completion of the new office, at a total cost of £158,791 3s 8d, was no sooner achieved than the Prudential began planning to add to it. The additions, also by Waterhouse, were carried out in three more phases, as the purchase of properties in Brooke Street, Greville Street and Leather Lane became possible, between 1883 and 1905.[20] The last and most substantial phase was that involving Furnival's Inn and old hotels adjacent to Leather Lane, from which emerged the long Holborn facade with its turreted roofscape that is still today such a dominating feature of the skyline in this part of London. This last phase will be described more fully in a later chapter.

In the meantime, keeping pace with the continuing expansion of the business, the Company began to erect its own office blocks in a number of provincial cities. This was a logical sequel to the acquisition of properties for investment purposes which began in a systematic way in the late 1870s.[21] The pattern that soon evolved was that of acquiring a site in a good location and putting up a large office block which included space for the Prudential's own divisional or district office and, in separate parts of the building, a variety of commercial suites that

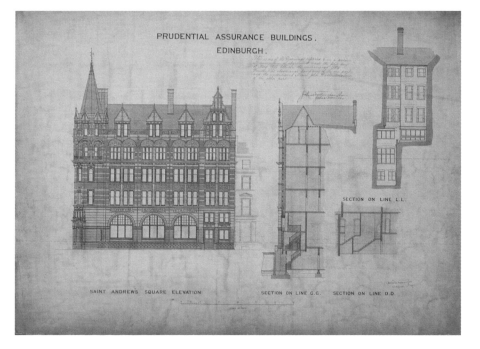

Waterhouse's designs for the provincial offices bore a recognisable similarity. The structural features, decoration and colouring of the Edinburgh office were distinctive, yet it was an unmistakeable example of the 'Prudential style'.

could be let. The first of these developments was the Prudential's Liverpool office, built in 1885. Thereafter, Waterhouse's Gothic-derived, brick and terracotta 'Prudential style' was carried all over the country: to Portsmouth and Manchester in 1886; Glasgow in 1888; Birmingham and Bolton in 1889; Leeds in 1890; Cardiff and Newcastle in 1891; Leicester in 1892; Bradford and Nottingham in 1893; Sheffield, Dundee and Edinburgh in 1895; Huddersfield and Oldham in 1898; Bristol and Plymouth in 1899; and Hull and Southampton in 1901.[22]

After buying Staple Inn at auction in 1886, the Prudential had it restored by Sir Alfred Waterhouse. Today it numbers the Institute of Actuaries among its tenants.

There were a number of Prudential offices that were never accommodated in Waterhouse buildings. Perhaps, had ill health not forced the architect to retire from practice in 1901, more of the provincial towns where they were located – places like Exeter, Brighton and Dublin – might have been graced by his designs. In those buildings for which he was commissioned, the details varied with the locations and the size of the sites. While brick and terracotta were the most frequently used materials, the colours of these varied too, and in a few instances terracotta was replaced by local stone.[23] There was great variety, also, in the amount of commercial space, and in the tenants to whom the Prudential rented parts of its buildings: a third of the office blocks included accommodation for shops, but there were also three which contained restaurants belonging to the Ye Mecca chain in their basements. Among the tenants of other district offices were a private hotel, an art gallery and a Turkish bath for which the fittings were also designed by Waterhouse.[24]

Two other developments entrusted to Waterhouse that deserve mention were the commercial block built by him in Brooke Street, and Staple Inn. The Brooke Street block was put up in 1880, facing the new Prudential office, and contained shops and flats. The flats were let to the women clerks at reasonable rents. Such an arrangement, which saved the cost of transport or the effort of a dusty walk to the suburbs, must have been among the most attractive in London for a woman earning an independent living. Staple Inn, a medieval survival on the other side of Holborn, bore a plaster facade when acquired by the Prudential at auction in 1886. Waterhouse removed the plaster in the course of fulfilling the company's intention of preserving the Inn as a historic building, restoring 'the ancient character of the front' to reveal the sound wooden beams, and adding medieval-style windows.[25] The Institute of Actuaries leased two rooms and the Hall of Staple Inn as its headquarters. The site next to Staple Inn was also purchased for a further Waterhouse commission, Staple Inn Buildings. This too was a commercial development, and one which eventually numbered Waterhouse's own practice among its tenants. Its combination of terracotta and Gothic-inspired decorations made it immediately identifiable.

Waterhouse's creations, taken together, proved to be 'one of the earliest and most widespread examples of the corporate image in Britain'.[26] As was asserted in a recent study, although the Prudential does not seem at the outset to have sought to create such an identifiable 'house style', in effect that was what its relationship with Waterhouse achieved. Despite the variations in the buildings, they possess a singularly unified character that quickly came to be identified with the Company.[27] Waterhouse's designs found such favour with the Prudential because, consciously or unconsciously, the Directors recognised that they expressed in a kind of visual shorthand the image and ideals the Prudential sought to promote. The size of the buildings and their monumentality suggested stability; the pointed Gothic arches and the soaring pinnacles symbolised an approach to the matter of assurance that proclaimed the values of a more spiritual age, giving an uplifting tone to the energetic pursuit of business. (The author of a piece in the *Ibis Magazine* even claimed that '... the design of this building is expressive of absolute truth ...'.[28])

The 'Prudential style' stated in brick and terracotta the conviction that life assurance was a right and godly remedy for the uncertainties of life. Life assurance was security, and the appearance of the Prudential's first Chief Office, an imposing sight even in 1879, suggested security – eternity, even. This visual fusion of matter and message was the Prudential's great debt to Waterhouse. It is doubtful whether, at this stage of the Company's life, any other means of self-promotion could have established it so positively, and so powerfully, in the minds of ordinary people as its buildings came to do.

EPILOGUE

The finale to the entertainment at the Prudential Clerks' Dinner, 1879 (*Ibis Magazine*, vol. II, May 1879).

Mr. Fisher.	Oh ! Schooling, don't you think before the audience goes away,
	That either you or I ought just a word or two to say?
	Suppose you do.
Mr. Schooling.	Oh ! no ; I can't ; I should break down I fear.
	You'd better try, and when you stick I'll give a loud "hear, hear."
Mr. Fisher.	I can't.
Mr. Dewey.	Ask Lancaster.
Mr. Hughes.	Just the man I meant to name !
Mr. Harben.	All you that are of that opinion signify the same.
All.	Agreed ! agreed !
Mr. Harben.	Unanimous ! Now W. J. L.,
	Stand up, and let our friends in front hear what you have to tell !
Mr. Lancaster.	Mr. Chairman, gentlemen, old friends and fellow-clerks,

It's been arranged, you see, that I should make a few remarks
About our Clerks' Society, it's [*sic*] future and its past,
For time rolls on and we must leave old Ludgate Hill at last.
How many of us in this house commenced our business lives,
Prudential boys, grown men and married good prudential wives.
How many a joke these walls have heard, how many a fearful pun !
How many a fight has there been fought, how many a kind act done.
This room is noisy, hot and low, yet how the applause has rung,
At many good recitations, and at many a song well sung.
Ay, Holborn Bars is large and grand, its architecture fine,
Yet who amongst us will forget the days of "Auld Lang Syne."
Of all our Clubs, our Cricket Club's the oldest—perhaps the best,
I speak in no disparagement of any of the rest,
It started first, for years was small, but still the pluck was there,
And now the match-list shows it's [*sic*] wins grow greater every year ; . . .
With boating, swimming ought to be allied, 'tis wrong of him
Who would attempt to row a boat before he's learned to swim ; . . .
But please don't think from these remarks that I wish to maintain,
That muscles are not often found in company with brain ;
Who thinks so let him but one hour in our Gymnasium pass,
And if he thinks so after that, why write him down an ass.
No, use your muscles, and in games of strength don't fear to train 'em,
Mens sana you will never have without the *corpus sanum.*
Our Musical Society have sung and played to night
With great success, if I interpret your applause aright, . . .
Last, but not least, our Library demands a word or two,
But not of eulogy from me, for it gets that from you;
How frequently you use it, this fact alone will speak–
More than three hundred volumes our librarians change each week;...
These, gentlemen, are all our clubs. We've prospered in the past,
The future's bright with promise too, may our good fortune last;
Yet while we're proud of what we've done, and what we hope to do,
Let us take care we don't forget to whom our thanks are due.
Our Board's kind thought about our health when business hours are gone,
Enables us to carry on these clubs as we have done,
For many a year may they be spared, these six men good and true,
Come wind, come storm, come fair, come foul, they'll bring the old ship through;
With cheerful hearts and willing hands let us our tasks fulfil,
Till our success makes Holborn Bars outshine old Ludgate Hill.

SECTION THREE

A National Institution

with the Prudential; by the end of the century, one person in three. To contemporaries, the Prudential during these years seemed less like a company than a phenomenon.[2]

In the mid-1870s – at about the same time that the Directors of the Prudential began their search for a new site – the subject of assurance for the working classes was once again under public scrutiny. Perhaps it would be more accurate to say that since Gladstone's dissection of the subject in 1864, interest in it had never really died away. Many of the country's estimated 32,000 friendly societies were still held to operate unsatisfactorily. These ranged from the smallest local societies and the burial clubs that were often indistinguishable from them, to the large collecting societies that covered whole areas of the country.[3] The financial unsoundness of many of them, their high expense ratios, the risks to funds when societies amalgamated – all these seemed out of keeping with the genuine service the better ones provided, and with the societies' boast of being the poor man's friend. There was still a widespread belief that abuse in the assurance of children was practised by the burial clubs.

Between 1871 and 1874, during W.E. Gladstone's first administration, these issues were examined by a Royal Commission, charged to make a full inquiry into the workings of friendly and building societies. The country was passing through a period of deep economic gloom as the century's worst depression brought the doctrine of *laissez-faire* that had dominated economic thinking since the 1840s under systematic attack. There was considerable support for regulation, even direct involvement, on the part of Government in what was seen to be a disordered area of the marketplace.

The Royal Commission identified 17 different types of assurance society which operated with reference to the Registrar of Friendly Societies; beyond them there were the host of unregistered friendly societies, and the industrial assurance companies.[4] As the halfway houses between the friendly societies and the ordinary life companies, the industrial assurers had not up to this time formed part of the Registrar's brief. Though it criticised some aspects of the way the large collecting friendly societies worked, the Commission – echoing the Select Committee of 1852 – spoke well of them, and of the companies, for filling a social need, encouraging thrift and providing useful actuarial information. The unregulated burial clubs, however, were heavily criticised. The Royal Commission recommended the opening up of the field of industrial assurance: an extension of the Post Office insurance scheme that would have meant adopting the system of agents that Gladstone in 1864 had sworn not to adopt, and changing the law to bring the companies under the same regulations as the friendly societies. Besides measures to ensure the provision of sound financial information, it also advised that these institutions not be permitted to insure children under the age of three.

The publication in 1874 of the Royal Commission's Reports casts a new light on Henry Harben's delegation of the Prudential's day-to-day affairs to Thomas Dewey, William Hughes and William Lancaster. It may be that, in addition to spreading the Prudential's administrative load, this was intended to allow him the time to act on the Company's behalf in the matter of the Royal Commission – even to protect the Company's interests in the wider field of politics. A few months after he stepped down as Secretary the board minutes recorded:

> *... the Directors having taken into consideration the present unsettled state of the law with regard to Industrial Life Assurance and in anticipation of fresh legislation enactments being brought forward based upon an imperfect knowledge of the facts ... it would be desirable for their late Secretary Mr Harben to enter Parliament and they undertake to explain their views to the Shareholders at a Special Meeting to be called for the purpose and to support a proposition to provide the amount required to secure his election if it can legally be done.* [5]

The Special Meeting was not called, however, because Harben, rethinking the matter, decided that his family commitments would not permit him to stand just then.[6] But during sittings of the Royal Commission Harben met and corresponded with Sir Stafford Northcote in an attempt to acquaint him with the singular features of the Prudential's business, especially with regard to the assurance of children, and to provide statistical information on infant mortality. The Commissioners did come to appreciate the Prudential's unique position, and included a Special Report on it in the final document.

A change of government in 1874 had brought the Conservatives under Disraeli to office, armed with a programme of socially reforming legislation in education, public health and local government. Northcote became Chancellor of the Exchequer and introduced a Friendly Societies Bill which steered a course between the recommendations of the Royal Commission and representations received from the industrial assurance companies. During the Bill's passage through the House of Commons in the spring of 1875, Harben continued to correspond with the Chancellor and secured some modification of Section 30 of the Bill, which covered aspects of the relations between societies and their agents, or 'collectors', and with their policyholders. Its two main provisions related to lapses and transfers. Policyholders had now to be given at least 14 days' written notice that their payments were in arrears. Similarly, written notice of the transfer of a policy from one society or company to another had to be given, and the policyholder's written consent obtained, before a transfer could take place.

The Bill became law as the Friendly Societies Act 1875 and brought all the institutions transacting assurance for the working classes together under one Act by virtue of their common activity. It rejected the Royal Commission's suggestion that the Government involve itself in the provision of assurance for the masses, which would have brought Post Office agents into direct competition with those of the friendly societies and the industrial assurance companies. There were not then (nor ever, as it turned out) to be Post Office agents. But the recommendation to bring the industrial assurance companies under the umbrella of friendly society legislation was adopted.

The Act defined industrial assurance as had the Life Assurance Act 1870, firstly, as the assurance of small sums by modest premiums, and secondly, as operating by a method involving the regular collection of these premiums from the homes of the assured. An industrial assurance company was classed as one which 'grants assurances on any one life for a sum less than £20, and which receives premiums or contributions ... by means of collectors, at periodical intervals of less than two months'. The recommendations of the Royal Commission for a proper, standard form of accounts and the need for quinquennial valuations were adopted. The Act provided that policyholders who fell behind with their premiums were from now on to be given notice in writing that any benefits so far accumulated would be lost in the event of non-payment. They were also to receive a statement of how much was owed and how to pay the arrears. A fortnight was to be the minimum time granted to repay any missed contributions. Similarly, policyholders were to be advised in writing when they were to be transferred from one company to another, and had to give their consent, also in writing, to transfers and to amalgamations.

Regarding the assurance of children, the emphasis was on amount rather than age. Children of any age could be assured, but the amount of benefit payable on death was restricted to a total of £6 for children under five years of age, and a total of £10 between the ages of five and ten, regardless of whether the child was assured with more than one company. Only a parent or guardian could propose a child, and only the proposer could collect the assurance money if the child subsequently died. The intention was to reduce the possibility that anyone might profit by a child's death. These measures temporarily allayed public concern about the purported link between assurance and the temptation to child murder, although the issue would prompt a further and more searching official inquiry in 1889.

The Act was important for the Prudential in that the industrial side of the business fell within its scope. Compliance required only minor alteration in the Company's procedures. As in 1870, the Company was well within the Act's guidelines on accounting, valuations and the provision of information, but it had now to submit its returns in the form laid down by the Central Registrar. The regulations on the assurance of children, especially the adoption of a limit on the amount of benefit, rather than on the age of the child, reflected the Company's own practice as communicated by Harben during the preparation of the Bill.

From the insight he gained into the way industrial assurance was officially regarded, as well as from the Prudential's own experience, Harben considered that service to industrial policyholders under the Act presupposed greater legal control over its agents than the Prudential currently possessed. He also foresaw that the differences between ordinary and industrial assurance were bound to become more exaggerated in the years to come, and viewed the separation of the two sides of the Prudential's business as essential to the unfettered development of each. This second course required a change in the Company's 1861 Deed of Settlement. During the same few months when the Friendly Societies Bill was before Parliament, the Prudential's own private Bill, the instrument which would effect both this aim and that of gaining greater control over its agents, was also receiving its successive readings.[7]

It was always referred to familiarly by the Directors as 'our Special Act', but the full title of this brief piece of legislation was *The Prudential Assurance Company Act, 1875*: An Act for removing difficulties attending the conduct of the business and the exercise of the powers of the Prudential Assurance Company; and for other purposes'. The 'difficulties' derived from the Company's experience with agents who, on leaving the Company, refused to hand over the 'book' that detailed the weekly transactions of their agencies. These records of new business, premium payments, arrears, lapses, revivals and claims, together made up the Company's relationship with each policyholder. Clause 10 of Section 30 of the Friendly Societies Act laid down the procedure for the settlement of disputes between assuring institutions and assured parties via the civil courts. The Prudential needed a quicker measure, since

The over-assurance of infants and children was rumoured to provide the motive for neglect and even murder.

> *... from the nature of the business of the Industrial Branch the Company are obliged to employ numerous agents, and it has on many occasions happened that persons who had been employed as, but had ceased to be, agents of the Company in that branch have refused and delayed to deliver up books and documents of the Company in their possession when required to do so, and by means of the books and documents so detained wrongfully by them have been able to inflict and have inflicted serious injury and loss not only upon the Company but upon persons assuring in the Industrial Branch ...*

Assured persons whose interests were jeopardised by agents who made off with their records had, at least in theory, common grievance with the Company, and it was in the interests of both 'for the purpose of preventing such delay and injury that provision be made for enabling the Company to recover such books and documents in a more summary way than by civil process'.[8]

To achieve this, several measures contained in the Companies' Clauses Consolidation Act 1845 (8 Vict. c.16) were incorporated into the Prudential Act.[9] These stated a company's right to require at any time from its officers a written account, supported by receipts, of all monies received on its behalf. In the case of an officer who failed or refused to do this, and to hand over all documents relating to the transactions, a company's complaint could be enforced by a Justice of the Peace, authorised to have the offender committed to gaol until he complied.

As Harben put it, the Company obtained its Act of Parliament '... to enable them to deal with its agents in the same way that railway companies can deal with their servants ...', which suggests once again that he viewed the Prudential as the provider of an essential service that in the public interest should not be held to ransom by its employees.[10] The Act would in no way deprive the Company of further remedies at law that it might have. It was merely a strong deterrent and a swift recourse in cases which, given the increasing numbers of agents engaged and the correspondingly high proportion of them dismissed, were becoming more numerous and hence more costly to pursue.

The Act's other objective was to clarify the way in which the Prudential could alter its Deed of Settlement. This would be by means of a Special Resolution passed in a General Meeting, and would empower the Company to enact new measures relating, among other things, to the separate valuation of the two branches of the business.[11]

Continuing statistical study was revealing just how very dissimilar the ordinary and the industrial sides of the business were. In contrast to the average ordinary policy, assuring £100 or more for a set term with premiums payable annually or six-monthly, the 'average' industrial policy assured £8 8s 9d, with a weekly premium of 'rather less than 1¾d'. The overwhelming majority of industrial premiums – 83% in 1876 – was payable on policies that had been issued during the previous five years. Of the remaining 17%, more than one quarter were for assurances on lives not exceeding 15 years of age. The level of expense was higher than for ordinary assurance, to cover the cost of weekly collections, outdoor staff salaries, more administrative paperwork and stamp duty. (This last penny-a-policy charge was one from which the friendly societies were exempt.) The cost, naturally, was covered by higher premiums over time than were payable for ordinary assurances. As to the high rate of lapse of industrial policies, of those valued in 1871, only 58% were still in force five years later, a fact that was directly related to the number of juvenile lives assured by the Prudential. The high rate of infant mortality decreased as the children grew older, and the tendency in working-class families was to let the policies, intended to pay for burials had the children died, lapse once they passed the critical ages and began to contribute to the family economy. These characteristics – added to the rationale for industrial assurance, the tables devised to cater for the mortality of an altogether different social class, and the basis on which the valuation of industrial policies was made – distinguished industrial from ordinary business, and suggested the sound administrative sense of creating separate entities. This separation was effected under the terms of an altered Deed of Settlement on 31 December 1876.

The year 1877 was the first for which the revenue accounts and balance sheets were prepared separately for Ordinary and Industrial Branches. The change was made in the year following the quinquennial valuation of 1876; given what was involved in making the valuation, this too made sense. The five-yearly reckoning was a staggeringly burdensome task for a company the size of the Prudential. In 1876 it involved multiple calculations on 17,751 ordinary and 2,643,665 industrial policies. Valuations are undertaken with two purposes: that of ascertaining the solvency of the company, and that of determining the surplus that can reasonably be distributed to participating policyholders (by way of bonus additions) and to shareholders. For each policy a calculation is required of the reserve (or liability) which needs to be held to meet future benefit payments, a deduction being made for the value of future premiums (net of expenses). For this purpose certain assumptions have to be made as regards future rates of mortality and net earnings from investments. Additional reserves for special contingencies may also be held. In so far as the aggregate value then put on the assets exceeds the aggregate value of the liabilities, there is a solvency margin from which surplus becomes available for distribution.[12]

The previous valuation in 1871 had been made on the basis of the Carlisle 3% Mortality Table, for both ordinary and industrial policies. With the publication by the Institute of Actuaries of findings based on its investigations in mortality among assured lives (meaning selected, middle-class lives), the Directors adopted this more up-to-date experience – the 'Institute Healthy Male 3% Table' – as the basis for the valuation of the Ordinary Branch policies in 1876. The industrial policies were dealt with differently. The Company did not yet use as its basis for valuation the mortality experience collected by its own Statistical Department, believing that the results of this should be confirmed by further experience.[13] The Farr English Life Table No. 3 was preferred as having been drawn from the mortality of the population at large, and hence as being 'very closely approximated' to the Industrial Branch's own experience. Calculations were made at 3% interest. The policies for each year of issue since 1852 were grouped separately and separate valuations were made for males and females – a total of 50 separate sets of calculations.

An appreciation of just how large a task this was emerges from the Quinquennial Valuation Reports. A.H. Bailey, the Prudential's Consulting Actuary, referred to the 1876 one as 'a work far surpassing in magnitude any similar operation in the history of Life Assurance in this country'. He dealt first with the affairs of the Ordinary Branch before going on to comment more fully

be manipulated'. One machine was purchased, for £21, the decision as to whether to buy more 'for general use in the office' being deferred for further consideration.

Another convenience was an internal communication system, 'an elaborate system of electric signals' designed to save steps rather than the effort of hand or brain. The *Insurance Guardian*'s visitor to Dewey's private office in 1874 recounted:

> *The signals in question were on the system of Julius Sax, and give instant communication with every department in the office. The audit department, for instance, wants to see him; the signals ring, and a disc appears upon the index board to show which department desires to communicate. An elaborate series of speaking tubes allows Mr. Dewey to hear what is wanted, and to convey instructions, or to summon the parties to his room. This being done, a simple pressure upon a corresponding button on the desk enables Mr. Dewey to reverse the disc till some further occasion for its use arises. Should he be absent from his room, he finds on his return, by means of these discs, who have desired to communicate with him in his absence, and as he disposes of them one after another, he reverses the discs for future use, as above described.[22]*

In April 1878, with the prospect of the move to the new building in Holborn on the horizon, it was decided to try out alternatives to this system. 'Wheatstone's telegraphing machine', recently patented, was considered, and at a meeting of the Directors Lancaster reported 'that a pair of them had been worked between the Manager IB and himself and had been found very satisfactory'.[23] But the speaking tube system was chosen for Holborn Bars in the end, probably to save expense. Once there, Dewey, as head of the Industrial Branch, was 'in direct electrical communication with more members of the Prudential staff than any other individual chief; in fact, one side of his private room is monopolised by a vast array of knobs, indicators, and other signalling contrivances'.

At Holborn Bars there was also a sophisticated pneumatic tube network ('so complicated that it is almost impossible to convey a clear idea of the working without the aid of diagrams') for conveying messages on paper. A central station was the point where 31 tubes converged; 'one tube from each room will suffice to convey messages to any part of the building' in metal cylinders forced through the tubes by pressurised air. The saving in clerk-miles and time effected by the message system worked out to prodigious sums.[24]

Electric lighting was another convenience that was introduced only after deliberation. Ludgate Hill was gas-lit, which must have made eye-strain a common complaint among the clerks engaged in figurework or correspondence all day long, and especially during the valuations. Electric lighting was still very new when the Prudential moved to Holborn Bars, and the Directors were not yet convinced of the need for it. Not quite two years after the move, in February

1881, the directors accepted the offer from the Electric Light Agency to put up 15 electric lamps free of charge as an experiment. Later that year the Audit Department was ordered to be lit after the clerks had affirmed that their work was eased by it.

While the Directors were evidently prepared to consider innovations, there seems to have been no hurry to adopt them where the existing mode of operation – in this case the hundreds of copy clerks and the system of ledgers and cards – functioned smoothly. The Company was able, by simply expanding its clerical departments, to carry out the same procedures by traditional methods as the business increased in size. Apart from periodically adding to its stock of arithmometers, it processed an ever-larger volume of data by multiplying personnel, rather than by adopting mechanised time-saving devices in large numbers. By 1891 the valuation was an almost unmanageable task, which 'pushed at the very limits of what was possible in an unmechanised office'.[25] There were over 10,000,000 policies in the Industrial Branch; as Bailey observed,

By the last Census it was ascertained that the total number of persons living on the 5th April, 1891, in the United Kingdom was 37,740,283; so that ... it appears

that the lives of about one-fourth of the population of Great Britain and Ireland are assured by your Company. The numbers have increased by more than 37 per cent. during the Quinquennium now under review.[26]

The computations attendant on valuing these had, according to Dewey 'involved an immense amount of labour and would have been almost impossible of accomplishment without the aid of the Arithmometer, no less than fifty of these instruments having been employed'.[27]

This valuation cost £70,000 and required the whole clerical staff of 700 to work overtime for seven months.[28] This was the last of the five-yearly valuations; thereafter they were done annually, under a new system of keeping the valuation cards up-to-date, which resulted in a much shorter period of intense work. As an unknown spokesman for the Company asserted in the *Insurance Journal* in 1893, 'the perfection of organisation has always been a strong point at the Prudential – we now have a system so perfect that we could start a valuation tomorrow and be done in five weeks'.[29] There was no lack of able minds to undertake such work, given the strong emphasis on actuarial training and qualifications in the Company. Frederick Schooling, who joined the Prudential as a lad and worked his way up to become a Fellow of the Institute of Actuaries, was appointed Actuary in 1892 to share the task with Dewey and Hughes.

The Reports for the valuations between 1871 and 1891 chart the progress of the Company in terms of growth of the business, and the income, profits and expenses related to this; they also show how the surplus of each five-year period was distributed. The Assurance Fund, the name given to that portion of the assets which had been accumulated to cover the liabilities, stood at £383,110 in 1871 and by 1876 had risen to £869,259. The difference between the amount in the Assurance Fund and the reserves required to be set aside (in 1871, £307,014 and in 1876, £761,571) showed the surplus available for division among the policyholders and shareholders. Under the Deed of Settlement the Directors were at liberty to divide the whole of the surplus, or set aside part of it to meet contingencies. Their habitual caution prevailed in this period of extraordinary increase, leading them to establish a Contingency Fund in 1871, placing in it £16,096 of the surplus of £76,096 and distributing the remaining £60,000 in a proportion of four-fifths to the policyholders and one-fifth to the shareholders.[30] In 1876 the Contingency Fund received nearly £24,000 of the £107,688 surplus, leaving £83,784 for division among the policyholders and shareholders.

Up to now the emphasis was still on accumulating enough in reserves to cover any possible adversity, rather than courting the policyholders with unduly high bonuses, though the bonus (27.1% in 1871 and 28.5% in 1876, on all the premiums paid since the previous valuation), apportioned as reversionary bonus or equivalent permanent reduction of premiums, was impressive enough. By

1881 not only had liabilities been amply provided for, with the Ordinary Branch Assurance Fund standing at £744,583 and the Industrial Branch Assurance Fund at £1,721,492, but even with generous transfers to the respective Contingency Funds, surpluses of £90,000 (Ordinary) and £200,000 (Industrial) were available for distribution, producing an average reversionary bonus of 40% to 60% on the premiums paid since the last valuation, depending on age.[31] It was still possible to carry forward a portion of the surplus amounting to some £25,000.

Ten years later the combined Assurance Fund stood at £14,000,000 as against liabilities of just over £12,000,000, and the total surplus of £1,800,000. Nearly £1,700,000 was distributed in the same proportions as before among the policyholders and shareholders, but the way of apportioning the policyholders' portion had been altered. A system of reversionary additions to the sum assured, irrespective of age, for every £100 assured for each of the previous five years, was adopted; in 1891 this amounted to £1 12s.[32] Not only could the Prudential boast iron-clad security for its policyholders, but a steady increase in benefits to them that was highly attractive and which competitors could not readily match.

The Prudential's approach to the investment of the funds accumulated during this period was naturally very conservative. As part of his secretarial function, from 1874 William Lancaster supervised investments other than property, in which the Company had begun to invest in an ordered way under the guidance of Edgar Horne a few years earlier. The investments in Consols and other British government securities were by 1880 almost equalled by its investments in freehold and leasehold estates, and in house properties. By 1900, total assets amounted to £14,623,627, and, apart from property and British Government stocks, there were also large investments in foreign Government stocks, as well as in the long-held colonial stocks and, from 1876, large amounts (£1,900,000 by 1900) in railway debentures and shares. There were also sizeable investments in domestic and foreign municipal stocks and bonds: in 1884 the Company held nearly £1,250,000 in Metropolitan Board of Works stocks, City of London Corporation bonds and other similar assets but by 1900 this had decreased to £320,785. (Its interest in these may have owed something to Henry Harben's place on the Metropolitan Board of Works from 1880 to 1889 and the London County Council until 1894.) The prime criteria for investment during the whole of this period were derived from the canon laid down by A.H. Bailey in a paper to the Institute of Actuaries in 1862, stressing absolute security of capital, and as good a rate of interest as was consistent with that security. Given the long-term nature of insurance business in a pre-inflationary age, this classical approach to investment went almost unchallenged until after the First World War. It is not surprising, then, that the Prudential's Directors did not invest outside those areas that offered an iron-clad guarantee of a fixed rate of interest. They never seem to have subscribed to a new issue, or to have been tempted by any of the passing fads – the goldfields of South Africa, for example – that set the City humming.

One seemingly paradoxical characteristic of the Prudential, an identifiable element of its corporate personality in these burgeoning years, even if hard to define, was its quality of reserve, of seeming distance, from the hive of commercial energy that was the City of London. Management emphasis was placed, in the first instance, on the perfecting of the disciplines that had evolved, and secondly, looking outward from Chief Office to the provinces, on the implementation of method through the agency force. The Board of the Prudential was composed of self-made men, or the sons of self-made men, not eminent City names or masters of high finance. The geographical situation of Chief Office, as far from the hub of activity around the Bank of England and the Stock Exchange as it was possible to be and still be part of the City, enhanced the sense that the Prudential was at one remove from the hurly-burly of the Square Mile. The fact that from the 1880s onward the Company employed a staff at Holborn Bars equivalent in numbers to the population of a small town, and operated from a building in which it was literally possible to walk miles, contributed to the impression that the Prudential was something of a world unto itself, that it had its own dynamic.[33] By now, too, it had created departments to carry out functions that earlier had been delegated to outsiders. A case in point was the decision in 1885 to replace Barnard and Co., the Company's solicitors since Charles Hanslip's departure in 1871, by an in-house legal department headed by Daniel Wintringham Stable.

Apart from the factors above, some of this had to do with personalities. The Reverend James Gillman, who died aged 69 in 1877, continued to hold a Church of England living during the first ten years that he was Chairman of the Prudential. He does not seem to have made any pronouncements about the social value of assurance or about the Prudential in particular, although he was an active member of the Board. It would be consistent with what is known of him to suggest that he regarded his position as one of service. His successor Edgar Horne was a man with business and family roots in the City of London that went back generations, but who deliberately 'abstained from participation in public and political life' and was personally self-effacing. He worked steadily at building up the Prudential's property holdings while keeping one hand on the tiller of his auctioneering and surveying firm, Horne & Co., but left insurance matters to Harben.

Even Harben (who, as Resident Director and, after 1877, Deputy Chairman, continued to exercise overall control of management through his deputies) seems to have accepted offices outside the Company through a sense of duty inspired by his evangelical conscience rather than the desire to project himself, or the Prudential, as a player on the wider public stage. The four occasions on which he stood as a Conservative parliamentary candidate might seem to contradict this, but the ability with which he explained and defended industrial assurance suggest that his motive was the desire to have a positive influence on legislation likely to affect it, and with it, the Prudential. Harben gave up the idea of politics on his wife's death in 1883, not because he had been unsuccessful four times, but in deference to the fact that she had never favoured it. The outside commitments he took on during the 1870s and 1880s were in the areas of public health and social improvement, and took up in committee time the hours freed by having devolved Prudential branch and secretarial management to others.[34]

The overriding reason for the Prudential's comparative insularity, however, was that its shares remained in the hands of a comparatively small number of shareholders. Many of them had been associated with the Prudential from its earliest years, and the majority were related in some way to the Directors. Until 1881 the Prudential was still an unlimited company, with a paid-up capital of only £24,920 and just under half of its 20,000 shares of £5 issued.[35] Conformity with the Limited Liability Act which became law in 1880 was the pretext for registration as a limited company, but an account of the Extraordinary General Meeting of the shareholders held on 28 April 1881 to consider the matter makes clear how advantageous their position became as a result. Edgar Horne reiterated a point made by a large shareholder at a previous Annual General Meeting: the difficulty experienced by some of them in finding trustees who would administer estates which included shares in an unlimited company. The Directors had resolved on registration as the solution to this, but only if the whole of the share capital – £100,000 – was subscribed at the same time.[36] The 10,060 shares still unallotted were accordingly offered to the existing shareholders, still less than 100 in number, and bought by them at £2 10s paid up. New shares were issued to shareholders pro rata at par (one for one) and paid for out of the bonus due to shareholders in 1882. In 1883 a further 30s was paid on each share out of bonus, bringing the amount paid up per share to £4 and the paid-up capital to £80,028.

Between 1883 and 1893, the Company's nominal capital was further increased on two occasions, with corresponding increases in the number of shares issued: in 1887, when it was raised to £500,000 in 100,000 shares of £5, of which 40,000 were issued and fully paid up, making a paid-up capital of £200,000; and in 1891 when it was increased to £2,000,000 in 400,000 shares, of which 100,000 were issued to raise the paid-up capital to £500,000. In 1893, a further 20,000 shares were issued and fully paid up, bringing the total paid-up capital to £600,000. All of these issues were to existing shareholders, pro rata at par on a one for one basis. In 1875 the purchase of shares was opened to senior office holders, such as Hughes, Dewey and Lancaster, and to selected members of the outdoor staff. (A very few of these, such as Alfred and Charles Willis, John Moon and others who had come into the Prudential with the British Industry, had owned shares since before the 1861 Deed of Settlement.) Agents and clerical staff were permitted to hold up to 100 shares from 1897, but transfers had still to be approved by the Board.

A note dated 1889 from Thomas Dewey's Memorandum Book identifies eight Directors as the owners of 15,107 shares, five officers as owners of 4,250, ten

Chief Office staff as owning 879 and six senior outdoor staff as owning 1,263. In 1893 the Prudential still had only 170 shareholders. Some possessed only a few shares; others, mammoth holdings. Of the 24 shareholders owning 1,000 shares or more, all but two were Directors or members of their families, or men associated with the Company from its early years. The largest single shareholder, with 10,380 shares, was Dr Patrick Fraser.[37] The holdings of Henry Harben, his son Henry Andrade Harben and his daughter Mary Woodgate Harben together amounted to 12,936 shares. The Horne, Hughes, Dewey and Lancaster interests also numbered several thousand shares, as did those of the Reid, Pugh, Cole and Allanson families.

One contemporary newspaper portrait of the Company took the trouble to analyse its accounts since 1867 and calculate the shareholders' profits over the 27 years between that date and the year of writing, 1894. It came up with some astonishing figures, which are fairly borne out by the Company's records. Recognising that part of the surplus was usually carried on, and making a fair estimate for the year just gone, it presented the following sums, 'earned on a capital which at the beginning of the period in question stood at £5,839':

Dividends and bonuses actually received by shareholders between 1867 and 1894	– £1,315,770
Amount allotted but not distributed (estimated)	– £ 600,000
Proportion of amount unallotted (£460,000) that is shareholders' profit (estimated)	– £ 250,000
	£2,165,770

Profits apportioned over the years to the shareholders gave people who held even a few hundred shares a comfortable living, and made those who owned thousands very well-off indeed.[38] But that was not all. The true measure of what had been achieved had to take into account the increase in the capital of the Company by £594,000, which had 'increased the stability of the undertaking, and added to its claims the confidence of the millions of people who are directly interested in it as policyholders'.[39]

This stability was more than just financial. By retaining such close control of share ownership, the Prudential's Directors and senior office holders were assured of the future direction of the enterprise. Inevitably, the Prudential began to acquire a dynastic aspect, as the sons of Directors and Managers were brought into the Company to acquire the knowledge of the business that it would be their responsibility to exercise as shareholders.

First among these was Henry Andrade Harben, who had been made a Director in 1879. His was an altogether less dominating personality than his father's, and he was very different in temperament and interests from the elder Harben. The two years he spent in the office without pay as a youth were followed by London University and Lincoln's Inn, from which he was called to the Bar in 1871. In the Prudential's Solicitor's Department, dealing with the legal aspects of property investments, he could indulge his interest in the history of medieval London that would find expression in the *Dictionary of London* that is still a valued reference work today.

It is not known whether the rest of the younger Directors had direct experience of the business before being elected to the Board. William Thomas Pugh took his father Richard's seat when the latter died in 1885, as did Percy Reid on the retirement of his father in the same year. Dr Fancourt Barnes became a Director in 1884, the same year in which his father, Dr Robert Barnes, was re-elected to the Board, having served 35 years as Medical Officer – the only man to be elected twice. Edgar Horne and William Lancaster had sons in the Company by 1890; Thomas Dewey had two, if not three, nephews. Stability and continuity, the aims to which, insurance itself was directed, were reflected in the composition of the Board in the last decade of the century.

The inherent problems of industrial assurance – expense, lapse, the evasion of existing legislation and the over-assurance of children – had a further airing during that time. In 1889 a Select Committee of the House of Commons was appointed to examine the operation of the Friendly Societies Act 1875 and recommend ways in which it could be improved. Many loopholes in the law had come to light. The legal requirement that new companies deposit £20,000, for example, could be flouted by acquiring inactive insurance companies whose registration under the Companies Act 1844 was still in force. At the level of the big collecting societies and industrial assurance companies, agents' malpractices were usually (but not always) detected, but below this there was still much abuse of the system.

Henry Andrade Harben, a Director from 1879 and Chairman from 1907 to 1910.

The Committee was mainly concerned with the collecting and friendly societies, especially the unregistered ones, but the companies were also considered. Thomas Dewey gave several days' evidence respecting the Prudential's industrial business. Since the Prudential transacted three-quarters of all such business, his demonstration of the progress that had been made in lowering its expense ratio was of great interest. The claim that insurance money was an incitement to child murder was much in the news at this time, owing to several lurid cases in which children insured under multiple policies had died of evident neglect.

address', under 45 years of age, and 'under no circumstances to be connected with the business of a publican, or an undertaker' as agents. The superintendent was not to appoint his own relatives, or men who had been agents of other companies. By the 1880s, in contrast to earlier practice, he was told to encourage his agents to devote the whole of their time to their task (as he himself was required to do) and to prohibit them from taking on another company's fire, sickness or medical aid business.[3] The local doctors appointed as medical officers were also to be 'gentlemen of standing'; heavy drinkers, the grossly obese and the morally suspect were not to be considered. Medical officers were to attend the district offices for a number of hours each week, and to be absolutely independent of the agents, communicating the results of their medical examinations of proposals directly to the manager of the office concerned.

Responsibility for a district was no sedentary occupation. The superintendent visited each agent once every thirteen weeks, checking that the 'Agents' Instructions' were being carried out, 'both in the letter and in the spirit'. Canvassing with the agent from time to time gave opportunities to observe his dealings with policyholders (the handbook recommended 'Tactful suggestions' here!) and the ways each man had devised of finding new business. Certain Ordinary Branch and Industrial Branch proposals called for a personal visit from the superintendent. His opinion was considered necessary to protect the Company from 'over-assurance of old lives, or on the lives of persons in humble circumstances, and from any attempt on the part of persons to effect assurances of a speculative character on the lives of relatives and friends'. This last point was particularly stressed. The Prudential's instructions were clear on the subject of so-called 'life-of-another' policies: 'It is most important that the Proposal should be properly signed. In Adult cases it must be signed by the person whose life is to be assured, and in Infantile cases by one of the parents, and no other person under any consideration whatever may sign for or on his or her behalf.'[4]

Agents' accounts were to be verified weekly, when lists of the policies issued, lapses and claims were sent by Chief Office to the superintendent for checking against those furnished by the men in the field. He received a monthly report on the business secured by each of his agents. This allowed him to identify those who were introducing the most and the least business and to evaluate the general condition of each agency. Until 1886 agents transacted ordinary *or* industrial business, but not both; from that year they could transact both if they wished. This reflected the new tendency for better-off working people – those who could count on being able to put aside enough on a regular basis to pay their premiums quarterly or biannually – to prefer an ordinary policy to the penny-a-week industrial one as more socially desirable as well as more economical. (It was interesting to observe near the end of the century, however, that most of the people who took out small ordinary policies of between £50 and £100 still preferred to pay their premiums weekly.)

The superintendent was the local buffer between the Company and its clients, the Company's 'public face' at a level above the agents, and its official spokesman in his district. On coming into a district he was expected to choose a good area to live in, and to cultivate personal relationships that could assist the business. Similarly, his time and individual attention could make the difference between a confident, energetic agency force and one that was full of disaffection. Superintendents were instructed to show particular regard for those agents who had been with the Company for a long time and were identified with it in their areas. The *Instructions* suggested that if such men left, they would probably join rival companies. On occasions when an agent decamped taking his 'book' with him, the Company could resort to its 'Special Act', but in practice it only did this after the superintendent had exercised his tact to try to get it back. It was, as Dewey put it, 'manifestly unadvisable that the name of the Company should appear before the public in petty disputes with dismissed Agents if it can be avoided'.[5]

Some of the *Special Instructions* show the Company's preoccupation about apparent threats to its reputation or authority. Agents were expressly forbidden to call meetings of their fellow-agents, or attend them. Such meetings as Chief Office might authorise the superintendent to call were to be 'as much of a sociable character as possible', with the making of speeches restricted to himself or chosen nominees. 'No advantage can result from any formal debate or discussion on the rules and regulations of the Chief Office ...' and a difficulty was to be aired 'only with a view to show how it may be overcome'.[6] On the formation of the National Union of Assurance Agents at Bolton in 1884, a Prudential agent called Cooper became its first Secretary and lost his agency as a result.[7]

Discretion was considered the better part of any dealings with the local newspapers. An open letter from Thomas Dewey in August 1888 on the subject of 'pic-nics and similar entertainments to which the Assistants, Agents and their friends are invited' indicated the Company's awareness that having these well-attended, convivial occasions reported in the press, '... especially in the Insurance Press, cannot fail to attract the attention of the public and of the Company's competitors, who will not be slow to make unfavourable comments on the proceedings'.[8]

Chief Office was well aware of the ease with which rival companies could take umbrage, a fact that was expressly singled out in edition after edition of the outdoor staff's rules. Competition for new industrial proposals, especially in the big industrial cities where there were dozens of agents, was fierce. Tactics such as plastering a town with anti-Prudential handbills were sometimes resorted to by the representatives of other companies, as happened at Birmingham in 1878 when the agents of the United Kingdom Assurance Society and the Royal London Friendly Society together concocted a handbill entitled 'Astounding Revelations Respecting the Prudential Assurance Company' which claimed that the latter was insolvent. Throughout the 1870s and 1880s there were dozens of instances in which competing agents invented stories that the Prudential was unsound and circulated them in ways that ran the gamut from 'libellous postcards' to letters to the press. Others plagiarised the reports of the Prudential's Annual General Meetings and put them about under the name of their own less admired institutions. Such activities could create much extra work for the superintendents, especially when they resulted in prosecutions for libel, as a number did.[9] The Prudential's staff were themselves forbidden to publish anything, in the press or elsewhere, on the subject of assurance. If their activities became the subject of a rival's calumny, they were reminded that 'the Company owes a great deal of its success to the opposition and difficulties it has had to overcome without ever using other than the most legitimate means'.[10] The following instruction, conveyed by Dewey and Hughes in May 1892, even warned of the 'circulars addressed to their agents, with a view to affording them assistance and encouragement' produced by some superintendents. In certain cases, 'It has happened that the circulars have contained statements and expressions neither accurate nor judicious: and it has been necessary to order their immediate withdrawal, as in the hands of the agents of other companies it was quite possible they might have been used against us.'[11]

Disregard of directives emanating from the London headquarters brought swift action. In the early 1870s John Moon was Superintendent in Manchester and Preston, and had the highest weekly debit, at around £435, of any superintendent then employed by the Prudential. Moon was an exceptional man, highly regarded by management and agents alike as 'loyal to his office, without being blind to justice'. When he placed advertisements in the local newspapers and circulated an assurance pamphlet in his area, there was a swift complaint from his opposite number at the Refuge Friendly Society. Summoned to Chief Office, he declared 'that on this occasion if the Directors would look over his offences he would on all future occasions observe faithfully the conditions of his Agreement ...' and offered to accept a month's notice should he fail in any way to do so; the Board 'deliberated' and agreed to let him carry on.[12] Less fortunate was one Hillier of Wolverhampton, whom Dewey found to have 'taken part in and

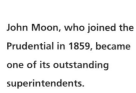

John Moon, who joined the Prudential in 1859, became one of its outstanding superintendents.

allowed his Agents to act for a certain local Sickness Society'; he was fined one month's pay, and his assistant, Gillott, who had known of the business but not reported it, was called to London to explain his conduct.[13] A less-than-truthful monthly report, made with the aim of 'screening his assistant', lost a man called Somerville his Dublin superintendency in 1878, and Rakestraw of an unknown district lost his for having been party to a testimonial – expressly forbidden – to one of his assistants, though the dismissal was later rescinded. Instances drawn from the Company minutes suggest that a man stood a reasonable chance of reinstatement if he had the courage to go up to London and face Harben and the Directors: no mean test of nerve.

The even tenor of a superintendent's working life depended much on the characters of the men he engaged, since their misdemeanours could literally cost him dear. Much depended too on his own physical stamina, as – at least during the years when the Prudential was seeking to establish its network of district offices and agencies – a man who proved himself able might be asked to take on more and more. The reminiscences of one such man survive. Benjamin Botley was a self-styled 'teacher and teetotaller' who began as a collector in 1863 and from 1867 worked as an agent in Bradford. Within a few years he caught the eye of his Superintendent, J.C. Witt, and was given the task of salvaging a 'book' that was being conveyed by a disgruntled Prudential agent to the rival Integrity Society.

Success at this brought him an appointment as Superintendent for Bradford and Keighley. Within two years Wakefield, Pontefract, Boston Spa and Wetherby had been added to his area, and in a further year, Leeds. At this point he was allowed two assistants. He spent more than half his time on trains and was away from home for extended periods, leaving his wife to manage the house and handle the local business. In the early days she had acted as his collector and he credited her with having kept him going while they built up his debit between them. Looking back on his career in the 1880s, he recalled how his exertions had increased the number of Prudential agents in Leeds from 25 to 75 and the weekly debit from £110 to £444. The total debit of his districts when he took them on he calculated at £10,348; at his retirement dinner, he reported that it was £50,752, and commented to his audience, 'Now my friends ... think of the time I must of necessity have been travelling and otherwise working when agents have been sleeping.'[14]

Despite the rigorous impression conveyed by the handbooks of the district offices, by the 1880s superintendents were getting two weeks' annual holiday and assistants one week, though the rules specified that such absences could only be taken at 'a time most suitable to the exigencies of the business'. There does not appear to have been a set scale of remuneration for superintendents. Their pay depended partly on an annual salary, partly on a commission on the ordinary business done in the district, and partly on an adjustable share in

Riley Lord was one of a number of Prudential field staff who entered local politics.

the debit of each agent. Annual salaries varied greatly. The remuneration of the superintendent who battled to maintain a district's debit (who did his best, in other words, to ensure that his agents maintained theirs) – and administered it well – would still have reflected external factors such as its size and population. On the death of a Mr Gaul, the Superintendent for Leinster and Ulster, a Mr Riley was appointed to replace him at £350 a year, but the industrious Benjamin Botley took on Leeds with no extra commission and no increase for two years, his £220 per annum to cover this and the areas he already held. A Mr Welch was appointed Superintendent for Cheshire at £180 a year in January 1876, while his colleague Mr Nixon, appointed to North Wales in the same month, received £110.[15]

Where an exceptionally talented man made the most of a populous district, the rewards were equal to the responsibilities he might be asked to assume. The case of Riley Lord was a good example. Lord, based in Newcastle, was another of the Prudential's leading superintendents, one step behind John Moon but still with an average weekly debit in 1870 well in excess of £400. In December 1876 he met with Thomas Dewey to discuss his impending appointment as Travelling Inspector of Agents for the four Northern Counties about to be separated from the 'A' Division to form a new 'B' Division. Lord was by then making something in the region of £800 a year as a superintendent. As Travelling Inspector he accepted a salary of £1,500 a year plus hotel expenses and first-class railway fares, and 'a further salary equal to the amount he now receives as commissions on renewals in the Ordinary Branch & ... commission at £5 perCent per annum on new business in the Ordinary Branch but without allowance for renewals on such new business'. Lord was a self-made man in the Harben mould: he began as a 19-year-old Lancashire agent; before he was 40, the financial recompense for his ability as a superintendent had enabled him to buy a handsome villa at Gosforth and furnish it with a library reported to be one of the best in the north of England.[16]

Riley Lord's contemporary, John Moon, was another whose singular ability was rewarded (the incident referred to above being an isolated one). Moon's debit was rising by £1,000 a year in the 1870s, due partly, no doubt, to his good judgment in the selection of agents and assistants, and partly to his personal reputation in his district; he retired on a pension in an era when very few men were granted a retiring gratuity.[17] He was able to introduce his sons to the business and they – James and another John

– became agents, superintendents and inspectors in their turn. John junior left his superintendency in 1883 to become an inspector at £2,000 a year, with an additional £500 for his father, who lived until 1888. A note in Thomas Dewey's Memorandum Book calculates the younger man's earnings as a superintendent at £15,000, though £7,500 of this was paid out to his assistants. James, who began as an agent in 1876 and became an inspector ten years later, was the first member of the outdoor staff to achieve a seat on the Prudential Board (1915), by which time he was Mayor of Birkenhead.[18]

Like the younger John Moon, superinten-dents were obliged to pay half of the commission they received from ordinary business to their assistant superintendents in the district, whose subsistence was also made up in part of a salary – anything from 35 shillings to £3 a week – and in part of commission on the business brought by the agents. The main occupation of the assistant super-intendents – of whom there were about a thousand by the mid-1880s – seems to have been to work closely with the agent on the administrative side, and to oversee the smooth running of the office. The number of assistants was dictated by density of population within a district, and thus by the number of agents whose affairs had to be supervised. It was probably the assistants who suggested, from their personal observations, the point at which agencies could be divided and new agents engaged. (The division of an agency was not often popular with the man who had built it up and now saw half of his debit – and income – hived off and given to someone else.)

James Moon was the first member of the field staff to join the Board, and remained a Director until 1930.

By 1900, there were about 1,770 assistant superintendents, 500 super-intendents and a varying number of inspectors, who together comprised the senior echelons of what had come to be known as the field staff. They even had their own educational and debating society, which met at the time of the Annual General Meeting at a hotel in London's Charterhouse Square and was thus known as 'the Charterhouse Party'. Below them were the agents, who in sheer numbers came to resemble a small army; by the turn of the century there were nearly 16,000 of them, and by 1902, 18,000. These were the men at the rock-face, as it were, who had the daily task of enlarging, and in the case of industrial policies, maintaining, the business. They could employ collectors or sub-agents if they chose, in order to spend more time on new proposals, but had to pay these employees' wages themselves, just as they had to pay for the policies and rate books issued to new policyholders. The collectors were absolutely forbidden to assess proposals. Some agents, like Botley, the veteran mentioned above, enlisted the help of their wives as collectors, or even their

FACING PAGE

The Prudential agent was
supplied with instructions,
account ledgers, forms and
leaflets, which he carried in a
leather portmanteau rather
like a doctor's. Steady
increase of his debit gained
him a Merit Award.

children: an agent against whom the Company brought the force of its 'Special Act' in 1892 was found to have been sending out his seven-year-old son! (The father admitted that this was reprehensible, less on account of the age of the child than because of the ease with which he might have been relieved of the money collected.) Most agents' rounds consisted of visits to homes situated all over a city, or scattered over a wide area of countryside. The miles covered by some men each day – on foot, by horse-drawn omnibus, pony-trap, the new 'velocipede' or penny-farthing – often worked out to double figures. By the 1890s the favourite and most affordable mode of transport was the bicycle, for which many advertisements appeared in the insurance press. The Prudential agent so mounted, with his brown despatch case in the basket, became a common sight in all weathers, even in remote areas.

From the 1870s it became less and less common for an agent to combine his work for the Prudential with another job, as earlier men combined it with a trade, or some other activity that could be carried out from home. In some populous areas, however, that were dependent on one staple industry, such as cotton manufacture or coal-mining, men were still justifiably wary of concentrating all their time and experience on agency work when a cyclic downturn could all but eradicate the weekly premium collections, but this became increasingly rarer. The Prudential emphasised to the newly engaged agent that 'the office of Agent to an Assurance Company is one of considerable responsibility, and requires the utmost care and discrimination to discharge its duties with judgment and success ...' and required him to pay a deposit of £25 into the British Mutual Banking Company as a security against any future debts to the Company.[19] He was then presented with a detailed code of rules and procedures that by the mid-1880s ran to 223 clauses relating to industrial business alone. Strict adherence to procedures itself inculcated professionalism and reduced the ratio of error, temptation and expense. The regulations make it clear how closely the agent's record-keeping dovetailed with the checks performed by the Audit Departments at Chief Office. The stationery required for industrial business by then amounted to 32 items ranging from prospectuses to coroner's death certificates.[20] The rules for transacting ordinary assurance were much simpler, given that there were no weekly door-to-door collections, sums of money to submit, and accompanying paperwork. Both sets of instructions were produced as small booklets; the differences between them – the Industrial Branch ones utterly plain, with the information numbered for easy citation, the Ordinary Branch ones printed on slightly better paper, embellished with a floral motif and with the information gathered under headings – reflect the differences between what had come to be called 'mass assurance' and 'class assurance'.

Most agents no doubt found the outdoor round, free from immediate supervision, another attraction of the job. (The emphasis on absolute conformity

with the voluminous regulations may have reduced this sense of independence.) Whether a man's debit took him into industrial slums or country lanes, he had to learn to make his circumstances work for him, sharpen his powers of observation, and take the initiative. Making the same circuit week after week, calling on the same families, he could inform himself about impending births and the state of health of the elderly. Small details could tip him off to the presence of new prospects in his area: a different mat in a tenement stairwell, or a freshly whitened cottage doorstep. To achieve more than a nodding acquaintance with the local doctor and vicar was considered judicious (the church porch was always worth a momentary detour, to read the banns). So, apparently, was visiting a bereaved family that had just received payment for a claim – not to mention the relatives of someone known to have died uninsured! The agent on his weekly round was as much a part of the local scene as the policeman on the beat. He was often the recipient of leads picked up in a moment's chat – assuming he had the true agent's predilection for following them up. Even inclement weather could be made use of, for he could do worse than to spend a quarter of an hour in the corner-house – though not the *public* house – with the day's births, marriages and deaths columns spread out before him. What he was not encouraged to do was canvass so aggressively as to bring himself into conflict with other agents, or draw undue attention to the Company. A certain sensitivity was clearly also a prerequisite of 'taking lives'.[21]

The need to reduce the high ratio of expense to premium income inherent in the collecting system was throughout this period almost the highest priority on the part of the Prudential's management. Given the periodic criticism of high expense ratios, it appeared that the Company could enhance its position as the dominant assurance institution in two ways: by keeping its expense levels well below those of rival companies, and by making its product ever more competitive. In discussing the latter of these objectives first, it is important to recall that the remarkable growth of the business during the 1870s, which made the Prudential the largest of the institutions providing industrial assurance, was itself a factor in fuelling the immense expansion that followed. The policy improvements effected in the 1870s were the first of a sequence; as the Prudential lengthened its lead over its rivals, it could afford to provide cheaper assurance with fewer restrictions. This in turn attracted more proposals.

The course of these improvements can be seen, firstly, with reference to ordinary assurance. In 1887, the year in which agents could elect to sell the assurances of both Branches, new tables were introduced, increasing the amounts assurable under the adult and infantile tables, improving endowments and introducing a system whereby a small amount was payable at death even after the maturing of an endowment and the cessation of premium payments. All policyholders under the adult tables were entitled to half benefit after three months instead of six; they had been entitled to immediate quarter benefit since 1882.

All existing policyholders (not just future ones) were covered by these alterations and, as Dewey put it in the letter sent out with the new edition of the *Agents' Instructions*, it was the agent's 'pleasing duty to point out these increased advantages to all your policyholders who may be benefited by them'. In stating that, 'no doubt you will find that the popularity of the Company will be greatly augmented, and that in consequence you will be able to obtain a very large accession of business', he touched upon a fundamental point. Since the Company completely dominated the industry, the Prudential agent had an advantage over the agents of other companies, simply by virtue – if one can put it this way – of representing the Prudential.[22]

There were other improvements: a further series of geographical and occupational restrictions for both ordinary and industrial policyholders were modified, or disappeared. They could now reside anywhere in the world except the tropics; soldiers could now go abroad at ordinary rates. In 1899, volunteers enlisting to fight in the South African War were exempted from any additional premium for war risk up to £250 in the Ordinary Branch. Reference has already been made to the steady improvement in the bonuses paid to policyholders.[23]

Making assurance ever more attractive had to be achieved while keeping the expenses of the outdoor staff as low as possible, but at the same time keeping their motivation high. On this seeming contradiction the whole success of the enterprise rested. Over the years a number of ways of motivating the agents

Prudential field staff of an unidentified division, c.1890. Note the number of women.

were devised. Early on, when obtaining new business was a matter of survival, money prizes for those whose weekly debits consistently exceeded a certain amount were given.[24] These were succeeded by other kinds of encouragement as the industrial side of the Company grew and the agency force increased to match it. Sometimes rewards were offered, not by Chief Office, but by the local superintendent. In August 1888, for example, when it would appear that the condition of the district administered by the brothers Welch was one of stasis, they sent a circular to their agents, sympathising with the difficulties that had been caused by a recent falling off of business, especially those caused by 'rival Agents, who seem to be allowed to take any class of lives ...'. Any of their own men who could produce an average net increase of 6d a week on the debit, or £50 of assurance in the Ordinary Branch, would be presented with a railway ticket to London and 10s towards hotel expenses for a visit to Holborn Bars, which would give 'an insight into the working of the business, that must prove very advantageous in conducting their agencies'. Some agents were already so highly motivated that they needed no 'push' from a superintendent. One from Orkney, John Glen, made 'A Startling Offer (to Orcadians only)' in promising 'a handsome FREE GIFT of a real SILVER WATCH' to anyone taking out a with-profits policy in 'the Largest and Best Assurance Institution in the World – a Home Office – and confirmed by millions to be the PRUDENTIAL'.[25]

The creed of quasi-paternal encouragement and personal responsibility dominated relations between superintendents and agents. It was expected that an agent would work hard, not only for his survival as an agent, but for the reputation of his district and his superintendent. His harvest, in the form of larger debits and increases, was acknowledged through a remuneration structure that rewarded those who proved most successful, in a manner reminiscent of the parable of the talents. Early on, agents were paid for new ordinary business by a commission on the money received by them on behalf of the Company, usually 20% of the first year's premium, though this varied depending on the table under which the assurance was transacted. The way of paying for new industrial business gradually altered, as the early system of commission only gave way to one that combined commission on new business and a salary linked to the amount of the collectable weekly debit.[26] From 1869, the salary formed the basic component. The scale was revised so that it began at 3d for a weekly debit of 2s 6d and climbed to £5 5s for a debit of £30. The special payments which covered quarterly increases – thereby acknowledging the effort expended to achieve new business – continued, and were known by 1875 as 'Quarterly Remuneration'. There was also 'Special Salary', calculated on every clear 2s 6d weekly increase in the debit – a most important element, since a high rate of lapse was inconsistent with 'increase'. The Company could, if it chose, wait up to eight weeks after the close of a given quarter to see whether the increase reported by an agent in that quarter were genuine or not. From 1869, postal expenses were deemed to be payable by the agent, as opposed to being paid by the Company.

While there is much information on what men could earn for specific kinds of business, there is less available, and this more difficult to interpret, on what the average agent actually received in a given period. For one thing, there probably was no 'average' agent. By the 1880s most took on the job full time, but some still worked only in the evenings, some employed collectors and others did not, some represented both the Industrial and the Ordinary Branches, others one or the other. Some picked their way through the courts and tenements of the industrial cities, where numerous families lived closely together, while other men's territory might cover a prosperous county town. Still others cycled the dusty thoroughfares from one hamlet or cluster of labourers' cottages to the next.

A *Commercial Diary*, unsigned but almost certainly the property of Thomas Dewey, notes on 2 November 1881 that 68% of Industrial Branch agents were earning less than 25 shillings a week.[27] Another set of figures covering the years 1862 to 1938 confirms this, and calculates that the average weekly debit in 1881 was £5 3s. Ten years later when there were nearly 12,000 agents, the average weekly earnings still hovered around the 25-shilling mark, the average weekly debit being £6 3s. These figures compare not unfavourably with the earnings of clerical staff, even those of several years' standing, at Holborn Bars.[28]

In the period of intense penetration of the whole country by the network of agencies that went on from the mid-1870s, emphasis came to be placed, not just on obtaining new business, but on maintaining the business gained. The way of dealing with lapses, that other most problematical aspect of industrial assurance, was by now seen to demand improvement for reasons of internal economy, quite apart from public disapproval of high lapse ratios. This was because the processing of proposals cost money, and if policies lapsed before they had acquired a value, it was money lost. Another was the desire to avoid what had evidently become a favourite bit of agents' duplicity. The lapse of a policy after only a short time allowed the agent to pocket the first four weeks' premiums, wait a few months, and reintroduce the proposal as 'new', thus rendering himself eligible to receive this payment again. To avoid these losses, the Company introduced a regulation that required the agent, if a policy lapsed within the first eight weeks, either to return the payment of the four weeks' premiums, or to find a new proposal to replace the lapsed one, forfeiting the four weeks' payment the new proposal would normally carry.[29]

These measures were fair in so far as the policy or the lapse had resulted from any collusion between agent and policyholder in the first place, but were clearly less so when misfortune lay behind a family's inability to find the weekly penny. The precarious economic state of so many of the Prudential's industrial policyholders posed the agent with an unenviable choice. Many households able to set aside premiums regularly when the breadwinner was in work, could not do so when he was struck by illness or unemployment. An agent was often moved to pay these premiums himself rather than let a family's policy lapse, as much for his own sake as out of compassion. A state of affairs in which the Company was deceived could not be right. Nor could one in which the agent, even at his own risk, ended up out of pocket if the premiums defaulted on could not be repaid. The Company, recognising that the agent was always going to be appealed to in this way (and unless a man were made of stone, he would probably respond on some occasions), set a lapse credit limit of nine weeks for a policy in force six months or more. Thereafter, the agent had to declare the policy lapsed in his weekly returns.

Concessions designed to deter lapsing, or to prompt the revival of lapsed industrial policies, began in the 1880s. It had always been possible to revive lapsed policies by paying the premiums in arrears (something for which the Prudential was commended in the Special Report included in the Reports of the Northcote Commission in 1874). Due to 'the continued depression in trade', in 1886 it was decided, when people wanted to revive their policies but could not afford to pay arrears, to issue policies for the same amount of premium in immediate full benefit where the previous policy had been one year in force and had lapsed within the previous two. Agents could only treat the policies issued as revivals and so could not claim the four weeks' fee for new business, but the 'considerable addition to their weekly debits' would supposedly make up for this.[30] Similar concessions were made to help those whose policies lapsed during coal strikes in 1894 and 1904.

Between 1875 and the end of the century, the Prudential made gradual improvements in the terms offered which were intended to encourage people to keep their assurances in force. These included reductions in the probationary period before full benefits could be claimed (for adults) and cash surrender values after the assured had reached a certain age and paid premiums for a determined period of years. From 1878 a system of free policies was initiated, to be applied to policies that had been in force ten years or more, whose holders were aged at least 21. Under this arrangement, a free policy for a reduced amount could be obtained without the need for further premiums. The term was reduced to five years in 1881. More than 256,000 of these policies had been issued by 1891.[31] In 1899 people assured for 25 years or longer could obtain a free policy for the full amount assured as they reached the age of 75.[32]

These measures had the effect of gradually reducing the temporary nature of so many industrial policies, so that their average duration began to lengthen. In 1874 it was stated to be between one and two years (but this was partly related to the high proportion of children assured, as touched upon earlier). Thereafter, the Valuation Reports record progressive increases: from 5½ years in 1886 to 6¾ years in 1891, and 8¾ years in 1899.[33]

Not surprisingly, some reductions in expenses were achieved during the same period. In his *Commercial Diary* Thomas Dewey kept a running tally of the yearly expense ratios of the Prudential and a long list of its competitors. The ratio of expense to premium income of most of them in the early 1880s was seldom less than 50% and in some more than 60%. The Prudential's ratio in 1882 was 46%. Taking three of its larger competitors at random, the Refuge's was 53%, the Liverpool Victoria's 50% and the Royal Liver's 44%. By 1885 the Prudential's rate was 39%, and those of the others 60%, 53% and 48% respectively. By 1889 Dewey was not even bothering to list most of the institutions he had included earlier; the Prudential had reduced its ratio to 37%, the above competitors' ratios were 39%, 43% and 55% respectively.

Comparative job security, the increasing probability of being awarded a retirement allowance after long service, and the power of the Prudential name were all positive features of the agent's job, which went some way to counterbalance levels of remuneration that were considered too low by agents who either had the ill-luck to live in poorer parts of the country, or who could not make the system work for them.[34] It was universally recognised that the nature of industrial assurance entailed high expenditure, and that reducing this was commendable from every point of view. By the end of the 1880s, however, feeling had arisen among Prudential outdoor staff in the London area that the reductions in the expense ratio had been gained largely at the agents' cost. This, together with the Company's requirement that its agents make good their lapses, were the main grounds for complaint in 1890, when a group of the Prudential's London and Suburban Agents sent a Memorial to the Directors. Some of their requests related to weekly salaries for collecting Ordinary Branch premiums and pay for specific procedures; the example of other companies that paid 25% for the collection of their premiums was cited, and the flat rate of 20% was asked for instead of the Prudential's current 17%. A corresponding increase in Ordinary Branch commission, from 20% to 30% of the first year's premium, was sought.

The most important point, though it appeared third in the list, was 'Responsibility for Lapsed Business', under which heading it was asserted that 'the question of agents being required to make good all policies in their agencies that become lapsed … is a vital point, which has probably caused the loss to the company of more good men than all other reasons combined'.[35]

The Reply to the Memorial, drawn up after the Directors had discussed the men's requests and signed by Edgar Horne, left the way open for future concessions in the matter of remuneration but conceded nothing immediately. It reminded the deputation that

One of the chief criticisms directed against Industrial assurance has been that it involves such a high rate of expenditure; and in settling the remuneration to be paid to agents, together with the other working expenses, the directors have to bear this objection in mind. Public opinion would not tolerate a continued heavy rate of expenditure, and it is almost certain that, had the rate of the Prudential's expenses been as high as that of some other companies, some serious interference with the system would have taken place, which, operating adversely to the company, would have greatly affected the agents' position also.

The Prudential's vast number of policyholders made 'its successful management a matter of national interest', and

Agents need hardly be reminded that, in dealing with the finances of an assurance company of such magnitude as the Prudential, an apparently small concession may really mean the expenditure of thousands of pounds, and for this reason it has always been a fundamental rule with the directors never to make alterations until some test has been applied, such as is afforded by the periodical valuation. It is by a firm adoption of this policy that a feeling of security has been engendered, and so large a measure of popularity obtained.

On the vexed subject of lapses, reference was made to the Prudential's success in reducing their numbers, but it was still widely believed that 'agents sometimes neglect old policyholders in order that they may re-introduce them as new entrants, the fees on new business making this course profitable to them'.

The Directors were 'extremely anxious to prevent lapses taking place which can be attributed to any cause other than the deliberate act of the policyholder', and since their regulations had been adopted with the aim 'not only of protecting the assured, but also of preventing this accusation being brought against their agents', they were unwilling to alter the existing instructions.[36]

This was not to be the end of the matter, however. The rules regarding lapses, especially those taken over when a 'book' was transferred from one agent to another, aroused particular resentment among outdoor staff affected by the collapse or shut-down of a particular trade. The formation of the National Association of Prudential Assurance Agents took place in 1893, following a prolonged period of labour unrest in the spinning and coal industries. This had resulted in a very high rate of lapsing in the area around Blackburn and Accrington, Lancashire. Temporary extra lapse credit was the main request in a list put forward by a deputation which journeyed to London in November 1893 to seek redress for 'the abnormal experience of the past twelve months, and ... a permanent removal of the irksome conditions under which Prudential Agents labour', but it also requested concessions such as free premium books, a uniform rate for collecting industrial debit, the increase of commission on ordinary business, and an allowable interest in an agency's 'book'. The union's First Annual Report also suggests that there had been problems with overbearing superintendents in Lancashire, and that part of the deputation's mission was to achieve 'direct contact with Chief Office without the intervention of local officials'.

The deputation was taken seriously: it obtained a three-hour interview with Thomas Dewey, who granted the request for full lapse credit for all lapsing due to the recent coal lockout. The other requests were not granted. Dewey gave the men £1 each towards their hotel expenses in London and made a personal contribution of £3 to the funds of the fledgling union (which stood, at the end of 1893, at £86 1s).[37] The union, which adopted a militant stance early on, had the outspoken David Jones, who advocated nationalisation of industrial assurance, as its Secretary. Its membership, ten years after its formation, was about 3,000 or one-sixth of the field force, mainly from the industrial north-west.[38]

A good deal of the explanation for the union's apparent weakness probably derived from the Company's antipathy to militant combination. But part may lie in the very nature and character of the kind of men who became agents. If a generalisation may be ventured, it is that agents on the whole were individualists, and the abilities they needed to do well militated against combination. In the words of an earlier writer, an agent's 'productive capacity ... making two

'My Old Section': Prudential agents in 1902. It may be that the man wearing the donkey jacket, centre, having retired, is visiting his former colleagues.

blades of grass grow where only one had existed, is the primary standard upon which the worth of his services is based'. If a man excelled at this, and possessed the necessary persuasive ability and staying power, 'his advancement is certain – more so, perhaps, than in any other kind of business'.[39]

There were also the periodic concessions to the outdoor staff, made in much the same way as those to policyholders, that may have eroded any generalised discontent. Such grants were made following the quinquennial valuations of 1886 and 1891 to all agents who had been in their posts longer than a year, 'as a mark of appreciation of their services, and in recognition of the share they had taken in bringing about such satisfactory results'. The funds were apportioned by a system that took into account an agent's years of service, collectable salary and quarterly and special salary, and, for superintendents and assistants, increases in the debits of the agencies in their districts. As usual, the higher achievers received the greater rewards. Remuneration for the collection of premiums was improved in January 1891, probably as a result of the London agents' request two months earlier, though no mention of this appears in the relevant notice. Ostensibly it resulted from a 'great and general revival of trade', but applied only to debits of £10 a week or more – again benefiting those agents who were already the most successful. In 1894 a grant towards postage was made, thus partially reviving the situation that had existed up to 1869, when these costs had been paid by the Company.

These concessions were promoted as an attempt to reward the most capable members of the outdoor staff, while holding out a carrot to the less successful. A more far-reaching measure was provision for old age in a form that embraced the whole outdoor staff. Retirement grants, awarded at the Directors' discretion from 1879 onwards for long service (though just how long we do not know), had come to be the practice rather than the exception by the 1890s. Such grants seem to have been half the amount of final monthly debit, payable monthly.[40] Gratuities were paid to men who left the Company's service early through illness; it is not known whether leaving for other reasons was acknowledged in this way or not. The widows of agents who died also received a gratuity or an allowance. If the widow's age permitted it, she might be invited to take over the agency, as might a son who was of age.

The novel departure came in 1898 when, in the year of the Company's fiftieth anniversary, the Directors established the Staff Provident Fund. This was a voluntary contributory retirement scheme to which the Company would pay 6d for every shilling paid by the member of staff. This was soon altered so that the company matched the staff contributions shilling for shilling. All outdoor staff in post for more than a year and earning less than £400 a year were eligible. A Jubilee Cash Bonus was also awarded, of varying amounts depending on length of service.[41] In 1906, agents were granted extra weeks' salary – four, three, two or one – depending on their length of service. Finally, from 1907 onwards the surplus on the industrial business, after payment of a fixed dividend to share-holders and transfers to various reserve funds, was apportioned between policy-holders, shareholders and the outdoor staff, the staff receiving one-sixth.

Measures such as these cemented agent loyalty, as they were meant to do, and encouraged long service. In the era before any kind of national provision for old age, they represented an enviable security. Unless a man were idle (in which case his district officials would find him out) or dishonest (in which case the Audit Department at Chief Office would) there were few threats to his position while there was so much business to be done.

Of course there were agents who *were* idle, dishonest or both. Thomas Dewey kept a tally of agent dismissals, which in 1895 listed 55 for 'misappropriation of cash', 17 for 'absconding', 12 for 'intemperance', 10 for 'proposal irregularities', and 6 for other causes: 100 in all. Among superintendents, 4 men lost their jobs through intemperance, 7 for proposal irregularities, 8 for cash offences and 7 for other causes, although many more in each case were cautioned.[42] On being found out or dismissed, some of them were sufficiently disaffected that they acted against the Company, either by publicising their discontent, or by mounting some fraud against it. The Prudential's system of fines and suspensions (not to mention outright dismissal) sometimes engendered explosive resentment. Though not an unduly litigious company, the Prudential usually threatened legal action when its good name was at risk. The most common trigger for a prosecution was failure on the part of an agent leaving the Company to hand over the documents belonging to his debit. Some offices did in fact allow the agent to treat his 'book' as property, with a market value, but the Prudential had never done so. Against a man who viewed the

The collapse of the Tay Bridge in 1879 resulted in many claims for the Prudential.

Thomas Dewey's notes on
deaths and claims in specific
years, and claims resulting
from colonial wars.

book as his own – and there were many who considered that the Company
should reimburse them for the increase they had effected in the value of their
'books' – the Prudential therefore brought the strength of its 'Special Act' of
1875.[43] There were also agents who chose to pay premiums themselves rather
than to declare policies lapsed, and ended up out of pocket when it became clear
that the policies really had been abandoned. Such men often saw the retention
of the 'book' as a means of forcing the Company to reimburse them. The best-
documented case of this kind was brought against an agent called Benjamin
Walmsley, who claimed to have paid in to cover lapses over a long period, knowing this to be contrary to regulations; he falsified his returns to cover what he
had done and at first refused to hand over the book belonging to his debit until
the Company repaid him the money he claimed to have advanced. After a magistrates' hearing the books were handed over. The amount of arrears was not
grave – some £65 – but the degree of deception exposed, together with the
unfortunate involvement of the NAPAA, were factors in the case brought by
the Company before the Queen's Bench of the High Court in January 1898;
the Prudential obtained the verdict on all counts.

Apart from cases such as these, and actions brought against former agents
who sent blackmail letters and murder threats to the Directors, most criminal
proceedings centred on theft by one means or another. Court cases involving
the Prudential frequently received press coverage, often in the national papers
as well as those of the relevant locality. Such publicity, considering that more
often than not the Company won its cases, only served to bring it to the

attention of the reading public rather as the furore over Post Office assurance had done in 1864.[44]

The degree to which, by the end of the century, the Company came to be recognised as financially unshakeable put the Prudential agent – to reiterate the point – several steps ahead of his rivals. But so did the impressive statistics he could recite regarding the number of claims – calculated at 600 a day in 1894 – paid by the Prudential, especially when these related to some recent local disaster. In the eight years between 1878 and 1886 the Company paid claims on 18,494 deaths from accidents of various kinds. From the Tay Bridge disaster of 1879 onwards, there was hardly a major accident in the United Kingdom which did not involve persons assured with the Prudential. In the large loss of life in such events as colliery explosions and lifeboat disasters, inevitably it emerged that a high proportion of the dead who had carried life assurance were Prudential policyholders. Out of 87 deaths arising from the Pen-y-Graig colliery explosion in 1880, 20 claims were paid. When a factory chimney collapsed at Bradford in 1882, 22 of the 50 dead were assured with the Company. Sunderland's Victoria Hall catastrophe of 1883 in which 191 children lost their lives by suffocation resulted in 35 claims, and the horrendous fire at Exeter's Royal Theatre in 1887, in which 160 died, in no less than 53. A Prudential advertising handbill of 10 November 1890 on the loss of HMS *Serpent* off La Coruña with 176 aboard proclaimed that the Company paid claims worth £1,441 19s on 58 lives.

The *Sun* newspaper's profile of the Prudential in 1894 devoted a section to statistics of this sort:

> *... no serious accident occurs among the masses of people without including in its death-roll persons who are assured with the company. When a South-Eastern railway train ran into a wagon filled with hop-pickers the other day and killed seven of them six were assured in the Prudential. During the summer 26 lives were lost by the capsising [sic] of a pleasure boat at Morecambe; 14 of them were assured in this office. The great gale of November 18 and 19, 1893, caused the death of 111 policyholders. By the terrible colliery explosion near Dewsbury last year 72 persons who were assured in the Prudential lost their lives. When the* Victoria *went down on June 22, 1893, she had on board 102 members of the Prudential. What anything approaching an epidemic means to the company may be gathered from the fact that during the last four years 20,528 claims have been paid on deaths certified to have been caused by influenza.*[45]

The Company paid out nearly 1,000 claims on street and railway accidents in 1899, and in this, the year that war began in South Africa, some 540 claims on British soldiers there. Figures like these point up the extent to which the Prudential's agency force enlisted the nation's working population during the last quarter of the century. The total amount paid out in claims by 1900 amounted to more than £38,000,000. The number of industrial policies in force stood at nearly 14,000,000 by then, and continued to increase by an average of around half a million a year for the next decade.

But while there were many innovations and improvements in the assurances offered over this lengthy period during which the Prudential was acquiring the status of a 'national institution', there were no significant changes in the method by which the outdoor staff carried out their tasks. There was merely the fine-tuning of the procedures established in the mid-1870s, which had been shown to work. The system of divisions, districts and agencies formed a simple structure that could be divided and sub-divided as the increase of the business dictated. Not until 1911 would a rethinking of this system be undertaken, and even then only under the pressure of new, if not entirely unforeseen, demands on the assurance industry.

Chief Office:
More Than Just a Building

The continued progress of the Prudential Assurance Company is simply marvellous. For more than fifty years we have read its annual reports, and whoever, in another fifty, has to comment on them for this journal, will almost certainly have to deal with totals in billions of pounds sterling. The company's total assets today are close on forty millions sterling! Its premium income last year was more than eight and three quarter millions, and the total number of policies in force was 13,891,667. Its Staff Provident Fund alone reaches £86,742. Many a company would be glad to boast such a total income. It is our firm conviction that the Prudential Company will, one of these days, pay off the National Debt, as a free gift to the nation.

The Building News, *15 March 1901*

THIS somewhat fulsome account of the condition of the Prudential in the year 1900 set the scene for a review of the monumental extension to the 1879 building that was then in its final stages of completion at Holborn Bars. That the new headquarters, known as 'Chief Office', should be as imposing as its financial profile was entirely in keeping with the status of a 'national institution' which the Prudential had by this time achieved. The building was also a victory for the confident working relationship between the parties: for the Prudential Board's single-mindedness, and for the architect's vision of what was possible at every stage of the piecemeal acquisition of the site.

It had taken 20 years, the original commission having scarcely been completed in 1879 than plans had been made to extend it. During that time the penetration of even remote parts of the British Isles by Prudential agents was being steadily matched by a corresponding increase in the facilities needed to service the business. By 1901, 21 district and divisional offices built in Alfred Waterhouse's distinctive 'Prudential style' had established the Company's presence in major centres all over the country. Both practicality and precedence demanded that the headquarters at Holborn Bars be bigger and grander than

Behind the monumental Holborn facade, and reached by a central, vaulted archway opening onto a small antecourt, lay the large interior courtyard – today known as Waterhouse Square – around which rose the main office blocks: four storeys high, also in glazed red brick ornamented with terracotta. Visually, the most important of these blocks lay on the north side of the courtyard. It followed the building line of the former facade of Wood's Hotel, and was the natural focus of attention when passing from the antecourt under the span of a bridge-corridor heavily decorated with Gothic tracery. The north block had a projecting, dormered entrance and rows of round-headed windows that owed more to Romanesque than Gothic. Patterned brickwork and banded friezes in terracotta provided visual interest on a potentially daunting expanse of wall. The rest of the complex was less rich in decoration, except for the small East Court that formed the centre of the block built on the late-acquired Ridler's site.[5]

The Prudential Chief Office was completed in 1906. It has dominated the Holborn streetscape ever since.

Decorative features drawn from a variety of architectural styles appear in the Holborn Bars facade; *clockwise from top left*: Prudence; *putti* and crests of towns where Prudential offices were located; Romanesque and Gothic adapted for terracotta.

If the building was imposing from the outside, certain of its interiors were even more so. As in the 1879 building, the most important rooms, such as the public office, Shareholders' Hall, board room and Directors' rooms, were located in the block facing Holborn. The storeys in the Holborn block were higher than those of the blocks behind: ever after there was a change of level on entering or leaving it, the first floor at the front of the building being equivalent to the second farther back. The public areas, together with the Directors' staircase linking the public office on the ground floor with the managers' offices on the mezzanine and the other important rooms on the first and second floors, were predictably the most highly decorated. The old board room became a clerks' reading room with the inauguration of the new one, which had lancet windows, two magnificent alabaster and tile fireplaces, one with a carved statue of Prudence by Paul Waterhouse above the mantelpiece, and an ornate clock.

The archway from Holborn, its terracotta vault evoking some medieval cloister, made a fitting entrance to the public hall. Divided into eight bays by columns faced with glittering green and gold faience ('ochre' and 'mustard' do not do it justice), this generously proportioned salon had a fine moulded plaster ceiling, glazed cream brick walls, Spanish mahogany counters and a marble fireplace, and small glazed windows with touches of coloured glass. The handsome light and door fittings in this area, as throughout the building, were designed by Waterhouse or by his son Paul. Like the cavernous Shareholders' Hall, its oak hammerbeamed roof a full two storeys high, and the main staircase (ablaze with faience floral motifs, vaulted with richly decorated tracery and floored in marble mosaic), this was space designed to overawe, to cause voices to drop to reverential whispers. A visitor to Eaton Hall, the country seat rebuilt by Waterhouse for the Duke of Westminster, is said to have exclaimed on entering the vaulted breakfast room, 'Good God! I never expected to eat bacon and eggs in a cathedral!' The Prudential policyholder, visiting Chief Office, might well have uttered something similar about paying his premium in such a setting.

The rest of the interiors of the Holborn block were also decorated and furnished to the highest standard. Windows and doors bore Gothic leaded tracery, and oak or marble parquet gleamed underfoot. Particularly notable was the panelling – English oak for the corridors, board room and the Directors' rooms; Spanish or Cuban mahogany, Korean teak and other quality hardwoods, some rare, for the private rooms. Each room had a fireplace; the board room's oak and alabaster creation had more modest equivalents in those of the Directors and managers, decorated with marble or with Waterhouse's favourite Burmantoft faience tiles.

In basic furnishings such as panelling and fireplaces there was, even at management level, an established hierarchy of decoration and materials, best documented today in the architect's surviving drawings. Some examples of the furniture Waterhouse designed for the new Chief Office survive, as do numerous drawings. An ornamental flower within a circle was a motif that identified the furniture of the elder Waterhouse. In addition to certain features such as the south-east staircase, simpler in decoration than the main one, Paul Waterhouse was responsible for much of the building's furniture. Items such as desks, chairs, cabinets, coatstands and light fittings differed in the material used or in degree of elaboration, according to the status of the user. Drawings of chairs for a Director's room, a waiting room and an office area, for example, show the same basic design with turned legs and straight, with a leather-covered seat and the same seat in wood, and with a simple back next to one that has a 'Gothic' motif of pointed arches.[6]

Behind the Holborn block, in the long blocks running back towards Greville Street, large areas were given over to the clerical departments and to fireproof storage areas for records. The women's clerical departments retained

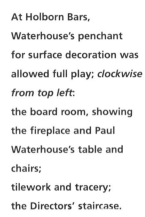

At Holborn Bars,
Waterhouse's penchant
for surface decoration was
allowed full play; *clockwise
from top left*:
the board room, showing
the fireplace and Paul
Waterhouse's table and
chairs;
tilework and tracery;
the Directors' staircase.

by Henry Harben. The symbolism that put work on a physically higher plane than prayer was not lost on the men who took part in either: prayer was the prologue to work, and work was prayer in action.

The mention of such areas leads naturally to a discussion of the tenor of working life in the Prudential in the years before the First World War. Adjectives like 'patriarchal', 'hierarchical' and 'deferential' were probably as applicable to persons or attitudes in the Prudential as to any other institution of the age, but where the Ibis Society was concerned, they are somehow misplaced. The 'Ibis' was the colloquial name adopted by the Prudential Clerks' Society from the mid-1870s. There are various theories about the derivation of the name, the best drawing on the cry of 'Come on, the IBs' that, due to the superior number of Industrial Branch supporters, habitually drowned out the supporters of the 'OBs' at team events.[13] Officially, 'the Ibis' was an association of employees under the aegis of the Directors: all Chief Office employees were eligible to join. (Henry Harben was its President from the beginning, and, together with Thomas Dewey, its greatest promoter. Dewey, Hughes and Lancaster were Vice-Presidents, and there was an elected Committee of 15 and two Secretaries.) In reality, it was far more. It was a sporting, literary and cultural fraternity that removed – at least for limited lengths of time – the distinctions of rank, status, age and department, in pursuit of excellence and good fellowship. As a unifying force in the rapidly expanding Prudential, it provided the recreational facilities that allowed the third-class clerk and the principal, the actuarial trainee and the sub-manager, to meet on common ground. The result was a network of acquaintance that counteracted the depersonalising tendency inherent in so immense an organisation.

The Society was, above all, organic. Given the strong tradition of long service that was typical of the age, it is perhaps not surprising that the names of men who joined the Clerks' Society as juniors in the 1870s appear on lists of Committee members in the 1890s. What is interesting is that, as principal clerks, sub-managers or even higher ranks at the later date, they saw no contradiction between the professional status they had achieved and continuing to play an active role in the Ibis. The annual lists of the prizewinners in the various clubs frequently contain the names of managers and office-holders.

William Lancaster had a knack for turning out the skits and good-humoured doggerel that reveal much about the Ibis spirit.[14] The range of interests represented by the end of the century would have done credit to a fair-sized town. The earliest – the Ibis Cricket and Rowing Clubs, and the Literary and Musical Societies – were joined by clubs devoted to other sports, such as swimming, tennis, cycling, running (the 'Harriers'), and gymnastics, and by associations devoted to chess, debating, choral singing and horticulture. The Ibis Dramatic and Operatic Society (IDOS) grew out of a production of *The Blind Beggars* organised in 1875 by two employees, Hallet Goodman and Harry Follitt, and went on to mount at least one major production a year, and several minor ones, for more than a century. The IDOS started small, but grew progressively more ambitious in the works it offered. By the century's end, professional standards applied in the sets and costumes, as contemporary photographs show. The Directors and their families regularly attended these occasions.

The performances took place, as did the lectures, debates, exhibitions of painting and photography, shows of handiwork, *tableaux vivants* and concerts by which Ibis members enlivened their winter evenings, in the Hall (described as being 'rather like a section of the Tube') of the original Chief Office.[15] Later on the Shareholders' Hall or the library were the preferred venues, if only because the events were so well attended. Displays of gymnastics, lantern slides, and performances of Gilbert and Sullivan took place in Waterhousian splendour; there was a shooting range on the roof and a photographic workshop (with equipment donated by Henry Harben) in the basement. The Musical Society's band and the male and female choral societies rehearsed in the Hall.

A high moral tone pervaded much of this activity. The Prudential Prayer Union, established in 1886, was soon inviting missionaries and evangelists to speak, and for a time even sponsored a missionary in China and another in Peru.[16] There was a Ladies' Prayer Union separate from the men's. Harben, as President of both, often addressed them; he claimed to be voicing his deepest convictions. On one occasion he spoke on the text of Romans 1, 16: 'I am not ashamed of the Gospel of Christ', declaring that 'our duty is not to be Sunday Christians ... but to be willing to stand up daily for the faith, and make all of our work of the best, because it is to be done to the Lord.'[17] He went on to recall that 'young men are especially liable to great temptations', and that the only way to prosper was by 'taking everything to God in Prayer'. On another evening, he expressed his personal views on prayer, which 'should and does strengthen and fit us for the due discharge of our daily duties and is as necessary to the life of the soul as daily food is to the life of the body'.[18]

The Prayer Union was one of the most active groups in the Ibis before the First World War. Usually some 30 meetings a year were held (though in 1906 there were 44). Its 'Special Meetings', with an invited speaker and tea provided courtesy of the Directors, were attended by between 350 and 450 employees; over 800 came to hear the Bishop of London speak on 'Personal Religion' in 1905. Thomas Dewey was a staunch supporter of the Prayer Union; one of his daughters went to India as a missionary and came to speak to the group before leaving.[19] An offshoot of the fairly ecumenically minded Prayer Union, which focused on an area of particular concern, was the Prudential Total Abstainers' Union. This invited doctors and other speakers to pronounce on the problems caused by drink. It continued to meet until the outbreak of war in 1914 and membership was restricted to male employees.

One club that became a central part of the Prudential's corporate life was the Literary Society, which administered the library and produced the monthly

Ibis Literary Magazine. The library by any standards was an exceptional facility. A grant from the Ibis allowed the purchase of about 130 books each year, so that between the Prudential's arrival at Holborn Bars in 1879 (already with over 1,000 books) and the end of the century, a circulating library of over 4,000 volumes was built up. Even in 1886, when it had about half that number, it was thought to be the largest of its kind in the City, with some 400 volumes in circulation at any one time.[20] The works were chosen by a committee with the aim of providing not only the best of current reading material, but also the most representative. There was inevitably some disagreement about priorities, some on the committee favouring the purchase of popular novels, others preferring non-fiction. (The subscription to Mudie's Circulating Library usefully provided more of the latter.[21]) The Ibis Library's accession list, which survived until 1989, mirrored the literary taste of the age, charting the careers of some 'name' authors, whose works were acquired as they were published, and of numerous individuals, now forgotten, whose novels evidently enjoyed a brief vogue. Subscriptions to reviews such as the *Cornhill, Edinburgh, Quarterly* and *Blackwoods* suggest that at least some of the staff read edifying material in their spare time.

Henry Andrade Harben in particular fostered the intellectual life of the Company through donations of funds to the library. In 1908 one of his gifts enabled it to buy 'a set of the Cambridge Modern History, the Eversley edition of Shakespeare, a Shakespeare Concordance, John Morley's Complete Works, Ruskin's Modern Painters, and the late Professor Jowett's Translation of Plato'.[22] Any Ibis member could borrow two books, or one book and one review, to take home. As usual in the Prudential until after the First World War, the hours when the women clerks could browse and borrow were staggered so that they did not come face to face with their male counterparts.

The *Ibis Magazine*, which cost 2d in 1902, was justifiably popular. The content before the turn of the century was more consciously 'literary' than at later dates; there were some short stories and serial novels of enduring quality, although much of the poetry was of the 'fairies and flowers' school, and so highly sentimental as to grate on the modern ear. Later on, as the bicycle and motor-car afforded greater mobility and staff became more accustomed to holidays away from London, accounts of travel, or illustrated articles on historical or architectural subjects, took space away from purely imaginative writing. There were always sections devoted to staff news, acrostics, snippets of humour sent in by the field staff, and observations related to assurance business – which likewise could provide amusement. There was no lack of ready wit among the contributors, as even the most casual browse through the volumes reveals.[23] The magazine was wholly written and produced by the Chief Office staff, with William Hughes as editor for the whole 30 years until his retirement in 1903. Hughes was a gifted satirist and often wrote for the magazine; its quality noticeably declined with his departure.

Apart from the Dramatic and Operatic Society, which invited outsiders to its performances, and the Musical Society, which occasionally gave concerts outside the Company under the direction of its conductor, Godfrey Young, the cultural societies were only active within the confines of 142 Holborn Bars. The sports clubs, however, had the added dimension of competition with the sides and teams of other institutions. In this way they helped to foster a strong Prudential identity. Ibis sporting activities were also considered by the management as a healthy complement to the sedentary, highly supervised working environment. The link between athletics and morality seemed self-evident to contemporaries, and thus working hard and playing hard were part of the Prudential ethos.[24] Clerks paid an annual subscription to the Ibis, which gave access to sporting facilities. Foremost among these were the grounds rented for cricket, tennis, rowing and athletic sports. The Boating Club, which began by using rented boats for its recreation on the Thames, bought its own sailing boat in 1878. Its rowing section, which kept boats at Richmond, Hammersmith and Kingston, held eights race meetings throughout the season, which ran from mid-March to the end of October. The rowers seem to have taken over from the pleasure-boaters, though the reports of their events sometimes reminded members that Rowing Club boats were on no account to be used for fishing. In the 1890s Alfred Corderoy Thompson, soon to be Joint General Manager of the Company, was the mainstay of the rowing fraternity.[25]

The Cricket Club, once installed at Dulwich, remained there for 20 years, moving to a ground at Penge in 1903. Among its leading players was Frederick Schooling, who captained the side nine times between 1876 and 1891 and who continued to play when he could after succeeding Dewey and Hughes as sole Actuary in 1892. The Prudential team had risen in the esteem of competitors in the wake of the Company's own rise and after the first few years did not lack for engagements. Names such as John Lidbury, Ernest and Stewart Dewey (Thomas Dewey's nephews), Septimus Daws, Tim White ('undoubtedly the best cricketer the club has ever possessed' according to its chronicler of 1905), H.G. Cath, George Clinton, and the 'slow left-hander' F.L. Parker were prominent in the batting and bowling averages in the years before the First World War. At the opening of the Ibis's new ground at Penge in 1903, W.G. Grace and his London County Club were the star attraction. In his professional capacity, Grace was a Prudential medical referee; the Ibis cricketers were elated that this somewhat temperamental celebrity considered them fair opponents.[26]

The Cricket Club always claimed to be the seed from which the Ibis had grown. Certainly it received more support, both moral and financial, than any other club, since the management were themselves passionately devoted to the game. Collectively the Directors voted successive grants: for improvements to the grounds, for the purchase of equipment, and for what came to be an annual tour. Individually, they turned out faithfully to matches. Dewey, Lancaster and

Fisher were by the 1890s too old to take an active part, but by now each man, possessed of a large suburban villa, had his own ground on which he entertained the Ibis team. These invitation matches became high points of the sporting year. Frederick Fisher's house at Farningham boasted magnificent gardens. The genial William Lancaster's liberality as host made excursions to his ground at Putney justifiably memorable.[27] Thomas Dewey, Charter Mayor of Bromley in 1903, in that year arranged for an annual match between the Ibis team and the town eleven. He was the oldest active supporter of the game in the Prudential, one of the group of young clerks who had come together to play in Battersea Park back in 1860 and formed the nucleus of the original Cricket Club.[28] Looking back on the matches played on summer evenings at Dewey's Bromley home, South Hill Wood, someone recalled that 'a pleasant after-dinner diversion had been hunting glow-worms in the shady walks in the grounds', and that the team-members were as adept at handling a billiard cue as a cricket bat.

W.G. Grace brought his London County XI to play the Ibis side at the opening of the new ground at Penge on 3 June 1903.

The most eagerly awaited events of the season, however, were the matches played at Henry Harben's private ground at Warnham Lodge. Harben bought the estate, set in the Sussex country-side near Horsham, when it comprised only 93 acres and proceded to add to it by the purchase of neighbouring farms until it took in nearly 400. Part of this he gave over to the creation of 'one of the finest and most picturesque grounds in England' which he inaugurated in 1891. Though it seems he was never himself a player, Harben's keen interest in the game meant that he was always a supporter of local cricket. He arranged an annual match between West Sussex and the City of London Police, and gave the county team and that of Horsham generous financial aid. Harben involved himself as deeply in local affairs when he was in the country as in those of Hampstead when he was in town, building the Warnham village hall and club and taking a particular interest in the village eleven.[29] The Prudential team played Warnham every year, Harben himself delighting to act as scorer. Any man who scored his century on the Warnham ground had his name inscribed on a roll of honour and received five gold sovereigns from its owner.

Harben's hospitality on these occasions was 'always ample, even exceptional'. The players were conveyed from the railway station to the estate in a chaise, and once there, 'were permitted to help themselves as they wished' to the superb peaches and apricots in the greenhouses and stroll in the grounds. Both teams dined – magnificently – as Harben's guests on the evening before a match and were shown any recent improvements to the estate resulting from the exercise of their host's technical ingenuity. In 1893, 'the peach houses were appreciated, but the novelty of the trip was the new clock. This curiosity strains credulity. It is alleged to have been electric with motive power supplied by a ton of coke sunk in the garden and destined to drive it for a hundred years'.[30] Another account mentions this clock and its ton of coke, 'buried with an ingot of copper ten feet deep in various gradations of substance', which at Harben's death in 1911 had been keeping perfect time for 18 years.

Harben's passion for applied science meant that Warnham Lodge was equipped with the latest apparatus for safety and convenience. It is hard to believe, from accounts of the cricketers' matches there, that Harben would not have shown off the house's electrical generating system – one of the earliest large ones in the country – or 'a novel arrangement, worked by electricity, for telling the direction of the wind'. Perhaps he treated the players to one of his practice firefighting displays. Soon after buying the house he had built a tower, visible for miles around, and disguising within it a water-tank for use in case of fire. The house was equipped with pumps and hoses and the staff well drilled; to keep them on their mettle he made 'occasional surprise calls, and he always timed the operations from the moment the alarm was given until the hose was ready to throw water upon the imaginary outbreak'.[31]

Cricket was played seriously but graciously by the Prudential side, with some fine players being invited by Harben to play for Warnham Lodge, among them 'Plum' Warner, 'Shrimp' Leveson Gower, Brodie Chinnery, Noel Curtis Bennett and Percy Fender.[32] Teams that visited included the Free Foresters, Eton Ramblers and Old Malvernians. Photographs show a proud Harben flanked by various guest elevens.

From 1890, Harben resided at Warnham for fairly long stretches, especially in the cricket season. He lived a well-regulated life, rising early and retiring on the stroke of ten; he neither smoked nor drank, though he permitted himself a glass of champagne on Christmas Day. Order and punctuality reigned in the house; daily, Harben and whoever of his family might be there assembled with the servants for morning and evening prayers. Sundays were strictly observed and amusements forbidden. When the cricket teams were staying in the Lodge on a Saturday night and a game of billiards was in progress, 'precisely at one minute past midnight, the old gentleman would come down in dressing gown and tasselled nightcap ... to inform us that it was Sunday morning and Billiards must cease.'[33] Comments such as this reinforce the picture of Harben as a benign autocrat, a stickler for the proprieties at home as at 142 Holborn Bars.

He was looked after at Warnham by his daughter Mary, and, after 1899, by her husband Thomas Wharrie, a nephew of Dr Patrick Fraser and a shareholder and Director of the Prudential from 1893. Mary Woodgate Wharrie had kept house for her father since her mother's death in 1883, and her marriage, when she was 52 and her husband 20 years older, apparently took place on the condition that she continue to carry out this role even though Harben himself had remarried in 1890. (The second Mrs Harben was Mary Bulman Cole, daughter of Thomas Bulman Cole, another Prudential Director.) Thomas Wharrie apparently did not object to this arrangement; according to Harben's grandson Guy Philip, Wharrie was 'a kindly genial old sportsman ... and took upon himself the running of the excellent Pheasant and Partridge shooting on the Estate'. It suited Harben to have 'the whole family under his eye and under his autocratic thumb'.[34] Henry Andrade Harben, his wife Mary and his five children were frequent visitors to Warnham, though they had a London house in Westbourne Grove and a country estate, Newland Park, at Chalfont St Giles in Buckinghamshire.[35] How the family resolved the confusion that must have resulted from all of its adult female members having the same Christian name is not recorded.

Neither his age nor his other commitments wrung from the elder Harben much reduction of his role as Deputy Chairman of the Prudential. This position, too, suited him well; in the hands of a less energetic man, who might have contented himself with the laurels of success and wealth, it no doubt could have involved less attendance at Holborn Bars than in practice Harben gave it. His physical presence there for part of every week reinforced the sense of continuity which he had always fostered in the Company. He himself had become a venerable figure – still straight-backed and straight-sighted, with a full head of white hair and heavy mutton-chop whiskers – regarded with respect by all and love by many. The fact that by the 1890s he had become a personage of some importance outside the Company served to enhance even further his prestige within it. By the century's end he was regarded as a kind of Grand Old Man, still enjoying robust good health at 77, having outlived all his colleagues of 40 years earlier except Edgar Horne and Dr Robert Barnes.[36]

Harben's activities outside the Prudential during the last 20 years of his life were largely philanthropic (as opposed to political or recreational). They were concentrated in the fields of health and education, the areas which he saw as the basic means, together with the promotion of a vigorous evangelical Christianity, of effecting a real improvement in the condition of working people. Of lasting benefit was his gift of 88 Prudential shares of £5 to the British Institute of Public Health, reflecting his lifelong interest in that subject. The donation paid for an annual series of lectures on a subject connected with public health, and the gold Harben Medal, still presented by the Institute.[37]

The best appreciated of Harben's personal initiatives was the convalescent home he established for working men on the Sussex coast between Rustington and Littlehampton. In this project many of his personal commitments – to the improvement of public health, to working people, to the county of Sussex and to his livery company – came together. His grandson later claimed that he originally wanted to build it in Hampstead, and offered an initial contribution of £4,000. The original plan was apparently one of raising further money by subscription. Harben came upon William Hughes and some Prudential employees discussing this one day at Holborn Bars and learned that hospital crowding led to many cases of people being sent home while still unwell to recuperate in equally crowded quarters. He decided to assume sole responsibility for the project, and to situate the home where it would serve a wider need than merely that of his own North London borough.[38]

'The Rustington Convalescent Home for Working Men', as the home was initially called, was to be established and maintained through a trust, the Carpenters' Company being responsible for its management. Its principal indenture states that 'the Institution shall be a Home wherein persons of the working classes and others may be received during convalescence or sickness either gratuitously or upon payment as may be from time to time prescribed ...'.[39]

Harben bought the 17-acre site, built the home and endowed it with a gift of £50,000, leaving the income of 300 Prudential shares to maintain it. Members of his family gave a further endowment of £20,000. The spacious Georgian-style house could take 50 convalescents in private rooms, most of which had sea views; there were medical staff and a chaplain in attendance and all the facilities to assist the patients in returning to active life. The Prudential staff had preferential access to the home, in keeping with the Company's well-documented practice of sending sick indoor staff away to rest homes.[40]

Rustington opened its doors in March 1897, the year of the Diamond Jubilee. On 22 June Harben was awarded a knighthood in the Queen's Jubilee honours list. He was already Deputy Lieutenant of Sussex; in 1898 he became High Sheriff, and set up a further benevolent association. This was the 'High Sheriff of Sussex Compassionate Society', formed to assist people awaiting trial by providing legal aid and support to their families, either during trial, or after acquittal in cases of need.

Harben patronised a whole host of local endeavours in the county of his

Sir Henry Harben built the Rustington Convalescent Home to provide healthful surroundings where working men could recover from accident or illness.

ancestors, from cattle and flower shows to hospitals, but at the same time he took a leading part in the civic life of Hampstead, the part of London in which he had lived since purchasing Seaford Lodge in the 1860s. In 1898, nine years after the first campaign to extend Hampstead Heath (and by which time Harben had received his knighthood), a similar situation arose when Golders Hill, a mansion set in 36 acres of parkland adjoining the West Heath, was put up for auction on the death of its owner. A committee of guarantors was formed to try to purchase the property for a top price of £35,000.[41] As Chairman of the Hampstead Vestry Harben at once launched a campaign to raise the funds and headed the Acquisitions Committee. As 'Nemo' he donated the first £1,000 – then, when someone queried why his name did not appear on the subscription list, gave another cheque for the same amount to satisfy his questioner. On this occasion the money was raised quickly.[42] Golders Hill was added to the Heath and opened in December 1898.

Only once in all his many public roles is Harben recorded as having alluded to his formative years. This was in May 1905, at the opening by the Prince of Wales of a purpose-built hall donated by Harben and his daughter in Pond Street, Hampstead, as the headquarters of the 1st Cadet Battalion of the Royal Fusiliers (City of London Regiment), of which Harben was Honorary

The Rustington Convalescent Home on the Sussex coast celebrated its centenary in June 1997.

Colonel. In his speech of thanks, Harben, then 82 years of age, recalled his youth, when athletics were little known and schoolboys learned only a few simple games. He recounted 'the happiness of being at a school where a Drill Sergeant came once a week ...' and credited the training he had received with having given him his present good health. He then went on with total unselfconsciousness to recall: 'Seventy years ago I was drilled by that man. I remember well how, week by week, I looked forward to his coming, and ... he helped me to expand my chest, and to give me a demeanour which now, at the glorious age at which I have arrived, stands me in good stead ...'. The lessons he had learned, he said, had lasted him all his life: to 'think not so much of myself as of my next door neighbour, ... keep in line with those around me ... sink my own individuality, and, for the common good, work shoulder to shoulder with my neighbours'.[43]

A photograph of Sir Henry on this occasion, dressed in his Honorary Colonel's uniform, gives a remarkable impression of vigour for a man of his age.

The arms of the Prudential Assurance Company, granted in 1904. Prudence presides over crenellations representing Holborn Bars and martlets (birds) taken from the arms of the Furnival family.

He had recovered well from the minor stroke he suffered in 1903, which forced him to step down as Mayor of Hampstead part-way through his second term of office. Even at 82, there were clearly things he wanted to achieve, which as yet had not fallen to him to enjoy. One of these was to hold the paramount position, in name as well as fact, in the Company he had spent his life in building and which had given him so much in return. When Edgar Horne died at the age of 85 on 18 December 1905 after 28 years as Chairman, Harben could no doubt have stepped aside to allow Thomas Dewey or his own son to take over. The fact that he did not suggests that he positively desired to occupy the position, thus at last reaching the office that he was rumoured to have refused in favour of Horne in 1877.[44] But though his election must have been seen as a short-term expedient, deference to his feelings and to his power as a shareholder made it a foregone conclusion. That the younger Harben would succeed his father was also predictable. Sir Henry Harben presided over his last board meeting in June 1906.[45] For the next year meetings were chaired by Henry Andrade Harben, or by Dr Robert Barnes, the last of the Company's original Directors, still mentally and physically active at nearly 90.

Sir Henry finally and formally relinquished his post on 12 July 1907. At an Extraordinary General Meeting chaired by his son, a Resolution was passed

A Prudential calendar shows the provincial offices built in Waterhouse's style between 1885 and 1901.

which simultaneously made him a Director and granted him the title of President 'as a recognition of the conspicuous services' he had given the Company and 'with a view to creating for him an exceptional position' which was not intended to exist after his death. A draft of this bears a note in his handwriting and confirms that, whatever the reality of his situation, his intention was to remain active: '... none of the Regulations of the Company providing for retirement from the office of a Director or the vacation thereof by non-attendance at Board Meetings shall apply to him, and he shall take the Chair at every General

Meeting of the Company and at every Meeting of the Directors at which he shall be present ...'.[46]

Henry Andrade Harben, having acted as Chairman for months, was now elected *de facto*, and other changes provoked by Sir Henry's departure announced. Thomas Dewey, in his fiftieth year with the Company, resigned as Manager, to be replaced by Frederick Schooling and Alfred Corderoy Thompson as Joint Managers. At the same time Dewey was made a Director and Deputy Chairman.

Henry Andrade Harben commented on this occasion that it was 'greatly, if not mainly' to Dewey that the Prudential's great progress in recent years was due.[47] This was surely true: he had borne the weight of administering the Industrial Branch through the three decades of its immense expansion. To his day-to-day supervision the Company owed the successful application of the mode of operation devised by Harben (that 'most strict attention to the internal economy and to the method and regularity observed at the Chief Office') to the relentless multiplication of all the factors involved: policyholders, agents, staff and paperwork.

With the deaths of Edgar Horne in 1905, and Dr Robert Barnes in 1907, the last direct links with the Company's earliest years were broken, apart from Harben himself. Glimpses of him in the last years of his life are confined to a few accounts of cricket matches at Warnham, and a few photographs. He could apparently walk only with difficulty, but his mind remained unaffected to the last. Guy Philip Harben recounted how in his last years, 'no longer "Master" but under his Nurse's control' the old man seemed to mellow, enjoying his role as *paterfamilias*, not only to his own family, but to the whole of Warnham. In particular, his rigid sabbatarianism waned, and he is said to have delighted in spending his Sunday afternoons watching his great-grandchildren playing cricket from his Bath chair on the lawn. Thomas Dewey and Sir William Lancaster (who received a knighthood in 1906 for establishing the King Edward VII Grammar School in his native King's Lynn) were frequent visitors to Warnham, bringing news of Chief Office, the Ibis and the wider stage of Prudential affairs.[48]

Henry Andrade Harben's term as Chairman caused no perceptible changes at 142 Holborn Bars, which was no doubt his intention. '... Under the new conditions the machinery of administration runs as smoothly and, I believe, as efficiently as before' was the way he put it, in delivering his first Report at the

Four generations of the Harben family: Sir Henry holds his great-grandson, Henry Eric. Henry Andrade stands (*right*) with his son Henry Devenish, the baby's father (*left*).

Company's Annual General Meeting in March 1908. He was an unassuming man, despite his accomplishments. Though his aim would seem to have been the preservation in letter and spirit of the traditions established over the previous 60 years, he was far from a cipher. The impression of him that emerges from surviving records is of a cultivated man with private interests, who, had he been born in another place and time, would probably not have chosen a commercial career, and certainly not the role to which, as Harben's only son, he was virtually predestined. Temperamentally he differed from his father in that he was not at all autocratic. One of the few first-hand reports of him as a colleague (though not in a Prudential capacity) relates that '... his modest and conciliatory bearing ... made for peace and endeared him to his fellow-workers', though the writer speculated that these qualities may have led those who knew the father to underrate the son.[49]

Like the elder Harben, the younger had a life of public service and philanthropy outside the Prudential, but there is evidence to show that within it he sometimes took – and was asked to take – the part of spokesman in situations when legal knowledge and the tact of the born negotiator were needed.[50] On the assumption that he wrote his own Chairman's Reports, delivered in 1908, 1909 and 1910, he had a sensitive appreciation of the social trends underlying the course of the Prudential's business. With his linguistic gifts and his knowledge of London's topography and history, he had the widest intellectual horizons in the Company's upper ranks.

The pity of it was that Henry Andrade's health was never what his father's was. He had needed periodic leaves of absence on account of unspecified illnesses all his working life. During his time as Chairman there were a few periods of several weeks each when he was unable to attend the weekly meeting, but in 1909 he made an extensive and reputedly exhausting tour of the Company's district offices, meeting with groups of agents all over the country in the aftermath of the passing of the Assurance Act of that year. In August 1910 he is reported to have been ordered to undergo a small and fairly routine operation for what was described as 'an internal complaint'. This took place uneventfully on 16 August at a London nursing home, but two days later sudden heart failure cut short the younger Harben's life at the early age of 61. His funeral took place at St Saviour's Church, Eton Road, Hampstead, a few days later. The church was filled with mourners from all his professional and social circles, but Harben senior was too devastated by his son's death to attend.

Sir Henry Harben's own death came 15 months later. It would not have been surprising if, in addition to the recent tragedy, he was depressed by the knowledge that neither of his grandsons aspired to joining the Prudential (though in time one of them would come round).[51] The protracted and undignified assault on the Company begun by the disreputable tabloid *John Bull* in March 1911, a discussion of which forms part of the next chapter, could hardly have left him unmoved. He died suddenly at Warnham Lodge on the morning of 2 December 1911, having been well enough to go out in his carriage on the previous afternoon.

Harben's body was brought from Warnham to London by train so that he could be buried from Hampstead. The service held on Wednesday, 7 December at St Saviour's was attended by more than a hundred Harben relatives (though not, apparently, any of the Chamberlain cousins) and conducted by Sir Henry's cousin the Archdeacon of London, Dr Sinclair. The church was completely filled, hundreds of people waited outside, and the procession that made its way to Kensal Green Cemetery was more than 60 vehicles long, many helping to carry the mountains of floral wreaths. A service was held at the same hour at St Margaret's, Warnham, which was filled to overflowing with local people and those from the Warnham estate. The extensive appreciations of Harben's life that appeared in the press, from *The Times* to the *Insurance Record*, the *Hampstead and Highgate Express* to the *Sussex Daily News*, gave evidence of the span of his interests and his patronage. His part in the creation of the Prudential and the

Sir Henry Harben played an important role in the development of Hampstead. Here, wearing a Masonic cap, he lays the foundation stone of the library he donated to the borough.

industrial assurance industry took its place among his other accomplishments, *The Times* succinctly summarising this most far-reaching of them as having 'reduced to system what had previously been chaotic ... he proved that liberal benefits were not inconsistent with sound finance'.[52]

Though in one sense Harben's passing marked the end of an age for the Prudential, the conduct of business and the tenor of life at Holborn Bars for a time remained much as before. The 'system' Harben had created had been the key to prosperity for more than half a century. Continuity and tradition had been the watchwords while he lived, and, for some time after his death, management's emphasis was naturally on trying to ensure that the method that had served the Company well did not alter. This was not an approach that could prevail indefinitely, however; the pace of change – social, political and economic – outside the Company was quickening, and some adaptation would soon be necessary.

SECTION FOUR

The Dimensions *of* Strength

A Turbulent Few Years

THE brief period from 1909 to 1914 proved particularly challenging for the Prudential. Two of the many pieces of legislation passed by the Liberal Government which had come to power in 1906 were of major importance for the industrial assurance industry. These were the Assurance Companies Act 1909 and the National Health Insurance Act 1911. For the Prudential, the repercussions of the first coincided with a period of intense lobbying related to the second, but for the sake of simplicity they will be dealt with separately here.

****

The Assurance Companies Act 1909 was prepared and guided through its parliamentary stages by Winston Churchill, at that time President of the Board of Trade in Asquith's Liberal Government, in which David Lloyd George was Chancellor. Churchill and Lloyd George worked closely together on the Assurance Companies Bill. Its main provisions were aimed at accident, fire and investment insurance rather than life, and sought to give insurers in these areas the same security as those purchasing life assurance under the Life Assurance Act 1870. The stipulation that the sum of £20,000 had to be deposited with the Board of Trade before a company could begin selling life assurance was extended to companies carrying on these other types of business, so that those engaged in more than one had to deposit £20,000 for each. Other regulations required annual valuations, and laid down the form in which these were to be submitted to the Board of Trade.

Section 36 of the Act was of central importance for life assurance companies and, in particular, for the industrial assurers and the large collecting friendly societies, whose way of transacting business was so similar. The root of this importance lay in the principle of 'insurable interest', which had been enshrined in law since the reign of George III. In that era, when gambling was a popular diversion, it became as acceptable to bet on the lives of others as on

FACING PAGE

A 'life-of-another' policy.

horse-races or any other event whose outcome was uncertain. The form frequently taken by these wagers was a kind of life assurance policy. More often than not the assurer had no genuine interest in the life he insured, while the latter remained totally unaware that his life had become the subject of a financial speculation.

To put a stop to assurances '... wherein the person or persons for whose use, benefit, or on whose account such policy or policies shall be made, shall have no interest ...', the Gambling Act (14 Geo.3, c.48) was passed in 1774. Assurances in which the proposer had no genuine interest were thus declared null and void. In addition, in cases where the proposer had a valid interest, it was laid down that the assurance policy must show his name as well as that of the assured. No greater sum was to be recoverable under the policy than the amount at which the assurer's interest was calculated.

While the 1774 Act had remained on the statute book and was often referred to as one of the principles of life assurance, it had long been ignored in practice. The growth of movements promoting working-class thrift – the friendly societies, burial clubs and industrial assurance offices – often involved multiple assurances. It was common for members of families to insure each other: there might be several policies on the life of a child, or an elderly parent, to spread the cost of burial and the show of mourning that was regarded as essential to any decent funeral. While the 1774 Act recognised that husbands and wives had a legitimate interest in each other's lives, this did not formally apply to children or to other blood relatives. But in practice, members of what today would be called the 'nuclear family' – a parent, child, grandparent, grandchild, brother and sister – were accepted as having a natural and legitimate insurable interest in each others' lives.[1]

The 1909 Act legally extended the principle of insurable interest to these family relationships, recognising that in practice they had frequently served as the basis for assurance and that this had been socially beneficial even if not strictly legal. It also provided that no such assurance made before the passing of the Act, even on the basis of more distant relationships, was invalid for lack of insurable interest, as long as the person doing the assuring had *believed* that in due course he or she would be responsible for the funeral expenses of the assured. The number of policies formally legalised by the measure was estimated at somewhere around 10,000,000.[2]

Section 36 of the Act, however, was far from clear, and the degree to which it was open to potential abuse alarmed the industrial assurers. The Prudential took legal advice before introducing its 'life-of-another' policies in 1910. One of its questions concerned exactly what 'funeral expenses' should amount to, given that no guidelines appeared in the Act. If several relatives took out policies for, say, £50, on the life of the same family member, the total 'funeral expenses' claimed on a single life might run into hundreds of pounds.[3] 'Such expenses as may reasonably be incurred for the interment of the deceased' was

PRUDENTIAL
ASSURANCE COMPANY, LIMITED.

— CHIEF OFFICE - HOLBORN BARS, LONDON.

Industrial Branch.

Free Policy.
Whole Life.

Life of Another
(On surrender by specially authorised assignee).

Whereas the PRUDENTIAL ASSURANCE COMPANY LIMITED (hereinafter called "the Company") heretofore issued a policy of assurance (hereinafter called "the original policy") upon the life of the person named in the first column of the schedule hereto (hereinafter called "the person whose life is assured"). **And whereas** the person named in the third column of the said schedule (hereinafter called "the assignee") claiming to be entitled to the original policy has surrendered the original policy to the Company and upon such surrender it was agreed that this policy should be issued in substitution for the policy so surrendered. **Now these presents witness** that in consideration of such surrender as aforesaid the Company hereby agree that upon proof being given to the reasonable satisfaction of the Directors of the Company of the death of the person whose life is assured the Company shall pay the sum assured mentioned in the fourth column of the said schedule to the assignee or to the executors administrators or assigns of the assignee.

Provided always that this policy is subject to the conditions endorsed hereon and to the Regulations of the Company as the same were established by a special resolution of the Company passed on the 28th February and confirmed on the 21st March 1878 and as the same have been thenceforth modified up to the date hereof.

Provided also that this policy is issued out of the Industrial Branch of the Company and the Industrial Fund together with the Capital Stock of the Company shall alone be answerable for any claims under this policy in accordance with the 99th clause of the said Regulations of the Company.

Provided further that this policy is granted upon the express condition that the same shall become absolutely void if any of the conditions endorsed hereon have not been or shall not be in all respects performed and observed.

No.

WORLD WIDE.

SCHEDULE.			Ex⁴
I. Name address and description of the person whose life is assured.	II. Age next birthday.	III. Name address and description of the assignee.	IV. The sum assured
	years.		

As witness the common seal of the Company this   day of
one thousand nine hundred and

H. A. Harben

W. Pugh
⎫
⎬ Directors.
⎭

Thos. E. Dewey
General Manager.

the reply given to the Company, and so the limits were set by the Board at between £5 and £15, the latter being considered the maximum for a working-class funeral.[4] Policies on the same life whose total value exceeded the amount specified on the policy scale were not to be permitted. As Henry Andrade Harben explained at the Annual General Meeting in March 1910, this was in keeping with both the letter and the spirit of the Act. Although he did not specifically refer to what was by then a hoary issue, it must also have been intended to deter crime by preventing multiple policies on frail or aged lives.

From the Prudential's standpoint, these were protective measures, but neither they nor the Act were viewed very positively by the field staff. To the agents, both were potential restrictions on the kind of business that was for some men a mainstay of the weekly debit. An increase in salary depended on increase in the debit, and this, in turn, depended largely on new business. In dealing with families, agents had always sought as many assurances as they could get, regardless of blood relationship. Under Penalty Clause 3 of the Act's Section 36, they could now be fined £100 for exceeding the specified relationships. The way in which proposal forms were to be signed was also a point of contention. The Prudential Agents' Instructions had always been adamant about this, and it is worth repeating the rule that had been in force since at least the 1880s: 'It is most important that the Proposal should be properly signed. In Adult cases it must be signed by the person whose life is to be assured, and in Infantile cases by one of the parents, and no other person under any consideration whatever may sign for or on his or her behalf'.[5]

But in dealing with people who were illiterate, it was often common practice for the agent to fill in the proposal and ask only for the proposer's signature or mark. Where the proposer was taking out a policy on his own life, the regulations were not violated. But in many cases, when one member of a family was assuring another, only the signature of the proposer, who would be paying the premiums, was taken, though technically this violated the rules. Frequently such assurances were taken out on an aged parent by an adult son or daughter, without the parent's knowledge. Another instance was the so-called 'quiet' or 'private' policy taken out by a wife on the life of her husband, when he had made no provision for his family.[6] While agents might well recall the regulations when writing such proposals, humanly speaking they were more likely to encourage than deter the proposer, especially if new business that week had been slow. But now, the signatures of both proposer and proposed were required by law. Agents objected that with the lower social classes, establishing the relationship between the two often ran the risk of indelicacy. Except in re-lation to children, there had been no limit on the number of assurances an agent could sell to one proposer, nor on their total value.

By redefining these requirements, the Assurance Companies Act seemed likely to impede the agent's prospects for new business, and this produced resentment among some Prudential field staff. The year 1910 initiated a phase of tense relations between the Prudential and the National Association of Prudential Assurance Agents (NAPAA), which in recent years had come under the influence of a group of aggressively socialist trade unionists. The NAPAA's demands for a Charter of Rights, which included the right to an interest in the debit, meant that the Company's dealings with the NAPAA were already guarded.[7]

Opposing the NAPAA was the Prudential Staff Federation (PSF), formed in October 1909 as a counterweight to its rival's militancy. The PSF claimed that the NAPAA was unrepresentative, and that its own position, as an association embracing the interests of the field staff as a whole – agents, assistants and superintendents – was one which pragmatically identified these with the prosperity of the Company. Not surprisingly, it enjoyed the confidence of the management, though in years to come it would itself adopt a less accommodating stance. By the middle of 1910 it had a membership of over 4,000, and its monthly paper, the *Prudential Staff Gazette*, devoted much space to practical advice to agents as well as to interpreting the law and the Company's regulations.[8]

The NAPAA sent two deputations to Chief Office to argue the points arising out of the Assurance Companies Act. The first took place on 28 April 1910, when George Kelly, Walter Wyatt and William Francis, the President, Vice-President and Treasurer of the NAPAA, faced Henry Andrade Harben, Sir William Lancaster and Alfred Corderoy Thompson across the board room table. The agenda included the Prudential's limited interpretation of the term 'funeral expenses', the curb upon business within families, and the added time and work caused by the demand for two signatures. The fact that rival companies and societies were adopting a less rigorous position than the Prudential on all these issues was strongly put. The ensuing discussion was transcribed, and survives as a union leaflet.[9] The men resented the way that the new law tightened up practices that, they claimed, had been enacted from time immemorial, at what was proving to be (as Henry Andrade Harben was 'good enough and frank enough to acknowledge') the expense of the field staff. They requested a relaxation of the new strictures: a higher limit on the sum allowed for funerals, and a simpler proposal form that required only one signature. They wished also to eliminate the need for the questioning about family relationships that agents found time-consuming and often embarrassing.

The Company, however, was not prepared to relax its position. Harben judged it imprudent to put aside the legal advice on which the estimate of funeral costs was based. Nor could he concur on the proposed form of 'life-of-another' policies. Lancaster pointed out that 'the reputation of the Company would not be enhanced with the general public if it departed from the sound principle and practice of always having the consent of the person assured'.[10] The principle of having two signatures on 'life-of-another' policies was now enshrined in law, whatever agents had been accustomed to do earlier. Putting aside the Act's requirement on signatures would have rendered many new policies illegal, a fact which up to now seemed to have escaped the deputation.

During the rest of the meeting, Henry Andrade Harben in particular impressed the men by being prepared to listen, by even being open to persuasion. With regard to the chicanery of which the men accused various 'special canvassers', he promised to investigate, and with barely concealed anger demanded names and took them down. But on the changes arising out of the Assurance Companies Act, the deputation was left in no doubt about the Company's firmness.

Its appeal to management having failed, the NAPAA grew bolder.[11] During the autumn of 1910 it began a campaign for the allegiance of the field staff, circulating handbills and holding meetings. One such handbill, circulated throughout the Midlands, was addressed to 'Fellow Trade Unionists of Birmingham' and called upon them to 'See to it that the Industrial Life Assurance Agent that collects your Industrial Premiums is a bona-fide member of a bona-fide trade union, affiliated with the Trade Council. ... Confine all new assurance to Trade Union Agents, who are able to satisfy you that they are members of a bona-fide trade union organisation'. It also claimed that 'the Prudential system is anti-trade union in its policy, and is therefore a menace to all Trade Union Workers'.[12]

The Company rejected this as unfounded, inflammatory and unfair to the majority of Prudential agents who were not members of the NAPAA. The president of the Birmingham branch of the union, A. Johnson, was suspended, and T. Do Vey, the member of its Executive Council who had signed the handbill and chaired a meeting in support of Johnson, was subsequently dismissed. Do Vey chaired a further meeting in Birmingham on 3 January 1911, intended to air the union's grievances to Prudential policyholders and put public pressure on the Company. On this occasion he asserted that agents were now 'unable to procure sufficient new assurance business without adopting irregular and unlawful methods', and again accused the Prudential of discriminating against trade-union members. A further meeting on 3 March was advertised by another handbill, this time promising that 'startling revelations of the irregular and unlawful methods adopted to secure increase of new business will be made'.

This brought swift reprisal. In writing to the union, Alfred Corderoy Thompson conveyed management's refusal to receive any further deputation while the offending statements remained unretracted. The Prudential, he repeated, did not oppose unions *per se*, but viewed as hostile those which irresponsibly sought to damage its reputation and business prospects. At this point the Company was fighting hard for a place for the industrial assurance companies in the Government's proposed National Insurance scheme (which will be discussed below), and was particularly sensitive to the damage that could be done by dissident agents.

This was the end of the uneasy dialogue between the NAPAA and Chief Office, and the beginning, in March 1911, of the extraordinary episode that became known in the Prudential as 'the *John Bull* affair'. The weekly paper *John Bull* was the creation of the financial impresario Horatio Bottomley, whose erratic and unprincipled career had taken a new twist with his election to Parliament in 1906, when he became the Liberal member for South Hackney as 'the people's tribune'.[13] A year later he had founded *John Bull*. As Managing Editor, he often proclaimed that his editorial policy was to act as a gadfly, criticising institutions and affairs from 'an independent point of view'. This was a commendable enough objective as long as there were no monetary interests involved, but this was never the case with Bottomley, whose precarious finances were ill-served by his extravagance. A tactic for which *John Bull* soon became notorious was to vilify in print those companies that refused (having been invited) to take advertising space in its pages.[14] Sensationalism assured it a weekly circulation of 50,000, mainly among the lower classes. Its brand of innuendo and salacious allegation frequently involved it in legal actions, and by 1911 Bottomley was a veteran of the libel courts.

The chance to make capital of the NAPAA's charges against the Prudential was irresistible, given that Bottomley promoted *John Bull* as the exposer of institutional hypocrisy. His avowed purpose in attacking the Prudential was to provoke the Government into appointing a Royal Commission to investigate industrial assurance, but he cannot have overlooked the existence of the Prudential's 19,000,000 industrial policyholders: a potential readership for *John Bull* that comprised a third of the nation. Since the Prudential dominated the field of industrial assurance, it had an automatic claim on the attention of the working classes. With the National Insurance Bill in preparation, and the Assurance Companies Act still recent history, public interest in industrial assurance was high.

The link with the NAPAA came about through a dishonest solicitor, one Walter Wenham.[15] Wenham had many contacts among disaffected agents. When in 1910 the NAPAA engaged him as its legal counsel, it gained in addition the ear of his friend George Wedlake, the deputy editor of *John Bull*. Early in 1911 it seems that Do Vey and other union officials had a meeting with Wenham and Wedlake.[16] The assault on the Prudential in *John Bull* began on 25 March with the first of a spate of articles penned by Wedlake, and containing a set of charges against the Company that bore a suspicious resemblance to complaints voiced at the NAPAA's meetings: firstly, that it 'victimised' its agents by insisting that they pay the full amount of the debit each week; then, that the system in turn induced agents to victimise the policyholders by forcing them to employ dishonest means to obtain new business; and thirdly, that both Company and field staff – one for motives of greed, the other for survival – connived at procuring lapses on a large scale. In this and in successive articles until 19 August, the headlines ranged from the self-justificatory ('Our Charges of Fraud and Forgery Fully Established by Legal Decisions') to the histrionic ('The Toll of Agents' Suicides', complete with a list of individuals purported to have taken their own lives as the shortest way out of the Prudential). The articles relied heavily on fabricated personal accounts. The insults were vulgar, in vintage *John Bull* style: the Prudential was described – and drawn – as an octopus and a juggernaut; the Directors were labelled 'bloodsuckers of the poor', and Thomas Dewey depicted as a kind of rotund Dracula figure, complete with fangs. Chief Office was renamed 'Terra Cotta Palace, Holborn Bars'.

A less than flattering depiction of Thomas Dewey as Manager of the Prudential's Industrial Branch at the height of *John Bull*'s attack on the Company.

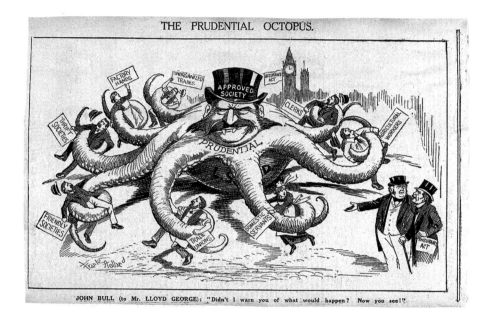

THE PRUDENTIAL OCTOPUS.

JOHN BULL (to Mr. LLOYD GEORGE): "Didn't I warn you of what would happen? Now you see!"

While the Prudential initially did not retaliate, the insurance community rose to its defence, rightly perceiving that the attack was really an assault on industrial assurance. Rejoinders appeared in the *Insurance Mail*, the *Insurance Record*, *Commercial World*, the *Agents' Journal* and the *Post Magazine*, as well as the national papers. Most of these pointed out the abruptness of *John Bull*'s change of tune: until 1911 it had often praised and even recommended the Prudential to its readers. Most also mentioned that the Prudential's lapse rate was the *lowest* of any of the large assurers, and the average duration for its industrial policies the *longest* at 12 years. It was praised for its concessions to those who kept their policies in force: its system of free policies, and the annual share of profits allocated to policyholders and agents, that were unmatched by any other company. The point mentioned by all was that it had never refused an honest claim on a paid-up policy where there was a genuine insurable interest. 'Once a Prudential policy was issued it was always deemed as safe as a Bank of England note … .'[17]

At the end of April 1911, Thompson and Schooling, as Joint Managers, issued a circular to the field staff, thanking them for their loyalty under such undignified fire. The Prudential's agents indeed had a good deal to contend with. *John Bull*'s signboards and posters were prominent on every street corner, every kiosk, where the paper was sold, and kept the mud-slinging in full view. Each week through the spring and summer of 1911 there were new accusations. *John Bull* laid claim to hundreds of cases of fraudulent or illegal Prudential policies. Bottomley even turned himself into a kind of agony uncle, inviting people who feared they might be holding 'worthless bits of paper' to send them in (enclosing a shilling), for him to pronounce upon. 'Ex-agents' were produced who described how they had forged policies, made fraudulent claims and pocketed the proceeds, 'fiddled' their weekly accounts and issued false contribution books to unsuspecting policyholders. Others admitted the old trick of deliberately lapsing policies so as to reintroduce them as 'new business'. Some of these individuals had indeed been Prudential agents at one time, and had been dismissed for these or similar offences. (One such man was William Edward Mashford (later to become a figure of dubious note in the insurance world) against whom the Prudential had obtained an interim injunction in 1907 for the return of his book and £96 outstanding.)

The tarnishing effect of all this publicity was keenly resented by the majority of the field staff. Most belonged neither to the NAPAA nor to the PSF, but by June 1911 all were finding new business thin on the ground. On 30 June the PSF held a meeting of some 1,000 London agents at the Tolmers Square Institute to protest the effect the campaign was having on their business and to urge the Company to take action against *John Bull*:

> *... the staff is now face to face with a crisis such as was never contemplated ... the constant posters exhibited by this journal on the walls are having an ever deepening and widely extending effect upon the policy-holders, with the result that the agents are finding it increasingly difficult to answer the very pertinent questions put to them by the assured and others. ... The most frequently occurring and the most natural question is – If the allegations made are not true, why do not the Company prosecute? and while at first we were able to assure the public, at the present juncture we are unable to make any satisfactory reply.*
>
> *The gravest danger arises from the rapidly diminishing confidence of our best and most respected policy-holders ... the prospect of doing further business with them is becoming more and more remote. This affair has been discussed in all its bearings, and we cannot forebear saying that the Company, on the publication of the first article, should have issued a writ and have "damned the consequences".*

The statement went on to make a plea to management on behalf of the much-maligned special canvasser, whose employment was the agents' responsibility:

'You must be aware that for many years past a very large percentage of increase has resulted from special canvassing. ... Under existing circumstances this door is now closed to us ... ' and for a circular letter ('couched in such terms as would nonplus even our mutual enemy') that agents could distribute to policyholders, with the view to recovering assurances that had been allowed to lapse under the influence of the damaging rumours.[18]

Neither the Staff Federation's petition nor Bottomley's latest discomforting tactic – open-air meetings around the country organised by the 'John Bull League' – were successful in persuading the Directors to issue a circular letter, as another course of action had already been decided upon. Intent on heightening his image as David challenging the Prudential's Goliath, Bottomley had brought an action for libel against the Company with reference to a statement in its earlier letter to field staff, the one thanking them for their loyalty. The letter contained words which, according to Bottomley's Statement of Claim, '... meant and were intended and were understood to mean that the Plaintiff was and is a corrupt, incompetent and reckless journalist, and had unfairly and untruthfully attacked the Defendant Company in the said paper *John Bull*, from corrupt and dishonest motives, and was notorious for improper attacks upon respectable institutions and persons'.

At a hearing on 3 June, the Prudential pleaded Privilege, claiming that the words were true in substance and in fact. It took a breathtaking sleight of hand for the editor of *John Bull* then to assume for the paper the role of the offended party:

> *Did the Company adopt our interpretation of their circular? Did they venture to say that our criticisms were corrupt? Did they dare to say that since the establishment of this journal, down to the present day, it had ever been party to a dishonest transaction? No. They specifically traversed our allegation. But that is not all. They set up the plea of "Privilege" ...* [19]

It became obvious that Bottomley did not in fact wish to press ahead with his action. The Prudential's Legal Department spent the summer collecting a voluminous body of evidence on his financial dealings. Having got word of the detail being assembled against him, Bottomley withdrew his action on 4 October, on the grounds that he was now at a disadvantage, since pleas of Privilege were 'certain death' to libel actions. This was announced in a flurry of scandalised prose that launched a second series of anti-Prudential articles. Quite coincidentally, extravagance and financial speculation now caused Bottomley's affairs to take a disastrous turn, and on 7 December 1911 he filed for bankruptcy. The Prudential found itself one of his many creditors – for the insignificant sum of £1,559 in costs, expended in preparing for the abandoned action.

The whole affair now trembled on the edge of farce. The Prudential made known its intention to examine Bottomley on the evidence it had collected, having opposed his scheme for an agreement with his creditors. As the date set for his public examination drew nearer, Bottomley's emissary Wenham sought to reach some accord with the Company behind the scenes. The second series of articles (similar to the first, but this time urging people not to join the Prudential Approved Societies, about which more will be said) was still in full flow. Wenham made the fatal mistake of threatening a third series, in an attempt to dissuade the Company from participating in the bankruptcy hearing. The Prudential's rejoinder was to bring an action against Bottomley and Wenham for contempt of court. It was tried in the King's Bench Division of the High Court before Justices Darling, Bucknill and Hamilton (with Bottomley – as usual – defending himself), and J. Astbury and H.A. McCardie acting for the Prudential. Judgment was given on 26 February for the Prudential, the convicted pair being liable for costs and a trifling fine of £100 each. With Bottomley's other creditors in mind, the judges considered it counterproductive to impose a higher one.[20]

The Prudential had the satisfaction of seeing Bottomley brought to book, but there was no doubt that the '*John Bull* affair' had a detrimental, if short-lived, effect on its industrial business. The Staff Federation complained that nervous and ignorant policyholders were abandoning their assurances because of what they read in *John Bull*. There were people who did so, though some apparently revived their insurances later on. Industrial Branch policies in force in the two years preceding the attack, 1909 and 1910, had totalled 18,375,229 and 18,820,427 respectively, with premium income of £7,171,770 and £7,426,317 and increases in premium income over the preceding year of £246,015 and £254,547. In 1911, 1912 and 1913, the figures showed the effects of the adverse publicity: new premium income began to suffer in 1911 at £205,091, dropped fairly dramatically in 1912 to £161,154, and showed the worst falling off of all in 1913 at only £81,894.[21]

In the absence of the volumes of the *Registers of Law Proceedings* and *Instructions to Solicitors* for the years 1911 and 1912, there survives only a casual passing reference to an increased number of summonses against the Company as a result of the affair. For the size of its field staff and the number of its policy-holders, there were usually remarkably few: 64 in 1909 and 46 in 1910. They rose to 104 and 180 in 1911 and 1912, falling to previous levels again in 1913 and 1914 with 52 and 36 respectively.[22] Ironically, in the light of the *John Bull* campaign, the problem of 'uneconomic' policies – the cause of many legal actions against industrial assurers – had in fact been addressed earlier in the Prudential than in any other company. It is doubtful whether the affair influenced the extension of the system of bonus additions to the sum assured, begun in 1908 for policies of five years' duration, for this seems to have been the direction in which the Company was already heading. In 1910, policies on which premiums had been paid for 10, 15 and 20 years and which became claims were brought into the scheme. By 1912, those that had been held for 30, 40 and 50 years received additions to the sum assured equivalent to the number of years in force. Bonus additions were the best answer to any criticism of industrial assurance, and for Prudential industrial policyholders, a form of profit-sharing no other institution could match.

****

The Prudential's reaction to the NAPAA and *John Bull* took place in the context of a far wider issue concerning the whole industrial assurance industry: the Government's plan to introduce national insurance. The background to the creation of the national insurance scheme is extremely complex. The measure encountered strong opposition from several quarters in the planning stages and during its passage through Parliament. The prospect of such wide-reaching state interference offended the traditional supporters of *laissez-faire*, but the most intransigent opposition came, at different stages, from the medical profession, the friendly societies and the industrial assurance companies, each of which opposed aspects of it to protect their interests. The lobbying behind the scenes has been much written about and speculated upon, but only those aspects which pertain to the role and aims of the industrial assurance companies, as well as to the importance of the Act for the Prudential, will be dealt with here.

The National Insurance Act 1911 was the first comprehensive attempt to insure the working population of the United Kingdom against the dual risks of ill health and unemployment. National insurance was the centrepiece of Lloyd George's programme of social reforms. Outwardly radical, it was in reality an attempt to ward off serious social unrest, especially after the election of December 1910 and the challenge to the Liberals posed by a block of 29 MPs sponsored by the Labour Representation Committee, which now began to call itself the Labour party. The population to be brought within the Act was largely that which formed the ranks of industrial assurance policyholders. What was described by Lloyd George as 'the relief of pauperism' meant, in practical terms, that the sickness, invalidity, death and medical treatment benefits that had been provided for the elite of the working class for generations by the best of the friendly societies were to be apportioned by the state to the rest of the working population. Though some friendly societies' financial instability had sometimes had disastrous results for their members, the philosophy of the great federated societies underlay much of the initial planning of national insurance.

During 1910 and 1911, when the National Insurance Bill was being prepared, the Prudential management's primary concern was to ensure that the Company's interests were not damaged by the intended legislation. Although not a member of the 'Combine' (the Association of Industrial Assurance

Companies and Collecting Friendly Societies, founded in 1901 to combat agents' malpractices), the Prudential shared with the other industrial companies and the three large collecting societies – the Royal Liver, Liverpool Victoria and Refuge – the objective of warding off possible state encroachment on the provision of death benefits, as well as on the employment prospects of some 80,000 agents. The existence of this veritable army of disciplined men, whose work took them into every hamlet in the British Isles, was to be an important factor in achieving the industry's aim.

Lloyd George had initially modelled his scheme for national insurance on that of Germany, and had included as one of its provisions a widows' pension. Though the earliest meeting between the Chancellor and the industrial assurance companies is undocumented, it would appear that such a meeting did occur in August 1910. Representatives of the 'Combine' explained on that occasion that widows' pensions would seriously diminish the attraction of insurance for funeral benefit. The enormous investments in agents' books would be virtually eradicated by state competition. The Chancellor had apparently not considered this, and was surprised to learn that adequate compensation to the companies would run into millions of pounds.[23] In a memorandum on the problems facing the scheme, he expressed deep indignation towards the industrial assurance system, which he saw as posing a major obstacle to the provision of benefits to those who most needed it. He noted '... the bitter hostility of powerful organisations like the Prudential, the Liver ... the Pearl, and similar institutions, with an army numbering scores, if not hundreds and thousands, of agents and collectors who make a living out of collecting a few pence a week from millions of households ... '.

He went on to castigate the high expenses and lapses that still characterised much of the industry, and went so far as to suggest that it should be 'terminated at the earliest possible moment' in favour of state insurance. This would be more economical, as both state and employer would contribute. He had been made to recognise, however, that

... however desirable it may be to substitute state insurance, which does not involve collection ... any Party that attempted it would instantly incur the relentless hostility of all these agents and collectors. They visit every house, they are indefatigable, they are often very intelligent, and a government which attempted to take over their work without first securing the co-operation of the other Party would inevitably fail in its undertaking; ... compensation on an adequate scale is well-nigh impossible, inasmuch as it would cost something like 20 or 30 millions at the very least to buy off the interests of these collectors, and such a payment would crush the scheme and destroy its usefulness. On the other hand, the agents cannot be absorbed within the new system, there being no door-to-door collection contemplated.[24]

The question of widows' pensions hung in the air during the autumn of 1910. Rumours that the Government intended to introduce, along with measures related to unemployment and sickness assurance, a form of life assurance in direct competition with industrial assurance, kept the industry on the defensive.

All of this was taking place against the backdrop of the much better known struggle over the Budget, and Lloyd George's threat to bring the House of Lords to heel through the creation of peers. In the autumn of 1910 Lloyd George was exploring the possibility of forming a coalition with the Unionists which, had it succeeded, would have made national insurance a proposal on which Liberals and Unionists could have united to withstand the interests opposed to the scheme. The coalition, for a variety of other reasons, proved impossible to achieve. Parliament was dissolved and a general election called for 19 December 1910.

With an election imminent, the industrial assurance companies swung into action. The 'Combine', supported by the Prudential, decided to canvass parliamentary candidates with a view to obtaining pledges that, if elected, they would oppose any Government proposal harmful to the insurance interest. The circular which went out to candidates asked:

> *Will you pledge yourself to oppose any measure of State Insurance which is likely prejudicially to affect the interest of the great affiliated orders and friendly and collecting societies and companies, or to jeopardize the livelihood of the very many thousands of persons engaged in the business of industrial life assurance, and will you oppose any exceptional treatment of any order, society or company to the prejudice of others?*

The press and the insurance journals were full of speculation. In the last week of November 1910, a number of articles appeared which claimed that a Government scheme which would virtually replace industrial assurance was on its way. There was also a rumour, supported by some of the agents' unions, that one or more of the industrial assurance companies was about to be nationalised. (This, it will be recalled, was the period when the NAPAA was suggesting that this was a desirable objective.) These rumours were quashed on 1 December, when Lloyd George issued a letter, published in the *Daily News* the next day and reprinted in the *Insurance Mail*, denying that the Government's proposed scheme included a form of death benefit and assuring that 'the proposals which the Government have in view ... are not likely, so far as I can judge at present, to interfere in any way with the business now carried on by industrial life assurance companies or societies'.

The industrial assurance interest was less than content with this, the phrase 'so far as I can judge at present' being viewed with apprehension. Even the result of the canvass of Members of Parliament, from which pledges were obtained from 490 of a total of 670 members, did not allay the dread of future state competition. During the next few months the assurance press remained on guard, speculating about the various interpretations that could be put on Lloyd George's letter of 1 December. The *Insurance Mail* suggested to agents that combination in the face of the threat to their livelihood was the best course of action, and that this was already well advanced: 'Organisations Being Formed' – 'Insurance Men Arming For The Struggle' – 'Petitions to Parliament To Be Prepared'. Superintendents' 'fraternals' or local associations were reported to be forming all over the country to plan local campaigns. In addition,

> *... the powerful organisation of industrial offices and collecting societies, popularly known as the "Combine", has been actively at work for some time, and will meet to form a kind of Parliamentary Committee, and to determine on a course of action ... petitions, resolutions and the like, to Parliament and to Members of Parliament, will be formulated, signed and presented whenever the time is ripe.*

These actions were justifiable, as

> *... a definite and deliberate movement for mutual protection against a positive menace. The Chancellor of the Exchequer intends to make a provision for widows and orphans in the near future. The benefits may be called pensions to the widow on the death of the bread-winner, but they are payments following death – and so are indistinguishable from industrial life insurance.* [25]

The leading spokesman for the industrial assurance interest was a young solicitor, Howard Kingsley Wood, whose firm was appointed legal counsel to the 'Combine' in 1911. He had first drawn the industry's attention to the threat posed by the Government's proposals on 27 September 1910 in a lecture to the Bristol chapter of the Law Society, the text of which shortly appeared in two parts in the *Insurance Mail*. Kingsley Wood is credited with having suggested to the 'Combine' that the assurance companies assert their right to a share in administering any scheme of state insurance. This was put forward by the 'Combine' at a meeting with the Government on 12 January 1911. [26]

In the aftermath of the meeting, widows' benefit was in fact removed from the scheme, but this was far from the end of the companies' worries. The formula that had been devised to administer all benefits other than medical and sanatorium benefits was that of the 'approved society'. The main characteristics of these insurance societies were that they were not to be run for profit, and that they were to be under the absolute control of their members. These criteria were already met by the friendly societies, trade unions and similar bodies, but obviously not by the industrial assurance companies. The 'Combine' set about securing modifications in the original concept of approved societies so as to make it possible to set up separate entities, under a company's aegis, that did comply with the rules.

There was a further point of contention. The friendly societies would have the advantage, in attracting members, of being able to offer funeral benefit, one of their main *raisons d'être* from time immemorial. As well, one of the clauses in the Bill would have allowed them to make additional death benefits periodically available out of profits. The threat to the insurance industry, then, came from two directions: the state, should it include death benefit in the scheme, and the friendly societies, which already provided death benefit and under the proposed legislation could enhance this. The *Insurance Mail* expressed the continuing alarm of the vast field-force:

> On behalf of insurance workers we ask the Government to say finally that it will not give temporary annuities to the widow and children after the death of the bread-winner, but will leave this field permanently open to the activities of a body of men who have done wonders in it already, and who are as much entitled to consideration as any other body of business men in the world. There is absolutely no need for any Government to set up against us a State-aided compulsory scheme. ... We have 40,000,000 policies in force. The nation will be all the better if anything it needs in this line is done voluntarily.[27]

And at the Prudential's Annual General Meeting on 2 March 1911, Thomas Dewey voiced the concern shared by the other companies. The industrial assurance industry had a legitimate claim to a role in administering the national scheme:

> We of the Prudential feel that we have an organisation capable of dealing with the payments under the proposed Bill as economically and efficiently as any other body, and if it is determined that the payments are to be made by other than Government officials, we feel that we ought to be given the option of employing our staff for that purpose, at any rate as far as our own policyholders are concerned.[28]

The nation's insurance agents, who viewed the proposed legislation as the possible death-blow to their profession, carried their protest into the homes of millions of policyholders. Letters to the press and public meetings produced a groundswell of opinion. The Bill was already facing great opposition from the medical lobby, which feared losing many patients to friendly societies if it became law, and which in its resentment of the societies was ready to align itself with the industrial assurance interest. Finally, the pledges secured by that interest from Members of Parliament, not to permit any measure injurious to industrial assurance, were a powerful asset in persuading the Chancellor to confine his measure to sickness and unemployment.

The National Insurance Bill was finally introduced in the Commons on 4 May. The Chancellor explained that due to the vast provision for death benefit that already existed through the friendly and collecting societies and the industrial assurance companies, '... we do not propose to deal with insurance against death. It is no part of our scheme at all, partly because the ground has been very thoroughly covered. ...' and he admitted that the operation of the scheme would rely on the experience of the companies and the army of agents that was already in place.[29] Whereas in fact Lloyd George could not afford to alienate the insurance interest, in accommodating it he gained its support, and so turned intransigent opposition into an alliance. The industrial assurance companies were

... managed with great skill by means of consummate business ability ... I say that not because I want to buy off opposition, but because I want their help. We do not want to interfere in the slightest degree with their present business as death benefits do not come in. The assistance of these societies would be an advantage to the State.[30]

As to the rest of the two-part Bill, Part I related to sickness, and outlined a contributory scheme. Funds were to be built up either by a combination of state, employers' and assured person's contributions, or by those from the state and the assured person alone. The benefits outlined in Part I were basically those traditionally provided by friendly societies: sickness, disability and maternity allowances, together with medical treatment. The plan covered all employed persons between the ages of 16 and 65 whose income from employment was below the income tax limit of £160 a year, and manual workers of whatever earnings level. There were large categories of workers that were exempt or treated separately, and the possibility for others of joining the scheme voluntarily.[31] Contributions were to be paid weekly by employers and those in work at a combined rate of 7d for men and 6d for women, in the form of stamps affixed to cards provided by employers. Each person was responsible for choosing an approved society to hold his contributions and for ensuring that his card, duly filled with stamps, was lodged with the society every three months.

The 'Combine' and the insurance press had also succeeded in gaining the inclusion of the industrial assurance companies among the organisations allowed

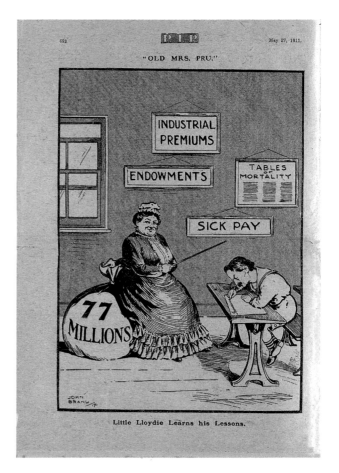

Lloyd George 'instructed' by the Prudential during the passage of the National Insurance Bill.

to set up approved societies. The clause in the Bill that might have allowed the friendly societies to distribute their quinquennial surpluses as additional death benefit was removed. The friendly societies not surprisingly resented the companies acquiring a place alongside themselves and the trade unions. 'Why?' queried the *Insurance Mail*, 'Because they know if we get in we shall take a great proportion of the public under our wing. In other words they are seeing their prey snatched from them.'[32]

The position of the friendly societies was rapidly deteriorating, as the doctors' lobby had wrested medical benefit, another of their age-old provisions, from the approved societies. The big issue that remained unresolved for the insurance interests was that of democratic election of the officers, representatives and committees of approved societies. This was the normal way of proceeding in friendly societies, but hardly in companies, and the latter feared the influence of the militant, pro-nationalisation union members among their agents. At a meeting at the Treasury on 19 October, Lloyd George met with spokesmen from the 'Combine' companies, the friendly societies and the agents' unions (the NAPAA attended, but not the PSF, as it was not a union). Alfred Corderoy Thompson, with his Assistant Manager, Arthur Rhys Barrand, and Frederick Schooling as Chief Actuary, represented the Prudential. Kingsley Wood was also there. The result of a heated debate was that the companies secured a rewording, known as the Goodship amendment, that allowed for the election of delegates where this was already the case, but which permitted the election of representatives in other kinds of institutions 'by the members, under the rules of such societies'.[33]

This amendment removed the last of the friendly societies' privileges and marked the final triumph of the 'Combine'. Equal terms under the law for the companies would in fact mean great advantage, and there was correspondingly great disillusion among those who deplored the powerful role that commercial interests would have in running the national scheme. However much Lloyd George had originally intended a scheme modelled largely on friendly society principles, the Bill had encountered such opposition, both in and out of Parliament, that the support of the vast industrial assurance interest was essential to effect it at all.

The Bill had its third reading on 6 December 1911, and received its royal

Frederick Schooling, FIA: Actuary, Joint General Manager, Director from 1912 to 1936 and Deputy Chairman from 1928, a cornerstone of the Ibis and one of the best-loved men in the Prudential.

assent on 16 December. Once it was certain that the companies would be co-administering the scheme, Kingsley Wood, representing the 'Combine', did attempt to reach an accord with the friendly societies on one further point. This was the vexed question of transfers, which was one of the worrisome problems that had brought the companies together to form the 'Combine' in 1901. But the friendly societies, smarting from the diminution of their own role, declined to join with their rivals to control transfers among approved societies once these were established. The result was that they were unrepresented when, in June of the following year, the insurance companies and the large collecting societies formed the National Amalgamated Approved Society and agreed not to accept transfers from each other.

The National Insurance Act came into effect on 15 July 1912. In the first six months of 1912 the Government created the entire administrative structure necessary to run it, while the bodies empowered to establish approved societies set about doing so. To meet the Act's criteria of being non-profit and under the absolute control of their members, the Prudential, like all the companies, was allowed to form separate sections of its own, which for the purposes of the Act were regarded as 'societies'. At the Prudential's Annual General Meeting on 7 March 1912, Thomas Dewey recounted some of the conditions underlying the action the Company was taking. The aim was that every Prudential policyholder should join a Prudential Approved Society. Since the Company was represented in every part of the country, no-one would need to transfer to any other, should he move out of his own area. The sections formed by the Prudential were to consist of one for men and one for women, so as to keep the funds for each sex entirely separate.[34]

In due course, additional Prudential Approved Societies were formed to cater for the notably large groups of people employed as domestic servants, laundresses and seamstresses, miners, and agricultural labourers. The fact that death benefit had been left to the existing commercial organisations was a powerful factor in increasing public confidence in industrial assurance. The Approved Societies, by definition, could not generate profit, but they did afford an exceptional new business opportunity. That they would do so, of course, had been recognised from the early days of the Bill. The agent who paid out national health benefits was in a position of unrivalled advantage when it came to signing up new policyholders. Through frequent visits – perhaps to pay out maternity benefit – he knew which members of a given family were insured with his company, and which still presented him with a canvassing prospect. The Government's evident approval of industrial assurance could be cited to good effect, especially where there was competition from a local friendly society. A circular to Prudential agents reminded them of the need to provide the best service possible: '... *his own two or three policies are, to a client, of special, personal and usually of urgent importance* ...' and an agent's attention to policyholders, even when stretched by the amount of new work, could only result in further goodwill.

By March 1913, the Prudential's 20,000 agents had succeeded in enrolling some 3,000,000 members in the Company's Approved Societies, with an average of 2,000 new applications a day coming in. The cost of managing the sections and record-keeping was covered by a set fee per member. As Dewey had emphasised in his speech at the Annual General Meeting, administration costs had to be kept within this, or the society would run at a loss. Since the agents frequently paid benefit claims on the same occasions on which they collected industrial assurance premiums, expenses 'in the field' were not expected to rise. It was the paperwork connected with the administration of the scheme and of the Approved Societies that was potentially costly. A bare nine months after starting up, the Prudential Approved Societies were handling between 40,000 and 50,000 cases of sickness benefit a week. Rather than allow the influx of this kind of work to disrupt the existing arrangements at Holborn Bars, the Approved Societies were housed in purpose-built premises in Brooke Street, and staff were rapidly hired and trained as needed. Dewey paid tribute to the 'splendid exertions made by our staff to master the intricate and complicated machinery set up by the National Insurance Act', and not without reason: the Act ran to 115 detailed clauses, 9 added schedules and 5 appendices.

The need to contain expense in operating the Approved Societies was the motive behind the rethinking of field staff organisation that took place in 1912. The originator of the so-called 'Block System' was Joseph Burn, newly appointed as Actuary to succeed Frederick Schooling, who retired to serve as President of the Institute of Actuaries from 1912 to 1914. Burn recognised that the addition of the tasks connected with national insurance to the agent's weekly duties could only be accomplished within cost limits if there were savings elsewhere to compensate for the extra time spent on each house-call and on Approved Society paperwork. The solution was to rationalise the agent's territory. Up to now a man could roam freely within a wide area: this was the system so beloved of Sir Henry Harben, who saw the working of it as a test of a man's drive and determination. The limits of an agent's beat were dictated by his energy and means of transport. The Block System proposed that he cover a given area, and that this area be exclusively his.

The greater efficiency to be secured by preventing overlapping of agencies was one attraction of the idea. The field staff were told that it was likely to boost earnings; there was already much effort being made to raise the minimum level of debits to £7 or £8 by combining small agencies. The Prudential Staff Federation was not so certain, fearing the possible loss of viable agencies. Some contributors to its *Gazette* viewed the enclosure of territories with suspicion, on the grounds that this would remove the main source of 'increase'. The PSF's policy was the opposite of the NAPAA's inflammatory approach; the latter was still preaching nationalisation. H. Birnage, the PSF's General Secretary, expressed himself satisfied with the Company's assurance that the Block System would

"The starlight night was beautiful"

Stern
2nd class
Section of ship

"The Titanic looked enormous"

Boat Deck clear of boats

"Every porthole & saloon was blazing with light"

"The bows & bridge completely under water"

"We had sixty or seventy on board"

Loose floating ice

"Sea calm as a pond" "There was just a gentle heave"

Prudential Assurance Company, Ltd.

HOLBORN BARS, LONDON.

'TITANIC' DISASTER.

14th April, 1912.

Claims have already been paid by this Company in respect of

292 PERSONS

(262 of the Crew and 30 Passengers)

who lost their lives in this disaster. The total amount paid
to date is

£12,834.

9th May, 1912.

A. C. THOMPSON, *General Manager.*

K. 50m. 5/

only be applied in agencies made vacant through death, retirement or leaving the Prudential's service. That the gradual introduction of the system encountered some resistance was inevitable in an agency structure that had remained virtually unchanged since the mid-1870s. By early 1914, however, the *Prudential Staff Gazette* was of the opinion that 'the Block System is a necessity, however it may evolve ...', and some agents who had been allocated 'blocks' were extolling the comparative ease and productivity of the new way of working.[35] The outbreak of war a few months later was to be a decisive factor in hastening its extension. Field staff numbers were suddenly and forcibly reduced, and there was much to be said for a compact territory that could be more easily worked by an older man, a youth, or a woman.

The Prudential in the Great War

TWENTY years after the end of the First World War, with all signs pointing ominously to a second, a book entitled *The Prudential Staff and the Great War* was printed for circulation within the Company. This account of 'Prudential people in a time of national crisis' may have been intended to inspire the staff of 1938 as much as to commemorate the generation who served in the armed forces between 1914 and 1918. The book is a collection of verbatim accounts spliced into a narrative text. 'How the Staff of one of the great business institutions of the Empire stood up to the shock of war' still makes stirring reading.

By 1914, the idea that war with Germany was probably inevitable had long been accepted, even if the train of events that provoked its outbreak on 4 August caught the British public momentarily by surprise. The mood of the country was confident and resolute; most people thought the war would be short and sharp, and the troops home again quickly.

Many male Chief Office staff already belonged to the Territorial Force, created following Lord Haldane's reorganisation of the Auxiliary Forces in 1908. The Prudential had long had a tradition of spare-time military service, which received fresh impetus when men returning from the war in South Africa organised a general interest in practice shooting into the most popular of the Ibis sports in the years before the First World War. The 'A' rifle range, located on the roof of 142 Holborn Bars and opened by Lord Roberts in June 1906, had facilities for up to 80 people at a time to practice. By 1914, three-quarters of the male staff belonged to the Rifle Club, but proficiency in shooting and the handling of weapons was considered a skill that everyone, including the women clerks, should acquire.[1] Similarly, from 1910, the British Red Cross's scheme for Voluntary Aid Detachments – intended to fill the gap between the Divisional Royal Army Medical Corps and the Home Hospitals – had encouraged the formation of two Prudential VADs, the first to be raised in the City of London. They received regular training and participated in the annual Prudential Field Days, the last of which took place at Sir William Lancaster's cricket ground at Putney on 20 June 1914, a bare six weeks before the war began.

On 12 August, a week after war was declared, Thomas Dewey and Alfred Corderoy Thompson called a meeting of male Chief Office staff in the courtyard of 142 Holborn Bars. By then more than 500 Prudential men had already joined the regular forces; the rest were told that jobs and salaries would be safeguarded, and that no man would be at a disadvantage for enlisting. The field staff was asked to help with a house-to-house canvassing campaign on behalf of the Prince of Wales's National Relief Fund.[2] H.S. Thompson, the elder of the General Manager's sons and a Recruiting Officer in the early months of the war, set up his headquarters at Holborn Bars. Initially the call was for men between 22 and 35, but 'too old' and 'too young' proved to be somewhat elastic terms, as plenty of men in both categories managed somehow to enlist by adding or subtracting a few years. Falling short of the physical requirements could also be got round. Some of those rejected for being an inch too short simply waited an hour and presented themselves to another doctor.[3]

The Prudential Board shared the prevailing view of the war as a temporary emergency: Dr John Boswell was given a leave of absence 'for the period of six months or of the war, whichever may be longer', after offering his services to the War Office at the outbreak.[4] Having clarified the position with regard to staff joining up, the Directors turned their attention to the Company's 21,000,000 policyholders. Some 700,000 of these were men of enlistment age, for whom war risk was now very real. The decision was taken to abrogate the War Risks clause and not to increase the premiums on existing Industrial Branch policies for either servicemen or civilians. Premiums on existing Ordinary Branch policies of £250 or less likewise remained unchanged, though policies of more than that amount were to carry a surcharge. For those on active service wishing to take out assurance or increase it, a new table for soldiers and sailors was introduced, payable after 15 years or on previous death, and providing cover for the duration of the war at 25s and after it at 12s 6d, for each £10 assured.[5] The concessions made by the Prudential and other insurance companies were to some extent pre-empted by the Government, in its haste to legislate quickly for the eventualities of war. The Courts (Emergency Powers) Act of 31 August 1914 prescribed that no lapse of industrial assurance premiums due to causes connected with the war could be enforced except by court order. By deferring their premiums, it relieved policyholders of the risk of lapse because of any temporary inability to pay. The insurance companies were liable for claims as if the premiums had been kept up to date. Thomas Dewey considered this Act highly damaging both to the industry and to the moral fibre of the nation, fearing that it would encourage men still engaged in civilian work to withhold their premiums for no other reason than that the law allowed it. Quite how onerous the consequences of the Act were to prove could not really be calculated at the outset, but the Board feared the worst and set up a reserve against contingencies of this kind that amounted to £350,000 by the end of the war.[6]

The earliest Prudential men to enlist soon found themselves facing the enemy. One of them was present when the first shots of the war were fired in France; another was aboard the *Lance* when she sank the German mine-layer *Königin Luise* off Harwich within hours of war being declared. Some, after brief training, fought in the earliest battles of the war: at Mons, and the retreat from that town, and on the Marne and Aisne. Others saw naval action, with the newly formed brigade of Naval Volunteers at Antwerp. The autumn and winter of 1914–15, when the Allied and German armies massed along the Somme dug themselves in, marked the beginning of trench warfare and a long military stalemate. The letters sent back to the *Ibis Magazine* were invariably censored, but the magazine printed the truncated and sometimes mysterious communications it received. There were a few lucky groups who had remained together, one reporting that '... the P.A.C. fellows are all well and fit. There are eleven of us with the regiment ... I am not permitted to state where we are, or give any other information. We are getting plenty of excitement, however, and we are there or thereabouts' (this presumably meant that the men were on or near the front).[7] Dr Boswell was sent to a base hospital in Boulogne. It was not long before the first casualties struck at the heart of the Company. The much loved Frederick Schooling lost a son, Captain Eric Schooling, in October 1914.

Thanks to *The Prudential Staff and the Great War* and the *Ibis Magazine*, the experiences of many of the Prudential staff who served in the First World War are still a part of the recorded history of the Company. Ordinary clerks, young men who until then had known nothing more competitive than the Ibis cricket pitch, described how they found in themselves an astonishing capacity for endurance that quickly came to be second nature. A member of the British Expeditionary Force in France observed that 'although our sleeping accommodation consists of a sack thrown on the floor in a garret, I am quite at home, and ask for no softer bed ...'.[8] The 200-mile retreat from Antwerp provided the theme for another clerk, who endured a day's march of 50 miles fully laden, with no solid food except the windfalls collected as he trekked past some orchards. Another wrote matter-of-factly of danger, exhaustion and hunger:

The soldier about to depart for the front has assured his life, and so made proper provision for his dependants.

We went into action the day before yesterday ... We had to take a trench, and to do so we had to cross a large potato-field that was absolutely swept by shrapnel. ... We crawled along a ditch that was full of nettles; it was hard work crawling about a quarter of a mile in our overcoats and with our packs. ... We dug ourselves into trenches for the night in anticipation of an attack at dawn, right on a road, and of course no sleep and no food except a few biscuits. We have had no sleep for about three days now ... .[9]

Once the Allied armies had dug themselves in on the muddy fields of Champagne, Prudential men sent back impressions of their living conditions. Life in the trenches during these early months was not too unpleasant. G.J.M. Best (who was later wounded and gassed but lived to become General Manager of the Prudential's Australian branch, undreamt of in 1914) wrote:

You may like to have more of an idea of what our dugouts are like, as they form our home for a quarter of our time. The new ones we are having built in our trench have wooden floors and sides, with corrugated iron roofs, on which sand-bags (or rather, canvas bags filled with clay) are packed closely round the edges, with mould dug from the front of the parapet to fill up the centre. This makes it proof against shell splinters and shrapnel (I am glad to say our trenches have not been shelled so far). The size of our dugouts is about 6 feet 6 inches, and 4 feet high. Then we improve on them ourselves, by putting up shelves (for accommodating our eatables), bracket for candle, etc., etc. In this we have to accommodate three men and one on guard, so that when we snug in together we are quite comfy and warm.[10]

F.L. Parker, in a trench that was closer to the German lines, described the dugouts as spaces in which 'it is just possible to lie down or sit up', but as he was a tall man, reported that 'my legs stick out of the end and recline in an inch or two of mud and water'. Sentry duty and the hazardous nightly task of going to collect rations compounded physical discomfort to militate against an unbroken night's sleep.[11] A fellow-clerk provided a note of wry humour on the perils of moving around at night: 'Getting in and out of the trenches is one of the most dangerous jobs, the Germans are always sending up flash-lights; when these go up one has to fall flat on the ground, which very often is not so dry as High Holborn'.[12]

The discomfort of trench life seldom elicited complaints, though powers of description were taxed by efforts to convey what it was like living up to the ankles and even the knees in the sodden Flanders clay. Several Prudential men wrote of the pleasure of being issued with proper raincoats; others of some unexpected opportunity of a hot bath and a change of clothing after weeks spent in soaked and mud-stiffened uniforms.

A few were taken prisoner early in the war. At best this meant farm labouring: outdoor work which, while physically taxing, at least meant a billet with a family, and a reasonably healthy way of life. At worst, it meant incarceration, with crowding and appalling food. One man wrote, of the internment camp at Gröningen in Holland in which he found himself, that the huts held 450 men each. 'We each have a small bed, upon which we sleep, dress, and in fact almost live – if such is living,' he recounted, going on to say that the tedium of camp life, and the sense of being useless to the war effort, were equally hard to bear.

At home, the *Ibis Magazine* voiced the prevailing mood of suspended animation as 1914 drew to a close: in a sense, the war seemed not to have started yet. Just after New Year, descriptions of the Christmas truce between the entrenched armies in France, sent back by men who participated in it, astounded *Ibis* readers (as similar, more widely published reports did the wider reading public) with their suggestion that the German soldiers were not so far removed in habits and feelings from their British counterparts. There were numerous accounts of how the opposing armies agreed not to fire on each other during the Christmas and New Year. Instead, they fraternised and sang carols across the lines. One Prudential soldier described how

... our fellows paid a visit to the German trenches, and they did likewise. Cigarettes, cigars, addresses, etc., were exchanged, and everyone, friend and foe, were real good pals. One of the German officers took a photo of English and German soldiers arm in arm, with exchanged caps and helmets. ... On Christmas Eve the Germans burnt coloured lights and candles all along the top of their trenches, and on Christmas Day a football match was played between them and us in front of the trench. ... They even allowed us to bury all our dead lying in front, and some of them, with hats in hand, brought in one of our dead officers from behind their trench so that we could bury him decently. [13]

The correspondents expressed their surprise at finding that many of the German soldiers spoke English; one Prudential man met an enemy soldier who had been a porter at Victoria Station and another who had played football for a Nottingham team; another met a German who had worked in the City for several years and travelled up to town each day on the same train as himself! In the course of the ceasefire, as C.L. Jefferson reported, '... we made arrangements with them to bury some dead cows that had been lying between the trenches for weeks; it was funny to see English and Germans working side by side'. [14] But within days the idyll of the truce was over; the bombardment and sniping recommenced, and the armies were enemies again.

At Christmas 1914, a precedent was set for the next three years, in the despatch of parcels from Holborn Bars to the men serving in the forces. On this first occasion, some 1,300 packages were sent, each containing a pound of De Bry's chocolate and a letter signed by Alfred Corderoy Thompson. In it he wrote

FACING PAGE

Prudential women featured

in a popular daily paper

during the First World War.

of the 'hundreds of officers and men who have forsaken the relatively uneventful Prudential life' for wartime service.

Memories of that 'uneventful' peacetime life, of work complemented by Ibis sports and activities, sustained many a man in the trenches. The initial expectation that the conditions in which they were living were temporary gave way, in the winter of 1915, to an acceptance that the mud, the noise and the cold were semi-permanent. The principal theme of letter-writers had by now become the fighting: the bombardments, the artillery fire, the shelling, the incessant noise and the grim suddenness of death. Men struggled to describe the new and awful realities for which, as yet, no words existed: the 'crump' of shells ploughing into the ground, and the 'sort of dull, low, mourning note which is inexpressibly sad' that was the sound of distant big guns firing day and night. They wrote of things that chilled the blood of readers at home. One told of a shell landing in the midst of a group standing chatting in the trench, and the instant of frozen horror before it exploded, killing half of those present. A wounded clerk wrote from hospital of having seen a stretcher-party, four men and a wounded comrade, blown to pieces only yards in front of him. The desolation of the battlefield was made appallingly real. The bombardments 'fling up trees just as if they were matchsticks', while the sight of broad tracts of farmland transformed into lifeless quagmires made a profound impression.

Far worse than the devastation wreaked upon the land was the carnage and suffering men saw all around them. M. Foulger (who later died in the attack on Hooge) recorded passing through Ypres in the autumn of 1915: 'We came to the famous Cloth Hall, and I could hear my men exclaim at the terrible scene which confronted them. There was a café a few yards from it, where four months ago I had dinner. Alas! I tried hard to find it, but a few bricks only marks the spot.'[15]

L.W. Lewis was describing the same place when he wrote in his diary of 'the smoking and stinking ruins of Belgium' and the plight of the civilians left to starve as the city burned. But greater attention was naturally devoted to the suffering of men under fire. Casualties soon became routine, and those who wrote from hospital gave scant attention to their own injuries. More often they wrote of Prudential colleagues killed, wounded or missing. Two such accounts, one concerning a clerk called Albert Keen who was wounded, found on the battlefield and ultimately lost again in the mud as night fell, and one describing the death of Duncan Bedbrook, a Prudential principal clerk, stand out as particularly moving. 'There is no romance in war now,' one writer concluded. 'Even the rifle has given way to the bomb, and the whole thing is cold-blooded murder.'[16]

Not all the letters recounted dire events. Some told of near miraculous escapes. The random way in which lives had been saved by seconds or inches was often transmitted to Chief Office, usually to allay the anxiety that men knew was felt on their account. (There were plenty of instances of men reported dead,

THE DAILY GRAPHIC, MAY 6, 1916.

LONDON
EDITION

The DAILY GRAPHIC

One Penny

LONDON: SATURDAY, MAY 6, 1916

No. 8741—Vol. CVI.

Registered as a Newspaper.

THE WAR-TIME CITY "MAN" AND "HIS" LUNCH.

Wherever possible the City man, and in particular the clerk, has now been replaced by the City girl. A typical instance of the change is to be found in the Prudential Assurance Company, which now employs 2,000 women war workers. As an economy for them, and to give them greater efficiency, special luncheon rooms have been provided, where they receive an excellent hot meal for a few pence. They have also a pleasant roof garden and library for recreation. 1. A few of the 2,000 girls who lunch-in every day. 2. A corner of the kitchen. 3. At lunch.

("Daily Graphic" photographs.)

who – their departments at Holborn Bars were later overjoyed to learn – were very much alive.[17]) One member of staff survived through having providentially left his dugout a moment before a shell crashed through the roof and landed on his bed. Another escaped death when the bullet that struck him lodged in the copy of the Bible he carried in his pocket. The stories of the strange fortunes of war that were reproduced by the *Ibis Magazine* often focused on this kind of incident, as well as on the unlikely meetings of Prudential men far from home. The circumstances in which these took place were as varied and as amusing as anything in fiction. It became a commonplace for men to identify one another through noticing a Prudential diary protruding from a tunic pocket, but there were far less likely encounters.[18] B.H. Cooper, writing from HMS *Proserpine*, described how he discovered that one of his several hundred shipmates also worked for the Prudential: 'When the mail-bags come on board they are emptied out on deck. While the Master-at-Arms was sorting out the lot in question, Deacon's hawk-like vision detected two similar packages with the Prudential label on them, one addressed to him and the other to me … .'[19]

Another clerk crossed paths with a fellow-officer in the aftermath of battle, and recognised him as the member of Chief Office staff who had given him his induction training as a junior in 1909.[20] One of the most delightful stories, though it turned on the relationship between agent and policyholder rather than on that of fellow-staff, was related by H. Golding, a Prudential agent who found himself in an Allied army camp in Salonika:

> *The Officer commanding the camp inspected the new draft and on passing me ordered the Adjutant to take my name. I was instructed to attend the C.O. Orderly Room at 10 a.m. When I did so the officer asked the others to retire, which they did. He then stood up and put out his hand saying, "Pleased to meet you, Golding. How was my mother when you last called upon her?".*[21]

By October 1915, with a national debate over conscription at its height, the Prudential was operating with its indoor and outdoor staff reduced by some 9,000 men. Of its Chief Office clerical staff who were eligible to enlist, 76% were serving or had volunteered for service. The numbers employed at Holborn Bars totalled 4,750, of whom 1,000 were temporary, 2,000 were women, and the other 1,750 men who were over- or under-age.[22] Except to ask for temporary deferments in a few cases, the Company was still encouraging staff to enlist. For men in the ranks the difference between their pay and their Prudential salaries was made up and paid to their families. In the case of the outdoor staff, the revision of salaries was calculated on the basis of what a man would have been likely to achieve had he not gone to war.[23]

Those who were ineligible for service were reminded frequently that, while the burden of carrying on the business might seem a task unsung and insignificant, 'seeing to it that the machinery of the National Institution continues to run smoothly' was no inconsiderable task. The basic problem in the first half of the war was captured by an *Ibis Magazine* sketch portraying two 'original' Prudential clerks lunching together:

Have you got too much work to do?
Work! Why my dear chap, we shall be three weeks behind in a fortnight if this goes on. Now who do you think I have to run my section with?
I give up.
Gladys Cooper and Methuselah.
What do you mean?
What I say. I am being assisted by an old man of ninety and a girl of fifteen ...

The number of women employed full-time increased dramatically. Before the formation of the Prudential Approved Societies there had been about 400; partly due to the Societies and partly to the war, there were 2,000 by 1915. Aiding the conduct of the war through their work was a case of 'every little bit helps'. Office hours were extended by half an hour at the beginning and an hour at the end of the day (an expedient which lasted until March 1921).[24] There were frequent calls for women in the Chief Office divisional clerical departments to volunteer for overtime until 7.00 or 8.00 p.m. to clear some temporary backlog. On occasion the call went out for '100 or 200 ladies' to undertake monumental tasks. One, significant as the initial step in the transfer to automated working, was copying the details from the Ordinary Branch audit registers onto addressograph slips, done after hours at 14s per 1,000.

The war marked a watershed for women's employment, in the Prudential as elsewhere. Generally speaking, the Prudential's women clerks traditionally held jobs that entailed copying in some form or other. Individual secretarial jobs, involving a degree of initiative and responsibility, as well as the use of the typewriter, had always been held by men, as opposed to the female copyists' jobs in the correspondence departments. Women were now entrusted – of necessity – with 'primary' tasks involving recording and calculating, perhaps on one of the divisional Audit Departments, and regularly invited to take tests in typing and shorthand with the prospect of more responsible work and better pay. Clerical departments ceased for the first time to be segregated by sex as women not only took on jobs hitherto the preserve of men, but for efficiency's sake came to occupy the same physical space. That the men were little more than boys or little less than retirement candidates was beside the point: a boundary had been crossed, and the women's ability to do the work and their willingness to put in long hours were undeniable.

More will be said in due course about the Powers Samas machines acquired in 1915 to administer the national insurance scheme through the Approved

During the First World War women took over the Ibis entertainments. This tableau dates from 1917.

Societies – 40 card punches, 7 tabulators and 7 sorters – which were operated by women from the beginning, and would continue to be so after the war.[25] The use of office machinery by the women of the Approved Societies paved the way for the wider use of automation in the insurance departments after the war, with a consequent widening of women's employment.

Apart from their jobs, Prudential men and women undertook a variety of activities in support of the war effort. Staff at Holborn who belonged to the Red Cross VADs were on call outside working hours to undertake the transport of homecoming wounded soldiers and their belongings. This involved meeting trains at Waterloo and Charing Cross stations, and conveying the wounded to hospitals and convalescent facilities all over the Home Counties. The pressure of this work increased greatly as the war went on, from a total of 8,000 casualties at the end of 1914 to nearly 140,000 two years later.[26] A special telephone line was installed and a rota of clerks permitted to sleep at Holborn Bars to deal with emergency calls.

The VADs also organised the transport for the Saturday afternoon entertainments given to convalescing soldiers in the Hall at Holborn Bars, which replaced the IDOS productions of happier years.[27] The Finsbury Square VAD Hospital was one of several medical facilities maintained and staffed by the Prudential. Some employees volunteered for Sunday munitions manufacture, while members of the female staff took on nursing and canteen work. There were also the correspondence and packages to organise for Prudential men in the forces. All manner of 'sales of work', teas and produce sales were held by Ibis clubs to raise the money for the periodic issues of warm clothing and reading matter.[28]

Members of field staff in the Home Counties raised £900 to buy and maintain two ambulances for the Red Cross. The Prudential Board subscribed to a host of minor relief funds, from Belgian Refugees to Indian Soldiers' Welfare, though its most important donations were to the larger royal or military charities.[29]

The Company's most ambitious support was for the several War Loan schemes and, in particular, its subscription for £25,000,000 of the Victory Loan promoted by the Government in 1917. It had already taken on £3,000,000 of War Loan in 1915; the conversion of its holdings of Consols and other stocks brought its War Loan holding to over £5,000,000. On 5 December 1917, as part of the fresh Victory Loan campaign, a tank arrived at Holborn Bars to collect a donation of £628,000 in dividend which the Directors had decided to invest in National War Bonds. Holborn filled with onlookers as the 76-year-old Thomas Dewey clambered onto the top of the tank to present the cheque to a representative from the War Savings Committee. Films made of the occasion formed part of the news-footage in cinemas all over the country, as the donation was the largest single contribution to the campaign thus far.[30]

Several senior members of the Company were requested by the Government to apply their experience at national level. Actuary Joseph Burn was appointed to the National War Savings Committee and the Royal Commission on Decimal Coinage following the promotion of the War Savings Schemes in the Prudential, with funds advanced to the staff at low rates to enable them to participate. Burn reputedly persuaded everyone at Holborn Bars from the Directors to the messengers to purchase war savings certificates and organised the agents, *en masse*, to sell War Loan vouchers in denominations of £1, 10s and 5s in a concerted drive.[31] Thomas Dewey became a member of the War Office Expenditure Committee, and Alfred Corderoy Thompson was assisted by Ernest Dewey in

SIR THOMAS DEWEY
CHAIRMAN
PRUDENTIAL ASSURANCE Cᵒ
PAYING FOR
£628,800. WAR BONDS
THE PURCHASE

Sir Thomas Dewey hands over a cheque for the purchase of War Bonds from the top of a tank as thousands throng the street in front of Chief Office.

acting as a consultant to the Treasury in an enquiry into the staffing of Government departments.

The most significant appointment, in view of the assistance the Company was able to render, was that of George May, who succeeded Daniel Wintringham Stable as Secretary of the Prudential when the latter joined the Board in February 1915. May had come into the Company as a lad of 16 in 1887. He suffered from poor sight and trained his memory to compensate for this. (His use of a monocle gave him a patrician air.) Attached to the Investment Department of the Secretary's Office, he became an expert on the investment of life assurance funds, and presented an important paper outlining his theory of diversification to the Institute of Actuaries in 1912. This theory offered an alternative to A.H. Bailey's standard criteria for investment, which focused on absolute security. May claimed that spreading investment over a wide range of securities would produce at least as good a result in terms of yield, while the comparatively small size of individual investments meant that exposure to risk also remained small. His interest in securities somewhat outside the predictable canon led to the Prudential's purchase of many American securities. Early in 1915 May was seconded to the Treasury as a member of the American Dollar Securities Commission, taking with him as his Assistant, P.C. Crump. In the summer of 1915, a Government desperate for munitions and food faced having to buy them from the United States when the American exchange rate was highly unfavourable. May conceived the idea of selling to the Government the Prudential's large holding of American securities, so as to provide it with a source of ready funds in the United States. A long note in the board minutes for 29 July 1915 records that the proposal had been presented informally to the Directors several weeks before, and permission then given for May to put forward the Company's offer of help as and when an opportunity arose.

It came a few days later during a meeting about War Loan between May and the Chancellor of the Exchequer, Reginald McKenna. The Prudential was prepared to loan or sell all its American investments, provided that it incurred no substantial financial loss. The Chancellor accepted the offer with a telephone call to the Prudential on 22 July. George May, Joseph Burn and Alfred Corderoy Thompson were invited to meet him that day to discuss how the transfer might be effected. The same evening the group met again, strengthened by Thomas Dewey on the Prudential's side and Lord Cunliffe, Governor of the Bank of England. It was agreed that the transaction should be made by means of an absolute sale on terms to be arranged. The group met a third time the following day to review the Prudential's entire holding of American securities – bearer shares amounting to some $42,418,000 nominal value. Their actual cash interest income of £378,344 was valued at 4½%, giving a value of £8,407,650, plus accrued interest, as the price at which they were to be sold to the Government.[32]

At the Annual General Meeting of 2 March 1916, Thomas Dewey revealed the practical dimensions of what had taken place:

> *It is our practice to detach the sheets of coupons from our bonds in order to facilitate the cashing of them as they fall due. These coupons had again to be attached to the bonds, and it is interesting to note that within a period of 48 hours over 44,000 bonds of a nominal value of over £8,750,000 were checked, removed from our strong rooms, had their sheets of coupons attached, and were dispatched to the Bank of England. Merely to state that we did this work in 48 hours may not seem very remarkable, but if I give you a few more particulars you will better appreciate what the work really was. The actual bonds themselves made up six motor-omnibus loads. The adhesive paper used to affix the sheets of coupons to the bonds measured well over eight miles. A staff of about 100 was engaged until nearly midnight. The work was carried out under the personal supervision of the directors, and when all was finished the Bank of England informed us that everything had been found to be correct, except that a single coupon of the value of only a few shillings had in some unexplained manner apparently vanished.*

Sir William Lancaster could always be relied on to present the incongruous aspects of anything, and his retelling of how the mountainous quantity of paper was handed over was no exception:

> *I daresay [sic] you all know that there are times in our lives when we are placed in positions in which we would rather our friends did not see us. ... Well, if any of you had been passing down Cheapside at a time near to midnight one day in August last you might have seen me in a Red-Cross motor-car which was filled with parcels, and Mr Thompson sitting opposite to me, together with two City detectives, one on either side of the door. It might have given you a shock to see me in such an ambiguous position. {Laughter.} When we arrived at the Bank of England the doors were opened for us into the court-yard. Soldiers were there with fixed bayonets, and there were three or four military wagons in waiting with a squad of soldiers to protect them. As soon as all the bonds had been checked they were loaded into the various wagons, and, attended by a squad of soldiers, taken to a particular ship, the destination of which was kept secret, and I am very happy to say that that ship avoided German submarines and arrived safely with its precious cargo at New York. {Cheers.} As you have already heard, one coupon for a few shillings was missing, and if any of you should happen to run across it we shall be glad if you will kindly send it to us.*[33]

As security was such a priority, few people apart from those directly involved knew about the sale of American securities until the facts of what had happened were related six months later. May, appointed Business Manager of the American

Dollar Securities Commission in January 1916, went on to organise the collection and transfer of the American securities held by other British companies so that they could be used in the same way.

Regardless of the war, the volume of business transacted by the Prudential continued to mount. That of the Industrial Branch had recovered from the *John Bull* affair, aided by a strong effort by the field staff to attract members to the Approved Societies. A novel life policy on which the premiums were collected monthly, new children's policies that provided a lump sum on marriage (the first 'marriage assurance', as Thomas Dewey observed), and a new short-term endowment policy which dispensed with the need for a medical examination were proving popular. The outbreak of war had brought a surge of assurances as men hastily tried to make provision for their families before enlisting. The result was that 1914 showed the largest increase yet in industrial business and premium income. Ordinary business was also up, due partly to the same war-related causes and partly to the increased attractiveness of insurance once the rate of income tax had been doubled and super-tax introduced.

This upsurge in new assurances coincided with the departure of the most energetic members of the field staff to the battlefields. The continued extension of the Block System, still regarded in 1914 as experimental, was seen to be, as Dewey put it, 'wise and timely'.[34] Greater efficiency, the original motive for the scheme, was quickly achieved in the agencies where it was introduced. Six months into the war some 1,300 blocks had been created, comprising about £1,000,000 of premium income. A year later these figures had more than doubled: 3,000 blocks comprising some £2,400,000 of premium income showed a 7% reduction in agency turnover, half that deriving from the old-style agencies, and a rise in agent salaries in the block agencies of 11s over the three years the scheme had operated.[35] By the last year of the war nearly half of the total industrial premium collections of £14,892,571 had been reorganised into 13,107 block agencies. The number of industrial policyholders continued to rise throughout the war, though not at the initially high rate, so that the annual income requiring collection had increased by £2,273,016 over the amount collected in 1913, while the expense of collecting it had fallen.[36]

There was another element in the overall equation, and that was the reduction in the actual number of agents. The Block System was not imposed forcibly; if an agent wished to continue along the lines he was used to – perhaps because he had built up a clientele over the years with which he was on particularly friendly terms, he was left to do so. The circumstances brought about by the war, however, facilitated the extension of the Block System. Agencies serviced by temporaries or by agents' wives were more easily managed as a block. The experienced field staff who remained at their posts were often older men who appreciated a reduction in the time and effort needed to make traditional rounds. The Block System required less supervision – an important factor in the several district offices that were manned single-handed, or where two districts were put under the control of one superintendent for lack of assistants. The economies made in districts where the Block System was implemented allowed them to absorb the loss of men due to promotion, retirement and death to a total of 4,504 by 1918.[37] From now on the number of agents no longer automatically needed to keep pace with the growth of industrial business; the Block System meant that an agent's 'book' increased as he signed up more policyholders within a well-defined area: in a sense his field of action became 'vertical', as opposed to 'horizontal'.

Given the scope of the Prudential's business, it was inevitable that the national calamity of war would have a strong financial impact upon it. The decision to bear the cost of war risk on the great majority of policies had expensive consequences, added to which were the effects of the Courts (Emergency Powers) Act, and the soaring rate of mortality, civilian as well as military, in the early years of the war. As Thomas Dewey reiterated later on, when speaking of the Industrial Branch, '... our business is so vast, and our 22¾ millions of policies so evenly distributed throughout the length and breadth of the land that it is not surprising that our mortality experience very closely follows that of the general population'.[38]

According to rates of mortality shown against census returns in a table covering the war years, the Prudential's rate of mortality just before the war reproduced almost exactly that of the 3rd English Life Table. The rates for 1915, 1916 and 1917 were, however, 'abnormal to a degree which it is difficult to realise'. The mortality rate for age 21 in 1915 was five times higher than the prewar experience, that for 1916 nine times, and for 1917 twelve times. In the case of all policies effected before the war, the Company paid the claims without additional premiums or deduction from the sum assured. War claims paid out by 1918 amounted to £5,000,000, a sum before which 'the boldest of us might have hesitated' had bald commercial factors outweighed patriotic feeling in August 1914. In sheer numbers of claims the figures were staggering. The Prudential paid 230,000 war claims out of the total of 674,000 deaths actually confirmed by the British Government: more than one-third of the British soldiers killed during the war.[39]

Heavy claims for civilian mortality (particularly in 1915 and in 1918, the latter being the year of the great influenza epidemic that laid low the whole of Europe), together with war claims, reserves against contingencies and the depreciation of securities, and the need to offset the effects of the Courts (Emergency Powers) Act by creating a reserve, effectively cancelled out the record increases in premium income during the war. Most of the surplus in both branches went to reserves. This meant that the bonus payable under the profit-sharing scheme of 1907 was reduced in 1914 and, apart from small distributions to the policyholders, not paid normally in the Industrial Branch until 1922. Small amounts were paid in the Ordinary Branch in most years, apart from policies that became claims, on which full bonus was paid.[40]

Some of those claims, of course, were on men and women employed by the Prudential. By the spring of 1916, 200 had been killed, and as war is no respecter of persons, the dead included Frederick Schooling's two sons, one an army chaplain, and both of Alfred Corderoy Thompson's sons. The sons of four other Directors fell in battle or were taken prisoner. By the time the Armistice came on 11 November 1918, 786 Prudential staff had been killed in action or on active service, of the total of 9,161 who had enlisted. More than half of those who had joined up had become officers, the class of serviceman disproportionately slaughtered in contrast to their number. The war brought military decorations for valour to 127 Prudential men and women, the awards ranging from the CMG (awarded to Lieutenant-Colonel Anthony Windsor), the DSO and the DFC, to a selection of Allied decorations. George May was made a KBE in 1918, as much for his work of reorganising the forces' catering facility throughout the country as Deputy-Quartermaster General of the Navy and Army Canteens Board, as for his earlier part in the sale of American Securities. As May's chief assistant, and for managing the American Dollar Securities Committee when May was ill, Percy Crump was awarded the OBE. Joseph Burn also received the KBE, and his assistant, E.J.W. Borrajo (delightfully known as 'Barge' by all), the OBE, for promoting the National War Savings Committee. Thomas Dewey was made a baronet, as the foremost representative of the Prudential, for the service it had provided to the Government in the course of the war. It also recognised Dewey's generosity in having turned his Bromley home into a reception centre for refugees, and his home in Sidmouth into a hospital and convalescent home for wounded servicemen.[41] Just before the war, Dewey had established the Dewey Trust, intended to aid male Chief Office staff in the same way that, since 1905, the Horne Jubilee Fund aided the women. Just how many men based at Holborn Bars benefited from the Trust is hard to say, as discretion was the watchword for the way it functioned. The point is that no member of the Prudential, male or female, was without resource in times of illness (Rustington) or financial difficulty.

News of the Armistice set off peals of churchbells and a frenzy of celebration

A menu for the Prudential's Annual Dinner in 1916 with scenes evoking the war.

throughout the country. In Holborn a jubilant crowd formed in the street. Of Chief Office, H.E. Boisseau recorded that 'At one moment all was normal: the next ... the air seemed charged with emotion. ... We looked out of the windows on to Brooke Street, and down it swarmed the girls from the Approved Society, laughing, running, waving little flags'.[42] The staff streamed down the staircases and out into the courtyard. From the top of a Red Cross bus, Alfred Corderoy Thompson addressed a crowd that overflowed the square to perch on the railings, the windowsills, anywhere. The atmosphere of elation and thanksgiving was tempered for his audience by the knowledge of his terrible personal loss. Tribute was paid to those who had sustained the Prudential at home, and a commitment made to erect a fitting memorial to those who had died. In the afternoon, a service was held for Chief Office at St Alban's Church and the working day suspended.[43]

After four years of austerity the Christmas of 1918 saw the revival of seasonal decorations and entertainments at Chief Office. The process of demobilisation continued into the following year, with the men sent to Germany with the Army of Occupation remaining there until October 1919. The return to civilian life was not always an easy transition. Not least among the adjustments that had to be made was the reintegration into office and agency life of men who had risen to greater levels of responsibility in the forces than they had enjoyed in peacetime. In many cases the conformity and predictability of civilian jobs must have seemed humdrum. Others returned having paid an enormous cost in physical and mental suffering. Contributions to the *Ibis Magazine* for the next several years reflected the degree to which people's lives in the aftermath of the conflict continued to be overshadowed by it.

To what degree restlessness played a part in the decline in the number of agents in the immediate postwar period is difficult if not impossible to gauge. There were many who retired early through ill-health, and who, in line with the economies being sought through the extension of the Block System, were not replaced. Those who returned were reinstated and, in many cases, promoted. Temporary field staff and clerks (both male and female) who wished to stay on were permitted to do so, though this meant a temporary surplus of several hundred employees. It was expected that the increase in business and the consolidation of agencies would counterbalance this overstaffing.[44]

The end of the war was seen as the beginning of a long period of readjustment. In the wake of the cataclysm that had just passed, the social and political issues that had dominated civic life in the years before the war were all but forgotten. Those who had been prosperous before the war assumed the eventual return to a *status quo ante*, to what they saw as the stable and well-regulated way of life that had prevailed before 1914. Too much had changed for that to be possible, although this was not something that was at once perceived. At the same time there was great disillusion, especially among the young, with the established order, and a strong feeling that the previous four years had done away with the old stereotypes and class divisions forever. The result was a new idealism, not only in the determination that the Great War should be the last, but in a more open addressing of social concerns.

Symptomatic of this in a Prudential context was the formalisation of management commitment in three areas. In 1919, a Consultative Committee was established, composed of members of the Prudential Staff Federation (which had become a trade union in 1915), representatives of management and officers representing the clerical staff, to come together periodically for the airing of employment matters. The increased scope given by the war to women's capabilities was acknowledged, with a relaxation in the rigid separation of the sexes and improvements in salary, especially for those operating the new machinery. (One small but significant detail relates to the recent conviction among Ibis Club members that women members should have a vote in electing the Ibis Committee. There were protests from a few diehards, but they were overruled and the proposal was adopted at the Club's Annual General Meeting in January 1920.) Finally, Sir Joseph Burn took in hand the gradual phasing out of the Staff Provident Fund in favour of a Staff Pension Scheme. This was planned during the last year of the war and came into effect from January 1919, and more will be said about it in the following chapter.

These innovations apart, there was a natural tendency in the organisation to revere the things that had endured. The Prudential was innately conservative, in that the nature of its business obliged it to take a long view, and in that even the youngest of its Directors were by now in their late middle age. They had all come to adulthood in the previous century; by and large, their values and ways of running the Company were those they had absorbed from Sir Henry Harben and Edgar Horne. In 1919 Sir Thomas Dewey was 79 and Sir William Lancaster 78; apart from James Moon, who was elected following the death of Lieutenant-Colonel Odo Cross in 1915, and Guy Philip Harben, who joined the Board in 1918, there were few Directors under 60. Sir Philip Spencer Gregory died a fortnight before the Armistice, aged 65. The 63-year-old William Edgar Horne, Unionist MP for Guildford since 1910 and a Director since 1904, became Deputy Chairman. (In deference to his father, he would be still referred to as 'Young Sir Edgar' at his death more than 20 years later.) Alfred Corderoy Thompson was chosen to replace Thomas Wharrie (who died at 89 in 1917) but retained the position of General Manager.

The basic methodology of the Ordinary Branch and the Industrial Branch had likewise remained fundamentally unchanged. Such influence for change as there was derived from Sir Joseph Burn, comparatively young at 47, whose standing in actuarial circles was at its zenith and whose role as a spokesman for the Company and for the assurance industry was well recognised. The war delayed the full implementation of the Block System and the transition to automated data processing, both initiated by him prior to it, which had been the first major attempts to address the endemic problem of expense ratios since before the turn of the century. They were also notable as examples of a more radical approach to the economy of industrial assurance than merely striving to improve on the 'Harben model' – total efficiency as the sum of individual efforts – that had characterised the business during the whole period since the 1870s. In securing priority for these developments in the first few years after the war, Burn was to bring a creative influence to bear at a point when ossification might otherwise have been a real risk.

Burn was also the one member of the Prudential's senior management who emerged from the war with his physical and emotional energies unscathed.

The unveiling in 1922 of the Memorial to Prudential staff who died in the First World War.

No amount of gracious reserve could hide the profound grief that blighted the last decade of Alfred Corderoy Thompson's life.[45] Sir George May, seriously ill from strain and overwork for three months in 1918 (during which time Percy Crump had carried out his duties), suffered thereafter from periodic bouts of blindness. More than either of these, Burn was to be the motive force in the years to come.

The act that formally laid the experiences of the First World War to rest for the Prudential did not in fact take place until a few years later. This was the erection of the War Memorial, which was intended, like hundreds of others up and down the country, to commemorate in some visible way the honour paid by the living to those who had died. The work was commissioned from the sculptor F.V. Blundstone, RBS, to occupy a place immediately in front of the great arch that spanned the courtyard of 142 Holborn Bars. The 10-foot-high bronze statue depicted two angels with wings outspread, supporting a dying soldier, while bronze panels on a plinth of pale rose granite bore the 786 names. The unveiling and dedication took place on 2 March 1922. The reordering of the courtyard in 1992 involved moving the sculpture to a new position in its north-east corner. The ceremonial two minutes' silence and placing of a wreath on the memorial was for many years observed on Armistice Day, but was later transferred to the day of the Annual General Meeting, as it remains.

The Triumph of System

I N the immediate aftermath of the First World War, the return of what seemed like prosperity induced a kind of febrile restlessness in a nation still suffering from emotional exhaustion. Though the postwar boom was to be short-lived, the revulsion against the war and what were held to be its causes was not. In the air there was a palpable desire for change. Sir Thomas Dewey, in his last speech as Chairman of the Prudential at the Annual General Meeting of 4 March 1920, closed with an observation that captured this postwar mood. 'In these days,' he said, 'we hear on all sides the cry for reconstruction, the cry for new methods, in fact for a new world.' His counsel for weathering the bumpy transition to the normality that he assumed would return was reliance on experience: the ways that had served well in the past.

A year later, as the national economy sank further into depression, Dewey had retired to become President of the Company, and his successor as Chairman, Alfred Corderoy Thompson, delivered a speech that was less sanguine in assuming a return to prewar stability. The war had 'violently disturbed the financial equilibrium, not only of the belligerents themselves, but of the whole world', and in a context so drastically altered, experience as a guide had its limitations. A surer strategy for dealing with the prospect of change was to pre-empt it: to be in the vanguard rather than the rear. It was this approach that would see the Prudential through the 1920s.

With the retirement of Sir Thomas Dewey and his exact contemporary, Sir William Lancaster, the election of Thompson was a tribute to the finesse

Alfred Corderoy Thompson.

with which he had piloted the Company through the war as General Manager. (Within a year, he would also be elected Chairman of the British Insurance Association, founded in 1917.) Sir Joseph Burn, who succeeded Thompson as General Manager while retaining the position of Actuary, was able to proceed with the three programmes held back by the war: the launching of the General Branch, the conversion of the field staff to the Block System, and the large-scale automation of office procedures. Before dealing with these, and with the other initiatives of the decade after 1918, it will be helpful to review the background to the legislation that regulated the conduct of life assurance during that time.

****

The setting up of the National Insurance scheme and the Approved Societies in 1912 did nothing to reduce the hostility of social reformers to industrial assurance. Its popularity continued to rankle, as did the wealth of the largest of its providers. The coming of war in 1914 eclipsed all else, and in the anxious mood of the following year, with all attention fixed on events in France, the publication of a detailed critical study of the industrial assurance industry went all but un-noticed. Its importance lay in the influence it came to have after the war, when its conclusions prompted the appointment of a further Royal Commission, and in the fresh legislation that would regulate the industrial assurance industry during the inter-war years.

The study was never published in book form, but appeared only as a Special Supplement to the *New Statesman* of 13 March 1915 – another reason for the scanty attention it received. It was written by Sidney Webb, soon to become Lord Passfield, and drew upon the investigations begun by the Fabian Research Department in April 1914.[1] With such a genesis it was hardly surprising that what purported to be a fact-finding study concluded that industrial assurance was not the 'notable achievement of thrift' claimed by its defenders, but rather, 'a costly preying upon the poor for the benefit of shareholders'. The Prudential received individual treatment. Close scrutiny of its long history of reforms exempted it from the serious charges made against the industry as a whole. But although the Prudential, controlling half of all industrial assurance business, received considerable praise, Webb's conclusions about industrial assurance were largely negative and the industry overall was condemned. Webb's solution was nationalisation, a sweeping recommendation that obviously posed great potential danger to the Prudential. For this reason and for its later influence, his study is worth examining more closely here.

A nine-page overview defined and explained industrial assurance – basically, as funeral assurance. There was little attention paid to the gradual shift, since about 1900, away from whole life policies and towards endowments, as a better-off working class came to use insurance more and more as a savings mechanism.[2] The field was described as dominated by 'one commercial colossus

– the Prudential Assurance Company', which, with 11 other large organisations, vied for control of virtually all the industrial business of any note.[3] Their 'armies' of agents, totalling some 70,000 men, accounted for 90% of annual new industrial business. Webb deemed these agents to be a 'new social type ... one of the most striking results of the beneficent revolution in the nation's schooling'. Literate, numerate, independent by temperament and highly motivated, often by a kind of idealistic, crusading zeal to promote the social usefulness of insurance as much as by the prospect of making a reasonable living, they carried the insurance gospel to the people in the most direct way:

> *Going in and out of six or seven million separate homes; visiting much more frequently than the clergyman, the doctor, or any official of the State nearly the whole of the working-class households of the land; bound by his calling to keep on terms of friendly intimacy with hundreds of different families, the Industrial Insurance agent has inevitably come to be a potent influence in British working-class life.*[4]

The author made it clear that, while investigations had not shown this influence to be particularly elevating, neither had it been shown to be negative or harmful. He believed that at the root of much unnecessary expense lay the fact that there were far too many agents, and he speculated about whether some amalgamation of offices might be desirable. But there was 'no indictment of Industrial Insurance agents as a class', only of the pressure for 'increase' inherent in the system, and the ills to which this pressure led.

The bulk of the report focused on the industry's traditional besetting sins: lapses, excessive cost, and what were identified as the common agents' malpractices of 'twisting' (transferring business on joining another company), special canvassers, abuses related to children's insurance, and absence of insurable interest. Lapsing was put down to the pressure for 'increase', and far worse than the financial consequences for either policyholders or the offices was said to be the damage done to working-class trust and the motivation to save.

Webb's case for removing industrial business from commercial hands rested primarily upon the unjustifiably high expense ratios generally prevalent in the industry. His point was graphically presented in the contrast between the rates of expense for ordinary assurance, at 13% of premium income, and industrial assurance at 43.9%. The trouble was that there was no other business with which industrial assurance could be compared. The cost per *transaction* was less for industrial than for ordinary business, but the total cost of *management* – commission and expenses taken together – was three times as high for industrial assurance as for ordinary, in relation to premium income:

> *The handling of 40 millions of Industrial Insurance policies, averaging £10 each, must necessarily involve a heavier ratio of expenses to premium than the handling*

of three millions of "ordinary" policies averaging £280 each. It must cost a great deal more to receive seventeen million pounds in no fewer than two thousand million minute payments, mainly in coppers, than thirty million pounds in something like forty or fifty million much larger payments, mainly in cheques.[5]

Webb affirmed that this disparity was due almost entirely to the personal house-to-house collection of premiums, the single most characteristic and essential feature of industrial assurance. As the industry had always held, it was only by such close personal attention that the vast reservoir of working-class policyholders could be led to insure at all.

From the bulk of this adverse comment the author made a point of singling out the Prudential, acknowledging that it was far ahead of its competitors in having introduced and gradually improved the terms for the granting of free policies in cases of lapse, and in the various measures it had taken to discourage lapsing. The distribution of bonus to policyholders and field staff through the profit-sharing scheme was admired. The Block System, which at the time the Report was published had been implemented in some 1,300 agencies, was expected to reduce by 10% in the near future an expense ratio that in 1915 was already the lowest of any company at 38.8%.[6]

Recognising that it had been built up through 'a prudent and skilful and extremely economical administration remarkable for its continuity', the study went on to take a closer look at the Company's history, including the evolution of its capital structure. Statistics were cited regarding its size, and its profitability to shareholders; here the author's disapproval was very clear. In his description of the industrial side of the business he expressed frank astonishment: the Company now had 'in number of policies in force and in premium income, more than half, and in accumulated funds over three-fourths, of the total for the whole kingdom'. These accumulated funds now amounted to £90,000,000, which was '... much more than is owned in any business by any British firm or joint-stock concern other than the largest railway companies, and is nearly four times as much as is possessed by any other British insurance office'. It also invested another £1,000,000 monthly '... a larger sum than any other single investor in the United Kingdom other than the Postmaster-General or the Public Trustee'.[7]

That the concentration of so much wealth in the hands of one commercial entity offended Webb's socialist principles can be understood. To acknowledge the Prudential's success in reducing the problems of industrial assurance, and then to label the system as incorrigible (having previously attributed to the Prudential the control of half of existing industrial business) nonetheless seems illogical. It is hard to resist the conclusion that before him – far larger in his reckoning than the system's faults, and infinitely more important than the Prudential's success in rectifying them – hung the vision of the accumulated wealth of the industrial assurance industry. His analysis was the prelude to a radical solution. Various alternatives to the house-to-house collecting system were proposed, based on the friendly societies, the trade unions, the Post Office, and the co-operative societies. By demolishing the case for each of them in turn, he reached – given his starting point – a predictable conclusion. Industrial assurance should not be left in the hands of 'frankly profit-making concerns, distributing dividends to their capitalist shareholders ...', but assumed by the state as a benefit to which all were entitled by right. This should be accomplished, firstly, by the inclusion of funeral benefit among those covered by the National Insurance Act 1911; and, secondly, by amplifying as far as possible the Post Office scheme and those operated by the voluntary agencies. The final measure designed to 'suppress, as socially inconvenient ... not necessarily the organisations carrying on Industrial Assurance, but that part of their work which is found detrimental to the community and which can now be more advantageously performed by other agencies ...' was outright nationalisation. The providers of industrial assurance were to be compelled to transfer all the funds relating to it to the Government, together with their obligations on existing policies. Agents, Directors and shareholders were to be compensated for their loss of emoluments, even though this might amount to a colossal sum. So as to remove any competition with a state-run system, the companies were to be forbidden to employ the collecting system for policies of less than £20. They were, in other words, to content themselves with ordinary business.[8]

None of this is to deny that abuses survived in the industry at large. Neither is it to claim that Prudential agents never stooped to 'twisting' or other dishonest tactics, the rigour of the Company's audit procedures apart. With an example before him of how the system could be made to work, Webb presumably could have recommended that the rest of the industry adopt the measures introduced over the years by the Prudential, but here he was faced with a dilemma. Great improvements had been achieved, but recommending that they be copied would merely increase the degree to which the Prudential dominated the industry, since many smaller offices could not have implemented them without serious financial difficulty. It was also an affront to his collectivist principles to concede that the Prudential's 22,000,000 industrial policyholders were a better indication of what the public actually wanted than the pathetically thin ranks of the Post Office system. A state monopoly along Post Office lines could only be viewed as a remedy for the defects of industrial assurance through the rosiest of spectacles: in 1914, after functioning for nearly 50 years, this sole example of state-operated life insurance had precisely 12,347 policyholders.[9]

Webb's study, which came to be known as the Passfield Report, had little effect until the war was over. In 1918, his 'Labour and the New Social Order', which advocated the elimination of capitalism and the nationalisation of a range of industries, was adopted by the Labour party at its Nottingham conference. In 1919, with the advent of a Coalition Government under

Lloyd George, the Chairman of the Board of Trade appointed a Departmental Committee chaired by Lord Parmoor to consider whether the deficiencies of industrial assurance outweighed its benefits and make recommendations as to the need for revised legislation. It was the first Government inquiry into industrial assurance in its own right. Sir George May gave evidence before it, together with representatives from other companies.

The Report of the Parmoor Committee was published in 1920 and made a number of recommendations.[10] These included the limitation of the expense ratio to a set percentage of premium income, the adoption of the Prudential's Block System by the other offices, elimination of the 'special canvasser' and the so-called 'procuration fees' receivable by agents on new business, and the introduction of profit-sharing schemes similar to the Prudential's by the other offices. Industrial assurance should be supervised by the Chief Registrar of Friendly Societies as well as by the Board of Trade. The Committee was also of the opinion that the hapless Post Office system should be brought to an end.

The Bill that became law as the Industrial Assurance Act 1923 was introduced early in that year by the Conservative Government that succeeded Lloyd George's administration. It incorporated the recommendations of the Parmoor Report, while tempering them with the considerations recently presented by the industrial assurance offices. Particular notice was taken of the smaller ones, which needed time to achieve the financial stability that would enable them to comply.[11]

The 1923 Act unified the regulation of both the companies and the societies providing industrial assurance under the Chief Registrar of Friendly Societies, who received the additional title of 'Industrial Assurance Commissioner' and powers to enforce the Act. While the Board of Trade continued to supervise the conduct and returns of ordinary business, the annual returns and legal matters relating to industrial assurance were henceforth to be the province of the Commissioner. Industrial assurance was made a separate class, and subject to the same deposit of £20,000 from each office transacting it, as ordinary business. Some of the Act's more important measures concerned lapses. The offices were compelled to grant free paid-up policies (though for a reduced amount) after five years' premiums, to give 28 days' notice before lapsing a policy, and to grant surrender values. Other measures related to insurable interest, with the term 'child' (strangely omitted from the permitted relationships in 1909) added to that list. The total sum assured on children's lives was raised to £6 at age three, £10 at age six, and £15 at age ten.[12] A five-year period was allowed for the implementation of the provisions regarding lapses, so that the smaller offices could build up the necessary financial cushion. The Act also did away with the Courts (Emergency Powers) Act, always a source of complaint, but particularly so since the end of the war.

The Act of 1923, with only small modifications in 1929, governed the conduct of industrial business in the interwar period. Apart from compliance with its rules about information, the Prudential had to do little that it was not already doing. At the Annual General Meeting in March 1923, Alfred Corderoy Thompson pledged the Company's support for any legislation that sought to improve the conduct of industrial assurance. A year later he observed that in its basic effects the Act merely 'extends to Industrial Assurance generally the principles which have actuated ... the conduct of our business in the past'.[13] The industry as a whole, however, had not heard the last of Lord Passfield's solution.

****

Returning to the immediate postwar period revives the subject of the three initiatives that had, even in their incomplete state, already given signs of their future importance to the Prudential's business. The first of these was the establishment on a firm footing of the General Branch, created in 1915 to transact fire, accident and aircraft personal insurance at a time when war damage looked probable. This field was already well-stocked with competitors, but it was believed that the possession of so large a force of agents would give the Prudential an edge, particularly for business where personal contact could be decisive.

Despite the expectation of a rapid influx of business once the war ended, the Company adopted a cautious approach in accepting risks and sought to build up a reserve for the Branch as quickly as possible. The changes to the Prudential's Memorandum and Articles of Association that allowed it to transact general assurance had been made in 1915. In 1919 permission was sought from the Treasury to issue the £1,000,000 of the Prudential's remaining authorised capital, in shares of £1, pro rata to existing shareholders, the nominal amount of only 2s per share to be called up. These new shares were called 'B' shares, and their owners were to receive 75% of distributable profits from the General Branch. The remaining 25% was to go to the existing, or 'A', shareholders.[14]

The first General Branch prospectus was issued in 1919, and offered to insure private homes against the risks of fire and natural disasters such as lightning, flood and earthquake. This prospectus, known as the 'GB 37', proved popular, and was followed by the 'Hearth and Home' policy, which offered, in addition to the above-mentioned cover, comprehensive protection against burglary, theft and domestic accidents. Premium income for 1919 was £92,968, and for 1920, £222,665.

The year 1921 saw the addition of foreign fire and marine insurance to domestic business, with the appointment of a Foreign Fire Superintendent. H.H. Redman's 'district' was the world, and within a few months he began the first of the tours that would result in the General Branch being represented by local agents in 16 countries. Whether individuals or companies, their essential qualification was that they be well placed to attract business. The first chosen was the firm of Blom and Van der Aa of Amsterdam, brokers, which also had connections in the Dutch East Indies. Redman found representatives in Antwerp, Hamburg and Copenhagen. Travelling around the world he appointed others in Buenos Aires, the Philippines, Shanghai, Singapore, Yokohama, Kobe, Auckland, Batavia, Cairo, Alexandria, Calcutta and Bombay, Paris, Montreal and Winnipeg. A subsidiary company, 'The Prudential Insurance Company of Great Britain', was formed to operate from New York to handle fire reinsurance

This card house advertised General Branch fire insurance by producing realistic 'flames' when the chimney-tab was pulled.

treaties in the United States.[15] To fund all this, a further 2s call was made on the 'B' shares. General Branch premium income in the very active year 1921 reached £686,299, about half of which derived from marine premiums.

After three years the growth of the General Branch, though respectable, was not felt to reflect the opportunities available. Selling general insurance through the field staff had produced rumblings of discontent at the amount of paperwork involved. The agents were paid at the end of the year for general business, as opposed to monthly or weekly for life business, and this was also disliked. The Prudential Staff Federation reported that the small number of general proposals accepted by superiors, out of the many put forward by the field staff, was felt to be discouraging.[16]

In 1922 the way of selling general insurance was revised. The country was divided into eight geographical areas, each under a District Controller (one of whom was the dynamic F.W. (Frank) Morgan, who had entered the Company as a Postal Department junior and would become General Manager, Chairman and President). These men had a motivating – almost a teaching – function, since most agents, used to sizing up every kind of physical symptom and health risk, had so little experience in evaluating risks relating to buildings, motor cars, animals and machinery. The work pertaining to the General Branch was centralised in one administrative department at Holborn Bars. Determined to become a Tariff Office, the Prudential sought election to the Fire Offices' Committee and the Accident Offices' Association. There was a concentrated effort to build up the Branch during these early years, with even the Chief Office clerical employees being asked to canvass their families for prospects.[17] Many articles on how to go about selling general insurance appeared in the recently founded *Prudential Bulletin*. The ease with which an agent could interest his existing policyholders in general insurance made it a potential source of extra income. Similarly, the process could operate in reverse. The transaction of domestic and motor insurance – and of fire and accident business – offered a chance to raise the question of life assurance.

From January 1924 Redman took on the Home Fire Department in addition to his foreign responsibilities. Abroad, the Prudential worked closely with the Liverpool and London and Globe on fire reinsurance, and with the Royal Exchange Assurance Corporation on marine underwriting. Local knowledge was essential in both types of business, as not only language, but climatic conditions, construction materials and methods, kinds of goods stored, and prevailing laws varied so widely. Unfamiliar ways of doing business also had to be taken into account. The local representatives were therefore given a good degree of discretion in accepting risks, though they had to comply with the rules of the local association under the authority of the Fire Offices' Committee in London.

The slow but promising development of the first few years gave way to less certain progress in the faltering economy of the mid-1920s. In an era of rampant unemployment, claim ratios inevitably spiralled upwards, hovering between 41% and 44%; marine assurance in particular passed through an unfavourable period. This experience showed the need for added caution in the acceptance of risks, though this precluded the desired rapid increase in premium income. The latter passed the £1,000,000 mark in 1923. No dividend was paid on the 'B' shares until 1929, all surplus being carried to reserves. By 1925, reserves had been built up to 81.8% of premium income, this having reached some £1,500,000. The purchase of a Polish life and general assurance company, the Przezornosc Assurance Company of Warsaw, was funded by the General Branch with a view to extending its business on the Continent. The underwriting agreement with the Royal Exchange Assurance was brought to an amicable end in 1927 when the Prudential decided that more detailed statistical study was the key to conducting successful marine business.[18]

Important though it was to place the General Branch on a solid footing, the latter was as yet only the junior complement to the mainstream Industrial and Ordinary Branches. Reducing expense in the life area far outweighed any other aim during the 1920s. Of the three areas from which profits might be made – improved mortality, improved return on investments, and savings in running costs – the first to aid this effort, quite apart from any action deliberately taken by the Company, was a mortality rate that declined sharply following the war and the disastrous influenza epidemic that swept Europe in 1918.

The gradual reduction in the national death rate since 1900 had of course come to an end in 1914, but it immediately began to decline again with the peace. The years 1920 and 1921 showed the lowest mortality rates yet recorded. The Prudential's experience reflected the same trend, with an Ordinary Branch death claim ratio in 1920 that was 8% lower than in 1913, its best year up to that time, and an Industrial Branch rate that was only 92% of the expected mortality under the most recent English Life Table No. 8. The decrease in the mortality of young children since 1900 was particularly noteworthy.

The postwar fall in the number of deaths may have been due in part to the generalised resistance to disease and the ravages of age that often follows war, and which is a demographic phenomenon not entirely understood. The more gradual reduction since the 1890s can be largely explained as the result of improved sanitary and living conditions.[19] Given the size of the Prudential's business, the reduction in mortality rates was of great importance. The prediction of the need for less stringent safeguards against future claims was one factor that allowed the Prudential to improve the conditions it could offer to policyholders in the years immediately following the war.

Initially, these improvements consisted of new types of policy, seen as meeting changing needs. The trend in favour of endowment assurances – a traditional mainstay of the Ordinary Branch – in the Industrial Branch, at the expense of its traditional 'funeral' policies, had been growing in line with the improvement in working-class living standards since before the turn of the century.[20] The demand was now for assurance that offered a means of saving, and that, assuming a normal lifespan, would result in the policyholder's reaping the harvest of his own thrift. The 'Progressive' policy, which combined life and endowment assurance, was launched in 1922. As an enhancement to its standard Industrial Branch policies the Prudential began to offer cheaper policies for which the premiums were payable monthly. These were more economical for both policyholder and company, and soon became a 'phenomenal success'.[21] In 1921, 41% of total Industrial Branch premium income and 77% of its new premium income came from these monthly tables. A new Industrial Branch endowment assurance carrying a fixed bonus proved attractive at a time when currency values were fluctuating. The profit-sharing scheme begun in 1907 but suspended since 1914 was restarted in 1921, and the Industrial Branch tables were recalculated to give more favourable benefits.[22]

Improved rates of mortality and the trend towards larger assurances also prompted a response in the Ordinary Branch. The Ordinary Branch tables, calculated years earlier when the average sum assured was less than £100, were recast in 1925 to reflect the growing number of assurances for £1,000 or more that the Prudential was receiving, and reissued with reduced premiums. Another innovation of the early 1920s was optional freedom from medical examination for new Ordinary Branch policyholders in favour of filling out a questionnaire. This had a particular appeal for thousands of women faced with the need to be financially independent, due to the deaths of fathers and husbands in the war. An advertising campaign for the 'Everywoman' policy, a combination life and endowment assurance, recognised that war losses had altered the traditional social patterns. The advertisements were strikingly modern in their emphasis on the need for women to take charge of their financial security and in the options available to a woman who received a capital sum at the end of her working life.[23] Women made up 25% of all new Ordinary Branch policyholders in 1920, a proportion which remained steady during the interwar years.

In contrast to the practice of many offices, the Prudential also made a point of offering assurance to under-average lives. Here was an instance where the size of the Prudential allowed it to absorb the risks that many smaller companies dared not take on. On the grounds that life assurance was fulfilling only part of its social function if its benefits were restricted to the healthy, the Company was prepared to accept proposals on men suffering the effects of wounds or gas, as well as persons with chronic illnesses, for an appropriate reduction in the sum assured.[24]

The economic instability that characterised the 1920s made this to all appearances an unpropitious time to effect major changes. The Prudential Board nonetheless chose to embark on the other innovations delayed by the war. In this the Directors were guided by Sir Joseph Burn. In him, as in Sir Henry Harben and Sir Thomas Dewey, the Prudential and the field of industrial assurance found their champion. His fervour when speaking of it was often referred to. He recognised the defects that marred its image and invited critical studies like the Passfield Report, but he was determined that the Prudential's standards should be those that shaped the industry's future.

To both the actuarial and managerial functions in the Prudential between 1920 and 1925, Burn brought breadth of experience and a freshness of approach. He often mentioned that he had entered the Prudential as a clerk in the Ordinary

One consequence of the First World War was an increase in the number of women who had to look after their own financial affairs. The 'Everywoman' policy was devised to fill this need.

HER FUTURE?

Branch at £20 a year, and that it had taken him three tries at his actuarial exams to pass them – through nerves, not lack of brainpower. Transferred to the Actuarial Department in 1895, it had taken him barely 12 years to become Frederick Schooling's deputy and then his successor when Schooling became Joint General Manager in 1911. Along the way he had worked closely with George May on investments, written two books and become completely captivated by industrial assurance, which he saw as affordable security for all, and the dignified way to break the cycle of deprivation that afflicted successive generations. He accepted that the subject was one about which there was much misunderstanding and tried to get the simplest points across in his many speeches, and later, radio broadcasts. The concept that the regular payment of small premiums over time would produce a set sum at death was easily grasped. Two other ideas were less readily understood. One was that death actually had to take place for the sum assured to be made available (apart from the possible advances made against it as short-term loans). The other was that the *certitude* that the sum would be paid at death was itself a thing of value. The weekly premium purchased both that certitude – the much extolled sense of security that assurance was said to give – and physical provision of it in the form of house-to-house collection, the agent's advice and record-keeping, and so on.

The problem that faced Burn in the 1920s was the perpetual one of how to bring down the Industrial Branch expense ratio without sacrificing the essential features of industrial assurance. Time had brought the added danger that among Labour politicians there was now considerable support for nationalisation. Burn went about trimming the Prudential's costs in two ways: through the Block System, which dramatically reduced expenditure at field staff level, and through the changeover to automated working, which revolutionised the Company's handling of data.

Burn understood that having the confidence of the staff when major changes were being introduced was not merely an advantage, but a necessity. He had the benefit of almost universal popularity, and an ability to infect others with his own enthusiasm. Being elevated to the rank of 'Sir Joseph' had made no difference to his approachability. Nor did it alter his way of life very much.[25] Open-handed in his dealings with others, he was personally frugal and continued to walk from King's Cross to Chief Office every morning, as much to save the fare as for the exercise. He had the city-born romantic's love of the countryside. At his home, a rambling farmhouse called Rydal Mount near Potters Bar, he kept bees, and enjoyed milking a cow for his children's breakfast before setting off for the Prudential.

Like Sir Henry Harben in the years when he was building up the Company, Burn spent several days each week travelling up and down the country, talking to agents about their work. (He often claimed to know everyone at Chief Office, from messengers to managers, through the annual review procedure. His frequent tours were intended to acquaint him with the field staff in much the same way.) One reason the field staff liked him was that he had the fine points of the business at his command and could explain them in language the men could understand. Moreover (as one agent put it), 'He could get up in a big place like the Memorial Hall, Farringdon Street, and in a clear and resonant voice deliver an impressive speech full of practical hints and useful arguments to his friends of the great outdoor staff.' In 1927 the *Prudential Bulletin* published an account of an agents' tour of Holborn Bars which provided a first-hand impression of Burn – then at the summit of his profession as President of the Institute of Actuaries – who, the writer concluded, 'must have felt very tired when he had shaken hands individually with the whole hundred and sixty of us'. Such gestures were typical of the man.[26]

When the Block System was first introduced in 1913, it had been greeted warily by the Prudential Staff Federation, fearful of a reduction in agents' earnings. After the war, the fear was more for the loss of jobs; in a period of rising unemployment, the PSF naturally sought to defend jobs at all costs. With the Parmoor Committee in session, Burn spent much of his time visiting the Divisions, talking to groups of 20 or 30 agents, pointing out to them the absolute necessity of reducing the expense ratio if the Industrial Branch were to survive in the long term.[27] This he did with such earnestness that any thought of 'us' and 'them' his hearers may have entertained was rapidly dispelled. On one occasion in Glasgow, feelings were running so high that he was warned not to hold a meeting because of possible violence. Catcalls and shouted interruptions died away as

Sir Joseph Burn, KBE, FRICS, FIA.

he put the case for change, and the meeting ended with a vote to adopt the Block System. He had been lecturing for years to students at the Institute of Actuaries, respected for the lucid way in which he presented complex subjects. These postwar tours were a challenge of a different sort: large and not always friendly audiences, that demanded inspiration. This they apparently got. As one Scottish agent put it, 'I never heard a speech that made me so want to be up and doing!'[28]

Burn never attempted to deny that the Block System aimed at a reduction in the size of the field staff; considering the uneconomic nature of the system it was replacing, there could hardly have been any other objective. From 20,475 agents in 1913, the numbers had fallen to 12,289 by 1924. Advantage was taken of each year's deaths, retirements, resignations and the inevitable dismissals to keep numbers down, though the Company continued to boast that no agent ever was or would be coerced into adopting the Block System. In 1923, for instance, 249 men retired, 431 resigned or were dismissed, and 60 died: a total of 740, offset by 254 new appointments, but still leaving 486 former jobs unfilled.[29]

The new system brought a few adjustments, mainly to divide clerical from field work in the middle ranks. The job titles of superintendent and agent remained the same, but that of assistant superintendent gave way to two new grades, 'superintendent's clerk' (a purely clerical office, as the name suggests) and 'divisional assistant' (an interesting development of the loved-or-hated special canvasser formerly employed and paid by the agents, but now employed and paid by the Company). Burn concentrated on making of these an in-house cadre of professional advisers, available to tackle particularly difficult cases with any agent who requested help.

While numbers were set to decrease, it was envisaged that earnings would first stabilise, and then rise. The Prudential Staff Federation ceased to protest when it became clear that the Block System was more likely to produce higher and more stable earnings than the old system. Replacing the wage based on individual combinations of 'special salary', 'commission', 'increase' and the like, was a stated salary based on the average of an agent's earnings during the previous three years, and augmented yearly.[30] The average wage was £2 5s a week in 1913; in 1925 it was £4 18s, with an increase in the average bonus to agents payable under the profit-sharing scheme of 11s a week, a considerable advance on the 2s a week of 1913.[31]

By 1921 the Block System had been instituted in 70% of Prudential agencies, and by 1922 in 89%. By 1925 almost 97% of Industrial Branch collections were being made by agents working 'blocked debits'. The figures, for a rising premium income collected by a decreasing number of outdoor staff, reveal the sweeping economies that conversion to the system had made possible.[32] While the 20,475 men of 1913 had collected £12,806,090, the 14,408 of 1922 collected £24,051,754 – in ten years, twice as much in premium income was being collected by two-thirds of the men. This had been achieved without, as the Chairman put it, 'forcibly disturbing' any agent, not even the 400 who in 1925 still resolutely clung to the roving style of running their agencies.

In Burn's view, the Prudential's business was 'only just large enough' to obtain maximum advantage from the innovation. It is obvious that the Block System would only work for companies that were already large enough to have heavy concentrations of policyholders in defined areas. Rural areas, where the inhabitants lived miles apart, were clearly not suited to it, and although there are no figures to support the theory, it is reasonable to suppose that the agents who remained outside the Block System were country-based.

Progressive reductions in the expense ratio during the 1920s (from 36.9% in 1921 to 32.1% in 1922, 29.7% in 1923, 27.8% in 1924 and 26.5% in 1925) fulfilled Burn's expectations, though his aim was eventually to reduce it to 20%. In 1924 the Board decided on an 'epoch-making event in the conduct of our business': a system of reversionary bonuses in the Industrial Branch for all policies of 15 years' duration, the bonus to become a permanent addition to the sum assured.[33] The ability to do this was explained to the Annual General Meeting as 'directly traceable to the introduction 10 years ago of the block system of collection'.[34] On the same occasion Burn prophesied that the benefits of the changeover to block working, and of reductions in the expense ratio, were far from complete.

The introduction of automated working, which went on simultaneously with that of the Block System, was the other factor in reducing expense between the end of the war and the late 1920s. Before 1918, the way of dealing with the veritable Everest of forms, registers, ledgers and cards generated by the ever-expanding industrial business had been simply to increase the number of clerks. This was in keeping with a seeming reluctance to admit new technology into the Company once the devices needed to manage the tremendous growth of the business in the 1880s and 1890s had been adopted. The system up to the First World War continued to be the manual one of copying financial details from the agents' records onto cards, and of duplicating information by hand. In the basement of Chief Office the foot-treadle numbering machine still reigned, while innovations such as the typewriter and the telephone were not in general use below principal clerk level. Actuarial calculations still depended heavily on the arithmometer. American visitors were apparently left speechless at the sight of Prudential juniors struggling to lever registers the size – and weight – of tombstones onto trolleys for nightly conveyance to the vaults. In that the vast volume of data was managed by such methods, the system could be considered efficient, but hardly economical.

Conservatism, coupled with inertia in the face of technical innovation, were attitudes that were almost characteristic of insurance companies until well into recent times. The availability of a punched-card system from 1904 – the Hollerith – apparently did not arouse any immediate interest among British insurers.[35] The exceptionally long time during which they had to keep records (for the lifetime of a policyholder, which might be 60 or 80 years), as well as the size of their operations, were factors that precluded rapid transitions from one method of record-keeping to another.

Burn was exceptional in being impressed with the Hollerith machines, which had been used in the British census of 1911.[36] His appointment as Actuary in 1912 signalled a change of approach in the Prudential. With the advent of National Insurance and the Approved Societies, the challenge of administering the latter alongside ordinary and industrial life assurance prompted interest in newer methods. Burn visited Germany with a group of officials from the

National Health Insurance Committee in 1913 to attend a demonstration of the punched-card machines invented by the American James Powers. The Prudential's lease of these machines from the Powers Accounting Machine Company of America (the large order of 40 card punches, 7 tabulators and 7 sorters mentioned in the previous chapter) meant that from 1915, the large, discrete task of administering the Approved Societies was being carried out by automated means.

The application of the Powers system to the Prudential's main business was the obvious next step, except for the fact that the country was at war, and at the time, such a large investment, sweeping away time-honoured methods that required little training, may not have seemed the prudent course. After the war, with the machines still only being leased from the Powers Company of America, two considerations shaped the somewhat radical management decision taken. One was that the machines required adaptation if they were to be of maximum use in dealing with insurance records. The other was the need for a reliable supply of the machines at a stable cost if the Prudential were to make the transition from manual to mechanised record-keeping. Rather than be dependent on a far-off source for such essential machines, Burn urged the Board to *become* the source. In 1919 he negotiated the British and Empire rights to manufacture Powers machines, and was appointed Chairman of the British Powers Company, subsequently formed to do so.[37]

In the following year the Prudential invested £150,000 in a Powers manufacturing facility at Croydon. The aim at first was to produce machines for its own requirements, but as Burn explained in 1923, the time and money expended in adapting the machines was gradually being recouped through rentals and sales to other commercial entities, often other insurance companies. The British Powers Company had by then gained fully half of the British market for punched-card systems. The Wesleyan and General Assurance Company, the first industrial assurer to buy the system through the Prudential, became its agent for the sale of Powers machines in the north of England.[38]

The transfer to mechanised working in the Industrial, Ordinary and General Branches took place between 1921 and 1928. Instrumental in adapting the machines for the task was E.J.W. Borrajo, who had worked closely with Burn on the National War Savings Committee and in the Prudential's Statistical Department. The Company's punched-card technology consisted of 100 punches, 24 sorters and 35 tabulators in 1923; in 1928 it had 170 punches, reputedly the largest automated system in existence. All actuarial figures used in the valuations were tabulated by the machines at an early stage, saving innumerable human hours. In the Industrial Branch the process of transferring records was known as the 'Decentralisation Plan' and was only effected in districts that had completely gone over to the Block System. The actual process of conveying the policy details held on the millions of handwritten cards (some produced as long ago as the 1870s when they had begun to replace the original ledger-based system) to the punched cards was done by a battalion of more than 100 clerks at a rate of 90,000 policy-cards per week – a quantity equivalent to three average-sized districts.[39]

Under the Decentralisation Plan, some of the work of agency administration that had until now been carried out at Chief Office was shifted outwards to district offices, of which there would eventually be some 200, each created to serve one or more districts. The machines had been adapted to be capable of printing various kinds of documents. A new collecting book, even for the largest debit, could be printed by machine in less than two hours. Valuable space was saved at Holborn Bars: so much that the extra storey added to the Brooke Street block to meet the postwar pressure on space was no sooner finished than it was found to be unnecessary. Devolving much record-keeping to the districts also reduced correspondence between agents and Chief Office, and machine-checking at district level caught and rectified more errors at source. The total number of clerks employed at Holborn Bars stood at 2,662 at the end of 1923, when Industrial Branch policies numbered 24,000,000 and Ordinary Branch about a million. There were also 271 district clerks. One group of observers considered this a relatively small number of employees, and accounted for it by mentioning that the Prudential seemed to have fewer transfers for its size than other companies, and that 40% of its Industrial Branch business was of the 'Monthly Premium' type. It also claimed that Prudential clerks demonstrated 'greater application to their work' and smaller turnover than those of the other big offices.[40]

These may have been factors in keeping numbers down, but the real cause was surely the use of the Powers machines. The 2,662 Chief Office employees at the end of 1923 included Approved Society staff; in 1915 the comparable inclusive figure had been 4,750. Sir Joseph Burn considered in 1926 that there were still 'far too many clerks', and noted that women were gradually replacing men. By 1927, as the agents who attended a conference at Chief Office were shown, the machines 'were being used for every possible purpose, everything was methodical through and through'. The old methods had been replaced by 'the delicate accuracy of the Powers machines', which were 'truly incredibly wonderful, sorting registration cards at 2,000 per hour, printing absolutely exactly the leaves for agents' ledgers, totalling same and giving every desired information at once and far more accurately than a full office staff would do in a full week's work'.

Not only were they much faster, but they were capable of '… actually ejecting any faulty registration card – and carrying on with the correct ones. The system evolved of registering the details of proposals by holes stamped in cards has indeed practically eliminated the human factor and the consequent errors in the Chief Office records'.[41]

By improving the quality of work done, the machines reduced the need for the repetitive checking that had always been such a feature of the clerical departments in the Prudential. One needs only to recall the descriptions of past valuations to see the impact of mechanisation.[42]

Machines that could handle such a volume of data obviously depended on a ready supply of cards and forms. The Prudential had always had an in-house printing department, but simultaneously with the greatly increased capacity offered by the Powers machines, this hitherto unsung facility came into its own. The 'Multigraph' printing machine was producing an average of 100,000 official forms a day in 1927, in as wide a variety of typefaces and paper sizes as anything the commercial printing trade could offer. A single page could be run off at a rate of 7,000 copies an hour and needed no drying; by running the machines 12 hours a day the entire quota of over a million Annual Bonus cards could be printed in less than a fortnight. Self-sufficiency was essential if real savings in time and money were to be made. The strain on the machines resulting from operating at this rate was reduced by skilled maintenance, and 'spare parts are made and running repairs executed without recourse to any outside help'. By the late 1920s the Printing Department was producing all the Prudential's forms, agents' requisites and literature. Particularly welcome was an attachment to the composing machine that reproduced signatures all but indistinguishable from those done by hand.[43]

Another innovation, heralded as 'Our New Ally in the Economy Campaign' was the photographic copier, or 'Photostat', of which the Prudential in 1927 was employing what was believed to be the only example in Europe.[44] The machine used mercury vapour lamps to highlight the photographing of documents directly onto sensitised paper, which then passed through a 30-second developing bath, a rinse and a drying process to produce negative images in a matter of minutes. A positive image was made by photostating a negative one. The applications of the machine were manifold: copies of documents could be made in 'a fraction of the time previously expended in laborious copying; while estate plans, superintendents' area maps and agents' block maps are but items in the list of Photostat possibilities'. But it was in the copying of figures that its greatest usefulness lay: 'Expense ratio sheets, great masses of figures, can be reproduced in one hour or less, where eighty hours of the most expeditious hand-copying were required before. Returns of all descriptions can be copied in a fraction of the time normally taken.' The saving in time and tedium brought about by devices such as the 'Multigraph' and the 'Photostat' changed the face of many clerical jobs, and in the long run contributed to reducing their number.

****

By 1925, with a Conservative Government again in power and the new Industrial Assurance Act in force, a more hopeful outlook seemed justified for the first time since the onset of the postwar depression. The Prudential had obtained a Stock Exchange quotation in September 1924 and there was a healthy demand for the 'A' and 'B' shares that found their way on to the market. At the same time, changes were made in the Articles of Association to allow the alteration of the profit-sharing scheme introduced in 1907. Once the sum of dividend and bonus reached a certain amount per share, the proportion of surplus allocated to the shareholders and field staff was to be reduced in favour of the Industrial Branch policyholders. In 1924, when the Prudential's total income reached a new high of £35,136,037, some £2,097,737 of surplus was allocated to the policyholders of the Industrial Branch, with shareholders and field staff each receiving £440,945. From 1925, reversionary bonuses on future Industrial Branch claims were increased (the period for which premiums had been paid being at the same time reduced from 15 to 10 years) from £1 5s to £1 10s per £100 assured, thus making Industrial Branch policies yet more attractive.

Unemployment was still extremely high and small-scale strikes common, both of which had challenged the Prudential to find ways of dealing with the increased rate of lapsing that went hand-in-hand with economic distress. As usual, the period allowed before policies were regarded as lapsed was lengthened for people in areas badly affected by stoppages or unemployment, or else they were allowed to restart their assurances and gradually make up their arrears once they were again in work. The measures adopted in 1926 to deal with lapsing in the aftermath of the General Strike were more novel, and showed the practical value of the bonus as a buffer against lapse. On 13 May, when the TUC had decided to end the strike, leaving the miners to continue, Burn impressed upon the field staff in an open letter the importance of keeping industrial business in force and as free from arrears as possible. The period beyond which policies were deemed to have lapsed was temporarily extended with the aim of 'reviving' rather than 're-entering' the endangered business. For policyholders affected by the miners' strike, which went on almost until the end of 1926, lapse notices were suspended and the concessions of setting arrears against reversionary bonus and, in the cases of without-profits policies, against the sum assured, were offered.[45] As alternatives to these, agents were instructed to make sure their policyholders knew about free policies, cash surrender values or immediate benefit upon re-entry, as appropriate. The mining districts, where continuing unemployment rendered many people unable to pay current contributions, were recognised as areas of particular hardship and concessions were extended on the advice of the inspectors.

Throughout the 1920s there was a noticeable emphasis, in any communication from Chief Office to the field staff, on the need for their continuing professional development. Once the Block System was fully operational, the Company got to work on bettering the standard of the trained field force, so as to mine each square mile of the British Isles. Young men coming into the field from school now served a probationary stage as 'apprentice agents', the length of which depended on age and the report of superiors; men coming in from other professions served 12 months' probation. To the whole field staff, a steady current of what can only be described as teaching literature flowed outwards from Holborn Bars. This was intended to increase the agents' knowledge of assurance law, imbue them with confidence in the value of their profession, and increase their practical and tactical skills. Agents' conferences were held regularly, affording the men of a particular division a chance to visit Chief Office and attend a series of talks on current topics given by the key men in the Company. Similarly, Sir Joseph Burn made periodic tours lasting several days to each of the divisions, in which he visited each office and the agents on their home ground. He was usually accompanied by his wife Emily, for whom some social programme was devised that involved the agents' wives. A favourite theme when he addressed the field staff was the raising of debits across the board by 10% or 20%. All of this was intended to increase the sense of belonging to a vast and far-flung but very unified family, and to engender responsibility and pride in being a Prudential representative.

Poster advertising carried the Prudential's message into every home.

In the mid-1920s, too, the Company began to advertise regularly in a wide array of papers and magazines. The emphasis was often now on the savings mechanism, in addition to the protection, afforded by Prudential policies. Following the success of a Prudential kiosk at the British Empire Exhibition in 1924, a Publicity Department was formed at Chief Office in February 1926, and systematically set about positioning the Company in the minds of the half of the population as yet uninsured. On occasion the Company would take an entire page in one of the dailies (as on 5 January 1928, when it took the entire front page of the *Daily Mail*) and enlist the help of the whole staff in drawing it to the attention of acquaintances. From *Blackwood's Magazine* to the *Jewish Chronicle*, from *Home Chat* and the *Daily Sketch* to *Athletic News* and *The Chemist and Druggist*, the Prudential reiterated the message that everyone could benefit from an assurance policy. If on occasion the message seemed out of keeping with the theme of the journal in question ('In each issue of *The Cinema* in which our advertisement appears there will be an editorial dealing with General Branch insurances', the *Prudential Bulletin* advised the staff), on others it was co-ordinated to perfection, with Prudential advertisements featuring 'A Talk with Mr Prudence' appearing in the *Radio Times* in the weeks that Sir Joseph Burn gave short talks on insurance from 2LO. (These broadcasts elicited numerous delighted letters from agents, prompted to write by the marvel of having heard Burn's voice over the airwaves.) This use of radio and advertising to educate the public further impressed upon the agent and the Chief Office clerk the responsibility of being better-informed.

The kind of professional support the agents received had no real counterpart at Holborn Bars, although the clerical staff also received circulars from the General Manager. These promoted education in assurance as a priority for men and women alike, so as to give better service to the public, but young clerks wishing to improve their prospects through formal training had to organise and fund it themselves. With the establishment of a Valuation Department in 1923 and the growth of the investment and pension areas as offshoots of the Secretary's and Actuary's offices respectively, the Company needed more qualified young men.

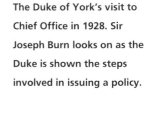

The Duke of York's visit to Chief Office in 1928. Sir Joseph Burn looks on as the Duke is shown the steps involved in issuing a policy.

Those best motivated, who perhaps had shone at mathematics at school but who could not afford to go to university, came to the Prudential as the next best option – not that with such high unemployment there were many options for most boys – intending to qualify as actuaries. The Institute of Actuaries courses had to be attended in the evenings, though candidates were given time off work to sit the exams. It was not until 1931 that the Company began to recognise success in the exams with an increase in salary.

One aspect of the Prudential's corporate life which has so far gone unmentioned is that of donations. The Company followed the example set by the Harbens, Dewey and Lancaster in supporting a variety of educational, medical and social causes outside the Company. There were, of course, privileges for Prudential staff attached to some of them, such as free beds at the Rustington Convalescent Home, as well as the Horne and Dewey Trusts that were specifically for Prudential employees. In 1923 Mary Wharrie added to these with the creation of the Wharrie Trust, for divisional and district office staff, and in 1930 Guy Philip Harben set up the Harben Trust for retired employees and their dependants.

Giving on the part of the Company, as opposed to individual members of it, had begun in the Great War, but in its aftermath, continued along broader lines. An adjustment to the payment of health-related benefits to members of the Approved Societies resulted in the donation of many hospital beds, cots for children and medical equipment. By 1930, 268 beds and 425 cots had been supplied and over £300,000 given to hospitals and laboratories. The Company did not publicise these donations, although gifts to other organisations usually attracted the local press. Such an occasion was the launch of the *Prudential*, given to the Ramsgate Branch of the Royal National Lifeboat Institution in April 1926. Both the Company and the RNLI were justifiably proud of the boat, which was built to the highest standards and possessed an engine that would function even when totally submerged.

****

Before leaving the 1920s, it would be well to touch on two further areas of activity, in both of which Sir Joseph Burn played a major part. These were the beginnings of the Prudential's life business abroad, the further development of which will be discussed in a later chapter, and the origins of its pensions business.

Following the setting up of the chain of agencies to transact general business around the world, there was a period of several years during which the Prudential Board considered the merits of extending the life business beyond the United Kingdom. The considerations behind the decision to do so were quite different from the simple motive of entering fresh markets upon which the earlier decision was based. Burn summed them up in a paper which he presented to his colleagues, probably in 1925, in which he urged them to consider the probable future of the Company's industrial life business.[46]

Trying to envisage the future from current trends, he predicted that 'an increasing proportion of the working classes of this country will be forced to emigrate to the Colonies'. In the first instance, this would be to Canada, where he predicted that 'a large number of people will be resident ... who otherwise would have been Prudential Policyholders and resident in this country'. Leaving them with no office and no personal attention in the new country was to leave them ill-served, and to miss the most obvious of business opportunities. Burn held that the Prudential had already forfeited much ground by having up to then refused to consider transacting life business abroad.[47] He also believed that the prevailing social climate made it likely that the danger of Government interference in the field of industrial assurance – the spectre of nationalisation – was far from diminished. For this reason too, venturing overseas was attractive, since 'The more our total business can be spread beyond the direct supervision of our own Government the more difficult will become the task of Government absorption'.[48]

Burn did not consider that commencing industrial life business, in Canada or in any other country, would necessarily be easy, and suggested that initially, ordinary business be sought, to be followed by a drive for industrial business where conditions seemed favourable. The first foreign representative offering ordinary assurance abroad in fact already existed, in the form of Messrs. Gillanders, Arbuthnot and Co. of Calcutta, initially engaged in 1923. It was recognised that conditions in India differed dramatically from those in Canada, but Burn nonetheless thought it worth reminding the Directors that the Prudential already had the legal power to undertake life business overseas. The question of how it should be financed should not be allowed to delay taking a decision on whether doing so would be of advantage to the Company.

The decision was not in fact made for another four years. In November 1929 an Extraordinary General Meeting was called to propose the creation of 250,000 'B' shares of £1, mainly for the purpose of embarking on overseas life business.[49] Ordinary business in India and Ceylon had by then been transferred to a Head Office in Calcutta, which had operated satisfactorily for over a year under Frank Morgan. On the face of it the moment chosen to begin overseas was hardly auspicious, but it was felt that at a time of such financial uncertainty, especially in North America and in the Empire, people would choose the security of a known British company over any other.

The Prudential's highly important involvement with pension management grew out of its pension arrangements with its own staff. From 1897 and the establishment of the contributory Staff Provident Fund, the question of providing for employees' old age had been put on a more formal basis, though ex-gratia retirement gifts continued to be made out of current revenue. According to Burn, recounting the Prudential's experience in 1923, the next step was prompted by his own valuation, to satisfy his curiosity, of the liability involved in providing pensions under the Staff Provident Fund. He had been astonished to discover that it amounted to £16,000,000. Burn maintained that pensions were simply deferred salaries, and were something that employees should be able to count on, and companies to promise. Putting this into practice clearly required more comprehensive planning than had prevailed until then. The Staff Pension Scheme for all those with 20 years' service or more was set up as the war was ending in 1918 to provide pensions at age 60 for men and 55 for women.[50]

Somewhat later, in the aftermath of the General Strike, came the influence of the first 'Group' employers' liability insurance made available through the General Branch. The Prudential first advertised this kind of insurance early in 1927 as a means of fostering good working relations between employers and their employees. It was but a short step to combine the provision of tailor-made group insurance schemes with the experience of managing the pension fund built up within the Prudential itself, to produce a capability for devising group pension plans for other organisations. The Prudential's Ordinary Branch was actively seeking group pension business by 1929, having set up a department under the Actuary's office to handle it. How this business fared will form the subject of a later chapter.

During the 1920s the Prudential embarked on a virtual revolution in methods, and branched out, firstly, into activities adjacent to the long-standing ones of ordinary and industrial business, and secondly, into new geographical areas. General, overseas and pension business, not to mention the increasingly important area of investment, would all be intensively developed during the next decade.

Sir William Lancaster, JP, FIA.

In his last year as President, Sir Thomas Dewey recounted to a journalist his memories of the Ludgate Hill offices in 1857 and of how, as a very junior clerk, he had been sent out, in a horse-drawn cab, by Henry Harben to round up shareholders for the Annual General Meeting. The Prudential's income from all sources was then less than £5,000. At Dewey's death at the age of 86 in July 1926, income from all sources was £38,621,753 and total assets stood at £185,140,143. Dewey was one of the last few men whose personal histories had been inextricably entwined with that of the Company since its first decade, another being his close friend for nearly 70 years, Sir William Lancaster, who died in February 1929 aged 88. Both had remained lucid in mind and intensely interested in the changing assurance scene to the end of their extraordinarily long careers: 69 years in the case of Dewey, counting his term as President, and 62 in that of Lancaster. Only Frederick Schooling was to match Dewey's years at Holborn Bars.

One consequence of long service, so much more common in an earlier age, was that everyone who came into a company at roughly the same time tended to retire or die at the same time. This was what occurred in the Prudential at the end of the 1920s. The Chairman, Alfred Corderoy Thompson, died in office at the age of 70 in November 1928. Another three Directors died in the next 14 months: Sir John Paget Mellor, KCB (who had come onto the Board in 1923), and Daniel Wintringham Stable early in 1929, and James Moon, the first member of the field staff to become a Director, in 1930. So many departures in such a short time reinforced the feeling within the Company that an era was passing, and the pace of events quickening, as the decade drew to a close.[51]

The Prudential Overseas

THE countries of the Empire that had been largely settled by British emigrants, where British troops were stationed and Prudential general business was already being transacted, were the obvious ones for the extension overseas of Prudential ordinary life business. Between 1929 and 1934 life branches were established in the major countries of the 'old commmonwealth', following investigative tours by Chief Office management. Generally speaking, the Prudential was a complete outsider to these markets, initially in the position of a gleaner where other, longer established foreign companies had already sown and reaped.

In only one did it have prior experience. This was in India, where, almost as an experiment, and coinciding with beginning the sale of general insurance there in 1923, the Prudential had given a life agency to Messrs. Gillanders, Arbuthnot and Co. of Calcutta. The first Prudential life policy written outside Britain was issued in March 1924: a £2,000 policy on the owner of a tea plantation in Assam. No market is easy to break into; India less so than many. In each of the agency's first few years the life policies sold could be numbered on the fingers of one hand. The British and European expatriate community formed the first client base for the Prudential. Even among the expatriates, there were some who viewed the Company only as the purveyor of industrial assurance to the British lower orders. Otherwise the Prudential name was unknown in India, and its true position in Britain had to be explained to every new contact made.

The population of the Indian subcontinent in the mid-1920s was about 330,000,000. The percentage of those for whom insurance was economically feasible, calculated at between 10,000,000 and 12,000,000, was infinitesimal compared with the overwhelming majority living in poverty for whom it was not.[1] The country presented a challenging panorama, with living conditions and climate as additional factors to be taken into account. Even among the Hindu professional and merchant classes, the mortality rate from disease and childbirth was far higher than in Britain, making it necessary to devise special tables for the native population. The opposition of Muslims to anything in which the element of chance plays a part, ruled out assurance for all but the wealthiest and best educated section of that community. The smaller religious denominations – Sikhs, Parsees and others – were on the whole more approachable.

It was soon concluded that with time, perseverance on the part of British staff might generate much business, but that what was needed quickly was new business among selected Indian lives in the provincial centres. Calcutta's geographical location, climate and culture left much to be desired. Finding sound medical referees was essential and, given the multiplicity of the subcontinent's

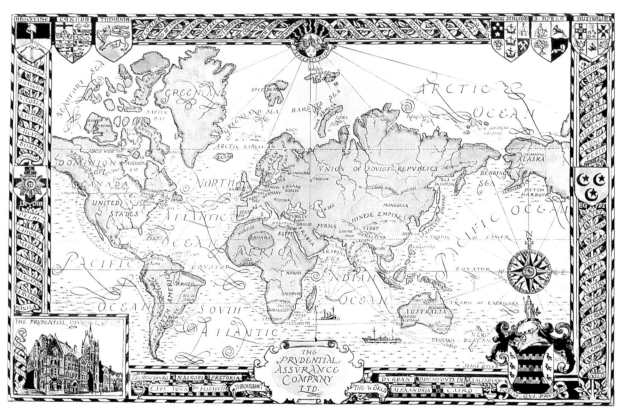

By 1934 the Prudential had offices or agencies in numerous countries.

languages and religions, only a trained, native-born field staff would do. To this end, C.F. Warren was sent from Holborn Bars to tour northern India in 1927. Agents were engaged and the first Superintendent appointed; his area covered Kashmir, the Punjab and the provinces of the North-West Frontier, and contained 30,000,000 inhabitants! He was instructed to create an agency force that drew upon the predominant religious communities. This strategy brought an almost instant explosion of business, with sums assured in the last half of 1927 exceeding £500,000.[2]

In the following year, F.W. (Frank) Morgan, as Manager for India, Burma and Ceylon, planned a programme of expansion, dividing the subcontinent into nine districts. These included Burma and Ceylon; outposts in East Africa and Malaya were also established, to be administered from the Indian branch's Head

Office in Calcutta. Over £1,000,000 of new business was written in 1929, and the total sums assured reached £1,750,000. Sir Joseph Burn took in Malaya, Ceylon and India on one of his tours abroad in 1931.

The Indian Branch of a British company was obviously not immune to the political forces at work in the late 1920s and the 1930s. Competition with Indian companies, which were steadily increasing in number, took on an added edge as the civil disobedience campaign gathered momentum. By the early 1930s, however, the Prudential had gained a reasonable footing. There were Branch Offices in Madras, Bombay, Jaipur and Delhi, another in Colombo, and a chain of inspectors and superintendents that oversaw an agency force several hundred strong.[3] Forms and literature were produced in more than a dozen languages and the company name became well known in the great urban centres. Only senior posts, such as those of the Manager, Assistant Manager and Actuary, were filled by men from Chief Office; the rest were filled locally, as far as possible by Indians, and as far as possible by graduates. In 1935, 11 years after Prudential life business was first written in India, the total of 24,990 policies for India, Burma and Ceylon assured a total sum of just over £5,000,000 and produced premium income of £286,938.

These figures, however, say nothing of market share, which was falling as anti-British feeling mounted in the late 1930s; only about a quarter of Indian

BALLARD PIER,
BOMBAY.
JANUARY 31st, 1931.

Mr. S. C. DARBY, Mrs. F. W. MORGAN, Lady. BURN, Sir JOSEPH BURN, Mr. F. W. MORGAN, Mr. J. R. I.

Sir Joseph and Lady Burn toured Prudential outposts in Asia in 1931, meeting expatriate and native staff, as in this visit to Bombay.

The interior of the Calcutta
office in the mid-1930s.

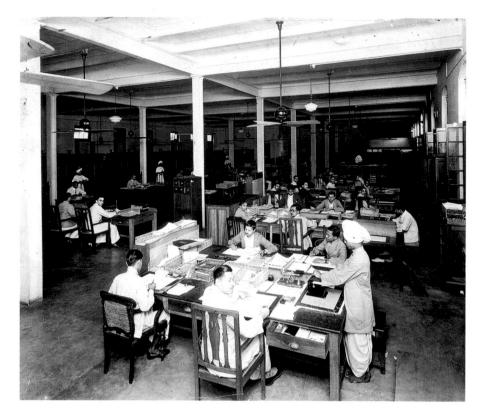

business was by then being transacted by British and foreign companies, and of this the Prudential had approximately one-eighth.[4] Rates calculated especially for the subcontinent, together with the careful selection of lives, kept claims within bounds, but the business was always exposed to the effects of tropical epidemics and natural disasters. Floods and famine in Bengal periodically killed massive numbers and the Quetta earthquake of 1935 left thousands dead and homeless.[5]

The point when the Indian life business turned a corner and began to repay the effort invested in it had almost coincided with the decision taken at Holborn Bars to develop life business abroad. The £250,000 of additional capital raised in 1929 to support expansion overseas, discussed in the previous chapter, funded the exploratory visits made to Egypt, Canada, Australia, New Zealand and South Africa. In Egypt, and in Malaya, investigated from Calcutta, the captive market consisted of British army personnel, and of expatriates, for the most part prosperous, residing in well-defined areas. For the men sent out from Chief Office (usually for four-year postings, but later on, three of these, a total of 12 years, became the complement), long days in the office were balanced by evenings of tennis, bridge or swimming at one of the social or sporting clubs, and by travel around the branch offices. Every four years men abroad were allowed a six-month furlough, with a first-class return voyage home by P&O.

In the 1930s, the Calcutta office was located in the building owned by general business agents Gillanders, Arbuthnot and Co.; there was no air-conditioning, and at certain times of the year concentration was severely strained by heat and humidity. Not until 1953 did the Prudential acquire its own premises, when it built a block called Walston Mansions; the office by then had 180 clerical staff, with living quarters above for the Chief Office staff. Business and social circles coincided to a greater degree than in England. Frank Morgan considered it absolutely necessary that the Prudential's representatives belong to the leading clubs. Each man sent out could choose three and have his subscriptions paid by the Company. Some of these were restricted to Europeans, others to professional and better-off Indians as well as expatriates. For a young man in such surroundings, life could be highly enjoyable. Chief Office held the reins, but loosely, so decisions referred to London would often be referred back again, to the judgment of the men on the spot. Professional challenge, independence, a ready-made community, and the stimulus of the country itself were each in their way satisfying. Only management's insistence (emanating from Sir Joseph Burn and the Board) that a man could not marry until he had reached a grade that carried an adequate salary, might cause a ripple of resentment.

In contrast to India were the 'white dominions', where the business potential of fast-growing, largely British populations outweighed the high cost of servicing such huge undeveloped areas, and the formidable competition from native and long-resident foreign companies. It also outweighed the effects of the New York Stock Market crash of October 1929. The Prudential's plans were already well advanced by the time this occurred. From London, the long-term repercussions of the crash were impossible to gauge, but the idea of making the Prudential 'indigestible' to any future government inclined to nationalisation acted as a spur to action, and the plans were put into effect all the same.[6]

The English-speaking dominions of Canada, Australia, New Zealand and South Africa differed greatly in geography, climate and customs, but shared a number of underlying characteristics. All of them had comparatively small populations, clustered in widely separated towns or spread thinly over large tracts of land, much of which still lacked communications. With economies that were still based on agriculture and raw materials rather than on manufacturing, their societies were more rural than urban. Each had a high proportion of British immigrant settlers, many of whom carried Prudential industrial policies and regularly remitted their premiums to London. The Prudential's fortunes in each country were greatly influenced by these conditions, though the distinctive cultural features of each country also came to stamp the conduct of business. How diverse this conduct became forms one of the more interesting aspects of the Company's history between the wars.

By the time life business was begun in Canada in 1930, a General Branch was already well established. On his global tour in 1923, H.H. Redman had chosen Montreal, a city that united Canada's major cultures, as the site of the

Canadian Head Office. He engaged a Fire Manager, Kenneth Thom, who in turn appointed local representatives in Halifax, other cities in Quebec and Ontario, and Winnipeg, covering western Canada. Brokers were later engaged in New Brunswick, Prince Edward Island and British Columbia, and in the then independent colony of Newfoundland. From the beginning the Prudential in Canada operated as a tariff or 'board' company, joining the various provincial underwriting associations formed to regulate insurance rates and practice. Fire insurance was the only line undertaken until 1928, but following Sir Joseph Burn's tour of the country in that year, vehicle and casualty insurance began to be offered.[7]

Canada was the only country in which the existence of two 'Prudentials', British and American, might have confused the man in the street. To signal its identity clearly, the Prudential distinguished itself from the start as 'The Prudential of England'. Although in the 1920s it was not yet competing with its American namesake for life business, British life policyholders began to come forward almost as soon as the branch opened, hoping to pay premiums locally rather than by post to London. This bore out Sir Joseph Burn's view that life operations in Canada would find a ready market. During these early years agents found much general and ordinary business among the holders of industrial policies, who were generally better off in Canada than they had been in Britain.

Then as now, Canada shared the economic fortunes of its vast neighbour to the south. When F.C. Capon and C.C.H. Drake arrived in Canada from London in February 1930, they found the prevailing mood one of disillusion with investment and the abrupt end of the boom years of the 1920s. This seemed likely to work to the advantage of life assurance companies – to which, in the current financial maelstrom, people looked for security – and to the double advantage of the Prudential, which had the benefit of being regarded as a cornerstone of the Empire.

At the same time, it was recognised that to build on these advantages, the Prudential had to offer products that reflected Canadian social and economic realities. One such reality was the sheer prosperity of the country: average personal wealth and earnings were far higher than in Britain and there was as yet far less unemployment.[8] In principle, practically every wage-earner in Canada could afford ordinary assurance; there was no massive underclass living in poverty, as in the United Kingdom.[9] In positioning the Life Branch in the Canadian arena, the Prudential therefore emphasised products aimed at the middle to upper end of the market, with ordinary assurance, group assurance and annuities. There was no thought of undertaking industrial business at this stage, though several Canadian companies were transacting it.

Space for both Head Office and local branch office was taken in central Montreal, though in separate premises from the General Branch office, and all speed was made to engage agents who were highly motivated and needed a minimum of supervision. Some of these came to the branch through channels that in London would have been considered unorthodox. Two such instances became famous in the annals of the Prudential in Canada. The first was a taxi-driver, James Bellin, who in the course of a fare so impressed a Prudential manager that he was offered a job as an agent. Bellin proved so successful at selling that he went on to found his own insurance company. The other was Paul Audet, one of the most prominent men in Canadian insurance after the Second World War, but in 1931 a 22-year-old McGill graduate who literally talked his way into being appointed Manager of the Quebec branch office. The insurance field in Canada was one in which the rules were still in the making.[10]

In addressing Canadian conditions, rather than seeking merely to transplant the British model, the influence of American terminology and procedure on Canadian practice was recognised: 'with-profits' and 'without-profits' became 'participating' and 'non-participating' policies; 'bonus' became 'dividend' and 'reversionary bonuses' became 'bonus additions'. The popularity of life assurance over endowment in Canada reflected the needs of a society with a high proportion of young families. By devising a plan that combined whole life and term assurance to give maximum coverage during the period of greatest earnings and family responsibility, the Canadian branch was able to offer something new at a time when other offices were cutting back. Canada's Family Income Policy introduced in 1931 predated its British equivalent, the Heritage Policy, by several months. On occasion, the Prudential's British practice was promoted as an improvement on the products offered locally. The usual means of distributing bonus, or 'dividend', for example, was as a cash payout or as a reduction of premium; the Prudential stressed the importance of adding dividend to the sum assured, to increase the amount payable in the event of a claim. 'Bonus additions' became a selling point for Prudential agents, and within a few years became so popular that fully 90% of policyholders chose them as a way of receiving dividend.

The growth of the life business during the early 1930s was reasonably steady, with about $500,000 of premium income by 1934, despite the depression which by then was affecting Canada severely. Branch offices were opened in Toronto and other centres in Ontario and Quebec, and a new headquarters in Montreal – still only rented premises – housed both general and life administrations. The Quebec City office was the first to operate in an entirely French-speaking milieu. As a British company operating in French Canada, the Prudential's policy was to engage French-speaking agents, to provide literature and policies in French as well as English, and to reply in French to correspondence written in that language. This contributed to the Company's eventual strength in the region.

In 1935 Frank Morgan came from Holborn Bars on the first of a series of tours of the Canadian Life Branch offices. As a result of his recommendations following the first tour, a programme of expansion was undertaken and a number of new offices opened in Ontario, Quebec and the Maritime provinces. Even by the time of his second visit in 1939, the entire life operation was still minute by Chief Office standards. Staff numbered only 143 (11 administrative and 132 field staff), the year's premium income was just over $1,000,000, and sums assured stood at about $31,000,000.[11]

During this developmental stage, Chief Office in London exercised tight control over all operations overseas. The Life Branch Manager and the General Branch Manager reported separately to London, so that the responsibility for Canadian business reposed in the hands of no single individual. While the day-to-day running was left to the local management, detailed reporting in such areas as personnel, actuarial and underwriting was regularly sent back to London. For the first ten or fifteen years, senior posts were invariably filled by British appointees sent out from Holborn. Professional insurance men born and educated in Britain were also sought; the Canadian branch's first actuary was Arthur Pedoe, who had already worked in Canada for another leading firm. The first relaxation of this attitude came in 1944, in the middle of the Second World War, with the appointment of Hartley McNairn, a Canadian, as General Manager for Canada. The Life Branch by then had 25,800 policies, over $62,000,000 assured and an annual premium income of $2,000,000.[12]

By the time life business began in Australia, the Prudential was represented by General Branch offices in all six states. Late in 1929 three managers – G.J.M. Best, C.F. Warren and F. Foskey – were sent from London to explore the possibilities for life business in Australia and New Zealand. As in Canada, once the Life Branch began to advertise – in the *Sydney Morning Herald*, in whose building the Prudential took an office in 1930 – policyholders who were remitting their premiums to London quickly came forward, providing a foundation for new business.[13] Between 1930 and 1933, a Head Office was established in Sydney under Warren and Best, with L.W. Offord as Actuary. Ordinary Branch offices were opened in Sydney, Melbourne, Adelaide and Perth, and a sub-branch in Auckland, New Zealand. Conditions and methods differed widely from state to state, but in general could not have been more dissimilar from those prevailing in Britain. Branch and agency structures had to be established from scratch and a field staff created from untrained men. There was no pool of experience on which to draw, little understanding of the way insurance worked or of the need for it, rather as in the England of 60 years earlier. Nonetheless, headway was made. A branch office opened in Hobart, Tasmania, in 1934, and, with the removal of a Queensland Government restriction on foreign companies, in Brisbane in the same year. By then, sums assured by the Prudential in Australia totalled more than £3,000,000. By 1939, life policies in force numbered some 25,000, assuring about £10,700,000. A new, 15-storey office block was built in Martin Place in the heart of Sydney to house the Head Office for Australia.

In these early years, most supervisors and managers came to the Prudential from other companies. One of these was E.D. (Ted) Smout, an avowed business-getter, longing for more independence than his previous employment allowed. Appointed as Agency Manager for South Queensland, he was charged with putting the Company on the map in that as yet untested territory. He chose his first half-dozen men for character, not experience, since there was so little of that; one was a teacher, one a sales manager, two were accountants ... 'They knew nothing about insurance, but they were extroverts, good honest people, fair people, all married with responsibilities. Anxious to make money and I was confident of being able to show them how to do it.'

With his immediate superior, who had experience of industrial assurance but not of ordinary, Smout developed a relationship that turned all the hierarchical assumptions of the business in the old country upside down. The pair tacitly adopted the activities that best suited themselves. The other man took on the office, leaving Smout 'to hire and fire and train, without reference to him'. The men he chose were 'goers', so much so that in 1938, when the then Manager G.J.M. Best came up from Sydney on a tour of inspection, he was astonished at how much business was being done. There was none of the deference that would have set the tone of the meeting in England. Ted Smout recalled a conversation along these lines: 'He said, "Don't you think you should slow down – it's time to consolidate." I said, "Look, I gave away £300 a year in salary to come here, I've got to make it up. ...You either grow or go in this business, and I'm not consolidating,

An Australian field staff practice manual from the late 1930s.

E.D. (Ted) Smout (*left*), one of the pioneers of the Australian Company, with T.S. Cullinan and a car driven by charcoal gas to save petrol.

I'm expanding".' Best apparently retreated in the face of this: 'All right, all right, Smout, go ahead,' he replied, and Smout did so, moving on to build up North Queensland as he had the South. By then Head Office in Sydney was eager for him to give intensive field staff training in the other Australian states. Smout produced the first manuals of agency practice in Australia, and a monthly life agents' newsletter that was then the only publication of its kind.[14]

No British agents' handbook could have covered the variety of circumstances presented by these antipodean agencies. Great distances were covered by a variety of means: car, bicycle, horse or trap – reportedly even by imported camel. Later, it became common for field staff to travel by light aircraft. Calling on the sheep stations, the cane plantations, the graziers' ranches, an agent might be on the road for weeks. Journeys by car of 100 miles to call on a prospect, then another 100 miles to the next, were frequent, and could be unpredictably adventurous. A river in spate forced one man to swim for his life, while another was reportedly chased up a tree by a crocodile, which then feasted on the documentary contents of his bicycle basket.[15] Rural hospitality combined with isolation might mean that the agent arrived in time for dinner, spent the next day going round the property, and left after breakfast or lunch on the day after that. The monotony of life in the outback could take its toll in alcoholism, for agents as well as policyholders. Some of the latter lived so far from anyone else that the agent's periodic visit opened floodgates of rambling discourse.

Distance and weather not only affected the agents' communications with their local branch offices, but also that of the branches with Head Office in Sydney, and with Chief Office in London. From Australia, Holborn Bars was six weeks away by ship, so that routine correspondence on important matters took months. Anything urgent was dealt with by telegram. Between Head Office in Sydney and 'Principal Office' (as the main office of a territory dependent on a 'Head Office' was called) in Auckland, New Zealand, there was a weekly packet-boat in both directions that sailed on Fridays and took four days. This meant that the fastest turn-around for correspondence requiring an answer was ten days. The tours made by Deputy General Manager Ernest Dewey in 1934 and Deputy Chairman Sir George Barstow in 1939 were of necessity fairly lengthy, and helped to cement the sense of identity between Prudential Head Offices in the Far East.

The Prudential's links with New Zealand went back to 1922, and the appointment of Horne and Bunting, land agents, to transact general business on behalf of the Company. By 1931, there were representatives in Wellington and other centres, and the New Zealand branch had taken over a fledgling treaty reinsurance business from London. With the advent of life business, Principal Office moved from Auckland to Wellington and a building on the site of the modern office on Lambton Quay, although much of the administration on the life side continued to be administered from Australia. As in Canada and Australia, once established, the Prudential embarked on the construction of an architecturally distinguished building that quickly became a feature of the host city.[16]

Like the other colonial branches, the New Zealand branch found that immigrants holding Prudential policies formed a nucleus of policyholders. Many of them, newly prosperous, could afford to pay their modest premiums annually, with postal orders for as little as 4s 4d. Ordinary assurances were generally for higher amounts than in Britain – between £100 and £300 in the early 1930s and £500 by 1940. During the 1930s the Prudential was the only company in New Zealand which carried on both life and general business. Although there were established District Offices in Christchurch, Dunedin and Napier, the operation was still small-scale by Chief Office standards: in 1934 there were 1,841 ordinary life policies in force, assuring £665,837 and with a premium income of £25,442. Two years later all these figures had roughly doubled, but by 1938 there were still only 5,972 policies in force, assuring the sum of £1,309,972 and with an annual premium income of £46,876. The General Branch in the same year had premium income from fire insurances of £18,715 and from accident insurances of £47,986.[17]

South Africa was another country to which the Prudential extended operations in the systematic attempt to build on the presence of British policyholders. Chief Office officials made a two-month investigative tour in October 1930 to examine the conditions affecting the assurance business in the Union. Their findings led to the appointment of L.D. Strong as General Manager and K.A. (Kenneth) Usherwood as Actuary for the South African Life Branch. Following their arrival in December 1931, a Head Office was set up in Johannesburg, and with the rapid formation of a field staff during 1932, branch offices were established in the Transvaal, Cape Town, Durban, Port Elizabeth, Bloemfontein and East London. The branch founded in Nairobi in Kenya in 1931 and administered from India was transferred to the control of the South African branch in 1933, though general business in East Africa continued to be transacted by the agents Mitchell Cotts & Co. South Africa was some five times the size of Britain. By 1935 the Prudential was represented in Southern Rhodesia, Uganda and Tanganyika as well, making the area overseen from Johannesburg some 4,000 miles long from Cape Town to northern Uganda.

In South Africa at this time, European lives numbered under 2,000,000, mainly British, Dutch and German. Although a certain amount of assurance might also have been written on Indian professional lives, the living conditions of the 5,500,000 Bantu made assurance out of the question. The Prudential's initial policy was to assure European lives only, under the conventional whole life, endowment, term and annuity assurances. Industrial assurance was not attempted, though, as elsewhere, the Branch Office acted as a collecting point for premiums payable to London.

The Prudential was fortunate in commencing business shortly before South

Africa's abandonment of the gold standard at the end of 1932. Boom conditions succeeded the dismal economic situation that had prevailed in the previous several years. While only 314 policies were written in 1932, by 1935 there were 7,419. The General Branch was separated from the Life Branch, as the latter expanded rapidly in promising conditions, one of which was continuing immigration from northern Europe, which quickened the demand for life assurance.[18] The country, as Sir Edgar Horne commented during a tour made in 1934, was 'like a vast storage battery waiting to be utilised' in its potential, with its wealth in gold and minerals, and its arable land ready for development.[19] Sums assured in the Life Branch exceeeded SA£3,000,000 and premium income SA£113,882 by the end of 1934; by the end of 1935 sums assured amounted to SA£5,000,000. On 30 October 1935, the Prudential's new eight-storey Head Office in Fox Street, Johannesburg, was opened by General (later Field Marshal) Jan Smuts.

In both South Africa, where new branches were opened in Pretoria, Springs and Pietermaritzburg, and in East Africa, where operations were extended to the Rhodesian copperbelt and Nyasaland, Prudential field staff and agency structure increased steadily during the late 1930s. Giving such men an affinity with far-off Holborn Bars and its ethos was one reason for the founding of the *Prudential African Gazette* in 1936. This was an adaptation of the *Prudential Bulletin*, and included sections in Afrikaans and monthly lessons on 'The Principles of Life Assurance' and 'Life Assurance Salesmanship' for the benefit of newcomers to the profession.

General Jan Smuts opens the Prudential's new office in Johannesburg in 1935.

Once there were enough full-time agents in a given area, it was constituted as a 'Branch', with a manager and regular get-togethers. In South Africa and the Transkei, the use of local men as part-time agents meant that full-time men, mainly based in the cities, concentrated on securing new business. The penetration of the country by the railways made travel over great distances somewhat easier than in Canada or Australia. The conditions under which business was pursued and transacted were not dissimilar to those in the latter country, however. The flavour conveyed by the stories that appeared in the *Gazette* cannot really be appreciated in the abstract; one, from the Transkei in 1939, captures the image of the Branch Manager and an agent 'wading waist-deep through a river with a lady between them whom they were assisting through [*sic*] to be examined by the Company's Medical Officer on the far side'.[20] In the farther reaches of East Africa the roads were appalling, and there was always the possibility of meeting wild animals a little too closely for comfort. One agent from Rhodesia reported gaining an unexpected trophy when an impala leapt from the verge to land across his windscreen. In Tanganyika, where such navigable tracks as there were often disappeared into 'elephant grass' six feet high, it was customary to pay a local tribesman to stand on the roof of the car to direct the driver. Agents who ventured into the bush had to be able to speak enough of the language to get by, handle a rifle, carry out fairly major motor repairs, and not mind spending the night under the stars if these failed to work. By 1939, after eight years of operation, there were life assurances in force in South and East Africa for SA£12,600,000, bringing in a premium income of almost SA£500,000. Income for the General Branch in the two main areas of fire and accident insurance in 1939 was SA£87,646. The country continued to enjoy a buoyant economy until April 1937, when the Johannesburg Stock Market crash brought about a readjustment. From that year the South African Branch kept any surplus funds on deposit until a suitable property investment could be made to absorb them.[21] It seems that investment in property was adopted sooner in South Africa than in either Australia or Canada, both because it made economic sense at the time and because of management's strong belief in the long-term potential of the country.

In Malaya, too, life business was grafted onto an established presence in general business since 1924, the agents in question being the Singapore office of Blom and Van der Aa. Frank Morgan as General Manager for India visited Malaya in 1929 and Sir Joseph Burn stayed there in 1931; the decision to open a branch office in Singapore came shortly thereafter, to transact ordinary life business under much the same classes as in the United Kingdom. L.A. Williams, who came to the Prudential after many years in Malaya, was appointed Branch Manager.

As in India, the difficulties presented by the ethnic, linguistic and religious mix of the Malay States were initially daunting. The three main groups were Malay, Indian and Chinese. Europeans formed only a small percentage of the population, but included a number of British army personnel holding Prudential industrial policies. Outside Singapore, the Prudential's representatives found that a literal translation of its name usually brought no sign of recognition. To appeal to the Chinese community, the one most active in commerce, a version of the name in Chinese characters was commissioned, the closest approximation to the English being 'Universal peace and security'.[22] The company was fortunate in finding several exceptionally capable and energetic Chinese businessmen to represent it. Branch offices were set up in Kuala Lumpur, Penang, Ipoh and Malacca. Given that a man could only sell to the people he could communicate with, the agents and inspectors were drawn from all the main linguistic and racial groups. Proposal forms were produced in various languages, although policies were issued in English to avoid legal difficulties. Operations were extended to Borneo in 1935. Progress was slow – by 1939 there were just over 2,000 policies in force, assuring £934,732 and producing annual premium income of £57,000 – but the country was felt to have great potential.

The last overseas market entered in this primary phase of the Prudential's overseas expansion was that of the Middle East, or as it was then called, the 'Near East'. Frank Morgan and others from Chief Office visited Egypt in 1929 and 1933, with the aim of writing life business alongside the fire insurance written by Messrs. Choremi Benachi, the Company's agents. Again, the presence of the British forces afforded a toehold in a difficult market. It was always envisaged that Cairo would be the base from which general and life agents operating in territories nearby could be overseen. The first of these were Palestine, where Messrs. Mulford and Co. were appointed agents, and Cyprus, where S. Marashlian was engaged, both from May 1934. General business emanating from Palestine had to be referred to Chief Office, whereas all life business, and general business from Egypt and Cyprus, was referred to Cairo. Having established the branch, Frank Morgan returned to London and was replaced as Operating Manager by Kenneth Usherwood at the end of his three-year term as founding Actuary in South Africa. His deputy was S.C. Canfield, who would later become Manager in Australia.

It proved extremely difficult to make headway in life business in the Near East. The presence in Egypt of a number of established companies, and the fact that the Prudential's commission scale was initially too low meant that the Company did not attract the experienced agents it needed. Most of the life agents appointed during the first year proved unsuccessful and had their agreements terminated, which likewise did nothing to enhance the newcomer's reputation. A practice with which the Prudential could not compete was the granting by other foreign companies – French, Swiss, Italian – of rebates amounting to 80% or 90% of the first year's premium. While gradual progress was made among the Jews of Palestine and among the Greek Cypriots, the Muslim distaste for assurance was an obstacle to dealing with the Palestinian Arabs, Turkish Cypriots and Egyptians. An attempt to extend the business to the Sudan in 1935 was abandoned after only a few months. In Egypt, poverty, disease and illiteracy meant that only a fraction of the population could be considered as insurance prospects.

The Company's representatives in the Near East carried out their task in an atmosphere unlike that in any of the other overseas markets. Because of the prevailing depression in world trade, the prosperity of the region was badly affected by the low demand for its exports, and business was even harder to come by than in other areas where the Prudential was a newcomer. Political tensions in Egypt frequently spilled over into rioting, with arson and the destruction of property. After the signing of the Anglo-Egyptian Treaty in 1936 the atmosphere was less threatening, but from about the same time, it became unsafe for Britons or Jews to move about freely in Palestine, which severely curtailed the movements of Prudential agents. Among the Jewish population, the precariousness of the territory's future produced an unwillingness to commit funds long-term, and frustrated the Branch's hope of increasing business there. Within a few years a counterweight to these factors was sought in the extension of the business to the Delta region and Upper Egypt, to the Sudan (this time successfully), and to Malta, where business flourished under the local manager, J.C. Degiorgio. By the end of 1937 there were 15 full-time and 83 part-time agents attached to the Near Eastern Branch, supported by a local staff of 15 and 3 senior staff from London. New business fluctuated considerably from one year to the next, but by 1939 the Branch had life business assuring £E872,050. The amount of fire and accident business written was curtailed by local instabilities, but as war appeared imminent, the whole region suffered from the apprehension that this would mean the isolation of the eastern end of the Mediterranean, possibly even occupation. In such a climate business fell off rapidly.[23]

International Congress on Life Assurance Medicine 1935

Reception by The Prudential Assurance Company Limited at their Chief Office Holborn Bars, London. England Friday 26th July

Chief Office kept watch over all these operations through the Overseas Life Department formed in 1931. The funds to establish each branch were advanced from Holborn Bars. Thereafter, each sent in meticulous sets of monthly or quarterly figures showing new business (obviously of prime concern in building from scratch) and premium income, broken down to show the business transacted under the various tables (whole life, endowment, both of these with and without profits, term, immediate and deferred annuities) and mode of payment (single premium, monthly, biannual and annual). India and the Far Eastern branches had to show the proportion of business done at tropical and sub-tropical rates. The proportion of business transacted in each quarter of the year was also calculated, as was the proportion contributed by each inspectorate, sub-branch and agency. Together with the standard figures showing new premium income, sums assured, claims, renewals, assets and liabilities, these were compiled by Chief Office into a comprehensive whole that gave a complete picture (along the lines of Sir Henry Harben's 'photographic portrait') of overseas business at a given moment. Charts and graphs were drawn up to show comparisons between the different territories.

For so large a responsibility, the Overseas Life Department was very small. At its apex was a sole principal clerk who reported to management; below him were two men and one woman, all second-class clerks, together with two juniors and two typists. Alongside the Overseas Life Department was the Actuaries' Office Overseas, consisting of one senior male clerk, a junior and a typist, reporting to an actuary, who in turn reported to a deputy controller. Vacancies in the overseas branches were advertised within the Company through the Manager's Office Memoranda, blue books eagerly scrutinised by the younger clerks with a longing to see the world. One clerk who joined the Overseas Life Department some years later records that even then, though the places were open to women clerks as well, it was assumed that no woman would want to go, and as far as he remembered, none ever did.[24]

Small as it was, the Overseas Life Department was itself occasionally a springboard to service abroad. The duties it required were more varied than the work of the home service departments, providing good training for a foreign post. It was also less hurried. The same man cited above recalls how he pored over issues of the *Overseas Bulletin* in the periods of rest between the weekly arrivals and dispatches of overseas branch post. Reading of the Prudential's activities in Calcutta, Sydney, Montreal and Khartoum, he began to grasp the enormity of this 'family' that extended around the globe. By 1939 net new ordinary business in the Overseas Life Branches had reached £8,156,278 and total annual premium income from these sources more than £1,500,000.[25] All but one of the branches had been founded since 1930, but in less than a decade had more than justified management's confidence in the value of carrying the business abroad.

'Strong roots, strong tree...'

T he Depression years, ushered in by the collapse of world trade that began in 1929, were a testing period for the Prudential as for any concern whose assets consisted largely of investments. Initially, in 1930, it was thought and hoped that the cataclysm of Wall Street and what William Edgar Horne called 'the Hatry sensation' would prove to be transitory incidents rather than lasting traumas. That the repercussions for the world economy would be drastic and recovery long was not immediately apparent. Initiatives such as overseas life and group pensions business went some way to maintaining a climate of confidence within the Prudential, something of a counterweight to the pessimism about the condition of Britain that grew as the Depression deepened.

The General Election of 1929 again brought the Labour party under Ramsay Macdonald to office, but so dependent upon the Liberals that moderation was the order of the day. Hostility to industrial assurance, however, had far from disappeared. Sir Joseph Burn was by now widely recognised as the industry's most cogent and engaging spokesman. The importance of his work at the Prudential during the previous decade would have made him the logical successor to Alfred Corderoy Thompson were it not that his services as General Manager were too valuable to lose. William Edgar Horne was thus the more prudent choice. In a sense Horne was born and bred to be Chairman, although at a robust 72 (he enjoyed golf and shooting until well into his 80s) he came to it somewhat late. His strength was that, despite his close links with the Company, he was not solely an 'insurance man'.[1] Having always combined political and independent business interests with his involvement with the Prudential, Horne brought an objective view of affairs to his position. He respected Burn greatly, and in 1930 reported having asked him (Burn was 60 by then) not to retire, leaving him alone to carry through the plans the two had so often discussed together. Burn, for his part, had probably never considered retiring — there were too many of his measures still in mid-flight for that, too much to defend in the wider forum of public opinion.

The deaths of several Directors in the late 1920s had brought newcomers onto the Board. The most important was Sir George Barstow, KCB, who joined in 1928 on his retirement as Controller of Supply at the Treasury. Barstow is thought to have known Sir George May when both were concerned with supplying the armed forces during the First World War. Sir Laurence Nunns Guillemard, GCMG, KCB, also a distinguished Treasury official, and since 1919 Governor of the Straits Settlement and High Commissioner of the Malay States, was invited to join the Board in 1929. The other three new appointees were already associated with the Company: Major William Guy Horne through his family shareholding, Frank Haycraft and Arthur Rhys Barrand through their former positions as Auditor and Deputy General Manager respectively.

Sir William Edgar Horne, Bt.

Besides pressing ahead with the overseas life business already mentioned, the year 1930 saw the Prudential Board embark on updating Chief Office despite the uncertain economic outlook: 'To launch an important re-building enterprise in a time of National crisis would appear to be boldness pushed to the point of indiscretion ... ' opines a booklet on the Company, referring to the decision to demolish the original Holborn block put up in 1879. This time – Paul Waterhouse having just died – the architect was Ernest Joseph, of the firm of Messrs. Joseph. His instructions were to produce a building whose facade was in keeping with that of the long Holborn frontage, while gaining height in the Brooke Street elevation. Between December 1930, when the demolition began, and February 1933, when part of the new building was used for the valuation, a seven-storey, steel-framed, terracotta-clad structure was constructed which, from the outside, admirably fulfilled the guiding principles.[2] Inside, there were clean lines, large unbroken spaces, much improved lighting; after the florid ornamentation of the surviving Waterhouse blocks, Joseph's interiors seemed almost stark.

The way the new space was organised reflected the altered demands of a modern office. There was a certain amount of rationalisation, to house allied departments together. The separate women's areas that had been the pride of the Victorian building were done away with. Segregation was a thing of the past, as by now each department had its complement of women typists and dining facilities were shared. 'The feeding of the 5000' was not a miracle but a daily reality at Holborn Bars, one henceforth made easier by the huge kitchen and dining complex constructed in the basement. On the top floor, one of the best-equipped small theatres in London provided a new home for the IDOS. Fittings and furniture throughout the building, in the streamlined 'art-deco' style, were designed by the architect. Perhaps the most attractive surviving artefact (most of the 1931 work having disappeared in the renovations of 1992) is his set of tubular steel tables and chairs for the new Muniment Room, manufactured by PEL (Practical Equipment Limited), which pioneered this type of Bauhaus-derived furniture in Britain.

The year 1931, perhaps the bleakest year of the century for the British economy, would be recalled in the Prudential for two events quite distinct from the dismantling of the oldest part of Chief Office. Press coverage of the first provided gripping reading for millions during the early months of the year. This was the celebrated Wallace case, described by the critic James Agate as 'the perfect murder' – assuming that the defendant were innocent.[3] William Herbert Wallace, a Prudential agent from Anfield in Liverpool, had been lured away from home by a hoax insurance call, and had returned to find his wife battered to death. When no other suspect came to light, Wallace himself was arrested for the crime. As he was a respected member of the Prudential Staff Union (he had been Chairman of the Liverpool Branch in 1919), those responsible for his defence sought the help of the PSU in raising the funds to pay for it. The Union's Executive Council pledged its help, not only because, in the words of the letter establishing the W.H. Wallace Defence Fund, '... we are a Trade Union and he is our member ... but on the broader, stronger ground of human brotherhood and Christian charity'.[4]

The trial, at the Liverpool Crown Court, St George's Hall, opened on 22 April 1931, and generated a great deal of publicity. Local presumption of Wallace's guilt was strong, although there were many discrepancies in the case for the prosecution. It was nonetheless a shock when on 25 April the jury unanimously found Wallace guilty, and he received the obligatory death sentence for murder. An appeal was quickly mounted on the grounds that the verdict was not supported by the evidence. The appeal was held at the Law Courts in London on 18 May, the leading judge being the Lord Chief Justice, Viscount Hewart of Bury. Having considered the evidence, the judges decided that since the case against Wallace admitted uncertainty, his appeal should be allowed and the original verdict quashed. Wallace walked from the courtroom a free man. On the following day he visited Holborn Bars, where he was given a month's paid holiday, and Gray's Inn Road, to thank the officials of the PSU. But in Liverpool a climate of hostility greeted him. Reassuming his debit proved impossible and he was found a job in the Prudential's District Office in Dale Street. Never a robust man, Wallace died early in 1933, but the unresolved nature of the case – no further arrest was ever made in connection with the murder – made it a classic of forensic studies.

The second noteworthy event of 1931 was the departure of Sir George May (having reached retirement age) to take up a very different task from that of Secretary to the Prudential. The soaring rate of unemployment benefit being paid out by the national Unemployment Insurance Fund was forcing it to borrow heavily, adding to growing fears that the economy was severely unbalanced.[5] The Labour Government, pressed by the other two parties, agreed to appoint an Economy Committee of financial experts to investigate the true extent of its budget deficit. Philip Snowden as Chancellor of the Exchequer invited May to chair it. Strictly speaking, May's activities once he left the Prudential are beyond the scope of this book, but given the importance of the May Committee's Report on the life of the nation, the briefest account of events will perhaps not be out of place.

May was an actuary and an investment expert, not an economist; he and the majority of his fellow Committee members held the predictably orthodox view that books should balance, and deficits, where they existed, should be rectified by stringent controls. They were anxious not to alienate business interests in their attempt to put the economy to rights. Besides May himself, the Committee consisted of two members nominated by each of the three political parties. The two Labour members appended a Minority Report (to which, in the maelstrom that followed, little attention was paid) to the main one. The May Report was published on 1 August, and calculated the Government's budget deficit as £120,000,000, although this estimate was subsequently increased. The crucial recommendation was a reduction of some £96,000,000 in Government expenditure, two-thirds of which was to come from cuts in the funding of unemployment benefit. Some £50,000,000 of war debt was also to be repaid to lenders of capital.

Whether Labour's policies were viewed as socially necessary or as irresponsibly inflationary was largely a matter of political opinion. The May Committee's depiction of them as the latter increased the misgivings of foreign investors about London's stability as a financial centre. Rather than restoring confidence, the Report fuelled the flight from sterling. During August there was continuing pressure on the Government to balance the deficit by cutting spending on social services. Gold stocks at the Bank of England were running low, and there was understandably no desire on the part of banks abroad to grant the Government the credit it sought unless it appeared that the economy would be brought under control.

Although there were other factors involved in the steady drain of Britain's gold reserves during 1931, the May Report caused this to accelerate. Its recommendations divided the Government, precipitating its dissolution on 24 August. The National Government formed under Macdonald's leadership the following day was committed to balancing the economy along the lines suggested by the May Report. This was to be done partly by a 10% reduction in the standard rate of unemployment benefit, and partly through taxation and other economies, including pay cuts for the forces. These measures were not enough to save the pound; the last-mentioned touched off the famous Invergordon Mutiny, the prelude to the Bank of England's loss of £50,000,000 in gold in a matter of days. On 21 September the Bank suspended the sale of gold, thus abandoning the gold standard.

The General Election that followed in October saw the return of the National Government on a platform of retrenchment and protection. Early in 1932 Sir George May was given the task of chairing the newly formed Import Duties Advisory Committee which formulated tariff policy. In the years that followed May was to make the reorganisation and strengthening of the iron and steel industry a priority for the Committee. The part that the industry was able to play in the war effort after 1939 owed much to this. May's time as Secretary of the Prudential had given him invaluable contacts with leading figures in finance and industry, experience that was of great benefit to the committees he later headed. Although his sight remained precarious, his extra-ordinary memory, the intense concentration by which he could master new subjects, remained undiminished.[6]

Apart from the effect on its investments, which will be discussed presently, the Prudential weathered the early years of the Depression reasonably well. Although a prolonged period of high unemployment – and for thousands of people, the descent into poverty – might have been expected to produce higher rates of mortality, this was not in fact the case. It is interesting to note that the four Prudential Approved Societies, with a membership by now of about 3,600,000, paid out decreasing amounts in National Insurance claims in the early 1930s – and, happily, increasing amounts of additional treatment benefit out of the Societies' surplus. (These, plus the amounts distributed to hospitals, usually amounted to well over £500,000 a year.) New premium income in the Life Branches continued to increase, although more slowly. By 1932 the adverse conditions for other kinds of investment were making the Prudential's higher annuity rates attractive. One of its better-known life policies was launched that year: the Heritage Policy, which provided dependants with both an income and a lump sum. Other innovations, such as a House Purchase Scheme and a Death Duty policy, offered secure means

The 'Heritage' policy proved extremely popular from the time it was introduced in 1932.

of protecting and increasing the value of personal savings at a singularly unpropitious time.

The Industrial Branch too continued to grow, even in the depths of the Depression, by over half a million policies a year. Its proudest statistic, however, was the steady reduction in the expense ratio, down to slightly over 24% by 1932. The average duration of policies was now 18 years. The role of the field staff in achieving this was acknowledged when the Prudential Staff Deferred Annuity Fund was set up in that year as a means of adding to field staff pensions.

A significant step was taken in 1930 with the introduction of Automatic Free Policies. Free paid-up policies had been granted since 1878 to policyholders whose premiums lapsed after a certain period. Initially this was ten years, decreasing to five years in 1882, three years in 1926 and finally to one year in 1928. But the policyholder had to request them; the difference from 1930 was that he need take no action. Once a year's premiums had been paid, a policy could no longer 'lapse' or be forfeited, since any notice of lapse sent and ignored resulted in the issue of an Automatic Free Policy.[7] Policies on children under ten which lapsed before a year's premiums had been paid already qualified for a cash surrender value. The field staff was directed to seek out policyholders whose policies had lapsed since the Industrial Assurance Act 1923 had come into effect, so that free policies could be issued to them.

The working out of the 1923 Act had involved the Industrial Assurance commissioner in considerable debate during the late 1920s, particularly over the point of substituted policies. Although the problems were eclipsed by more crucial ones relating to the economy by 1931, that same year (which saw the Report of the Macmillan Committee on the financing of British industry as well as the May Report) also brought the appointment of a further Committee on industrial assurance. Under the chairmanship of Sir Benjamin Cohen, it was instructed to consider the subject with particular reference to assurance on children under ten, 'including the question of whether any amendment of the law or any addition to it is desirable'.

Sir Joseph Burn prepared an extensive Memorandum on the Prudential's conduct of industrial business. He also gave several days' evidence during which he was questioned about its every aspect.[8] A close reading of this material today imparts a sense of contact with the mind of a man who had the minutiae of industrial assurance at his fingertips. Burn's evidence also conveys a genuine and detailed understanding of working people's lives. For all that, the Committee was not really concerned with the Prudential except as the benchmark office against which the practice of the others could be measured. Rather, its subjects were the companies whose expense ratios were still unacceptably high, and those which still, knowingly or unknowingly, permitted the sale of assurances that were frankly speculative or which otherwise contravened the law.[9]

Although small endowment assurances were increasing in popularity among industrial policyholders, the ease by which funeral policies could be sold indicated a strong continuing demand for them. A proportion of the business transacted no doubt still infringed the law as set out in 1909 and 1923, with the agent colluding with the client or being deceived by him. The better offices had long since adopted measures for reducing this risk and reinforcing the existing legal formulae. As Sir Joseph Burn suggested, using Prudential figures, the number of such cases among the 25,000,000 Prudential policies in force – one-third of all industrial business – during the period cited was very small. He was anxious to show as well that the Company did not profit from them.

'I have had an investigation made,' he wrote, 'into the number of illegal policies that have come to light in the Prudential since January 1924, ... and find that out of 3,228 cases, in 2,986 all the premiums have been returned and in only 242 has some payment less than the full premiums been made.'[10] In his evidence to the Committee Sir Joseph claimed that such instances arose more often through ignorance than through deliberate attempts to deceive (which, depending on their severity, could have resulted in prosecution). He reported four groups, the over-assurance of children being by far the largest at 1,964 cases. Then came life-of-another policies outside the permitted degree of relationship, and own-life policies taken out by someone other than the person named on the policy. Finally, there was a small miscellaneous category.

Whether such instances bulked larger in the business written by offices less tightly administered than the Prudential is not possible to gauge from the Committee's proceedings, but, despite Burn's figures, the assumption that this was so coloured its eventual findings. It appeared that funeral business was still too open to abuse for industrial assurance as a whole to be seen in a positive light. It could undoubtedly have appeared more positive had the high expense ratios reported by many of the offices not added to the Committee's misgivings. Its most important single recommendation was the imposition of a maximum ratio of 30%, which, it believed, would encourage offices to adopt the Block System and, in the long run, to amalgamate. This would reduce the undignified competition between agents which was thought to underlie many defects. The suggestion that children were still being over-assured, while bringing no suggested change in the maximum sum assured (£15 exclusive of bonus) up to the age of ten, led the Committee to recommend that the amount of weekly whole-life premium payable on the life of an individual child be limited to 1d. Endowments on or on behalf of a child taken out by a parent were to be limited, if the child died, to the return of premiums. There was a prohibition on children under 14 taking out contracts, except on their own lives through their parents, which was intended to prevent adults using juveniles as a means of insuring other relatives.

The Cohen Report appeared just before the end of the parliamentary session of 1933, and received little attention. In the end, since no legislation resulted from it, its importance was limited to the degree to which it was cited in subsequent studies: for having discussed, not nationalisation, which it considered too political, but three possible alternatives to nationalisation. The idea of a monopoly public utility corporation was rejected as fraught with difficulties (and these same difficulties were suggested as likely to accompany nationalisation): the disparity between the size, strength and range of activity of the offices, how to separate and protect the interests of shareholders and policyholders, the compensation payable to agents who would lose their jobs ... . The Committee considered welding the companies and societies into a finite number of large units, leaving aside the Prudential, for obvious reasons. This too raised more problems than it looked likely to resolve. The last idea was the limit on expenses mentioned above, which the Committee recommended should be complied with in not more than seven years. The fact that it had taken the Prudential a dozen years to get the Block System running smoothly and the expense ratio down below 30% made this a somewhat optimistic proposal.[11]

By the time the Cohen Report appeared, the worst of the Depression was lifting, but the Prudential, like other large investing institutions, was faced with new challenges. As Sir Edgar Horne recalled, the year 1931 had been 'the worst in recent history from the point of view of a company such as ours, with large invested funds', and several more years were to pass before the outlook improved.[12] Following Britain's departure from the gold standard, the Government sought to stimulate the economy through a cheap money policy. Although share values recovered from the shocks of 1931, the yield on gilts – the mainstay of the balance sheet – declined over the next few years to a low of 2.9% in 1935. As the Prudential's basis of valuation was 3%, the situation posed a serious problem. Yields on other fixed interest investment assets were similarly affected, forcing the Company to seek more adequate rates of return through other kinds of investment.

The most prudent choice in the circumstances was property, which, since the turn of the century, and notwithstanding its large holdings, had generally had a minor place in the Company's overall investment scheme. Historically, the Prudential had followed the investment canon of absolute security laid down by A.H. Bailey in the 1860s. Sir George May's theory of diversification (which, it will be recalled, held that the greatest protection from temporary fluctuations was afforded by distributing funds over as wide an area as possible) was wholeheartedly endorsed by the Prudential, but had a limited effect on actual investment practice until after the First World War.[13] In 1912, the year May presented his ideas to the Institute of Actuaries, the Prudential's property holdings amounted to some £9,000,000, but this was less than 11% of its total assets.[14] From the mid-1920s, May promoted investment in equities, there being a growing range of promising companies seeking development finance. Among them were a host of companies, such as Rootes Motors, Beecham's and ICI, which later became household names. Conversely, in the 1920s, the returns on property were less attractive than Stock Exchange securities, which offered potentially larger yields and could be realised quickly.

Multiple retailing, which had existed earlier but which only came into its own in the 1920s, was one area in which the Prudential invested heavily and which provided good opportunities for property investment in the 1930s. Among the Prudential's interests were – and are, since the Prudential is still a shareholder in most – some of the best-known names in British retailing. The limitations of scope and space preclude discussion of more than one of these, Marks & Spencer, although the subject as a whole would merit a detailed study. The Prudential had acquired a 15% interest in Marks & Spencer in 1926 when the Industrial Finance and Investment Corporation underwrote the public issue of shares in a new company that was absorbing the original family-owned undertaking.[15] Sir George May had been closely associated with the issue and he and Simon Marks, the son of one of the original partners, had become friends. At the time the new company was launched, it had 135 stores, about 40% of which were leasehold, and the initial plan was to remodel the shops in line with the retailing methods that Simon Marks had seen on a recent visit to the United States and wished to introduce.

Marks & Spencer raised additional finance on two subsequent occasions before 1931 to feed its expansion programme. It was becoming harder to lease properties at economic rents, and as remodelling rented properties had obvious drawbacks, the tendency was increasingly to extend existing stores, both those that were owned and those that were held on long leases. Much of this ongoing development during the 1930s was aided by the Prudential, initially as underwriter of successive issues of capital, later by providing mortgage debenture finance. But in some cases it also bought the sites for future stores on which Marks & Spencer took 99-year building leases. This to the latter was more attractive than the standard leaseback arrangement, given the frequency with which it enlarged and remodelled some of its branches. On occasion the Prudential would also advance funds for the modification of buildings on the sites.[16]

By 1935, Sir Edgar Horne could report that, 'During the past 12 months we have invested substantial sums in the property market, on which the return is somewhat higher than that obtainable from stock exchange securities.' The Company had in fact invested more than £3,500,000 in property that year, at a yield of 5.25%; besides investing in the expansion of multiple retailers, it had also intensified the programme of building residential flats begun in the 1920s with the construction of several blocks in Marylebone and Kensington. This may have originated in Sir Edgar Horne's knowledge of the London residential property market, but by the 1930s it was a response to the boom in flat-building that grew out of the low building costs and lower mortgages of the cheap money period. Many blocks of flats, mostly of the luxury category in the better parts of central London and its leafier suburbs, were built from 1932 onwards. Some were purely residential and some combined flats with parades of shops. Property investment of this kind brought the expansion of the Estate Department, since it was considered more economical and a better guarantee of quality if the buildings were maintained, decorated and repaired by the Company's expert staff. Quite apart from the demand for well-appointed residential flats, the standard of tenant relations, once flats were let, may have helped to keep occupancy high. In 1937 Sir Edgar Horne reported that only 4% of Prudential flats were unlet, and two years later the rate was down to 2%. By then, roughly £1,500,000 a year since 1936 having been invested in properties, the number owned by the Company was 14,434 and their annual rental income, after outgoings, was in excess of £1,000,000. The book values of the Prudential's holdings of landed property stood at more than £25,000,000.[17]

Property was the sedate end of the investment spectrum. From 1932, the National Government began to encourage institutional investors to support British industry by filling the 'gap' identified by the Macmillan Report. The Prudential responded positively to this; as well as providing finance directly in the ways mentioned above, it took an interest in Charterhouse Development Limited, set up specifically to finance promising smaller companies. In one area, apparently at the request of the Government, it was prepared to be more adventurous.[18] This was the British film industry, badly in need of financial backing in the face of American dominance.

The initial contact came through one Montagu Marks, an Australian businessman with links to the film industry. The Prudential wished to develop the new Hillman colour process owned by Colourgravure (a subsidiary of Gerrard Industries, in which the Prudential held an interest) but as yet had taken no steps to do so. Marks, having independently investigated the process, brought together Sir Connop Guthrie, a director of Gerrard, and the Hungarian film director Alexander Korda. London Films, the company founded by Korda in 1932, seemed best able to exploit the process but needed finance and Guthrie presented the situation to the Prudential.[19]

The reputation of London Films in the spring of 1934 was high. Korda's masterpiece *The Private Life of Henry VIII*, starring Charles Laughton, was breaking box-office records in the United States and the Prudential was encouraged by this to agree to fund an ambitious programme of films. For the first £250,000, paid in July 1934, the Prudential was allocated all the preference shares in London Films and liens on all productions, while Sir Connop Guthrie joined the film company's board. The Prudential advanced another £500,000 a few months later.

Korda could attract the biggest stars of the day: Marlene Dietrich, Merle Oberon, Robert Donat, Laurence Olivier, Vivien Leigh and many others. He made several films in 1935 and 1936, among them *The Ghost Goes West* and two collaborations with H.G. Wells, *Things to Come* and *The Man Who Could Work*

Miracles, at the Isleworth Studios. Returns at the box office did not, however, match expenditure and London Films lost £30,000 in 1935 and £300,000 in 1936. Korda was an extravagant director, and a worse administrator, incapable of keeping to budgets and insisting on the best in materials and facilities. His notorious charm was coupled with the ability to carry on unperturbed by financial thunderclouds.

Korda not only wanted to make films; he wanted a purpose-built studio in which to make them. Further Prudential backing made possible the purchase of a site near Denham in Buckinghamshire in June 1935. Less than a year later Denham Studios was finished. A grand reception was held at which Sir Edgar Horne acted as host. As 'Hollywood on the Colne' Denham aroused the wonder of visitors, but the following description conveys some idea of why, by this time, the Prudential's Joint Secretaries, Percy Crump and Ernest Lever, were finding their investment in London Films a source of concern:

> *Denham was the largest film production facility in the country, boasting seven huge sound stages, fifteen star dressing rooms, a studio restaurant, its own water supply and the largest private electricity plant in the country, reputedly supplying enough power to service a town the size of York. There were workshops for every kind of craft: a foundry, a machine shop, and a complete processing laboratory. ... And, of course, there were the employees, which numbered at least 2000 people – enough for the Great Western Railways to create a new fast service to London.* [20]

Not only had Denham cost three times the original estimate, but worse was the prospect of keeping such vast – and vastly expensive – space perpetually in use. By the end of 1936 the debts accumulated by London Films amounted to £1,794,222 and Korda had almost relinquished film-making to devote himself to studio management. (The last film he directed at Denham was *Rembrandt* with Charles Laughton.) The programme of films planned now had no chance of being realised within the financial constraints laid down. The Prudential was thus in the invidious position of having either to close Denham and recoup nothing, or keep London Films afloat in the hope that it would one day show a profit. Ernest Lever attempted the second course, insisting on the separation of the production and administration functions of London Films and installing a Prudential representative on the Board. By the summer of 1938 the Prudential had invested about £3,000,000 in London Films. Memoranda from this tense period survive and contain such observations (from Percy Crump) as

> *The fact that we have lost a great deal of money through our association with K must be faced ... . K's engaging personality and charm of manner must be resisted. His financial sense is non-existent and his promises (even when they are sincere) worthless. In other words, he is impossible to work with ... . Korda is a*

very dominant [sic] man and dangerous to converse with owing to (among other things) his powers of persuasion. ... We who have nursed his ventures have never received a penny out of them.[21]

By this time a funding crisis was affecting the whole British film industry and the impossibility of keeping Denham filled compounded the existing situation. The Prudential removed control of Denham Studios from Korda and enforced an arrangement on London Films that ensured that future film earnings were remitted to the Prudential. Besides the films already mentioned, the list included *The Scarlet Pimpernel*, *Sanders of the River*, *Elephant Boy*, *Knight Without Armour* and the still popular *The Private Life of Henry VIII*. In 1939 Denham, which represented about half of the Prudential's investment, was merged with J. Arthur Rank's Pinewood Studios in a new company, D&P Limited. Film royalties reduced the amount outstanding somewhat more, but in 1942 Korda bought back the rights to his films from the Prudential for £42,000.

The Prudential's promotional film *From One Generation to Another*, made in 1935, tells a story about the role of insurance in the prosperity of a family.

London Films was one of the few Prudential involvements which turned sour. It had not been a wholly negative experience: more than a dozen pictures had been made, and the reputation of the British film industry enhanced. On a minor level, it brought a whiff of glamour to Holborn Bars and the lives of the younger Prudential staff despatched on some errand to Denham.[22] In the early stages, captivated by the idea of film as a communications medium, management even commissioned a 45-minute feature purporting to show the human side of life assurance, entitled *From One Generation to Another*. (The story was contrived so that the second of its three sections centred on a tour of Holborn Bars, and the professional actor playing the main character was Edward Harben, one of Sir Henry Harben's great-nephews.) But it is significant that until very recent times, the Prudential avoided any further financial involvement with the film industry.

The business environment in the last half of the decade was less volatile than in the first, although rearmament hinted at chaos to come. The Prudential's life branches had continued to expand through all the vicissitudes of the previous six years. In 1937 the Ordinary Branch wrote the largest amount of new business in its history at £32,457,832. The Industrial Branch's new business amounted to £22,296,696 and the expense ratio had been wrestled down to 22.7%. The tiny British Widows' Assurance Company, with less than 10,000 ordinary policies and about 220,000 industrial ones, transferred its business to the Prudential in 1936; its staff was taken on as well.[23] In the same year the Company began the process of withdrawal from the Irish Free State, imminently to be known as Eire. Under a new Insurance Act four of the five Irish assurance offices merged to become The Industrial and Life Assurance Amalgamation Company Limited, which took over their contracts and staffs. The Prudential transferred its industrial business – some 350,000 policies – and staff to the Amalgamation Company, and its smaller ordinary business to the newly incorporated Irish Assurance Company Limited.[24]

Chief Office in the 1930s, evoked by those who spent their early working lives there, was still a secure and relatively happy microcosm within the wider financial community. The same sense of security prevailed as always had: the familiar figures of Sir Edgar Horne and Sir Joseph Burn were still to be glimpsed, though neither travelled far now from the panelled third floor. More in charge of day-to-day affairs between the wars was the esteemed Assistant Manager, Anthony Windsor, CMG. A veteran of the South African War and the Great War, Windsor habitually interviewed the candidates for Company posts, and his high standard of dress and bearing made a strong impression.

A venerable – almost legendary – figure disappeared from the Prudential scene when Frederick Schooling died in 1936. His was the longest service of any at 69 years, begun in 1867; to the younger clerks it seemed incredible that this 84-year-old man had played in the Ibis Cricket Club's first match in 1868 and seen the Prudential outgrow Ludgate Hill! Schooling's love of cricket had not diminished over the years, nor had the actuarial mind's advantage at the chessboard. Guy Philip Harben succeeded him as Deputy Chairman, and Sir Nigel Davidson, formerly Legal Adviser to the British High Commissions in the Sudan and Iraq, was appointed to his place on the Board. Another link with the period before the First World War was broken when Sir John Luscombe, a Director since 1906 and five times Chairman of Lloyds, died in 1937. He was succeeded by Sir George Stuart Robertson, following his retirement from the office of Industrial Assurance Commissioner.

Holborn Bars in the late 1930s is recalled as having had an atmosphere rather like a mature version of a public school. There was the inherent sense that the Prudential performed a great public service, and that the standard of that service had to be high. A Training Centre for the field staff set up at Holborn Bars was the complement to Sir Joseph Burn's 'Star' Dinners for outstanding agents held from 1931 on. For Chief Office clerical staff the pressure of work came from quantity rather than difficulty, as the pace demanded concentrated effort. The autonomy enjoyed by principal clerks meant that the tone of individual departments depended on the temperament of the man in charge. The principals were products of the previous century, for better or worse; hours were strictly kept, penmanship mattered and it was expected that correspondence would be dealt with promptly on the day it was received. That said, there were plenty of Company traditions, such as annual dinners of various kinds, annual sports days and Christmas celebrations, the Technical Society exhibitions and the IDOS shows, that cheered the seasonal round. The fact that Chief Office staff received a rebate equivalent to the amount of their income tax each year was an enviable perquisite that lasted until 1946.

The inter-war period, and particularly the 1930s, marked the heyday of the Ibis. It acquired a new 32-acre ground and pavilion at Duke's Meadow, Chiswick, through Sir Edgar Horne's desire to see the sports clubs settled in one place. The site of the boathouse was particularly envied at the time of the Oxford and Cambridge Race. The IDOS thrived, mounting a succession of ingeniously elaborate productions-on-a-shoestring in the wonderful theatre at the top of Holborn Bars. The companionship of the clubs spilled over into the lunch-hours and early evenings. The neighbourhood of Chief Office abounded in establishments frequented by Prudential staff. Mickey's (the forerunner of Henekey's, now the Citie of York, in High Holborn, which had 'a wine list that amounted to a catalogue' and box seating), the Old Leather Bottle (less salubrious but full of character) and the Haverstock (with its horseshoe bar) were especially popular. Almost anything could be bought at Gamages, adjacent to Chief Office, which had supplied generations of clerks with clothing and sports gear, and an annual treat in the form of the Christmas model railway displays.

With nearly 5,000 souls united under its roof, the Prudential was important to the economy of stores in the area. There was a close relationship between it and some of the small local businesses: Gibbs and Mast in Gray's Inn Road, for example, had supplied it with pen-nibs and red and blue inks (not green, which was reserved for the auditors) as long as anyone could remember. The dairy in Brooke Street… the Court Tailors, where clerks could go to have buttons sewn on (gratis, by the kindly proprietress) and discreet repairs made to suits that were wearing thin… these found a place in employees' memories of Prudential life.[25] Across from Chief Office stood Staple Inn, a veritable symbol of continuity, through whose courtyard had passed scores of Prudential men (and by now, a few Prudential women) *en route* to actuarial honours.[26] To them, as to their non-actuarial colleagues, the community around Chief Office confirmed the sense of permanence and security inspired by the Prudential itself. How soon the one would be shattered, how enduring the other was to prove, the next few years would show.

The Prudential 'Family' and the Second World War

WITH the signing of the Munich Agreement in September 1938, the nation breathed a collective sigh of relief and the spectre of war receded temporarily. The response of the Prudential Board to the situation on the Continent, however, was to take protective measures. Within days of Munich the Estate Department had begun the search for premises outside London to which the Prudential could resort if the scenario suddenly changed for the worse. In the event of war, enemy attacks on London were expected to be devastating, with hundreds of thousands of civilian casualties and destruction of property on a hitherto unimagined scale.[1] By the end of 1938, staff training in ARP and first aid was underway and a vast bombproof safe had been constructed in the sub-basement of Chief Office to protect deeds and securities. Records were duplicated and moved to the provinces, the basement converted to air-raid shelters and provided with alternative sources of power and air. Tanks for reserve water supplies were stored in the courtyard.

Maintaining in force the life policies of nearly a third of the population of Britain was the Company's first priority. The 'Decentralisation plan' drawn up during 1938 involved the evacuation from Holborn Bars of the departments administering the Divisions. The aim was to create what were conceived of as 'Chief Offices in miniature' away from the capital, so as to ensure the independent functioning of the business in the various parts of the country. Through the winter of 1938, the Estate Department continued the search for locations. In the face of stiff competition from Government departments, securing the premises identified was not always easy. Eventually the Prudential settled on ten towns: Darlington ('B' Division), Wakefield ('C'), Oldham ('D'), Derby ('F'), Wigan ('G'), Nuneaton ('H'), Slough ('I' and 'N'), together with Larbert ('A') in Scotland, Sketty Park House near Swansea ('E') in Wales and Belfast in Northern Ireland. Some of the premises were already owned by the Company, others were especially bought. They ranged from ballrooms to garages; the quarters at Wakefield and Darlington were country houses set in acres of grounds.

In an eleventh town, Torquay, the Grand Hotel, the Victoria and Albert and others were obtained for the Approved Societies. Their membership had now reached 4,250,000, and they were paying out nearly £4,000,000 annually in cash benefits, mainly for sickness and disablement. Given their national importance, and the certainty that war would see an increase in claims, it was felt that the 2,000 staff must be kept together for ease of administration. There was a tense interval at Chief Office for Manager Hubert Lane, who was organising the move, when the Grand Hotel was suddenly requisitioned only days before it. Some vacant land was found and 22 huts hastily erected to provide elementary office space; a bowling alley near Paignton was also taken over.

The refitting of buildings for Prudential use was still going on as the diaspora from Chief Office began on 26 August 1939. Convoys of chartered buses, laden with office supplies and duplicate records, left Holborn Bars for their provincial destinations. Special trains carried the Approved Societies staff to Torquay; the Ordinary Branch and Industrial Branch also left London in the last days of August. On arrival at their respective centres they were met by Prudential agents and conducted to billets. Their first task was to help to unload tons of divisional administrative records into the temporary quarters. The evacuation caused remarkably little disruption: barely a week later, the Approved Societies were again paying benefits, and the Life Branches, claims. Only the 'K', 'L' and 'M' divisions (the London ones) remained with the management and a skeleton staff at Holborn Bars. With the fall of France in June 1940, and an enemy invasion seemingly in the offing, the 'M' too retreated – to Bournemouth.

Unlike the early stages of the First World War, when everyone had been convinced that victory would be gained quickly, from the spring of 1940, as one country after another fell before the German advance, there were no illusions about the struggle ahead. The Prudential Board accepted that the war effort demanded the total dedication of manpower and assets. As in the First World War, it was decided to make up the difference between salaries and service pay for all Prudential staff on National Service.[2] A greater expense, and impossible to predict, was the level of claims that might arise. The Prudential had more than 28,000,000 policyholders in 1939. All Industrial Branch and many Ordinary Branch policies contained a clause which reduced a claim to the total of premiums paid if death were due to war causes. The Board decided on 7 September 1939 that for the time being all claims arising from naval, military and aviation causes be paid in full.[3]

Together with the other life offices, the Prudential agreed to protect Ordinary Branch policies from lapse due to hardship caused by the war. Industrial Branch policyholders were already protected under the Industrial Assurance and Friendly Societies (Emergency Protection from Forfeiture) Act, which prevented lapse if the circumstances arose from the war.[4] There were also state initiatives relating to the insurance of property. A body called the

Associated Fire Insurers was created to provide cover for commodities which came under Government control. Each of the commercial offices accepted a proportion of the total insured, the Prudential's share being 3%. In the operation of the War Risks (Commodities) Insurance Fund, which related to plant and machinery and household effects as well as commodities, the Prudential and other assurers acted as agents for the Board of Trade.[5]

The Prudential's most persistent problem, as before, was finding replacement staff to carry on the business. In the first few months after decentralisation, the huge Chief Office interiors seemed eerily quiet to the core departments that remained. Many of those taken on to replace enlisted men were married women, who put up with chaotic travelling conditions in the blackout, to commute between home and office. For most this was compounded by hours standing in food queues and further hours of war-related voluntary activity, yet they learned the necessary jobs and the work got done. The 'war on waste', and Paper Control Orders that allowed the Prudential less than a third of its prewar amount of paper, meant even tighter office procedures.

With the ending of the 'phoney war' in the spring of 1940, air raids became a fact of life. In theory, when the air-raid sirens sounded during working hours, everyone was supposed to leave their desks and head for the basement shelters. Each department was allocated a specific shelter, but as the staff became accustomed to the raids and the spotters more proficient at gauging the danger, people ignored the intermittent ringing that announced an emergency and carried on working. Gas masks had to be within reach at all times.[6] Everyone from General Manager to messenger took regular turns at fire-watching and 'spotting' enemy aircraft from the roof. In the event of incendiaries falling onto – or into – the building, extinguishing them in buckets of water or sand was the prescribed course of action. Devices that exploded or caused fires posed a visible danger; more insidious were those that struck without exploding (of which there were a number that penetrated the roof of Chief Office), but which were still 'live' as experts sought to disarm them. Later, when the sustained attack on London had passed, there were quiet nights, when leaning against a parapet under the stars produced in the men a feeling of watchful, meditative calm, a sense of the great edifice beneath them as an almost living entity. During the blitz, however, the need for vigilance battled with exhaustion. The fire-watchers worked in shifts, beds and meals being available at all hours in the ARP room. First-aid posts at Chief Office were manned day and night.

A number of bombs fell in the vicinity of Holborn, including one that severely injured two Prudential employees, but it was not until 29 December 1940 that a bomb actually damaged Chief Office, The incident occurred during the first severe raid on the City, when a heavy explosive bomb partially destroyed the Stores Department and set adjacent areas alight. Fire-watchers smothered the cluster of incendiaries that fell on 16 January 1941, but on 8 March six heavy explosive bombs did varying degrees of damage. Showers of firebombs on other occasions during that year were dealt with before they could do any great harm. Water from burst pipes and fire hoses often left as much devastation as anything dropped by the enemy. The water tanks in the courtyard, however, proved a godsend on repeated occasions, including one when the National Fire Service borrowed 12,000 gallons from the Prudential's reserves to fight a blaze nearby. Although Chief Office escaped major destruction, there was secondary damage, mainly to windows, as a result of the recurrent bombing of the surrounding areas. Sometimes the view from the roof was a panorama of flame to the horizon, and the heat from nearby fires intense. The residential neighbourhood around the building, including Leather Lane and St Alban's church, was badly hit on 16 April 1941. During the blitz the basement shelters at Holborn Bars, with sleeping space for about 120 people, were made available at night to residents of the area who had been bombed out.

Of the buildings owned by the Prudential around the country, 99 suffered fairly serious damage, and four offices – Coventry, Greenock, Hull and Swansea – were destroyed. The Coventry office was a new building, reduced to a blackened shell on the night of 14 November 1940 by the same fire-storm that incinerated the city's cathedral and historic heart. The Clydeside town of Greenock was bombed for two days in May 1941, the office surviving the bombing but falling prey to fire spreading from adjacent buildings. (The only remaining vestiges of the Prudential's presence on these sites were their respective office safes, found in the debris.) The Hull office was destroyed by fire in a terrible raid on 8 May 1941 that left 34,000 people homeless. As there was nowhere else from which to operate, an office – *sans* records, *sans* furniture, *sans* everything – was set up in a private house. The Company's caretaker and his family were killed in the Hull incident, but there was an equally tragic outcome at Swansea, where the Prudential building was lifted off its foundations by two bombs on the night of 21 February 1941, and collapsed, burying several members of staff in the rubble. Apart from the devastation and loss of life in these incidents, there was extensive damage to Prudential offices in Manchester, Yeovil, Plymouth and other centres. In all offices it was customary to move documents and registers to the shelters each night, but there were some heroic removals from burning buildings, such as the rescue of the Plymouth office records in a commandeered butcher's van.

Several Directors and members of management were loaned to the Government and the forces. One important secondment was that of Kenneth Usherwood to the War Office, where he took charge of the co-ordination of production statistics. This was an immense task, involving the elimination of much existing duplication of effort, and the formation of a highly qualified professional staff. Statistical sections on the War Office model were set up in the

Home Command HQ, the Expeditionary Forces and other overseas centres of command.[7] Most of the Directors were too old to be seconded. The death of Sir William Edgar Horne on 26 September 1941 was hardly unexpected, as he was 85 years old, but the sudden removal of such a venerable link with the past was a sobering event. The urbane Sir George Barstow, as the senior Deputy Chairman, was chosen to succeed him, and Ernest Dewey was appointed a Deputy Chairman alongside Guy Philip Harben. Sir Joseph Burn, by then aged 71, resigned from the post of General Manager and was elected to the Board on 9 October. At a shareholders' meeting on 6 November, he was named President, an honorary office held previously only by Sir Henry Harben and Sir Thomas Dewey. Ernest Spurgeon, a Deputy General Manager, joined the Board on his retirement and was succeeded in his former post by Hubert Lane. Frank Morgan took over from Burn as General Manager. Both Barstow and Morgan, who now assumed the Company's most public roles, were extroverts, although they were very different in background and experience. Each in his individual way was what the Prudential needed in this darkest period of the war. Both were inspiring speakers and Morgan in particular an articulate and passionate defender of insurance and the insurance industry. Barstow would pilot the Prudential with the classical scholar's equanimity as well as the managerial deftness of the senior civil servant he had once been. Morgan, whose breadth of field experience was unrivalled, kept up morale in the divisions, in so far as travel restrictions allowed.

Sir George Barstow, KCB.

As the war progressed and more and more men joined the forces, it became ever more difficult to find and keep replacement field staff. By the spring of 1942, 57% of the Prudential field staff were in uniform. A year later, only 4,350 of the entire permanent male staff of 18,473 were still in post.[8] The Company's views were sought (by the Committee chaired by Lord Kennet during the preparation of its Report on manpower in 1942) on a plan for the creation of a 'service company' to take over the amalgamated industrial assurance business of the various offices. The plan had been submitted from an undisclosed source. Within the Prudential, it was seen as having political motives, and to be similar to a plan devised for the Irish offices a few years earlier.[9] Frank Morgan as the Prudential's spokesman refuted the proposals as 'wholly impracticable' and more likely to bring chaos to the industry than the result ostensibly sought by the

Committee. The Prudential's evidence to the Kennet Committee showed the level of efficiency at which the Block System already functioned.[10] This was acknowledged in the Committee's Report, which complimented the Prudential on the Block System, recommending its adoption by other companies.

The Prudential, in turn, set up its own committee to consider how its manpower could be even further rationalised. By withdrawing requests for deferment for some men and by not replacing others, more than 600 assistant superintendents aged 35 and upwards were made available during 1943.[11] As part of the preparation for war, the District Managers had compiled lists of temporaries who could take over when field staff were called up. Most of them were agents' wives and relatives, though some were retired former agents. There were also elderly folk, or people with mild physical disabilities that kept them out of any more strenuous occupation, who were willing to give collecting a try. The first vacancies were relatively easy to fill, but any remaining civilians were by now being directed into war-related industries. In one London borough, of the 70 possibilities drawn from the Prudential's lists and trained, all but one had been reallocated to other jobs within a few months.

Nearly 10,000 women formed part of the larger number of temporary field staff – 15,000 by 1945 – engaged to carry out house-to-house collections. It became a common sight to see women collectors making the rounds with small children in prams. The ingenuity of these replacement staff was sorely tested once the evacuation of large numbers of people began to make havoc of District Office records. The Company's aim of maintaining service to policyholders was made exceedingly difficult if, for example, hundreds of people from one area were evacuated at short notice to another, with the result that they had to be transferred from the registers of one district to those of another. Instances such as the following were relatively common:

Women collectors and agents became more numerous during the war, and many, like Miss K.M. Long, shown here with her Merit awards, carried on working when it was over.

> *... in the summer of 1940, two thousand people were sent from Eastbourne to Cheltenham, with little chance of leaving a note of their future whereabouts. For a whole week the Prudential office at Cheltenham was thronged with people anxious to have their policies transferred. At length the business of transfer was arranged. Then, on the Friday, it was discovered that Cheltenham was a "scheduled military*

area". All the evacuees had to leave for another town: a week of wasted work, and more complications for Prudential staff![12]

On occasion, the populations of towns swelled or declined dramatically. That of Southampton fell from 181,000 to 122,000 as a result of recruitment and evacuation, and a Prudential collector there found only three people living in a street that normally housed 300.[13] There were all manner of additional complications such as receipt books lost or left behind or stolen, and people leaving a new district to return to their damaged homes without advising anyone. The problems were even more daunting following an air raid, when the collector might have to seek traces of policyholders among the ruins. Uncertain whether 'her' subjects were dead or alive, she would visit neighbours, local shops, relatives, or perhaps write out a plea for information to leave atop the rubble. Forms and posters were handed out to the survivors of a raid, telling them how to get in touch with the collectors. Similar advertisements were placed in the local newspapers, and the Post Office issued with lists of names and addresses to be returned to the collector when new addresses were recorded.

Collecting during the blitz was an activity fraught with near-misses and incongruous incidents. One woman collector was struck by the force of a bomb blast and carried the width of two gardens – where, as it happened, she landed unhurt, and found the family she had sought at the first house hiding in the neighbours' shelter. It was common for agents to collect the weekly premium from some preordained spot – the jar on the mantelpiece or the kitchen table – when policyholders were out, and in rural areas unaffected by bombing this system still served. In cities during the blitz, however, the shelter at the bottom of the garden became a safer alternative. Some collectors made a point of calling during raids. They 'trained' their policyholders to leave their policies and receipt books by the back door to be picked up *en route* to the Anderson shelter. This worked best in the northern cities where the 'back lane' was a standard feature in working-class districts. The collector could go from shelter to shelter down the back lanes and be sure of finding everyone 'at home'. The evening was the best time to call; earlier, and no-one was in; later, there was the blackout to contend with, and the risk of being robbed of a full purse.

The collectors were themselves in the 'front lines' in dealing with the effects of the war on ordinary people's lives. One young temporary assigned to a debit in Dundee recalled:

> *The housewives always left the doors unlocked for us, so we just rang the bell, opened the outside door and yelled "Prudential!", to be answered with "Come away in, lass …". Often we were delighted to see a husband home on leave, until we saw the foreign uniform. We didn't criticise these things, war had changed everything. Our business was to collect the money and stay friendly.*

Like the agents they replaced, the collectors were greatly trusted:

> *We were more than just collectors of money, the housewives liked having the girls calling and we became good friends. We exchanged recipes for making the rations go further, told jokes about happenings in the blackout, gave tips about which shop had got what, and helpful hints about altering clothes to make up for lack of coupons. The customers were very generous and I was often the recipient of something very precious like sweets, an egg, an orange or apple. This was kindness indeed during shortages.*

Sympathy with the people on the debit transcended the roles of Company representative and customer:

> *We made jokes about all the wartime problems, but never on the subject of the lads who were away, this was the deep worry we all had, and here I was able to help just a little. Often a tearful lady would tell me that no letters were coming from son or husband ... I would ask the lady where the lad was, and I would say, "There hasn't been mail in this week or last week, because I've had none ... . You'll get one by next week." This was a simple service, but the relief on the person's face was worthwhile ... .*

It often fell to these young girls to comfort the bereaved. One of their hardest tasks was to persuade wives or mothers in acute states of grief to sign the form that would allow the payment of death benefit. 'My only unhappiness in my job was when I had to pay out on a death policy on someone in the forces. I had to be strong when I was in the house, but I shed a few tears once I was outside.'[14]

Many of the collectors were themselves bereaved or bombed out, and kept on working, despite their distress. 'We remember our lady Collector friend – 65 years old,' wrote one District Manager, 'bombed out on Sunday and reporting as usual on Monday at 9 o'clock.'[15]

All kinds of nooks were used as temporary offices: one collector related how, when bombs fell on the District Office, he and his assistant dealt with enquiries and claims from seats at the Express Dairy across the street. Another set up a table in makeshift quarters to deal with two clients. Within minutes there was a queue stretching out of the door and across the yard. Dealing with claims all day – some of them heart-rending, such as the one in which four generations of the same family, all policyholders, died in the same blast – often preceded an interrupted journey home and a night's fire-watching.

Besides keeping assurances in force, the Prudential's other major priority was to pay claims promptly, and to those who were genuinely entitled to them. When calamity struck, Prudential collectors were able to provide rapid financial relief to beneficiaries, often without waiting for a final inquest on the assured, thanks to the care with which agency records were kept. There was even a case in which a claim was paid to the heirs of a man killed in an air raid barely an hour after taking out a policy on his own life. It was not infrequent for people making claims to possess no supporting documents at all, their birth and marriage certificates, policies and receipt books having been destroyed along with everything else they owned. The difficulty of determining the fate of individual policyholders was multiplied a thousandfold after a bad raid. Some of the worst-hit parts of London were areas where there were heavy concentrations of Prudential assured. The Prudential Districts of Stepney, Bow and Bermondsey, as well as 57 agencies in another district, were closed down because the blitz had killed or driven away so many: 2,000 a week from the East End alone, at the height of the bombing. Some survivors left notes for the collectors wedged into shattered masonry, but many others did not.

And what of life in the divisions to which Chief Office personnel had been evacuated? Some, such as Torquay and Bournemouth, were also subject to air raids, and the northern centres such as Darlington and Wigan to frequent alerts, but at nothing like the level of London. Like their colleagues at Holborn Bars, the staff of most centres joined the local ARP efforts, swelling the ranks of the Local Defence Volunteers (later the 'Home Guard'), the Special Constabulary and the Royal Observer Corps. Others became air-raid wardens, ambulance drivers, Red Cross volunteers and fire-watchers. Sunday munitions-making, agricultural work and transporting the wounded were also undertaken, depending on the area. Many of the women staffed YMCA Forces canteens, or acted as nurses. The centres faced the same shortages of manpower as in the capital. Of nearly 2,000 Approved Society staff evacuated to Torquay, there remained only 530 midway through the war, the rest having gone either into uniform or into industry. Local people were recruited, the disadvantage being that many no sooner learned the job than they were directed elsewhere.

The original 'Decentralisation plan' of 1938 had been much influenced by the expectation that destruction of London from the air would be much worse than in fact it turned out to be.[16] Each of the provincial centres was self-sufficient, with its own banking facilities and a complete accounting system, its own audit and claims functions. As the story of the Prudential at war later published as *Salute to Service* put it, the Divisional Manager in these circumstances was '... much more than an office "boss". He became the head of a tribe'. The 'tribe' usually numbered fewer than a hundred, each of whom, uprooted from his or her accustomed surroundings, looked to the Divisional Manager to provide something of that security, that atmosphere of the 'Prudential family' characteristic of calmer days. Given the smaller population of the centres, there was inevitably some combining of duties at every level. Office life without the amenities of Holborn Bars was a learning experience for everyone: from the Divisional Manager himself – who might find himself in the role of Chief Office maintenance man, repairing a leaky roof – down to the second-class clerk, appointed Staff Controller in the absence of anyone more experienced.

The sense of solidarity that developed in the centres was one of the happier aspects of a somewhat artificial existence. Some of the married men were able to rent houses for their families and live a near-normal life. For the rest, living out of suitcases in billets, dependent upon the same facilities, putting up with the same shortages and inconveniences, tended to create a sense of community that was some defence against loneliness and anxiety, especially for the young. The work to be done was the first claim on everyone's attention; out of hours, the absence of the usual diversions tended to throw people back on their own collective resources. One consequence of the blurring of so many distinctions was the reduction of formality. Dress became more casual: several of the centres were located in very rural surroundings – an agreeable change for people inured to London's noise and grime, but transport was often lacking and winter weather, especially in the north, could be unexpectedly fierce. Warmth and comfort became priorities as both sexes traded City suits for more casual outfits. Skirts gave way to trousers, thin-soled shoes to brogues or wellingtons. Those who walked a mile or two from billet to workplace, or who possessed bicycles, found that their health improved.

With the great exodus from London, Ibis activities virtually ceased at Holborn Bars, but the provincial centres soon saw the resurrection of the IDOS and many of the sports clubs. Almost every centre soon formed an amateur

Prudential Approved Societies staff in makeshift quarters at the Victoria and Albert Hotel, Torquay.

dramatic group. At Torquay, the Prudential evacuees were able to mount full-scale dramatic productions for public audiences at the Pavilion, raising substantial sums for the war effort. A surprising number of talented musicians came forward, some eventually playing with the nearest big orchestras. (One, Stanley John (later Sir John) Pritchard, stood in for Leon Goossens' accompanist at a concert with the Derby Philharmonic in October 1944.[17]) Choirs and music groups, clubs for whist and bridge, and knitting circles (to make warm woollens for the troops) were formed at some of the 'country house' centres lacking other means of amusement. Augmenting the rationed diet with home-grown vegetables was possible at the rural centres, and all kinds of sales were organised to raise funds for the war.

One of the few Ibis initiatives that lasted right through the war was the *Ibis Magazine*, edited without a break first by W.M. Parker, then by H.E. Boisseau. Paper restrictions reduced it to 12 pages, which consisted mainly of chat from around the country and servicemen abroad. As the *Prudential Bulletin* ceased to be produced in 1941 and was not revived until 1946, it was left to the *Ibis Magazine* to keep alive the sense of a Prudential 'family' for more than 15,000 British members of it in uniform, and especially the 300 odd who spent time in captivity. Frank Morgan's Christmas letter, written in his strikingly elegant hand and duplicated to the men in the forces, had the same effect.

There were now, of course, Prudential men from Australia and New Zealand, Canada and South Africa, fighting in various parts of the globe. Not infrequently they found themselves in or near another country where the Company maintained a presence. Morgan encouraged visits to the overseas branches by Prudential servicemen, sure that they would find 'a grand welcome', and proof that 'the Prudential spirit is not confined to the old country'.[18] In this respect S.C. Canfield, Manager of the Near East, based in Cairo, was often gratefully mentioned, as was S.G. Marashlian's hospitality at his 'Villa Prudentia' in Cyprus.[19] There were countless instances of Prudential men running into each other in unlikely places: Eritrea and the Sudan, the Outer Hebrides, Kashmir, the Bahamas and Madagascar, to name a few. Letters to the *Ibis Magazine* often provided nice vignettes of this kind, such as one agent–2nd Lieutenant's story of being approached in the bazaar in Lahore by a Sikh in full regalia who introduced himself as 'The Gentleman from the Prudential' and asked if the soldier were interested in life assurance.[20] Perhaps such meetings were not so unusual, considering the number of Prudential employees around the world, but those involved found them extraordinary.

They were considered even more extraordinary when they occurred behind barbed wire. On many occasions, and especially in the Near East and the Far East, British and overseas staff met by chance, as did British and Canadian Prudential POWs incarcerated in the same camps in Germany. As well as food parcels, some men obtained Prudential training books through the British Red

Cross; they then gave talks on insurance subjects to any fellow-prisoners who cared to attend. One member of the field staff imprisoned in Bavaria was astonished to find that the man in the next bed hailed from Chief Office: the pair spent a good part of each day for several months studying the books sent to the Chief Office man. (This particular account had an interesting sequel. In April 1945 the camp was evacuated by the retreating Germans, leaving behind the agent, still recovering from wounds. Unwittingly, they also left behind the Chief Office man – hidden in a hole the two had dug under the floorboards of the hut. Both men were liberated by the Allies.[21])

Every serviceman or woman who returned to a Prudential post after the war brought his or her own story, and for valour and strange coincidence these matched any from the First World War. It was a Prudential man serving as a radar operator on HMS *Norfolk* who first detected the *Scharnhorst* in the Arctic waters north of Norway, and another, in the Far East, who descended in diving gear to repair the hull of his ship, while the ship was under fire. Another helped to blow up Gestapo headquarters in Copenhagen. A Prudential agent navigated a 200-ton wooden minesweeper across the Atlantic in heavy seas after its steering failed – something of a contrast to the experience of a colleague aboard the *Delhi*, which was known by the end of the war as the 'stooge' ship of the Mediterranean, having been bombed 203 times. A Prudential agent who became a Wing Commander received the DFC and two bars for downing nine enemy planes and damaging another four; on his next tour he shot down two further planes and flew his damaged bomber home on one engine. A number of men escaped from German prison camps and evaded capture for weeks; several even made it back to London. Stories like these were only the tip of a very large iceberg.

The Prudential employees who had the most singular experiences were not necessarily the men or women in uniform, or even the POWs, but those of the branches in countries directly affected by the conflict. They bore the weight of protecting the Company's personnel and assets, and of trying to carry on the business, while faced with a gamut of difficulties. Under the noses of enemy surveillance, the Prudential manager in Occupied Jersey wrote regularly to his 'old Aunt Pru' in Southampton to let her know all was well.[22] The coming of war short-circuited all plans for home leave, so that some of the staff remained at their posts for six, seven, even eight years without a break, sometimes under the most trying conditions. These ranged from shortages of essentials such as petrol and paper, to enemy occupation and all the menace to life and property that came in its train. That said, the effect of the war on the Prudential's overseas business was not always wholly negative, even if it led to hardship for numbers of its personnel.

The staff of the geographically vulnerable Near Eastern Branch, for instance, endured long periods when it was not at all clear what course the fighting in the Egyptian desert would take. The Branch records were duplicated and

at Holborn Bars. In a time of few pleasantly absorbing activities, one – although it involved hard work – was helping out in the deep shelter at Chancery Lane tube station, which opened in 1943 and was staffed by Prudential volunteers. Instead of being used as a public shelter as originally intended, the station was reserved for off-duty servicemen, including hundreds of allied soldiers from occupied European countries. The rota covered the hours from 8.00 p.m. to 8.00 a.m. Each night 6 volunteers of the total of 56 (all women) provided bed and breakfast for several hundred men. In 1943 too, Chief Office was cheered by the return of the Approved Societies, but the advent of the V2s in 1944 was the signal for their second removal to Torquay. Apart from breaking hundreds of windows, these terrifying weapons did no major damage to Holborn Bars, but Staple Inn across the street was not so fortunate. A direct hit on 14 August 1944 destroyed the Hall occupied by the Institute of Actuaries, together with the Italian Garden so lovingly designed by Mrs A.C. Thompson; Sir Alfred Waterhouse's former office at Staple Inn Buildings was also ruined.

However lamentable any loss of property, there was a strong resolve to restore it when the war ended. More problematical over time, yet impossible to reverse, were the conditions affecting some areas of the business. The Prudential shared the burdens common to the insurance industry during these years, but its size meant a corresponding increase in its share of the burden. There were heavy annual claims for war casualties, totalling more than £3,000,000 by the end of 1943, and over £5,500,000 by the end of the war, representing claims on nearly 110,000 deaths; 21,000 of these comprised fully one-third of all British civilians killed in air raids.[27] More than half of these claims were on policies carrying war exclusions clauses, which, in line with the decision taken at the beginning of the war, the Company had disregarded so as to pay the full sum assured. From 1943, to save manpower in accordance with a Government directive, all canvassing for new life business had ceased. Motor and accident business felt the detrimental effects of petrol rationing and the blackout. For marine business, the reduction in premium income in the last stages of the war derived from the lower amounts it was necessary to charge once the Royal Navy had made the shipping lanes safer.[28]

Yet despite a somewhat static period up to 1943, both Ordinary Branch and Industrial Branch premium income rose by moderate steps to considerably higher levels by 1945 than in 1939. In the case of the Ordinary Branch, this meant nearly £18,000,000 as against just over £14,000,000; the Industrial Branch's figures were £30,000,000 as opposed to £23,000,000 six years earlier, and included several years of record increase. Efficient service to policyholders, including the payment of national health benefits, had been maintained against all the odds. Much of this was a tribute to the 'temporaries'. In Frank Morgan's words:

Had anyone ... predicted that we should not only be able to carry on with a mere nucleus of pre-war Staff but handle record increases in I.B. business, mass transfers due to the "blitz", and a substantial output of O.B. and G.B. business he would not have been believed. But then who could have possibly foretold the truly phenomenal success of the supervisory members of the Field Staff in training a veritable army of Temporary Collectors and Probationers ... ? Or of the remarkably efficient manner in which over 1800 Temporary Clerks under the guidance of veteran members of Chief and District Office Staffs would master the intricacies of the administration side of the business?[229]

The uncertainties of the war, together with higher taxation and the extra costs already referred to, inevitably led the Board to adopt a cautious policy in allocating bonus. Before the war bonus amounted to £2 6s per £100 for whole-life and £2 per £100 for endowment assurances in the Ordinary Branch, and £1 12s per £100 in the Industrial Branch. By 1942 the amounts of bonus had been reduced to £1 per £100 on claims in the Ordinary Branch and 16s per £100 on Industrial Branch claims: rates which were maintained until 1948.

Investment experienced particularly negative repercussions from war conditions. In 1939, the Board had foreseen the likely need to make funds available to the Government, as it had during the First World War, and had invested substantial funds on a short-term basis so as to maintain a state of readiness. This in itself involved a lower rate of interest than if the money had been invested in other ways, but as it happened, interest rates were already well down, as were the values of Stock Exchange securities. Between 1939 and 1941, the effect of the war was, as Sir Edgar Horne explained it at his last Annual General Meeting, 'to close down practically every avenue of new borrowing, not only from abroad but at home too, with the single exception of Government loans'.

Every aspect of the British economy was redirected towards producing the maximum for the war effort. The Prudential subscribed immense sums for successive Government War Loans, and for National War Bonds and Savings Bonds, all of which yielded rates of interest far below those of happier times. There was neither the wish nor the option of avoiding this: supporting the Government to the utmost was viewed as patriotic duty, but neither, for the time being, did there exist more attractive possibilities. Halfway through the war the Company's holdings of British Government loans and securities amounted to £151,000,000, some 39% of the Prudential's total assets. By the spring of 1945 the amount of Government loans and securities held by the Prudential stood at £196,988,000 – nearly 47% of total assets. It also supported the Government War Loans issued in the countries abroad where it had branches, to the tune of £5,500,000. By then, Stock Exchange values were recovering somewhat and the end of the war was in sight, with the promise of a more open market as the country made the transition to peace.

As in the First World War, the nation's dollar resources were of crucial importance. The Prudential made available the assets and earnings of its New York subsidiary, as did other insurance companies their American interests, as security for the loan agreed by the American Reconstruction Finance Corporation under the Lease-lend scheme. Furthermore, the value of the Prudential's Canadian and American securities and sterling loans requisitioned to fund the war effort amounted to £5,800,000. In addition to all this, the Prudential participated in over 800 local 'Weapons Weeks' and a thousand 'Warship Weeks' around the country in the early years of the war, subscribing £10,000,000 to the London 'week' of the same kind.[30] The later 'Wings for Victory' programmes were similarly supported. One singular property investment made just after the war, but as a result of the Prudential's connection with Torquay nearby, was the purchase of the entire village of Cockington Forge. This came about through an approach from the residents, on the decision of the village's owners to sell it in lots at auction. The Cockington Trust was formed and with an injection of funds from the Prudential, the unified freehold retained. The village is recorded in

The Devonshire village of Cockington Forge, purchased by the Prudential at the request of its residents to preserve its unique character.

Domesday Book, and with its thatched cottages, remains one of the prettiest in South Devon.[31]

With the declaration of victory in Europe, the Prudential began the gradual process of dismantling the divisional centres and reintegrating their permanent staffs into the Chief Office system. This, like demobilisation, was a slow process: by April 1946 only 7,000 Prudential men had returned to their jobs; the rest were still awaiting release from the forces. Some, having gained high rank, found it somewhat anti-climactic to return to the same department (if a rung higher on the clerical ladder) as they had left. This was Company policy, however, intended to ease the transition to civilian life.[32] Those decorated or

FACING PAGE
Chief Office seen through the ruins of the *Daily Mirror* building, 1945.

mentioned in despatches numbered 278; almost the same number – 265 – as returned from prisoner of war camps. All discovered a London changed forever. The area around Chief Office had been devastated, and the turreted red pile stood out against the sky, looming over the ruins and drab hoardings around it like some great ship riding at anchor. The *Daily Mirror* building across the street was a bombsite. Favourite shops, favourite eating and drinking establishments were gone; between Holborn Bars and St Paul's little remained standing apart from Gamages and the churches of St Andrew, St Etheldreda and St Sepulchre; the City Temple was badly damaged.

Those attending the first Annual General Meeting after the war stood in silence for a few moments in memory of the 603 Prudential servicemen and women who had died since 1939. Commemorative plaques bearing their names were eventually mounted on a new memorial in the courtyard at Holborn Bars. A more novel commitment was the scheme of educational and vocational grants established for their children, to the value of £200 each, to be made available as the children reached school-leaving age. It seemed fitting to those at the time that any memorial, as well as serving as a reminder, should also have a forward-looking component.

As postwar austerity permitted, the Prudential Board sought to revive in the returning field staff the confident approach to business of before the war. The *Prudential Bulletin* and the Star Dinners recommenced in 1946. In the same year, Frank Morgan set a target for each agent of £3,000 in Ordinary Branch new sums assured. A new ethos of fairness that was part of the levelling tendency of life in the forces demanded the reform of some anomalies in pay and conditions. One notable example of this was the justification of salary scales between Chief Office and the divisions, in the course of which the long-standing practice of paying the income tax of Chief Office employees was discontinued.[33] Abroad, Prudential offices got to grips with repairs and recruitment. Perhaps the most stirring example of 'Prudential grit' was displayed by L.A. Williams, who spent some time in England rebuilding his health before returning to Malaya. Once his presence there was known, the Prudential's agents and staff began to reassemble and the business was quickly rebuilt as the Company announced its intention to honour all policies in force at the time of the Japanese invasion, whether or not any premiums had been paid. In an article for the *Prudential Bulletin* early in 1947 Williams expressed his conviction that 'the sufferings of the war years are now best forgotten'. What was necessary was 'to take stock of the present and look to the future'.[34]

SECTION FIVE

———

Expansion *and* Evolution

Into a New Era

IN May 1945, the same month that saw the end of the war in Europe, a British general election brought to power the third Labour Government of the century in a landslide victory. Labour under Clement Attlee would hold office for the next six and a half years, though with a much reduced majority after the general election of 1950. The programme of economic and social measures introduced during those years, which took the form of the nationalisation of key industries and the creation of what has come to be called 'the Welfare State', looks more radical in retrospect than it did to contemporaries. For the previous five years Churchill's wartime Coalition Government had mobilised the nation's entire manpower and resources for total war, assuming responsibility for every aspect of national life, from the direction of labour to the foodstuffs grown on the land and the provision of health and emergency services. The bombing, evacuations and rationing were shared by the entire population, and the relief of distress, however and to whomever caused, came also to be seen as part of the Government's all-encompassing role.

Though the war brought full employment, the social evils of the 1930s were still greatly in evidence. Underlying people's growing acceptance of Government controls during the early part of the war was concern and shame at the poor health of the children evacuated from the urban slums. The desire for social reform, with the aim of eradicating the divisions and inequalities of the Depression years, was one which all political opinion had in common. The war thus did away with the view that relief from the state was only for the poorest. A basic standard of security, underpinning the well-being of the entire popu-lation, became part of the ideal for which the war was fought. One feature of Labour's postwar social reforms was the degree to which the groundwork had been laid for them by the wartime Coalition Government.[1]

The foremost example of this was the Beveridge Report, the predecessor of postwar social legislation. Sir William (later Lord) Beveridge's promotion of labour exchanges and theories on unemployment had influenced the working out of the National Insurance Act 1911. Thirty years later he was appointed to chair an Inter-departmental Committee to study and recommend improvements to the entire existing patchwork of social insurance provision. This was effectively a brief to produce a coherent policy of social welfare for postwar society, a task technically beyond the remit of a Committee composed of civil servants. Its 200,000-word Report, published in December 1942 under the title *Social Insurance and Allied Services*, appeared with Beveridge's name alone as signatory to the recommendations – hence the title by which the instant best seller has always been known.[2]

Beveridge's call to arms against the 'Five Giants' of 'Want, Disease, Ignorance, Squalor and Idleness' has been the subject of many studies, but there is no need to do more here than allude to the points that affected the insurance industry. Three main planks underlay Beveridge's plan for social reconstruction: the creation of a free and comprehensive health service, a system of family allowances, and full employment. Beveridge proposed that in return for a flat-rate contribution, everyone, regardless of status or circumstances, was to belong to a state-run social insurance scheme and receive flat-rate benefit by right. This in itself was radical, and did away with the last tattered remnants of the hated Poor Law, and with the means testing and qualifying conditions of the 1911 Act and its subsequent amendments. His plan consolidated much existing welfare provision, and was thus in fact less original than it appeared in the hopeful climate that greeted it in the middle of the war. But in remodelling the existing system to provide subsistence benefits for all, at every stage of life and in every critical circumstance, many discrepancies were eliminated and a plan proposed that was universal, remedying the fact that many provisions of the 1911 Act had only covered working people and not dependants.[3]

Following the Beveridge Report, a series of Government White Papers made known official thinking on specific social issues. The third, issued in September 1944 and entitled *Social Insurance*, endorsed Beveridge's recommendations, and eventually served as the model for the National Insurance Act 1946. Included in the Beveridge plan, reiterated in the White Paper and provided under the National Insurance Act were unemployment, industrial injury, sickness, medical, maternity, widows', orphans', and retirement benefits, and finally – 35 years after the original National Insurance scheme – death benefit.

This, of course, was one of the traditional *raisons d'être* of industrial assurance, although 'life-of-another' policies intended to cover funeral expenses had formed a declining portion of annual new business across the industry since before the First World War. (In the Prudential, for example, only about one-sixth of new premium income was by 1946 derived from this source.) Beveridge held that a 'burial' policy was nonetheless the thin end of the wedge by which agents could interest proposers in other types of insurance. He also distinguished between the 'direct' expenses involved in burial, and 'indirect' ones such as loss of earnings to attend a funeral or the purchase of mourning clothes. The state benefit was intended to cover direct expenses only. The wage-earning classes that traditionally bought 'life-of-another' policies had never made this distinction. As Beveridge pointed out, 'no person can have more than one funeral', but many people might anticipate costs on a person's death that had nothing to do with the actual interment. Strict funeral benefit was of course insufficient to cover all the expenses arising from the death of a near relative, and the need to top up the grant with voluntarily transacted insurance was assumed, both by the state and by the industrial life offices.

The inclusion of death benefit in the 1946 Act was accepted by the life offices without too much resistance. This was partly because, in the current climate, national social insurance was viewed so favourably, and partly because there were more important battles in the offing. Speaking at the Prudential's Annual General Meeting in 1946, while the National Insurance Bill was still before Parliament, Sir George Barstow cited the proposed national welfare scheme as 'a striking illustration of the advance of humanitarian feeling in the political sphere', but warned against the stifling of free enterprise and the strong British tradition of voluntary thrift. State funeral benefit, however, had as its logical sequel the limitation of the industrial assurance offices' right to compete by selling funeral policies. The Industrial Assurance and Friendly Societies Act 1948 specified that only parents and grandparents could be insured, and only for sums up to £20; the insurance of children under ten was prohibited.

Of greater importance to the Industrial Life Offices Association (as the AILO had been renamed in 1940) was the fate of the Approved Societies. The Beveridge Report admitted that the majority of the societies had carried out their task well during their 35-year existence, but considered that the great variety in the services they provided was incompatible with the creation of a unified system. Societies such as the Prudential's, with a membership of over 4,500,000, and disbursing a wide range of discretionary benefits over and above the statutory ones, had an advantage over the multitude of smaller societies, some with only a few hundred widely scattered members. The fact that the largest and most efficient societies were allied to commercial concerns was wholly unacceptable to Beveridge. The companies' view had always been that generous discretionary benefits were possible because of the surplus resulting from favourable sickness experience and good management; the Report's was that it reflected selectivity in the choice of lives, though in the Prudential's case, superlative administration was conceded.

There were contrasting views, too, about the role of field staffs in the administration of the societies. The societies allied with companies asserted, in their evidence to the Beveridge Committee, that their 'outstanding feature' was that 'there is placed at the service of their members at their own homes the extensive agency staffs of the associated offices'. The agents, they said, '... form that personal link between the system and the insured person which is so essential.

They convey information in a way that no official form ... can do regarding new legislation, and advise greatly on matters which are vital to maintaining title to National Health insurance and pension benefits'.[4]

While the societies were not legally permitted to make a profit, the agents of the offices who serviced the system on behalf of the state did of course receive a per capita fee for doing so. The Report saw this link as a possible stepping stone to 'increase' for the agents and hence as indefensible despite the fact that the more than 9,000,000 members of the societies represented by this evidence (or more than 46% of all insured persons in the country) received an exceptional standard of benefits and service.

The Prudential and the ILOA strove to save the societies and produced several pamphlets in their defence, but there were simply too many anomalies in the unreformed national insurance system to permit their survival. In accordance with the National Insurance Act, the Approved Societies took on no new members after July 1947. The staggering administrative task of effecting the changeover to state control took until 1 July 1948, by which time the Ministry of National Insurance had recruited thousands of employees (many from the societies being disbanded), acquired the records of the 6,000 societies, and allocated National Insurance numbers to well over half the population. The offices' agents received no compensation for their loss of earnings from Approved Society work, estimated in the relevant evidence to the Beveridge Committee at nearly 12s a week out of average earnings of £5 13s.[5] (To compensate its own agents, the Prudential introduced the Guaranteed Earnings Scheme, which made up the difference between an agent's weekly earnings and the sum of £6.[6])

The National Insurance Act, together with the National Health Service Act which came into effect on 1 July 1948, were the main components of what soon came to be called the Welfare State.[7] These measures, together with the first round of the Government's programme of nationalisations (the Bank of England, the coal industry and the railways), were enacted against a background of harrowing postwar economic ills. In the first few years after the war the battle to curb inflation was carried on simultaneously with the repair of war damage and the struggle to revive industry, war-weakened and long starved of capital, so as to regain export markets. Continuing rationing and shortages strained the nation's patience, while the bitter cold of the winter of 1947 compounded the misery.

By the end of 1948, the Government was past the halfway mark in its term of office and anticipating the day when it would again have to face the electorate. All of the recommendations of the Beveridge Report save one had by now been enacted. That sole outstanding proposal was the nationalisation of industrial assurance. In the space devoted to the industry, Beveridge had drawn heavily on the Parmoor and Cohen Reports, and had come to the conclusion that 'while the system remains ... a competitive business', the traditional criticisms of high expense and lapse ratios could not be met. These faults he laid at the door of the collecting system itself, and of overselling by agents – a point strongly contradicted by the ILOA in its evidence, which stressed that lapse was a feature of any transaction involving regular payments and not just of industrial assurance. Beveridge did not share the life offices' view of their business as what amounted to a social service, either in its insurance function or in facilitating the voluntary thrift of the less well-off. The contrast between the expenses reported by the Prudential and by the other industrial life offices convinced Beveridge that 'the cost of industrial assurance could be materially less if it were conducted on the lines of the Prudential by a monopoly corporation'. In place of competition, Beveridge recommended that the state establish an Industrial Assurance Board, with a statutory monopoly on the use of collectors, and a commitment to '... work steadily to substitute direct payment of premiums for collection'.[8]

Concerned about Labour's plans in the run-up to the next election, the ILOA and the Prudential produced a paper entitled *State Ownership and the Industrial Life Assurance Industry* in February 1949. But with the manifesto *Labour Believes in Britain*, issued in April, any doubts about the party's intentions evaporated. Noting the provision of basic minimum benefits that had already been achieved through the social security system, it asserted that

> ... *this minimum can and should be added to by voluntary thrift. One of the best ways for the individual to save is through insurance. The nation's social security plan will be completed when industrial assurance itself becomes a great social service. ... Labour therefore proposes that all the industrial assurance companies, the biggest being the Prudential and the Pearl, and the larger collecting societies, should be taken over as they stand.*

This proposal drew a swift response from the threatened life offices. A point-by-point reply to the manifesto was sent to Members of Parliament and to the offices' own staffs by the ILOA. Hundreds of volunteer committees were set up throughout the country, advertising space was taken and posters sited.

It was the Prudential's – and the industry's – good fortune at this time to have in Sir Frank Morgan (recently knighted for his contribution to the industry) an effective spokesman and an implacable defender. Morgan had prepared and given evidence to the Beveridge Committee and advised on the National Insurance Act, but his conviction of the social and economic value of industrial assurance set him firmly against any attempt at Government interference. As he told the Prudential field staff: 'To me something even more vital than the fate of the Prudential is at stake: this proposal, if implemented, would sound the death knell of large scale voluntary thrift and cause compulsion to rear its ugly head. Make no mistake about that.'[9]

The removal of competition and creation of a monopoly would, he believed, result in the ruin of the business that would see the end of security of employment. On 3 May 1949, an open letter on the subject appeared as a supplement to the *Prudential Bulletin*. This was the first of many such communications, for Morgan believed in keeping every member of the Company informed about matters of common concern, and there had never been a matter of such common concern as the danger made explicit in the Labour manifesto. He urged Prudential staff to have the points at issue clear in their minds: in their ability to explain them when required lay part of the industry's defence. The rest lay in the resistance that he was confident would be offered by the nation's industrial assurance policyholders:

Every third person in the United Kingdom is a Prudential policyholder; the industrial life offices between them have business in four out of five of the homes of the lower income groups. These people are our friends. They are in a position to value the services they are receiving. They have much to lose by this proposal. When they fully understand how their personal interests may be affected it is likely they will exert powerful opposition.[10]

Sir Frank Morgan, MC.

The letter preceded a 12-point rejoinder to the Labour document. One item in the manifesto aroused Morgan's particular resentment, as showing, to his mind, either a lamentable ignorance of the business or the deliberate manipulation of the facts for political ends. This concerned the way the industrial assurance companies invested their funds. The manifesto declared that, 'In the past, the hard-won savings of working people have been invested as the industrial assurance companies thought fit. The companies have often made extremely high profits for their shareholders. Private profit has come before the public interest. In future public interest will come first.'

To which Morgan retorted:

What are the executives of an office to do with the premiums if they do not invest them as they think right and proper? It is because of their skill in the difficult matter of investment that British offices have an unrivalled reputation for strength and security which enabled them to survive unshaken the huge claims made upon them as the result of two world wars. It is to their credit and not to their detriment that they have made good profits. In the Prudential Life Branches the dividends to shareholders are directly related to the profits distributed to the policyholders. In the Industrial Branch approximately 75 per cent. of the distributable profits go to the policyholders, 12½ per cent. to the field staff, and 12½ per cent. to the shareholders. In the Ordinary Branch 90 per cent. goes to the policyholders and 10 per cent. to the shareholders. "Private profit" has not and does not "come before the public interest".

And he went on to voice his suspicion that the reasons given for Labour's decision were no more than a smokescreen: the real motive was the desire to obtain control of the industrial offices' funds, amounting to some £1,200,000,000.[11] While the offices invested their funds for the benefit of the policyholders (and which, it went without saying, the latter trusted the companies to do), 'In the hands of the State this would not be the primary consideration. Investments might well be made for political or State reasons, regardless of the security of the funds which in effect belong to the policyholders. The offices do not seek power to interfere with industry through their funds and their aim is to avoid obtaining controlling interests.'

Morgan also pointed out the inherent contradiction in the several points suggesting that the state could carry on the business more cheaply than the present offices while retaining the collecting system, without sacrificing agents' jobs or compromising the level of service given. If 'Labour was satisfied' that such economies were possible, he concluded, 'then they must be the only group of people so deluded ...'.

Barely a year earlier, on 30 May 1948, the Prudential had reached its hundredth anniversary (on the occasion of which Morgan had received his knighthood), although in the prevailing economic climate the celebration of it had been postponed.[12] The Centenary dinner that was finally held in May 1949 was the occasion of some fiery rhetoric. Sir George Barstow had recently declared that nationalisation would be 'an unmitigated disaster to the insurance industry and the country'. On 2 June 1949, given a standing ovation at a mass meeting of field staff at Holborn Bars, Sir Frank Morgan went further, referring to the Prudential's traditional independence from any form of political allegiance, which in the face of the present danger was having to be put aside. This he found 'deplorable, but inescapable, for those who are for nationalisation ... must be for it on *political* grounds – there *are* no other grounds for it'.[13] The best safeguard was 'talk on the doorstep'. Of every five policyholders so far canvassed for their views, two were against the proposal, one was for it, and two were undecided. Many people who had supported Labour's programme so far were alarmed by the prospect of the state taking over the life offices. Influencing the large population whose views were still shifting was the field staff's task, strengthened by the knowledge that no other body of men could undertake it with better advantage, or more justification.

Throughout the summer of 1949 Morgan travelled around the country on a hectic schedule, aiming at making it possible for every member of the Prudential field staff to attend at least one meeting where he was present. (He was a compelling speaker, and 90% of them had done so by September.) These meetings were partly intended to inspire, and partly to argue the case to those agents who were themselves in favour of nationalisation. As the pages of the *PSU Gazette* reveal, there was an element within the union that did support the proposal, but how many men this meant, of the 64% of the field staff (then about 16,000 strong) that belonged to the PSU, is difficult to gauge.

The British Insurance Association took space in more than 60 newspapers to declare its aim of informing every life policyholder in the country of what was at stake, and 11 of the other life offices requested Morgan's 12-point broad-side to circulate to their agents. The combined field staffs of the life offices (at this point numbering about 65,000) were encouraged to carry the campaign into every household they visited. They were often asked straight out for their opinion, and avoiding heated argument was not always possible, given the strength of Labour support in some areas. Morgan continued to urge Prudential agents to talk openly about the issue, even if this resulted in some loss of business. 'Is it not better to hazard some business and possibly lose a little rather than to lose the whole – because that, I believe, to be the alternative?'[14]

The statement issued by the Labour party in November 1949, modify-ing its original proposal to one of 'mutual ownership', was the first sign that the opposition mounted by the life offices was being taken seriously. A booklet published in February 1950 and entitled *The Future of Industrial Assurance*, spoke of 'mutualisation' rather than nationalisation. But in the proposal for a state board, as in the control over the appointment of directors and the combination of offices, the basic tenets of nationalisation were preserved. As Sir George Barstow put it, 'The new proposal was merely a new method of approach to the objective of State control and ... the change of method was actuated solely by the desire to placate policyholders and staffs.'[15] The ILOA responded by publish-ing *Industrial Assurance. A Reasoned Reply ... to the Labour Party's Proposals*, which again roundly rejected state interference 'whatever name they give it'.

Lack of understanding had led various critics to attribute the defects of industrial assurance to the agency system of house-to-house collection, and to the 'thoroughly impracticable idea' that it could be abolished without also abolishing voluntary life assurance among the wage-earning classes. Neither had investigators grasped that the proportion of funeral expense policies was now of rapidly diminishing importance. The disastrous consequences for the overseas earning power of British insurance were overlooked by planners advocating control of the long-term investment market. That this was their objective was undeniable. Labour declared that the state would guarantee all existing policies. 'Is it conceivable,' the ILOA queried, 'that the State would

THE STATE WANTS TO POCKET £1,200,000,000

POLICY HOLDERS' MONEY

(ONE THOUSAND TWO HUNDRED MILLION POUNDS TO DO WHAT IT LIKES WITH)

From an anti-nationalisation leaflet published by the ILOA.

accept responsibility for the liabilities of the Offices without controlling their assets?'[16]

The strength of the life offices' protest was a factor in the comparative lack of exposure the issue received in the run-up to the election of February 1950. Labour's return to power with its majority reduced to only 17 meant that for the moment the tension eased for the offices. They carried on the campaign just the same, with a Prudential publicity caravan touring the country. The Prudential Staff Union rejected both nationalisation and mutualisation at its annual conference in May 1950.[17] Labour's popularity was waning. Economic woes (which had forced the devaluation of the pound in September 1949) and political ones (with costly rearmament, the Korean War and disaccord in the Middle East) conspired with evidence of waste and mismanagement (the ground-nut scheme) to exhaust the nation's appetite for experiment. When the Conservatives returned to power in October 1950 with a programme of measures to control inflation, the black cloud of nationalisation was seen to have passed over.

The campaign had drawn the offices together in a common struggle, and the threat was – at least temporarily – beaten off. The life offices had discovered, however, that their role in the nation's economy was less well appreciated, the rationale for life insurance less well understood, than they had assumed. The industry was 'too modest about its achievements' and had not done enough to inform the public about them.[18] In 1951, the year of the Festival of Britain, the

British Insurance Association (BIA), the Industrial Life Offices and the Life Offices Association mounted public education campaigns. Dozens of leaflets on insurance as a savings medium were produced by the ILOA. These covered every conceivable savings objective, from a child's education or wedding to a peaceful retirement and meeting death duties. The BIA mounted an exhibition called 'Risks Round the World' at the Royal Exchange in London to promote the role of insurance in generating earnings abroad.

For its part, the Prudential embarked on one of the most famous of its advertising campaigns, resurrecting a popular music-hall phrase from between the wars, 'The Man from the Prudential' (from the song about young Albert and the lion), and matching it with a photo-character modelled on a real agent, Fred Sawyer of Huxtable in Kent. An article in *Illustrated* appeared as part of

Fred Sawyer, the model for the original 'Man from the Prudential', chats with policyholders.

'The Man from the
Prudential' proved to be
an adaptable fellow: images
of 'the Man' from several
different countries, 1951–65.

the anti-nationalisation campaign on 11 June 1949, and showed Mr Sawyer on his daily round. His trilby-hatted, tweed-suited figure with its confident stride was criticised by none less than the Chancellor, Sir Stafford Cripps, on the grounds that his rumpled waistcoat was hardly the last word in sartorial refinement. Reissued in 1951 using the slimmer figure of Mr 'Brad' Bradley from Putney, better turned out in a dark double-breasted suit, 'The Man from the Prudential' was an immediate hit and lasted as an advertising device until 1965 – the Dutch used a bowler-hatted version until 1986. In some Prudential territories, such as Pakistan and the Malay peninsula, 'the Man' assumed local garb and colouring. The Australian company and others ran the advertisements for a number of years in the popular *Reader's Digest*. Some countries produced their own conception of the figure with 'Service in His Stride'. Canada's (with a nod to the Company motto, *Fortis qui Prudens*) was called 'J. Fortescue Prudens' and combined a breezy, tailored look that was very North American with the usual emphasis on the British connection. South Africa's 'Man' at one point carried a rugby ball!

Within the Prudential, the nationalisation episode had a considerable psychological impact. The Company's financial strength had become the very feature that rendered it vulnerable. Its usual stance in relation to the rest of the industry – friendly, but somewhat at one remove – had been transformed into one of active instigation and solidarity. This was reinforced by Sir Frank Morgan's presence at the head of the Industrial Assurance Council, and drew the Company reluctantly into a spotlight that it had never sought. In the reminiscences of the staff and agents of the day, there is a sense that the Prudential came of age through the campaign, far more than through reaching its 100-year milestone.

At the Prudential's Annual General Meeting in May 1950, Sir Frank Morgan stepped down as General Manager, badly in need of rest after a demanding year, and was made a Director at the same meeting. Replacing him as General

Manager was former Actuary W.F. (Frank) Gardner, recalled by colleagues as a somewhat austere man of absolute integrity and dedication. Two years later Gardner would be elected President of the Institute of Actuaries, the fourth Prudential man (following William Hughes, Frederick Schooling and Sir Joseph Burn) to receive that honour. F.M. (Frank) Redington (a highly respected figure in the actuarial world who would serve as President of the Institute from 1958 to 1960) brought a delightfully human perspective to his role when he took over Gardner's former post as Actuary. Gardner and Redington, so very different as personalities, served as models of their profession for the scores of aspiring actuaries who trained under them. The genial Edward Borrajo was made a Deputy Chairman in 1950. The practice, begun before the war, of inviting men prominent in politics and law as well as in the world of insurance to join the Board continued, with two appointments in 1948: Sir Patrick Spens, KBE, PC, Chief Justice of India until 1947, and Sir James Grigg, KCB, KCSI, Secretary of State for War in Churchill's wartime Coalition Government. Hubert Lane, MC, joined following his retirement as a Deputy General Manager in 1947.

Some venerable names disappeared from the ranks of the Directors at around this time. Deputy Chairman Guy Philip Harben, who had opened his house to Prudential staff in need of rest after the war, retired through ill-health and died in 1949. Ernest Dewey, a Deputy Chairman since 1941 (and, long ago, the successor to Frederick Schooling as the most revered name in Ibis cricket), retired in the same year. Sir Joseph Burn, President of the Company since 1941, died in October 1950 at the age of 79, after 64 years' service. Since becoming President (he had very much wanted to be Chairman but his age and the war were against him) in 1941, Burn's active role had been one of counsel rather than responsibility, but he continued to visit the office two or three times a week until days before his death. Rectifying as far as possible the defects of lapsing and high expense had been his life's ambition: at his memorial service, Sir George Barstow spoke of Burn's ability 'greatly to advance the reputation of industrial assurance by the reforming, almost missionary zeal with which he approached the problems surrounding the insurance of the poor'. Having scented danger back in the 1920s, Burn found the prospect of state control of the industry distressing and, sadly, did not live to see it recede. One who did was John Roy Lancaster, son of Sir William. He too was 80 years old at the time of his death in February 1951, a Director since 1920, and probably the only man able to recall the move from Ludgate Hill to Holborn in 1879. Sir George Barstow, more fortunate in his health, was still an articulate and energetic Chairman (it was he who coined the phrase 'Home Service' to replace 'industrial assurance') when he relinquished his office on 21 May 1953, the day before his 80th birthday. Sir Frank Morgan was elected to replace him.

While it is beyond the scope of this book to go very deeply into the Prudential's role in the wider financial and commercial communities, the effects of changing conditions on the Company are of course very much part of its story. The bleak economic climate seemed to intensify in the early part of the new decade, with 1951 reportedly the most difficult year so far. In the five years since the war, lower interest rates and yields on securities in the 'cheap money' era, the national-isation of industries in which substantial investments were held, the restriction of investment opportunities, and finally, the insidious evil of inflation, were all problems which the Prudential had taken in its stride. Inflation in particular produced unsettled financial conditions unlike any previously experienced.

For life business, based on the accumulation of funds over a long period and oriented towards stability, inflation posed a most intractable difficulty. While the Actuarial, Investment and Group Pensions areas grappled with its reper-cussions (actuarial and investment matters are discussed below, and pensions in a later chapter), its most immediate and visible impact was upon the expense ratio and on the relationship between management and staff. This had always been characterised by paternalism on one side and deference on the other, but both approaches were gradually eroded under the duress of postwar instability. From 1947 through the early 1950s, the cost of living was rising faster than the basic guaranteed earnings agreed by the Joint Committee. While increases in the agreed 'basic' field staff remuneration were granted in 1951 (agents' salaries went up by 13% and overall remuneration by 21%) and 1952, such increases were the main cause of the rise in the expense ratio to 29.6% by 1953. By this time the Government's policy of wage-restraint made management doubly conscious that staff-related expenses – remuneration, bonus and pensions – made up 87% of total Industrial Branch expenses. This scenario made the Company unwilling to grant the further increases and higher expense allowances requested by the PSU.

Discontent flared up at mass meetings of agents around the country during 1952, reaching a peak in October when a deputation of 1,000 agents marched to Holborn Bars to hand in a petition addressed to Sir George Barstow. The petition was not replied to, but the Joint Committee subsequently agreed on a scheme whereby 'basic' was to rise by 9s (pensionable) to £6 14s a week, in exchange for cost reductions based on the absorption of 1,250 agencies over the next two years. The expense ratio was gradually reduced to 27.7%, but from 1956 it began to rise again – inflation being by then a fact of life – as fresh concessions were made to maintain agents' earnings and the standard of service to policyholders.[19]

Petitions and confrontations were not the way things were done in the Prudential, but neither – not even in the worst times between the wars – had both Company and agents felt the economic pinch so acutely. It reportedly came as a surprise to management to find that the indoor staff felt it no less. The Prudential Staff Welfare Association (PSWA) was not a trade union as was the PSU; as an almost philanthropic body, it had no tradition of protest. In 1952 it took the unprecedented step of asking for a rise in salaries across the board for Chief and District Office personnel. Geoffrey Haslam (who would later become Chief Executive of the Prudential Corporation, but who as a second-class clerk was then Chairman of the PSWA) had the unenviable task of telling General Manager Frank Gardner that management's offer was 'quite inadequate' – to which, after an incredulous silence, came the promise to think again. Two weeks later the desired increment was authorised.[20]

W.F. (Frank) Gardner, CBE, FIA.

The other consequences of the financial environment were less dramatic than the one just mentioned, but their impact nonetheless caused Prudential actuaries much perplexity. The low interest rates (2½% at one point) of the 'cheap money' era shortly after the war meant that the yield on the Life Branches' funds was declining, while at the same time, new business was flooding in, giving a false impression of the relative values of assets and liabilities. This was important because traditionally, the management of assets and liabilities had developed almost as separate functions, although there had been broad agreement on the way the assets backing the life funds should be invested. (This was a natural result of the way the management of the Prudential had evolved, with the position of General Manager as *primus inter pares* of the group of experts constituting a Senior Management Committee that included the Actuary and Joint Secretaries.) Later, with the acceptance that inflation was more than a passing phenomenon, came the realisation that a more integrated approach should be taken to the management of the life funds.

The man who devised the theory that heralded a virtual revolution in this field was Frank Redington, the Prudential's Actuary. 'Immunisation theory' centred on the investment of assets in such a way that the existing business was immune to a general change in the rate of interest, since the values of assets and liabilities would alter to the same extent with changes in interest rates. The paper Redington delivered to the Institute of Actuaries in April 1952, in which the concept of 'immunisation' was revealed, was at once recognised as a landmark in the profession.[21]

Redington also devised a means of dealing with another actuarial conundrum. Investment policy in the Prudential since first investing in equity shares back in the 1920s had always been to avoid accumulating large holdings in any one company. The resulting spread of investments gave the Company an interest in, as Sir Frank Morgan put it, 'the great majority of companies of standing whose shares are quoted on the London Stock Exchange'. In the changed economic circumstances of the mid-1950s came a re-evaluation of equities, and a 40% rise in their value that was due, in Redington's opinion, to 'a permanent re-adjustment to inflation'.[22] If the resulting increase in dividends and capital values on ordinary shares had been allowed to produce large additions to current surplus, the Prudential's traditional simple reversionary bonus would have been inadequate. Inadequate because unjust: the increases in dividends largely arose from investments made in the past, and were thus attributable in greater measure to older than to newer policies.

Older policyholders had a prior claim on these increased dividends, and to meet it, Redington proposed the idea of the 'terminal' or 'special' bonus. It was decided that these bonuses would be paid initially on claims arising in 1956, only on policies issued in the United Kingdom (not overseas), and based, subject to certain maximum amounts, on the number of years the policy had been in force before 1 January 1954. The special bonus for each such year was declared at 6s per £100 assured in the Ordinary Branch and 4s per £100 assured in the Industrial Branch. The example given at the Annual General Meeting in 1956 at which special bonuses were announced showed what the innovation would mean on a 25-year term with-profits endowment policy for £1,000 taken out in 1931. Maturing before the end of 1956, it would receive 23 years' worth of special bonuses for the period before 1954, which at 6s per £100 assured, added £69 in special bonus to the £1,000 policy, in addition to any reversionary bonus it might attract. The point was made on the same occasion that bonuses, both special and reversionary, were proof of policyholders' share in the fortunes of the nation's industry. In the wake of the nationalisation debate, and in the face of growing competition from some of the big mutual societies, it had been decided to increase the Industrial Branch policyholders' proportion of available surplus. (The field staff's portion of 12½% was later diverted into the improved remuneration mentioned above, payable from 1952.) To do this required a change in the terms of the Profit-sharing Scheme that had been in force since 1907. The Prudential's Articles of Association were altered in February 1952 by an Extraordinary General Meeting, to enable Industrial Branch policyholders to participate in the profits on the same basis as policyholders in the Ordinary Branch – that is, on the basis of an allocation of at least 90%, the remaining

F.M. (Frank) Redington, FIA.

amount of not more than 10% to be allocated to the shareholders, at the Directors' discretion. The shareholders' proportion continued to be reduced in favour of the policyholders: to 8.8% and 91.2% respectively in 1953, 7.7% and 92.3% by 1956.

By the latter date, an interesting change could be detected in the composition of the life business. Total sums assured and new premium income in the Ordinary Branch had overtaken those of the Industrial Branch. This was less because the Industrial Branch was standing still than because the Ordinary Branch was burgeoning; where Industrial Branch premium income had increased by 95% in the previous 15 years, Ordinary Branch premium income had increased by 170% in the same period. Ordinary Branch total sums assured exceeded £1,000,000,000 for the first time in 1954; by 1956 they were £1,100,000,000 to the Industrial Branch's £1,062,000,000. A number of factors contributed to this tendency. There was a growing preference for single-premium business. Postwar social legislation may have liberated a certain amount of 'emergency money' and given people the confidence to invest a lump sum. Undoubtedly, the return to full employment by the mid-1950s meant that some business was written by the Ordinary Branch that in leaner times would have gone to the Industrial Branch. Some of the increase came from group life and pensions business, which was still classed as 'ordinary'. The major increase, however, came from the ever-greater share being written by the Prudential's overseas offices.

Unlike Britain's economy, the economies of countries such as Canada, Australia, New Zealand, South Africa and those of East Africa entered on a period of expansion right after the war that continued through the 1950s. The rapid growth of the life business in these areas was astonishing. By the end of 1949, the total overseas sums assured in force, including bonuses, had risen to £174,000,000 – more than four times the 1938 figure, with an annual premium income of £6,400,000. This represented about 20% of the Prudential's total ordinary life business. In the single year 1950, total sums assured abroad rose to over £200,000,000 and premium income to over £7,000,000, or 30% of total Ordinary Branch business. In 1951, the £39,000,000 assured by the 42,000 new overseas policies written that year exceeded the totals written in the entire Ordinary Branch for any year before the war. By the end of 1953, overseas business represented 42% of the total business of the Ordinary Branch. Total overseas policies in force by then numbered more than 360,000, assuring over £300,000,000 – more than the sums assured in the whole of the Ordinary Branch as recently as 1942.

Canada, Australia, New Zealand and South Africa together accounted for 85% of the Prudential's overseas life business by 1954. Canada was consistently the healthiest market, providing the largest figures for any of the overseas branches. Both there and in the other countries immigration had been encouraged since the war and the agency network extended. Particularly in South Africa, but in the other countries as well, group pensions business on a with-profits basis had grown in tandem with commercial and industrial expansion.

There were inevitably repercussions for the Prudential in areas abroad that became politically unstable for one reason or another. Palestine was the first of these. Civil unrest and hostility to the British presence surrounded the creation of the modern state of Israel. In Jerusalem, the Prudential's office was situated in a kind of no-man's land and had to be moved; life business, since it had to be actively canvassed, almost dried up, although general business suffered less. By 1950 the Company was no longer writing life business in Palestine, and affairs in Israel were again being directly administered from London due to the impossibility by then of overseeing them from Cairo. In Egypt and in the Sudan, periods of tension, with racial disturbances, strikes and martial law, were offset by calmer ones when the business thrived. The decision was taken to cease writing life business in Egypt and the Sudan in 1955, though the office remained to service existing policies and conduct general business.

The sequestration of British assets by the Government of the United Arab Republic in November 1956 at the time of Suez was a disquieting episode. The Prudential's representative in Cairo was briefly imprisoned and its property and funds, like those of other British and French concerns, transferred to a 'Custodian General'. Early in 1957 the news arrived at Holborn Bars that the Prudential's assets had been sold to the recently formed Egyptian Al Gomhouria Insurance Company. An injunction was obtained from the High Court to prevent the Egyptian company from taking over British Government securities belonging to the Prudential. Seven years of legal wrangling between Chief Office and the various Egyptian authorities were to pass before the Prudential's claim for compensation of £136,000 could be paid by the Foreign Compensation Commission.[23]

A similar fate befell the Prudential's interests in India, although for completely different reasons. The Prudential's Head Office had been moved from Lucknow back to Calcutta in the run-up to partition in 1947. Under Manager and Actuary A.J. Males the business carried on through the period of mass migration and intercommunal violence that followed. The Calcutta office continued to supervise affairs in Pakistan, Burma (though business was discontinued after that country became independent and left the Commonwealth in 1948) and Ceylon. In general, the period following partition saw life and general business prosper in both India and Pakistan as rural development and education advanced. Then, in 1956, alarmed by malpractices among local life assurance companies, the Indian Government took the decision to nationalise the life assurance industry. It was felt that this must include the offices of foreign companies, although there were no allegations of malpractice against them. After 30 years in India, the Prudential's sums assured and bonuses in force exceeded £18,000,000 (just under 2% of the Ordinary Branch fund) and included £2,500,000 assured under sterling policies on British and European lives. Frank Redington, then Deputy Chairman of the Life Offices Association, led a delegation of British and Canadian insurance representatives to India to discuss the exclusion from nationalisation of policies on non-Indian lives. Under the terms of the Life Assurance Corporation Act 1956, this concession was granted and compensation promised to the offices for their nationalised Indian business. The amount of £335,000 was repaid to the Prudential in recognition of the funds transferred to India in the early years of the business.[24] The loss of India was a considerable blow to the Prudential's confidence in its overseas business.

Palestine, Egypt, the Sudan and India were thus the territories where business was lost to the Prudential in the 1950s (others, such as Malaya, Cyprus and Malta, had their temporary difficulties but recovered when the political climate improved, though the Prudential would eventually withdraw from the latter two) and the fast-developing, English-speaking Commonwealth countries were the areas that gave greatest cause for satisfaction. Record amounts of new business were written in Canada, Australia, New Zealand and the African countries in almost every year during the 1950s. By 1960, total new premium income from overseas was £2,800,000, assuring sums of £102,000,000 and new annuity and pension business of £2,000,000.

In the early days of the overseas life business, the premium rates set for each country reflected local conditions, such as mortality, interest rates, expenses and legislation. The bonus declared in each, however, was the same as that declared at home, since trends abroad took time to become sufficiently clear to allow for differentiation. As the business grew, it became apparent that some countries generated more surplus than others, and the Prudential began declaring rates of bonus appropriate to each territory. In 1950, for instance, the reversionary bonus per £100 assured was £1 6s for policies issued in Australia, New Zealand and Canada, £1 14s for those issued in South Africa, East Africa, the Rhodesias and Nyasaland, and £1 for all the others. The rate for policies issued in the United Kingdom was £1 8s.

Each territory was visited with relative frequency by members of management from London. This might be brought about by some actuarial problem, or by the need to vet some major investment, the liabilities of each overseas branch being balanced by investment assets in the country in question. The visits of Chief Office men in the 1950s and 1960s were a contrast to the grand tours made by Sir Edgar Horne between the wars! His baggage had included guns for big game hunting and formal evening wear for the opera (though probably not both on the same trip), while the departure of Sir Joseph Burn and his wife Emily for the Far East in 1931 occasioned a send-off at Victoria Station from members of the Prudential management. (Reports of a spontaneous rendition of 'May God Be With You Till We Meet Again', sung as the train pulled away, convey the degree to which the world and corporate life had changed within a generation.) After the war the leisurely, semi-social trip became less frequent as shorter, more focused visits were made possible by air transport. Those who went abroad clocked up a dozen flying hours to cross the Atlantic, more to South Africa and far more to Australia or New Zealand, but could do the round trip in a week. Sir Frank Morgan, whose travelling career spanned the 1920s to the 1960s, experienced the contrast most vividly. He and the then Manager for Canada, Rupert Thorp, made a six-week train journey across Canada before the war, stopping for a few days in each of the major cities for a heady round of intense work and a full social programme organised months in advance. The two men made much the same kind of trip in 1958, visiting agents in outlying, snowbound parts of Ontario in a hired car, but by then it was also common for an actuary to fly to Montreal, carry out some specific task, and return to London.

In the territories themselves, surprisingly little changed in the way of life of the Company's representatives. Particularly in India and Malaya, where British Prudential staff were more visible and where business contacts and social ones still tended to overlap, life and work were hedged round with protocol and un-spoken rules. Prudential men in these territories still had the dues to three clubs of their choice paid by the Company. It was customary in Sir Frank Morgan's time as General Manager, as in Sir Joseph Burn's before the war, for overseas staff to wait until their earnings reached a suitable level before marrying. (Those who married without the Company's blessing might find themselves unceremoniously transferred home.) But increasingly, positions abroad were being filled by the nationals of the country concerned: in Malaya there were only three British senior staff in 1957, the rest of the staff, both clerical and field, being Malay, Chinese or Indian.[25] In Pakistan and the countries of East Africa, an educated middle class was emerging and could be drawn upon for supervisory and clerical posts. In Ceylon, a country where historically the assurance concept had flourished, the government established a monopoly Insurance Corporation in 1961, with the result that all privately written new life business, whether foreign or local, was prohibited after January 1962. No compensation was offered to the offices taken over but, as in Egypt, the sums concerned were not large.[26]

All overseas business was, of course, ordinary life or annuity and pension business; the Prudential did not transact industrial business overseas. The trend noted earlier in the United Kingdom, whereby new ordinary business had over-taken new industrial business, had become an accepted fact by 1960. What was also noticeable was that the general rise in the standard of living had eroded some of the differences between them. The Prudential's core business had always been assumed to be industrial assurance, but with the boundaries shifting, it seemed that the Ordinary Branch was destined to grow at the expense of the Industrial Branch. Death cover was still one basic purpose of industrial assur-ance, but the public was increasingly attracted to policies which combined it with saving.[27] The endowments that comprised the great majority of new business were for larger amounts; working-class policyholders were now able to afford higher premiums. The old way of paying them by tiny amounts once a week was also being replaced by monthly payments, an option available in the Industrial Branch for decades but never especially popular before. This change may reflect the growing number of people who were paid monthly, rather than weekly, and the number of women going out to work, and hence 'not home' for the agent's weekly call, as in times past. Now, most people could save enough to pay at less frequent intervals. The visit from an agent was still seen as essential, both for convenience's sake and in reinforcing the will to save. From 1963 weekly collections were done away with (though some agents are said to have continued to collect weekly from elderly folk for whom they knew themselves to be the only regular social contact), and all new Industrial Branch policies became payable monthly and carried a minimum premium of 2s.

A new emphasis on savings reflects social change in the 1950s.

This measure was a natural development reflecting social change, but it was also helpful in reducing costs at a time when the life area as a whole was under scrutiny. The Prudential had dominated the entire field of life insurance for almost a century, and there was a sense of inevitability in the record results reported each year. To some it seemed that the organisation was carried along partly by its own momentum. But by the late 1950s competition from other offices was intensifying. As Frank Gardner reported in 1957, the Prudential secured more than half of the new ordinary business written by the life offices in that year, yet by the early 1960s, its share of the market was declining. This was despite having correctly identified a new middle-income group coming into being through the postwar redistribution of incomes, and having successfully introduced a number of new products aimed at its particular needs. Some of this competition derived from new areas into which the Prudential was as yet unwilling to venture. For the Prudential to maintain its prime position would require tighter procedures, greater efficiency, and savings in costs and time.

When Frank Gardner retired as General Manager in 1960 to join the Prudential Board, he was succeeded by Deputy General Manager Kenneth Usherwood. Intellectually adventurous (some found his unpredictable manner and irreverent sense of humour daunting), Usherwood was fascinated by new developments in technology. He would comment in his Presidential address to the Institute of Actuaries two years later that 'The man who immures himself in his professional castle deprives himself of much'. Renovation of the systems that had grown with the Prudential – primarily information storage and working procedures – were seen by Usherwood as essential in meeting the current challenges, and he had already devoted considerable study to both fields. Data processing using electronic computers was not yet widely used, although for some years the Prudential had been using computers in the group pensions area and in compiling the payroll. In 1960 Usherwood ordered a large system based on the Ferranti 'Orion' computer for the Prudential. Two of these machines were delivered in 1962, and the records of the more than 1,250,000 Ordinary Branch policies then in force were subsequently transferred onto magnetic tape. The aim was to update the whole of these records daily, and to eliminate much of the routine work of the older punched-card system. The same procedure was then applied to the Industrial Branch cards, which up until this time had occupied an entire floor of the rear block of Chief Office.

The savings thus brought about were not confined to Holborn Bars. The reduction of Industrial Branch record copies from three (punched-cards at Chief Office, district office loose-leaf ledgers updated weekly and agency registers) to two (the magnetic tape record at Chief Office and another printed from it onto agency record cards (ARCs) held by the agents) eliminated the district office registers. Of the 200 district offices created in the 1920s as part of the decentralisation plan, only 60 remained. It was decided to phase them out, relying on natural wastage, retraining and relocation to avoid staff redundancies.[28] One long-term effect of the First World War was that there were few men to retire prematurely; district office men were nearly all young enough to be transferred to other work.

K.A. (Kenneth) Usherwood, CBE, FIA.

With the move to large-scale data processing, the Prudential was once more in the vanguard of new technology. While the changes mentioned were coming into effect, Usherwood was also grappling with the outmoded organisation and procedures at Chief Office. Since the 1930s little had changed – departments had merely grown. The jobs and methods of the 1930s were still effectively those of the era before the First World War, and some practices so entrenched that no-one really knew where their origins lay. It is interesting to note that Marks & Spencer was in the throes of 'Operation Simplification' at about this time, and Usherwood's interest may have been sparked by this. Applied to the Prudential, the result was an overview of the entire departmental functioning of Chief Office, known as the Owen Report after the man placed in charge of it, Deputy General Manager Ronald Owen. Desmond Craigen, having absorbed as much as he could in a year's secondment to the Treasury's Organisation and Methods Department, returned to Holborn Bars to set up a similar area. The 'O&M' was initially staffed by men who volunteered for the job. Among them were F.B. (Brian) Corby, newly returned from four years as an actuary in South Africa (who in his retirement claims that he did not volunteer!). The O&M's task was to identify duplication of effort or resource, areas where procedures survived where the rationale for them had disappeared, and where manpower might be saved or better used. As a hand-picked group carrying out a new function, it needed – and got – management backing in overcoming resistance to change. Inevitably, there was a degree of this, and of suspicion of O&M as an American-inspired novelty. A further innovation was the use of the outside consultants P&A to carry out systematic work measurement of maintenance and life administration staffs, and eventually of middle and senior management. A system of job evaluation for clerical and supervisory staffs was devised by Philip Meikle, who joined the O&M after years in India, Pakistan and Ceylon.

Long service – men with 40 or even 50 years were not uncommon – was still very much the accepted pattern in the Prudential, and the ethos of 'growing your own timber' still dominant. Young men who came into the Company in the 1920s or 1930s, often through a family connection, were reaching retirement age by 1960. Those who occupied the middle and upper management ranks were exclusively 'home-grown'. One might have said that the Prudential-bred held such posts 'to a man' were it not that in 1960 Monica Allanach, an actuary with 22 years' service and later the first woman to reach management rank as Actuary for the UK, was made a Deputy Controller. (Later she broke new ground outside the Prudential by becoming the first woman to serve as Vice President of the Institute of Actuaries, from 1976 to 1978.) From about the time that data processing and the O&M were introduced, the idea that a career in the Prudential properly progressed from entry to retirement began to bend, as the first specialised jobs arose for which experience within the Company was not available. Employees interested in computing had the opportunity to train, but having done so, often left for greener pastures. As computer applications increased during the rest of the 1960s, the practice of looking outside to fill designated positions gained ground. On the other hand, the advanced training scheme known as the 'Circus' (begun after the war and then halted) was revived. Those 'home-grown' men identified as having management potential were given intensive exposure to the various business areas, often as a prelude to an appointment overseas and a move onto the management escalator on return.

All of these changes gave the late 1950s and the early 1960s the sense that the pace of change in the Prudential was quickening to keep up with the changes outside. There were intangible, but very real, pressures upon the idea of home-grown timber and the wider extension of it that was the concept of the Prudential family. The loss of some overseas business had shown that the 'family' was not immutable; inflation, heightened competition and the urgent need to modernise had a similar effect on the individual sense of security. The shifting emphasis in the life business, for example, in due course brought about what seemed an almost cataclysmic change: the decentralisation of Life Branch functions, the first stage of which was the relocation of Industrial Branch administration to premises in Reading. Between 1960 and 1963, the departments dealing with new business and registration, comprising about 700 staff, moved first to various buildings owned by the Prudential in the town, then in 1964 to Forbury House in the town centre. The divisional audit departments were also moved, to the divisional offices in the parts of the country they served. While separation from the nerve centre of Holborn Bars – an inconceivable turn of events to the long-serving – was a wrench to some, others welcomed the chance to abandon the urban environment for a rural one. The transition was smoothed by financial help with moving and the construction of a new Ibis sports ground at Tilehurst for those working at Reading.

Coming within the same few years, decentralisation, the elimination of weekly collections and the decision to phase out the district offices ended the long era during which the Prudential was dominated by its Industrial Branch. The indications were that the relative decline of industrial assurance would continue, as the saving habits of the working population moved away from cash payments and towards bank accounts and direct debits. By the late 1970s, only 15% of profits would be derived from industrial assurance, while 40% came from ordinary life and pension business and 30% from general insurance, including reinsurance; the remainder represented profit on investments.

Something must be said about the investment of the Prudential's life funds in the postwar period and about the organisation and criteria for managing them. Life fund investment between 1945 and the mid-1960s fell roughly into three timespans. When the war ended, more than half the Prudential's assets were in Government stocks, although it was expected that peace would widen the investment panorama as reconstruction got under way. New opportunities, when they came, absorbed only part of the funds available. The result was that life funds continued to be overbalanced in favour of Government securities, a situation exacerbated by the compulsory transfer of holdings in the railway and electricity companies into Government stocks after nationalisation in the late 1940s. Given the low rates of interest and decline in the net yield from equities, this first period, from 1945 to 1951, was a worrisome time for life fund investment.[29] The search for higher yields prompted the Prudential to invest in substantial unquoted loan stock in industrial companies such as ICI (£1,500,000) and the Distillers Company Ltd (£2,000,000).

As confidence in national recovery returned, the second period, which broadly covered the rest of the 1950s, brought a dramatic rise in interest rates and the surge in the attractiveness of equities mentioned earlier in the context of terminal bonuses. The Prudential's investment in equities, particularly in the ordinary shares of industrial companies, increased to the point where its holding was the largest of any individual insurance company in 29 of the 40 largest British industrial companies.[30] It also enlarged its investment in property and property development companies, and mortgages. With the growing importance of with-profits policies, it became necessary for life funds to include a higher proportion of assets with the potential to provide a 'real' rate of return relative to inflation. The strength of equities and the relative decline in the importance of gilts continued into the 1960s, when in the third period, the proportion of assets invested in property and mortgages began to expand significantly, in the early stage of what became the property boom of the early 1970s.

By the 1950s the Prudential had been an investing institution for nearly a century and had a tradition of investment expertise, embodied in such men as Sir Joseph Burn, Sir George May, Percy Crump, Ernest Lever and C.W.A. (Allan) Ray. Leslie Brown was Joint Secretary with Allan Ray from 1942 until Ray's retirement in 1955, after which he carried on as Chief Investment Manager until 1970. Brown was at this time probably the most respected investment man in the City. From the early 1950s, the pursuit of a more unified investment strategy brought the investment and actuarial areas closer. Luckily, Leslie Brown and Frank Redington got on 'extraordinarily well' as representatives of areas that 'necessarily go together but don't necessarily think together'.[31] Broad investment policy, such as whether a high or low proportion of available funds was to be invested in a particular sector, took into account the discussions between investment and actuarial management and was subject to the final approval of the Prudential Board sitting weekly as a Finance Committee. Below the investment managers, the emphasis was on maintaining or buying in specialised knowledge in each of the investment areas in which the Prudential had an interest – ordinary shares, Government stock, industrial and commercial debt quoted on the market, commercial mortgages and other unquoted debt, house purchase loans, commercial, industrial and agricultural property (and, to a smaller extent, residential property), and the money market. Although the greater part of the Prudential's assets was British, a proportion derived from the Commonwealth and from other foreign countries. A geographical analysis reported at the Annual General Meeting in May 1951 revealed that 89.8% originated in the United Kingdom, 8.5% in the Commonwealth and 1.7% in other countries.

The revival of the equity market prompted the formation of an economic intelligence unit in 1958 under the auspices of the economist Harold Rose. This eventually became the largest such research team of any insurance company in Britain, said by the early 1960s to employ more economists on macro-economic analysis and forecasting than did the Treasury.[32] The analysts, specialising in a particular industry, regularly produced assessment forecasts for a five-year period of the 200 largest companies whose shares were held by the Prudential. As R.E. (Ron) Artus emphasised in his report to the Wilson Committee some years later, the share-evaluation-based structure of investment and portfolio analysis was never the sole or blind determinant of equity transactions, but rather, a useful guide and an important part of the discipline of investment management.[33] A broad spread was achieved by not allowing too great a concentration on any one area, nor within any one area. Other criteria, such as the marketability of a company's shares, or its dependence on a particular commodity whose price was liable to fluctuation, brought into play the expertise and judgment of the investment team.

As Sir George Barstow reminded his audience at the Annual General Meeting in 1953, the Prudential could not create opportunities for investment, but only avail itself of those that arose. The guiding aim of obtaining the best return consistent with security dictated that the industrial companies in which policyholders' money was invested be unshakeably sound. This had traditionally meant large to medium-sized companies, although the Prudential's wide portfolio included some smaller ones. (The Company's commitment to development and venture capital projects was still being exercised at one remove through its role in the Charterhouse Group, which since 1931 had been bridging the 'Macmillan Gap' of lack of finance for small and developing companies.[34]) Between 1954 and 1960, as well as making or increasing its investments in the shares of leading companies, prevailing conditions encouraged the Prudential to extend its holdings in the smaller company sector of the market. The percentage of its total assets invested in equities, many of them in smaller companies, increased from 14% to 25% (about £200,000,000) during this period of equity strength.[35] Other insurance companies were following a similar course, and some were developing investment-linked insurance contracts, based upon their wide spread of small to medium-sized investments. Initially the Prudential resisted this course, only entering the market for investment-linked products, about which more will be said later, in 1967.

In one sense, large institutional investors such as the Prudential found themselves in something of a dilemma during this time. The funds available for investment were immense; very often the companies coming to market were not. Ideally the Prudential preferred holdings of between 3½% to 6½% of a company's equity. A shareholding of that size in a small to medium-sized company might not be big enough in investment terms to be worthwhile, while acquiring a larger percentage might carry with it an undesirable degree of involvement in the management. The difficulty of finding enough suitable investments to absorb the funds available – some £2,000,000 a week by 1965 – brought some relaxation in the chosen percentage of ownership. By the 1970s the Prudential held more than 10% of the equity in over 50 companies and more than 5% in over 200. Besides investing in established companies, the Prudential played a significant part in the market for new capital issues. New issues were sometimes problematical in that they tended to be made as offers for sale rather than placings, and very often to be oversubscribed. Given that this situation usually favoured the small application over the large, obtaining a shareholding of the desired size was by no means a foregone conclusion. As well as investing in new issues where possible, the Prudential also acted as an underwriter. It was usually offered between 2% and 4% of the sub-underwriting on new issues in the London market, and, as Ron Artus recalls, it was widely regarded as the 'bellwether' office during the 1950s when insurance companies dominated the sub-underwriting of issues.[36]

While the Prudential tended to try to keep its shareholdings below 10% of a company's equity, even in this range it was frequently the largest single institutional shareholder. The allegation of undue influence that was so adamantly refuted during the anti-nationalisation campaign continued to be a sensitive point. In 1958, the Radcliffe Committee accepted the claims of the Prudential and other insurers that they neither sought nor exercised control over the managements of the companies in which they invested.[37] That the Prudential's advice and guidance was sometimes requested by them was acknowledged openly, and the good relations that made such dialogue a natural occurrence were valued. On the whole, however, companies asked for advice when problems arose, so that solutions, when they were offered, may have looked to the outside world more like interference than the intended helping hand. In cases where it was the largest single shareholder,[38] the Prudential's investment managers naturally kept an eye on the way the company in question was run, and very occasionally, where there was apparent mismanagement, felt an obligation to intervene to protect its own and other shareholders' interests.

The case that comes to mind in this regard is almost legendary in the Prudential and the City. Mention of the Birmingham Small Arms Company (BSA) and 'the Docker affair' summons up, even after 40 years, the image of Leslie Brown as a quietly spoken David in pinstripes facing the flamboyant Sir Bernard Docker, a latter-day Goliath backed by an entourage of hecklers. Sir Bernard was Chairman and Managing Director of the BSA, a company his father had done much to build up, and the Prudential was the BSA's largest single shareholder. The Dockers – Sir Bernard, with his yacht and his fleet of Daimlers (one of which was gold-plated), and his wife Norah, bedecked in furs and jewels – were the darlings of the tabloid press in the mid-1950s, personifying the triumph of glamour and plenty over the drabness of austerity. Unfortunately for the BSA, glamour seemed also to have triumphed over common sense. The degree to which the Docker lifestyle was subsidised by the company, over and above the Chairman's £20,000 salary, not unnaturally aroused the discontent of the rest of the BSA Board. The final straw was Docker's attempt (defeated, in the end) to force the election of Lady Docker's brother-in-law to the Board. Leslie Brown, aware of the concern of other BSA shareholders, first had a meeting with Docker to request an independent enquiry into the way the company was being run, but this was refused. Director John Sangster (who had sold his Triumph Motor Cycle

Company to the BSA) then approached Brown to discuss his colleagues' unease, and offered to put the request for an enquiry before them. Brown's letter to Sangster, outlining shareholder misgivings, was laid before the Directors. As the writer put it, the letter 'facilitated, rather than caused', the subsequent removal of Docker from office; Sangster was elected in his place.[39]

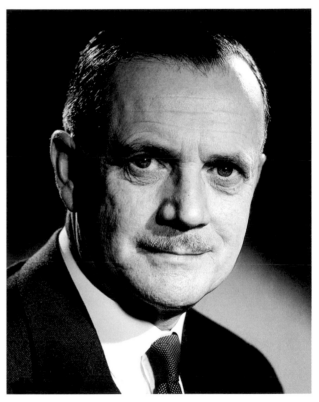

The ousted Chairman's campaign to regain his position went on for months, and even included the purchase of time on ITV to rally BSA shareholders to his cause. An Extraordinary General Meeting was finally convened at Grosvenor House to deal with his resolution for reinstatement. Many of the 1,500 shareholders who attended were Docker supporters, and made the fact known loudly both from the microphone and from the floor. Docker delivered an emotional hour-long appeal, denying the allegations of extravagance and mismanagement, after which there were numerous interventions, for him and against. For a time it appeared that he would have his way.

Leslie Brown, FIA.

Leslie Brown's eventual approach to the microphone produced pandemonium in the packed salon. The quiet words he uttered when he was finally allowed to speak – 'My name is Leslie Brown, and I represent the Prudential Assurance Company' – have passed into City lore. He explained that the Prudential Board had concluded that, out of duty to its own policyholders and to the other shareholders, it must make an exception to its policy of non-interference and support the directors of the BSA; for this reason the Prudential was going to vote against Docker's resolution. After Brown, Norah Docker and Sangster, among others, had each had a say, the votes were counted. The result was resounding defeat for Docker by four votes to one.[40]

The Prudential's role in the affairs of the BSA caused a stir, not only because of the publicity surrounding the Dockers, but because it was so rare for the Company known in the City as 'the sleeping giant' to flex its muscles.[41] In the future, however, the Prudential's reluctance to involve itself in the management of companies in which it had an interest would be increasingly challenged. Sometimes, as in the matter of the BSA, concern for the quality of management would be the precipitating factor. In 1959, for example, the Prudential's refusal to participate fully in the loan scheme worked out by Morgan Grenfell for the shaky GEC carried implicit censure of the management of that company, and was a factor in the resignation of its Chairman, Sir Leslie Gamage.[42] The need to take a larger-than-preferred percentage, or the advance of a particularly large loan, would make joining other companies' boards a more common step for Prudential investment men.

Increasingly, as the 1950s gave way to the 1960s, investment of the life funds ceased to be seen as an activity that was almost freestanding, and came to be viewed more as a response to the needs of the business in meeting its liabilities and maximising its profits. This was another subtle but major change, to rank alongside the erosion of the old distinctions between the Prudential's life branches, and growing competition in the marketplace from products such as investment-linked pensions and insurance contracts that marked the convergence of areas that had hitherto operated independently. How the Prudential countered or took advantage of these trends remains to be told.

Against a Backdrop of Change

So far, the life branches, as the main characters in the Prudential story, have held centre stage. By comparison, the General Branch has played a secondary role, overshadowed by the twin stars of the Ordinary Branch and the Industrial Branch. In the postwar period, its main subdivisions were still the traditional ones of fire, accident and marine insurance, though within these it offered a variety of policies catering for almost any day-to-day incident. Since many such events related to property in one form or another, it was a rare year in which natural or man-made disasters did not result in a high number of claims, if not in Britain, then in one or more of the 34 countries in which the Prudential carried on general business by the mid-1960s.

The years immediately after the war saw the unleashing of pent-up demand for general insurance which continued strongly through the return to prosperity in the 1950s. Record increases were achieved for several years in succession, starting with a premium income of £5,487,000 for 1947 that was double that achieved in 1938. The only shadow to mar this achievement was at first no bigger than the proverbial man's hand, but in time became a formidable problem. This was in the field of motor insurance. The number of cars coming onto the roads after the war brought a rise in the number of accidents. The cost of damage to vehicles and of third party claims rose for this reason, and was exacerbated, once inflation took hold, by the spiralling cost of labour and materials. Through the 1950s premium rates for motor insurance had to be recalculated again and again owing to the relentless increase in the accident rate, as more and more cars were manufactured and a rising standard of living brought them within the reach of more and younger drivers. Poor weather in a given year was an additional factor in high levels of accident claims. One of the concerns impressed upon the field staff was the need to persuade policyholders to revise their insurances to keep in line with current values, which were being driven upwards by inflation. A systematic revision of domestic policies became part of the home service offered by agents. Not infrequently they discovered that the insurance taken out before the war stood by the early 1950s at a quarter or a fifth of the replacement cost of the items covered. General insurance, it was often repeated in the pages of the *Prudential Bulletin*, was in many ways easier to sell than life, since in the latter the proposal was encouraged to insure for the benefit of others, but in the former, he was insuring for his own benefit. Frank Gardner as General Manager frequently emphasised the usefulness of a wide and varied general business account as a solid addition to earnings, and the fact that general business so often led to life business. Throughout the 1950s he periodically reminded agents to concentrate on non-motor insurance to offset the increasingly unfavourable motor experience.

General business, as Gardner put it 'can be said to touch human activity at almost every point' and seen like this, 'it becomes more human and interesting'.[1] The mid-1950s saw a plethora of new General Branch insurances that did indeed reflect the changing social scene. Prosperity, competition and advertising were conspiring to create new needs and new social groupings, and the nation's habits were altering under the twin influences of novelty and choice. Consumer durables such as washing machines and television sets found a place in more and more homes as hire purchase made them widely affordable. Foreign travel became more common. In response the Prudential's 'Hearth and Home' domestic contents policy was updated, and various travel, motor and baggage policies designed for the increasing number of people who could afford Continental motoring holidays were offered. Insurance for private planes and boats, television insurance, transit insurance to cover the household effects of people emigrating to Canada, South Africa and the Antipodes, golfer's policies, trailer caravan policies and even 'Third Party Insurance for Coronation Celebration Events' were a few of the policies on offer. Existing policies against fire, burglary, personal accident (which included oddities such as 'death by laughter'), third party injury and damage to goods were the subjects of intensified poster advertising in the High Street and on public transport. As the 1950s gave way to the 1960s, campaigns such as 'A Man and His Home' helped to raise General Branch new premium income to over £25,000,000 by 1962, about half of which came from overseas.

At Chief Office, the General Branch was divided between Home and Overseas, each with its own Fire and Accident Departments. A statistical department served the whole branch. Marine insurance was handled by the St Helen's Trust. City Office, by now located in Lombard Street near the Bank of England, was a self-contained unit, writing its own business (a good portion of it linked to the film industry), issuing its own policies, paying its own claims and keeping its own accounts. The business came through brokers, and was presented on slips showing the details of the risk to be insured. Acceptance of all or part of it was indicated by a signature. This was in contrast to the rest of the General Branch, the business of which, of course, was written by the field staff. While the underwriting limits of any contract were set by Chief Office, much administration was handled by the General Branch divisional offices (one located in each of the 14 divisional offices around the country). Each had fire and accident sections responsible for underwriting, reinsurance as required, claims, audit and accounts, and the preparation of statistical returns. There was also an accident claims section which investigated questions of legal liability and negotiated claim settlements, where necessary interviewing witnesses and dealing with the claimant's solicitor or trade union.

While the level of motor insurance claims was a problem common to Britain and to most of the industrialised countries, isolated disasters, such as the Winnipeg flood of 1950 or the devastating bushfires to which Australia was prone, could seriously affect profits from general insurance in a given year in the country concerned. General business was by its nature more volatile than life, and poor returns from a particular country were probably more often due to freakish weather conditions than to purely economic factors. In Britain itself the business was extensive enough to be able to absorb most shocks, but the four occasions between 1952 and 1962 when storms and floods wreaked havoc on specific areas of the country were a test of the local divisions. The first of these episodes was the memorable flood of February 1953, when the sea walls were breached along the Lincolnshire and East Anglian coasts all the way to the Thames, leaving some 150,000 acres of agricultural land awash. More than 30,000 people were evacuated and about 300 killed.[2] Prudential agents paid out over £300,000 on more than 3,500 claims, some within a matter of hours, to stricken policyholders. Five years later, when a hurricane struck the Home Counties, the damage under Fire (which also covered floods), Hearth and Home, Shopkeepers' and Homeowners' policies amounted to £71,000. When torrential autumn rains in 1960 repeatedly caused terrible floods along the east and south coasts and extensive damage to a number of inland towns in the West Country, the Prudential set up a claims office to speed payments to policyholders. Finally, in February 1962, another hurricane left a broad swathe of devastation across the north of England, striking the city of Sheffield with such ferocity that thousands of homes suffered some degree of damage. The industrial north was a Prudential stronghold, and in anticipation of an avalanche of claims, a claims office was opened to facilitate their payment with the minimum of delay. This particular disaster cost the Prudential over £125,000, and on this occasion as on the others, many payments were made in advance to enable urgent repairs to be carried out.

Such catastrophes, as always, brought out the best in the field staff and sowed a fresh legacy of goodwill in the afflicted areas. After each of the aforementioned disasters, gum-booted 'Men from the Prudential' waded, rowed, clambered, inched and cleared their way around their respective debits, often in appalling weather, handing out claim forms and paying claims. In passing, they shovelled mud and debris, ventured onto roofs after sodden pets and helped to put policyholders' homes to rights. This was 'home service' indeed, earning them the frequent accolade 'You'd not be doing this if you'd been nationalised!'[3]

Higher praise than this, the average Prudential agent could probably not have imagined. He usually knew more about the circumstances of the people on his debit – especially the elderly and infirm – than did the local fire and rescue

Disasters brought out the gallantry and commitment to service of Prudential field staff. Here, an agent helps a policyholder to safety in the floods of 1953.

services or even the health visitor. He often knew 'where to look' for some prized possession left behind in a flooded house, or the names of relatives in another town, purely through the confidence gained through years of weekly or fortnightly visits. The much advertised 'Man from the Prudential' acquired an individual face for the thousands of policyholders touched by their particular agent's response when calamity struck.

This, of course, was nothing new, but only the proof, under particularly trying conditions, of the trusting and genuinely friendly relationships that existed between agents and their policyholders. The human element in the agent's job was an inseparable part of it; his success hinged, no less in 1962 than a hundred years earlier, upon being able to build and justify that trust. Evidence that he was regarded as adviser and confidant as well as 'insurance man' shines out from the testimony of literally hundreds of agents. Selecting one example as representative is easier when the account brings a locality to life, as does that of S. Hickson of Spalding in Lincolnshire, writing about the market gardeners and bulb growers of his fenland debit in the mid-1950s. The distances between calls under those wide skies amounted to many miles each day:

Although at first, when I used a push-bike, I could not get home to lunch, there was never any need to take sandwiches. There was always a place set for me and I can still see those heaped plates of steamed apple puddings, followed by an equally generous plate of meat, often home-cured bacon, and vegetables. Invariably they served the pudding first. How many cups of tea I swallowed on a cold day rather than refuse the hospitality so generously given! ... Later, when I acquired a bright yellow Austin Seven of very ancient vintage – which the local folk referred to as "the flying bedstead" – it sometimes resembled a greengrocer's cart when I arrived home from my day's collecting. Then there were the places I used to get the key: in the spout over the kitchen window; under a piece of brick near the side door; on a nail in the shed; and then I would let myself into the house and find the books and premiums which had been left in some convenient place. All this was to save me a back call when the housewife was working in the fields. Many times I would find also a hastily scribbled note: "Please take an extra sixpence and post these letters" ... "Fill in this form" ... "Tell the doctor Johnnie is not so well" ... "Tell my mother I cannot get home this week" ... "Leave this parcel at Mrs Browne's" and many others of like sort.[4]

Agents were used to being of service in a host of ways distinct from the actual transaction of insurance, but in another sense, very much a part of it. Stories of agents who ferried policyholders to the doctor, unblocked drains and shifted heavy furniture were legion. One agent was honoured by a request from a young woman policyholder to give her away at her wedding. In a number of cases agents obtained widows' pensions for policyholders who had no idea how to go about doing this for themselves; one agent reported being asked in the strictest confidence to find out for a policyholder how to procure a divorce! The best of the errand-related stories (worthy to stand alongside that of the agent who delivered several bundles of a policyholder's washing to the laundry – *and collected it the following week*) came from J.J. Hughes of Colwyn Bay, who called at a house early in January 1955 to find the premium receipt book in its usual place with a message attached to it that read: 'Happy New Year to you. Will you please take the mice out of the traps by the dustbin?'[5]

This personal element in the work of the field staff, valued as much by the members of it as by the policyholders, was by the 1960s coming under increasing pressure. The 'amalgamation plan' of the 1950s was only the first stage of a process that was ongoing through the 1960s, as the Prudential grappled with the constant pressure to improve efficiency in the face of the changes in life business already mentioned. The lines that had once divided the Ordinary Branch and the Industrial Branch were by this time sufficiently blurred that management was taking the logical course in attempting to bring the two branches closer still. The basic intention was to augment the amount of life cover purchased by a given premium and so bring the facilities available to the Industrial Branch policyholder more into line with those offered under Ordinary Branch policies.[6] It took time to translate the realisation of change into action at agency level. The volume of business in all the branches was growing apace, so that agents had more calls and collections to make over larger areas. Many felt the job was becoming too regimented under the pressure of time; if men gave the habitual degree of personal attention, paperwork ate into their leisure hours. The Prudential Staff Union complained too that inflation, still running at about 4% a year, quickly eroded any increase in earnings. Out of a review of field staff workings and remuneration in 1960 emerged the 'Yardstick' scale. This was a time and productivity calculation of the time it took the average man to make 100 calls in various kinds of housing from slum to garden suburb, and of the paperwork involved in running an average agency. (It is interesting to consider that the Yardstick scale would not have distinguished between a house in the mythical 'Coronation Street' and No. 10 Downing Street, as both would have been described as 'terraced property with no front garden'.) The scale was revised every three years by a committee representing the management and the Prudential Staff Union. (The first revision indicated that agents were still spending half their time on Industrial Branch collections.)

New social trends lay behind the adjustments that were made. The rehousing of families from slums into high-rise tower blocks was by now a common occurrence. In a debit that included many such buildings (as in areas heavily populated by immigrants, and those where all the women went out to work) the time for collection differed from that required in a better neighbour-hood of detached or terraced houses. Material prosperity and readily available hire purchase facilities meant that the amount of General Branch insurance (which carried a lower commission) being written was steadily increasing, with a consequent effect on the agent's time and earnings. Agents' weekly salaries at the time the Yardstick system was introduced ranged from a minimum of £10 10s (£546 a year) to a maximum of £17 10s (£910), and were still based on a confusing array of commissions and payments.[7] The Yardstick simplified the basis of calculation, and provided a framework for the steady rise in agents' earnings to an average of £24 8s (£1,268 a year) by 1965.[8]

With the Industrial Branch expense ratio hovering between 30% and 32% between 1958 and 1965, management concluded that only the further reduction of agent numbers could keep costs under control. The Prudential was still by far the largest life assurer, but the decline in its share of the market showed no sign of halting: it was 17.6% in 1960 and 16.4% in 1965.[9] Management knew that the Company was over-dependent on the field staff, and potentially open to trouble should a major industrial dispute ever arise. A Committee was set up in 1965 'to review the Company's existing Field Staff Organisation and to consider whether it is still appropriate having regard to the changing social and economic circumstances of the general public and of our own staff as well as the employment pattern of our policyholders in all branches'.[10]

Following the report of this Committee a further amalgamation plan loosely based on the formula of '4 into 3' – creating three larger agencies from four smaller ones – was introduced. This was carried out over the four years from 1966 to 1969 inclusive, and resulted in the elimination of 1,000 agents' jobs. This came mainly through low recruitment, but part-time agency collectors were also called for, to take over the time-consuming and less remunerative Industrial Branch collections and free the agents to spend more time on new business. Additional savings were made in the supervisory grades by spreading increments over longer periods. Despite this tightening up, the Prudential's commitment to home service continued to be reiterated through the late 1960s. The emphasis now was on the person wishing to insure for a substantial pre-mium, but who was expressing a considered preference for home collection. By 1970, the Industrial and Ordinary Branches were considered to be on a par, the only essential difference being that premiums were collected at more frequent intervals from policyholders' homes in the former. The average new Industrial Branch policy carried a premium of more than £1 a month, and a sum assured of £250. The new prosperity of the working classes did not, however, mean that habits changed overnight: 'without home service, many people would not make any regular saving or provision for their dependants', and part of the service performed by the Prudential lay in facilitating this, in line with Government exhortations – but little action – to the same effect. But it also seems to have been tacitly accepted that the writing was on the wall for the Industrial Branch: inflation and Government policies would in time force the further rationalis-ation, and even the merging, of the labour-intensive life branches. The Selective Employment Tax (introduced by the Labour Government under Harold Wilson as part of its strategy to encourage manufacturing at the expense of the service sector), for example, fell heavily on the Industrial Branch, to the extent of £1,000,000 in 1968 and £1,600,000 in 1969; the cost to the two branches together in that year was £2,600,000.

It was somehow fitting that Sir Frank Morgan, the field staff's champion throughout his career, should come to the end of his time as Chairman in April 1965, just as the Committee mentioned above was appointed. After 62 years in the Company, Sir Frank became President, the fourth man to hold that honour, while Sir John Mellor, a member of the Board for the previous 21 years, was elected Chairman in his stead. Mellor, an unassuming yet highly astute and influential figure, had the ability to grasp the essence of any subject *and ask the right questions*, according to colleagues. This was one trait that made him the right man to take over at a time when many challenges to the Prudential's identity and direction were seen to be on the way. He was a popular man, both within the Prudential and in legal and political circles outside it.[11] In addition to Morgan's departure (a minor cataclysm for the many staff who still saw him as the incarnation of the Prudential spirit) there were other changes, brought about by the deaths of Sir James Millard Tucker, Sir James Grigg and and the genial Rupert Thorp (the last after 50 years with the Company; he had joined the Board in 1960 after four years as a Deputy General Manager). These directorships were filled by Leslie Brown on his retirement as Investment Manager, by retiring Deputy General Manager R.E. Montgomery, and by Sir Harold Caccia on his retirement from the Diplomatic Service.

Further changes took place in 1967, when Kenneth Usherwood and Frank Redington retired and were elected to the Board. Desmond Reid, already a Director, and the fourth member of his family to serve the Prudential, was made Deputy Chairman in succession to Maurice Petherick, who relinquished that post but remained on the Board. Ronald Owen became Chief General Manager and Ronald Skerman Chief Actuary. The latter two had worked closely together for most of their careers and complemented each other well. Both were highly respected actuaries – the adjective 'brilliant' has been used of each man by ex-colleagues, but there the similarity ended. Owen was intensely conscientious and highly strung, living for his work and always concerned to have mustered all the facts or arguments well in advance of any decision-making. Staff who knew him only slightly report having found him forbidding, but those who worked with him recall him as deeply and unobtrusively kind (he was, for instance, devoted to his old school, King's College School, Wimbledon, of which he was a Governor), a somewhat shy and lonely man, in whose life the Prudential occupied the central place. Skerman had a penetrating, intuitive mind that revelled in

Sir John Serocold Paget Mellor, Bt, MP.

the intricacies of problems, and a puckish sense of humour ('actuaries are not gods, but you can reach me on extension 403' – which, on the old dial telephones, spelt 'GOD') that enlivened his subject for the growing number of non-actuaries in the middle and upper ranks. His natural bonhomie made him an approachable senior figure where others, such as Ronald Owen or Kenneth Usherwood, could seem distant. (Skerman, like Frank Gardner, Frank Redington and Kenneth Usherwood, served as President of the Institute of Actuaries (from 1970 to 1972) and, like Redington, received its Gold Medal.) The upper echelons of management had widened considerably by now, due simply to the size of the enterprise. Below the rank of Chief General Manager there were three Deputy General Managers and three Assistant General Managers; the Chief Actuary headed a team of three Deputies and below the Joint Secretaries (now Angus Murray and Gordon Clarke) were three Deputy Investment Managers and several Assistant Secretaries. There was also a Group Pensions Manager with three Deputies, an indication of how this area had grown.

The searching revision of the Prudential's day-to-day workings initiated under Kenneth Usherwood continued under his successor as Chief General Manager, Ronald Owen. More often, however, credit for having 'dragged the Prudential into the second half of the twentieth century' is given to one of his Deputy General Managers, the highly popular John Maxted. Maxted had trained as a solicitor and brought his considerable knowledge of employment law to bear on the anti-quated departmental structures and differentials prevailing in the Prudential in the mid-1960s. As the O&M Department's recommendations were enacted, new organisation and pay scales were adopted, the latter tied to productivity.[12]

In particular, it fell to Maxted to deal with the impact of computerisation over a number of years: not only the redeployment of staff as clerical jobs disappeared, but the less visible effects such as employee unease stemming from the experience of a great deal of such change in a short time. The emphasis was still very much on retraining and redeployment, and allowing natural wastage to effect any reduction in numbers. Smoothing the entry of staff imported from outside the Company, while allaying the fears of those who had come up through the system, was part of Maxted's task in this period of transition. Regular reporting was one means of doing this; Chief Office staff suddenly found themselves informed and consulted about impending changes to a degree unimagin-able a decade earlier. Discussions within the two Staff Associations on matters such as pay rises and job security often took the form of open meetings in the 700-seat theatre on the sixth floor of Holborn Bars.[13]

Sir Ronald Owen, FIA.

Maxted also carried overall responsibility for staff training, which, from being regarded right up to the late 1950s as a sideline, had come to be seen by the Prudential management as an essential part of getting to grips with the changes being forced upon the insurance world. Staff training covered everything from induction courses to computer training (relating to the second set of Orions and the IBM 360s bought in 1967) to management courses for principals and train-ing for in-house instructors; John Prior was the man most immediately concerned with developing this area into a department, with an extensive programme of specialised courses. Prudential staff were also by now sponsored on day-release, evening and short courses and in seeking the qualifications of professional bodies such as the Institute of Actuaries and the Chartered Insurance Institute. Both indoor and outdoor staff received training, well in advance of the actual event, on how to deal with the massive impact of the decimalisation of the currency on the work of the life branches.[14]

The late 1960s, however, was a period of a great deal of change and of almost continuous adaptation for Chief Office clerical staff. It had begun with the O&M and work evaluation procedures. Computerisation initially aroused great curiosity among the rank and file, but no real understanding of its potential impact. The importation of numbers of outside programmers and operators, however, shook employees' sense of security. It was difficult for the Staff Associations to keep well enough informed of changes in the law and incomes policy to represent their members effectively. This was one factor that led its representatives to approach the General Secretary of the Association of Scientific, Technical and Managerial Staffs (ASTMS) and request membership. Clive Jenkins later commented that this was not as straightforward a matter as the Staff Association appeared to think; there was some deliberation at the TUC over whether it was proper to bypass the insurance unions, but it was decided to permit ASTMS to seek the approval of PSA members.[15] Clive Jenkins and Muriel (now Baroness Muriel) Turner addressed mass meetings held in the theatre at Holborn Bars and followed by a ballot. Both the Men's and the Women's Associations voted strongly in favour of the merger. The move

Ronald Skerman, CBE, FIA.

was not altogether unwelcome to the Prudential management, some of whom felt that in the complex and ever-evolving area of employment practice, dealing with a professional trade union was preferable to the somewhat paternalistic relationship with the Staff Associations. Following the merger in October 1970, a productivity agreement was agreed which gave the staff a share of the savings made through computerisation.[16] It was also agreed that those whose jobs were eliminated by new technology had the choice of redeployment or leaving the Company with financial compensation.

Computerisation, unionisation, the departure to Reading of the majority of Chief Office Life Branch staff – all contributed to the change in what (for want of a better term) might be called the Prudential's 'corporate culture' as lived at

Holborn Bars. Its staff still regarded the Prudential more as an institution than a company, and Chief Office almost like a town unto itself.[17] Until 1960, life there had not been far removed from that of the 1930s, a parallel to the technological time-lag described in the last chapter. It was highly disciplined and hierarchical; clerical staff were still classified as third-, second- and first-class, deputy principal and principal clerks (and an unofficial class known as 'stopped second-class clerks' comprised of men who had blotted their copybooks, so to speak), the distinctions reinforced by the details – a glass screen, a square of carpet – of their respective departmental space and furniture. The administrative departments still recorded information manually. Traditional courtesies were drummed into juniors: a man stood when a superior approached his desk and removed his hat in the lift. Male colleagues were to be called by their surnames, female by their titles. A minor thorn in the side of the several clerical employees married to members of the maintenance staff was the divide between these groups, marked by separate dining facilities and lavatories and a general disapproval of fraternisation.

Discipline was symbolised, as it always had been, by the red line that was still drawn across the signing-in sheets at 9.10 a.m. sharp (although there was one legendary individual who habitually arrived at 9.09 and 30 seconds and signed with an enormous flourish, leaving space for three or four signatures above his own; there was another who occupied a Prudential flat in Brooke Street who shuffled across in his dressing-gown to sign in early and then return to bed!). Lateness beyond the maximum of twice in a month or a dozen times a year brought the same stiff lecture from one's principal as before the war. The annual evaluation continued to be the formal meeting with a member of management at which praise, criticism, promotion and a pay rise were communicated to each member of staff. Rules were unvarying in the junior ranks, but it was accepted that those of first-class level and upwards had more leeway as to the length of lunch hours and overtime working.

Dress, too, was as traditional in 1960 as before the war. Prudential men still wore dark suits and white shirts; many wore waistcoats and bowler hats, in conformity with City practice. Each employee had a locker in the subterranean depths of Holborn Bars. Older clerks donned the 'office jacket' (a euphemism for the ink-splotched, shiny-elbowed garment kept for protective purposes) in place of the one worn on arrival, just as they had for generations. Fully integrated departments of men and women had been the rule since 1947, but even 20 years later the staff welfare associations were segregated. None of this was seen as restrictive. Employees were accustomed, and for the most part content, to follow the lead of those higher up. There was still a strong sense of Chief Office as a community, an acceptance that unless one were lazy or became hopelessly inept, the Prudential offered a job for life. This sense of security, together with the variety of benefits paid for by the

Company, had always produced corresponding feelings of cohesiveness and of loyalty towards it.

By 1970, much of this had changed or was changing. Ronald Owen confessed himself bewildered by the apparent demise of cordiality and deference that marked the changeover from the Staff Welfare Association to the ASTMS, and indeed, it did seem that in the past few years there had been an upheaval in social norms.[18] All except senior management and real sticklers were now addressed by their Christian names, and casual dress (favoured by computer staff working shifts) was displacing the more formal dark suits. The advent of trouser suits for women caused a stir in the mid-1960s. Eventually it was officially decided to permit them, though not trousers without a matching jacket. (The mini-skirt met nothing like the resistance to trousers, the battle in a sense having been won.[19]) The trappings of paternalism – the various Trusts, the Ibis clubs and sports grounds, the Christmas bonus and half-day for shopping, the subsidised lunches – were still in place, but the needs they had been created to serve had begun to diminish.

This was largely the consequence of a rising standard of living and a change in the pattern of life for the urban worker. By 1970 the Prudential clerk, whether married or single, Holborn-based or relocated in Reading, was less dependent than his pre-war counterpart on the facilities available through the Company. He very probably had a car of his own, a television set and enough disposable income to pursue his interests unaided. He was also less inclined to spend his free time at his place of work. Given that Saturday working was from 1958 a thing of the past, adjourning to the Ibis ground to spend the rest of that day playing cricket or rowing also lost its attraction for some. Ibis membership may not have dropped, but the active participants were perhaps somewhat fewer than earlier, and included fewer members of management.

Those for whom this period formed part of their careers recall that from about 1970, departmental socialising and celebrating seemed to slacken off, and the sense of knowing everyone – including being able to call on just the right person for help or information – to diminish. Home-grown timber was increasingly interspersed with 'timber' – punch-card technicians, computer operators, programmers and trained personnel staff – grown elsewhere. Such vestiges of formality as survived to 1970 were under siege within a few years. Flexible working hours ('Flextime'), introduced in 1974, pushed Ibis club meetings into the lunch-hour and thus further curtailed the camaraderie that had once filled entire evenings. The Ibis library, rivalled by the cinema and the discotheque as popular entertainment, saw its borrowings dwindle. Reg Barnard, who retired as the *Ibis Magazine*'s editor when it was turned into the chattier *PruView* in 1967, nicely caught the flavour of past and present when he told aspiring contributors, first, that 'if anything in writing is detestable, it is the alternating pomposity and jocosity of the unformed mind', and secondly, that 'the language of pop singers is not a good model for your own literary style'.[20] The Ibis Technical Society's Fair, the annual demonstration of employees' creative skills, continued but on a more modest scale year by year. Even the IDOS found it harder to get female actresses to stay late in town for rehearsals, as the streets came to be thought less safe. That said, the IDOS continued to inspire tremendous dedication, producing two or three sell-out shows a year in the theatre at Holborn Bars. It also hosted the annual Insurance Drama Festival in which the clubs of a dozen other companies participated. The soul of the IDOS was the irrepressible Barry Serjent ('I worked nine to five at my desk and five to nine in the theatre'), who wrote, acted and directed for Prudential players during 40 years in General Branch departments and the Publicity Department.[21]

Some of the changes noted above were, of course, the products of a general relaxation of social convention. Others were specific to the Prudential, brought about by the streamlining and modernisation of the life branches. This was ongoing through the 1960s, but at the same time, the Prudential's management recognised that it was not enough to modernise what was already in place (that is, try to expand the capabilities of the Ordinary Branch while the Industrial

An Ideal Husband, by Oscar Wilde, mounted by the IDOS in 1974 in its centenary season. Here Ray Sharman as Lord Caversham (*left*) and Barry Serjent as Lord Goring share the stage.

Branch was made to economise). A wider range of products was needed to keep abreast of competition and market developments. From 1964 the Company began to offer a number of new life contracts and pension products in an attempt to reclaim market share from the new competitors, including foreign ones, entering the British market.

But it was also becoming clear that the current vogue for unit-linked products was changing the market itself. Up until now, as Brian Corby put it some years later, '... competition in the life market was still of a somewhat gentle-manly and sedate manner' and the traditional divisions between the various kinds of financial institution still held.[22] From now on, thanks to the advent of new, mainly investment-linked possibilities, the demarcations would be less rigid, and the need for financial institutions to adapt ever more pressing. In the case of the Prudential, while members of the Board and management were aware of this, to actually effect such change was more easily said than done – 'an exercise comparable to trying to turn the *Queen Mary*' as several recall. Nonetheless, from 1968 attempts to widen the Company's range of activity began to be made, although initially without any specific strategy to speak of, through the purchase or creation of subsidiaries. The result over the next ten years was to transform the Prudential from a company with a tightly controlled and focused set of businesses into what was, properly speaking, a group of companies whose range was broader and more diverse.

The first departure came after years of deliberation, and with competition and public demand as the spur. This was the decision to enter the rapidly developing unit trust market through the Prudential Unit Trust, to be administered by a newly created wholly owned subsidiary called Prudential Unit Trust Managers Limited. Life policies linked to the Prudential Unit Trust were made available through the Ordinary Branch as 'Prutrust' assurances. They were immediately successful, belying the tendency on the part of Prudential management to view them as merely defensive, and producing premium income of £700,000 in 1968. In the following year they brought in annual premiums of £900,000, providing sums assured of £14,000,000. One reason for management's concern about embracing unit-linked products was that as they were so fashionable, they were easy to sell; the fear that the field staff might promote them hard without understanding them particularly well was countered by lowering commission rates and tightening controls on selling. Since the element of risk in unit trust investment was considered somewhat higher than that of traditional areas, Prutrust policies were advertised as being designed primarily for people who were already adequately insured but who sought an outlet for surplus savings. The Prutrust Life Bond, a single premium assurance policy enabling the investment of lump sums in the Prudential Unit Trust, was introduced at about the same time.

Next came the purchase of the Mercantile and General Reinsurance Company (Holdings) Limited, which, with its subsidiary, the well-known

'M&GRe', was largely owned by the Swiss Reinsurance Company of Zurich, or 'Swiss Re'. At the time it seemed possible that the M&GRe, Britain's only reinsurer of any size, might again pass into foreign ownership, and the Prudential Board was motivated at least in part by the desire to prevent this. The acquisition was also attractive in that the M&GRe could be run without increasing the Prudential's dependence on the field staff.[23]

The M&GRe, formed by a group of Glasgow businessmen and incorporated in 1907, had an interesting history.[24] Before 1914, the British reinsurance market had been dominated by large German companies, whose withdrawal when war broke out left a space which the M&GRe had sought to fill. This had not proved a viable course, but close links with the Swiss Re, which formally acquired an interest in the M&GRe in 1919, gave the latter the access to the business connections and technical expertise it needed to expand. It soon established treaty connections in Scandinavia and the Baltic States, the rest of Continental Europe (including the Balkans), Australasia, India and the Americas. Between the wars the M&GRe developed a distinctive international outlook through its expert knowledge of the countries in which it did business. This included an emphasis, singular at the time, on conducting business by personal contact and in the client's own language, rather than through intermediaries.

The M&GRe transacted fire, accident and life business, avoiding marine business, after an expensive early disaster in this area, until after 1945. In the postwar period it experienced the great expansion of its life business. Seeking to establish a competitive niche against the major British life offices, it set up pools of substandard lives hitherto rejected by the larger offices and became accepted as a specialist reinsurer, with close links to several of the mainstream life companies. An increasing proportion of marine and fire business, as well as life, came from overseas, and by the mid-1950s the company was active in 30 countries and its officers constantly on the move. Although the life side continued to do well, the M&GRe found that, like the Prudential's General Branch, its accident and fire losses were steadily worsening by the early 1960s. In addition, the M&GRe's expansion outside the United Kingdom was increasingly bringing it into competition with the Swiss Re, whose subsidiary by now it was.

This was the situation which led in 1967 to the search for a British buyer, culminating in the sale of the M&GRe to the Prudential in 1968 for £15,000,000. Julius Neave, the M&GRe's General Manager, wanted the company to operate as an independent reinsurer, and although Ronald Owen joined the M&GRe Board, few constraints were placed upon it by the Prudential. At the time this seemed appropriate. The new subsidiary was replacing one strong parent with another; its business was viewed as similar to the Prudential's, but its culture was very different, its management being used to operating autonomously. They also believed that M&GRe's position as underwriter of other life companies made it essential that the company be seen to be completely independent. In continuing as General Manager in the company his family had helped to found 150 years earlier.

By now Kenneth Usherwood was Chairman of the Prudential, Sir John Mellor having retired in 1970 according to the policy adopted in 1965 that chairmen should serve a five-year term. The early 1970s, as anyone who lived through them will recall, were politically, economically and socially an unsettled and unsettling time. Industrial relations in particular were seemingly at an all-time low, and in the divisive atmosphere following the passing of the Industrial Relations Act 1972, questions such as employee participation in the management process, and the role of trade unions, shareholders and institutional investors in British industry were widely debated. Some such issues would later prompt investigation by Government-appointed committees (the Bullock and Wilson Committees, which considered employee participation and investment in industry respectively, were cases in point). The role of the institutional share-holder gave the Prudential Board much food for thought. The Prudential had long been the largest single institutional investor in the United Kingdom, with more than £3,000,000 to invest every week. It was by now accepted that being the largest shareholder in a company made intervention inevitable if misman-agement or other difficulties threatened. The old fear of undue influence had gradually given way to the view that large institutions had a responsibility to maintain good management in the companies in which they invested.

This was also a view that implicitly endorsed the conviction voiced by the Prudential and other large offices on the subject of fiduciary responsibility. The Prudential claimed no inherent expertise in the management of industrial companies, but accepted that large shareholders should rise to the challenge of making sure that such companies were commercially sound and honestly run. At the same time, the Company's primary responsibility – to invest the resources entrusted to it by several million policyholders so as to obtain the best return at the lowest risk – was clearly reiterated.[30] Big investors were often accused of putting commercial considerations ahead of social or long-term economic ones in the decision to invest or to advance capital to industry. To this charge, Kenneth Usherwood pointed out that at a time when the level of inflation was about 10% a year and interest rates correspondingly high, the return on capital after tax-ation was miserably low. Industrial companies seeking finance were naturally apprehensive about long-term borrowing. The return on new investment barely covered the cost of raising the capital, and many companies were wisely deciding to finance their requirements by increasing short-term debt or by raising fresh equity capital. The Prudential's disinclination to lend or invest at this time was less a comment on the state of British industry than on the discouraging and uncertain economic outlook.

This grew no less bleak as events in the Middle East and the resulting oil embargo in the autumn of 1973 produced a crisis in the economies of the developed nations. In Britain this was exacerbated by the recession, and the measures taken to control inflation which had little positive effect. The complex background to the international loss of confidence in sterling and the marked decline in share values on the London Stock Exchange between the autumn of 1973 and the end of 1974 has been widely written about, and it is not proposed to review it here. Nor is it proposed to dwell on the memorable events – the miners' strike, the state of emergency, the three-day week – that preceded the change of Government in February 1974. Labour under Harold Wilson took office under the banner of the 'social contract', but settlement with the NUM and other unions was the prelude to a further bout of inflation and the worst half-year in the history of the London Stock Market. The perceived inability or unwillingness of the Government to bring inflation under control and curb the power of the unions caused investor confidence to evaporate, and there was a dramatic fall in the value of all the major kinds of investments held by financial institutions. The crisis, one component of which was the decline in the purchasing power of sterling by some 35% over three years to the end of 1974, brought many secondary banks and insurance companies into serious difficulty.

While the Bank of England organised the salvage of the viable banks, the Prudential participated in consortia to do the same for several insurance companies, property companies and small banks that were dangerously close to insolvency. It also rescued a small annuity office called the Vavasseur Life Assurance Company Limited, which ran into difficulties at the end of 1973. The Prudential acquired the whole of its share capital for a nominal payment of £100. The company was promptly renamed Vanbrugh Life Assurance Limited and its authorised capital increased to £1,800,000 with the aim of using the company to sell unit-linked insurance through the medium of insurance brokers. Vavasseur's policyholders were thus safeguarded and, from the Prudential's point of view, the acquisition provided a timely means of entering a growing area. Operating through a subsidiary company avoided the friction that might have arisen from the field staff.[31]

One effect of the chaotic conditions of the late 1960s and early 1970s was an increase in the degree to which the insurance industry became subject to official regulation. The collapse of general insurance companies such as the Vehicle and General and the Fire, Accident and Marine led to legislation to protect policyholders in the form of the Insurance Companies Act 1972 and the Insurance Companies Amendment Act 1973. The disasters of 1974 similarly spurred the passing of the Policyholders' Protection Act 1975, which served as an example for subsequent legislation in the financial services area. Under this Act, insurers were required to contribute to a fund to protect the policyholders of offices unable to meet their obligations. Prevailing economic conditions continued to be extremely negative, and confidence in eventual recovery to waver.

Although he remained on the Board, Kenneth Usherwood retired as four sources: the Ordinary Branch, the Industrial Branch, group pensions, and overseas life business, but in addition the Company could claim a spread of interests, as Ronald Owen put it,

> *... across virtually the whole range of business in the insurance market, both at home and internationally. In addition to the traditional areas of strength, the life business ... now includes important contributions from the group pension business, from the top end of the market for individuals (sold through insurance brokers), and from reinsurance business, as well as a small but growing amount of life business sold in Europe.* [37]

Investment trusts, property companies and worldwide general insurance rounded out the picture, so that it seemed to Ronald Owen more appropriate to speak of 'the Prudential Group of companies'. Total revenue premium income from individual assurances and annuities was £145,800,000 in 1976; that from group pensions had reached £125,000,000, and that from overseas £133,600,000. The premium income from general business, including reinsurance, stood at £180,000,000 – one-third of this arose in the United Kingdom and the rest abroad; M&GRe accounted for some £114,400,000 of it, and L'Escaut £27,300,000.

A singular conjunction of ability now existed in the executive ranks: below Chief General Manager Geoff Haslam, Brian Corby was appointed General Manager alongside Desmond Craigen, to head a team that included Derek Bourdon and Gordon Wood as Deputy General Managers, Ron Artus and Peter Moody as Joint Secretaries and Investment Managers, and Ronald Skerman as Chief Actuary. Corby's intellectual and managerial qualities had made his rapid rise – by Prudential standards – to the top rank a foregone conclusion to colleagues since his early years in the Company. Both he and Haslam were noted for an unassuming manner that charmed the staff, a fine wit, and a firm but softly spoken authority that married integrity and common sense. The Board, still entirely non-executive, included former members of management such as investment experts Leslie Brown, Gordon Clarke and Angus Murray, and actuarial giants Kenneth Usherwood and Frank Redington. There were a number of outside Directors drawn from commerce and politics, a group further strengthened by the appointment of Lord Carr of Hadley, the former Conservative Home Secretary, who had wide business experience.

One fact upon which all were agreed was the increasing awkwardness of directing the 'Prudential Group of companies' with a wholly non-executive Board operating along what were effectively prewar lines.[38] Although a good number of the Directors were drawn from outside, well over half were retired members of management, most of them actuaries who had come up through the Company together. Their long familiarity with the business, and in many cases their friendship, produced a relaxed atmosphere, but fostered the tendency to examine each item on the agenda in detail. The Board still met for two mornings each week: on Wednesdays it sat as a Finance Committee, dealing mainly with investment management, and on Thursdays it dealt with management proposals relating to life and general business. Minutes were taken in longhand and filed, rather than being typed out and circulated. This somewhat self-absorbed Board procedure had become outdated: what was needed was improved management control and greater efficiency. The Company was felt to need fresh perspectives, yet new men from outside it who might have provided these did not have two half days a week to devote to the Prudential.

Two considerations shaped the decision taken in 1977 to alter the structure of the Company. The first was the theoretical threat to solvency posed by a market collapse such as that of 1974. The sudden fall in the market value of the Company's assets had produced the paradox that, according to Geoff Haslam,

> ... although we were extremely strong, we had great difficulty in producing a balance sheet which showed that the assets covered the liabilities. We could have gone into any of the financial markets and borrowed £200,000,000 to £300,000,000 ... but if we borrowed money we'd have the asset but we'd also have a similar liability, so we would be back where we started from.[39]

A holding company could obviously borrow and finance the desired expansion of activities with far greater flexibility than the existing Company could. Difficulties in one or other of the subsidiaries could be contained. (As it happened, the M&GRe was shortly to provide an example of this, when in 1978 it announced massive losses and required an injection of Prudential aid.) The second consideration was that it had become clear that the future of the insurance industry, in the 1980s and beyond, lay in the transformation into the broader, more open field of 'financial services'. Further constraints were very likely to fall upon the insurance industry as the activities of financial institutions overlapped and converged. Increased involvement in the European Community would subject the Company to further legislation. A holding company would again offer a simpler formula for administering what was now a diversified set of interests. Pressing the case for strategic planning was Geoff Haslam, whose perspective as a non-actuary took in more of the competitive commercial scene.

For these reasons, the separation of the Prudential's non-insurance interests from its traditional life and general insurance areas seemed the wise solution. As Sir Brian Corby recalls, once the idea of a non-insurance holding company was aired, it was rapidly accepted as the best way to conserve the most valuable elements of the past while keeping abreast of the pressures for change. In May 1978 shareholders were advised of the plan, their shares in the Prudential Assurance Company to become shares in the new Prudential Corporation.

Following formal approval on 23 November, the Prudential Corporation came into being on 29 December 1978. Its operating subsidiaries were the Prudential Assurance Company, the M&GRe, Vanbrugh and L'Escaut. Smaller entities, such as the Standard Trust, an investment trust purchased in 1977, the Beaver Trust, bought in 1973, Edger, Stocklund and other small property companies, remained subsidiaries of the Prudential Assurance Company.

For the first two years the Boards of the Prudential Corporation and of the Prudential Assurance Company (PAC) were identical and it was not until 1980 that the first executives were brought onto the Board of the former. On the management side, in keeping with the earlier Maxted dictum of 'evolution, not revolution', Geoff Haslam became Group Chief Executive, and Desmond Craigen took over from him as Chief General Manager of the PAC. The senior management of the Corporation drew entirely upon the existing management of the PAC. Brian Corby, who as a General Manager of the PAC had done much of the work of bringing the Corporation into being, was already well advanced along the trajectory that would see him become both Chief General Manager of the PAC (in succession to Desmond Craigen) and Chief Executive of the Corporation when Geoff Haslam retired in 1982.

The creation of the Corporation was not a particularly dramatic move, but rather, a natural step in the ongoing process by which the Prudential became a worldwide financial institution. As a formal acknowledgment of this, however, it did mark something of a watershed for the Company, rather like a gate opening onto the broad meadow of recent times. The events of the past 20 years are still too close to permit much historical perspective: such a multiplication of themes, not all of which may prove significant, so many decisions of which the results are not yet clear, so many changes in the commercial context whose consequences are not yet worked out, so many men – and women – whose parts in the Prudential saga are still unfolding. An overview of the period after the creation of the Corporation can only touch on the most notable developments, order them, and bring the Prudential story up to the present day. But before that, there will be a brief diversion down an avenue as yet unexplored with the attention it deserves.

Focus on Group Pensions

'The lesson of history,' wrote Frank Redington in one of his actuarial reflections, 'is that few people are able to provide for their own old age. ... If we are to have a pensioned society, somebody has to make the arrangements for us.' Pension arrangements on behalf of employers began to be undertaken formally by the Prudential's Ordinary Branch from 1929, but it was only after 1945 that group pensions began to gain a wider importance and came to make a major contribution to the profile of the Company. By 1976, a subsidiary called Prudential Pensions Limited had been created to handle part of a business whose revenue premium income, at more than £125,000,000, was of the same order as that of the entire individual life business of the Ordinary Branch. Over 30 years, this was a remarkable performance. To trace how this came about was the aim of the following account, written by Derek Fellows, Group Pensions Manager from 1973 to 1981 and Chief Actuary of the Prudential from 1981 to 1988.

****

THE history of the Group Pensions business is one of the most fascinating, yet paradoxical, features of the Prudential. Nurtured in the traditional manner, the 'Group', as it was generally known, came to develop a momentum of its own and to acquire particular characteristics as it adapted to the harsh commercial realities of a competitive and changing scene.

For much of its life, the 'Group' tended to be regarded as potentially too volatile to become a reliable and key component in the Prudential's development. After all, a change of Government or of legislation could alter business prospects overnight, as could decisions by a few large companies to switch schemes. Moreover, the development of scheme business (often embracing several thousand members) through brokers was at the opposite end of the spectrum from the home service concept so successfully created in respect of 'The Man from the Pru'.

In the event, the Group became a significant part of the Company's operations. Later, its identity had to be moulded into a wider framework following the formation and development of the Prudential Corporation and the encouragement of personal pension concepts by Government.

Early pension plans

Pensions for retired employees originated on an ex-gratia basis and it was natural that they should be paid by employers out of current revenue on a pay-as-you-go basis. It was a long time before the realisation dawned that substantial potential liabilities could be involved in pension commitments and that such liabilities ought to be funded, at least in the private sector. Although pension schemes had long been established by some of the large companies, it was not until the 1920s that private funded schemes began to gather momentum.

At the other end of the spectrum, state benefits to those in retirement were originally paid only to those in serious distress, and from 1908 the benefits were subject to a test of need. In 1925 a compulsory scheme of contributory pensions (including widows' and orphans' benefits) was introduced for the greater part of the population but excluding higher paid clerical workers.

It was not until 1948, in the wake of the Beveridge Report, that a comprehensive scheme of social insurance – including retirement and other pensions – came into operation. The year-to-year costs of this scheme were met by contributions from employers and employees and by Exchequer grants, there being only relatively modest funds available to back the enlarged liabilities.

So the seeds were sown for two different systems – private employer-based funded schemes on the one hand and state pay-as-you-go arrangements for the lower paid on the other. Initially the two systems played a complementary role in the social fabric, but as each grew and gained strength they came on a collision course.

Group Pensions Department (1929–45)

It was against this background that the Prudential's Group Pensions Department was established in 1929, although only as part of the Actuary's office. Originally most insured pension schemes were arranged through ordinary individual policies, endowment assurances (with an annuity option at maturity) or deferred annuities being issued in respect of each member of the scheme. However, this meant that it was necessary to issue new individual contracts each year to cater for benefit increases stemming from improvements in pay. Later the concept of issuing master policies to cover groups of lives appeared, not least by way of year-to-year group temporary assurances to provide death-in-service benefits accompanied by group deferred annuity policies to pay retirement pensions.

Benefits accrued on a block basis from year to year, each block of benefits being related to the salary payable at the time (i.e. total benefits were, in effect, related to average salary throughout pensionable service). Offices were many years away from being able to offer so-called final salary schemes under which retirement benefits are related to pensionable salary over the period immediately prior to retirement.

So it was that the Prudential, with a few other offices, began to gain experience in the handling of pension schemes, and in establishing business through brokers and consultants, for a wide range of companies, many of whom were prominent in British industry and commerce. This experience was to prove invaluable later when the Prudential came to play a leading role in the shaping of the wider pensions scene.

As Group Pensions was part of the Actuary's office, it was natural that some of the pioneers of the pensions business were qualified or budding actuaries. They included John Shine, Hubert Briscoe, Jack Edey, Graham Haslam, Tom Tinner and Fred Lewis. There were naturally interruptions on account of service in the Second World War (when for most of the time the Group administration functioned from Torquay with other Prudential operations). Most of the team then returned to lay the foundation stones for postwar development.

Tariff rates (1946–50)

Prior to, and including, the immediate postwar years, group deferred annuity policies in the United Kingdom had been written on a non-profit basis only (apart from certain special contracts issued in this country by a United States office from 1928 to 1933). Indeed offices in the group pensions field generally conformed to a premium tariff.

The rate of interest used in the calculation of the tariff non-profit rates was 3% per annum. Even so, and not least because group deferred annuity scheme business was subject to tax as part of the general annuity fund, there was little margin for most offices; and those with a rapidly developing level of deferred annuity business were carrying forward large and increasing tax losses. At the same time the very long-term nature of group pension plans made them more vulnerable to future changes in interest rates than most other classes of life office business. The years from 1945 to 1948, with their very low interest rates (yields on dated gilt-edged stocks then being less than 3% per annum) produced an apparently healthy financial position through the appreciation in asset values of medium and long-term securities. But there was an insidious danger because the increase in long-term actuarial liabilities stemming from these low interest rates was much greater than the improvement in asset values.

By the late 1940s several hundred company schemes had been written by the Prudential. Group non-profit deferred annuity business had, in fact, developed to a stage where – because of low interest rates and an unexpected increase in the longevity of pensioners – the earnings for bonuses on ordinary with-profits whole life and endowment assurances could be seriously affected. Equally, if the pendulum were to swing the other way, an embarrassingly large surplus might arise. The hand on the tiller was becoming too heavy!

It was in these circumstances that the Prudential took the decision to withdraw from the tariff, to introduce more expensive premium rates for existing group non-profit deferred annuity schemes and, in general, to cease to write policies for new schemes (though some employers still insisted on placing business with the Company notwithstanding the higher costs!).

A move to with-profits schemes (1951)

Those decisions were made against the background that an innovative new concept was being developed by the Prudential. This was the introduction of group deferred annuities on a with-profits basis. Notwithstanding much careful planning prior to its introduction in 1951, the with-profits concept proved hard to sell in the group pensions market. Coupled with the decision in effect to withdraw from the non-profit sector, the result was seriously to deplete the inflow to the Prudential of new group pensions business.

Inevitably there was much daunting administration, actuarial and legal work – not to mention the sales and servicing aspects – to be undertaken behind the scenes in preparing the ground for the new group product. At the same time all schemes already on the books had to be processed in their existing format, at least until such time as employers were persuaded to change to the with-profits basis. Responsibility for handling all this change, with the limited data processing facilities then available, was borne partly by several of the early pioneers – Jack Edey had become Assistant Actuary in charge of Group operations and Gerald Williams and Graham Haslam were successive Group Pensions Managers. They were joined by others from elsewhere in the Prudential, including Michael Hill and Ronald Skerman. So a formidable team was assembled.

Group scheme contributions vary from year to year, partly because of changes in the workforce but also because of salary improvements of individual employees. This is in contrast to the position under individual life assurance policies where annual premiums usually remain unchanged for several years at a time. To cope with the variability of contributions, each premium paid under the new product was treated as though it were a single premium. Successive bonuses were then calculated on the accrued benefit secured by each such single premium rather than, as in the case of level premium assurance policies, on the prospective benefit (for example, the sum assured) secured by all the premiums to be paid. It was decided that the bonuses should consist of two elements: one an annual addition to the accrued pension as it built up and the other a special and final addition to the pension when it commenced. At first the attempt was made to sell the schemes on the basis that the bonuses would augment the benefits otherwise payable to the employees. But this was not successful. By 1953 it had become clear that the group with-profits deferred annuity would need to be modified. This was to meet the more general demand from employers that fixed benefits should be provided for employees, the bonus additions being applied to reduce employers' costs.

The period of transition in the 1950s was uncomfortable. With expensive changes in hand and little at that stage to show for it, coupled with a continuing loss of market share of pensions business, it was natural that there should be some apprehension as to whether the Group was on the right course. Management Committee minutes in April 1952 reveal that the Chairman and Deputy Chairman felt it necessary to question Frank Redington, the then Chief Actuary, as to the large amount of group pensions business, albeit in non-profit form, which was being written by several other offices. Frank's answer was clear – there was no wish to change course and development on with-profits lines was still wanted. A sales team – among whom was Geoff Haslam – was assembled to stimulate business through field staff as well as brokers. Even so, progress proved difficult for a time; but the tide eventually turned and gradually the with-profits schemes began to gain momentum, not least through many leading pensions brokers. The with-profits contract, launched with the lessons of low and declining interest rates very much in mind, would prove subsequently to be a most powerful medium for the development of insured group pension schemes through a long period of high and increasing investment returns. The launch was followed later by the issue of broadly similar products by the Prudential in Canada and South Africa; and through the rest of the decade many other offices in the UK began to follow suit, although with different premium and bonus structures.

It is difficult to gauge whether the Prudential, in persisting in its belief that its own course was the right one, ever fully recouped the ground lost to some other life offices. But there is no doubt that the Company helped to lead the way to the conduct of business on a sounder footing than had gone before. Moreover, in the process, a flexibility in handling group schemes was achieved which was to serve life offices well when facing the upheavals which were to come later.

Controlled funding (from 1953)

An important by-product of the with-profits plan, and of the switch from 'profits to employees' to 'profits to employers', was the concept of controlled funding. Some degree of flexibility in funding schemes had already been tried for non-profit schemes. But the arrival of with-profits contracts facilitated a more sophisticated technique whereby the value of scheme liabilities over a long period ahead could be assessed and met through a predetermined rate of employer contribution expressed as a percentage of the members' salaries, thereby helping employers to budget more efficiently in advance. A scheme's funding position would then be reviewed from time to time and the employer's contribution rate

EMPLOYERS – GET YOUR COMPANY PENSION SCHEME FROM THE PRUDENTIAL

THE PRUDENTIAL COMPANY PENSION SCHEME

adjusted as appropriate. Essentially it was a matter of using an actuarial tracking device to home onto a distant moving pensions target. Coupled with subsequent tax changes, the controlled funding facility proved to be a powerful tool in the hands of the Prudential (and other specialist offices) in securing final-salary-type pension plans for large groups of employees.

A tax lifeline (1956)

In 1953 the report of the Millard Tucker Committee, set up by the Government to review the taxation position of pension plans generally, appeared; and many of its proposals were implemented in the Finance Act 1956. Under the Act insured pension schemes meeting certain conditions could become fully exempt from tax on interest income and capital gains as far as policyholders' funds were concerned. Private self-administered funds had already been entitled to a fully gross build-up and thus the new legislation removed a competitive disadvantage from the insured sector. The 1956 Act led to wholesale conversion of schemes, with appropriate documentation, to the new exempt format and to the transfer of a large volume of reserves from the general annuity funds to the new pension annuity funds of life offices. The result was to alleviate, or remove, the tax burden on the general annuity funds of most offices. In the process of transfer most employers who had schemes with the Prudential were persuaded of the wisdom of converting to the group with-profits deferred annuity format. Suddenly, after the slow start, the with-profits business began to surge.

Another provision of the Act was the introduction of comparable tax concessions for individual retirement annuities for the self-employed. Many of the bonus and other characteristics of the with-profits group plan pioneered by the Group were invaluable in the development by the Prudential of the new retirement annuities and, with powerful support from field staff sales, the Company quickly became the market leader in the UK in the personal pensions field.

State pensions and growing pains (1959–64)

The comprehensive state social security schemes of 1948 covered virtually the whole population but at the level of subsistence only. Anything beyond that was the responsibility of the individual. Nevertheless, and despite some increases in contribution rates over the years, the National Insurance scheme began to run into heavy deficiencies in the late 1950s; and the outlook was that the financial position would get worse. This was due partly to the changing demographic structure and partly to the effects of inflation; but it also reflected the increasing weight of costs implicit in the 1948 scheme as it matured.

Both the Conservative and Labour parties had begun to realise that, as the demand grew for more substantial universal pensions, it would be impracticable to meet the costs by flat-rate contributions alone. The relative burden on the lowest-paid workers would become too heavy. At the same time private

FACING PAGE
Group pensions was the
Prudential's fastest growing
area in the postwar period.

pension schemes had been increasing rapidly and, by the late 1950s, more than half of employed men (including those in the Government sector) were in some form of pension plan. The Labour party suggested that this was dividing the country into two nations – the privileged and the underprivileged – and produced a plan for radical revision of state pensions. The Conservative Government accepted – if earnings-related contributions were to be introduced – that it would be desirable to introduce also some element of earnings-related benefits on top of the basic flat-rate pension provision. The result was the 1959 Act under which a relatively modest level of graduated benefits was implemented from 1961; but the graduated contributions were much more than were needed commercially to provide the enhancement in benefits and thereby in effect embraced a special form of tax. At the same time the earnings-related pensions became a promise left for future generations to redeem.

There was one important and unique feature of the legislation which was to become particularly significant for private sector provision. Although the graduated benefits in the 1959 Act were relatively modest, there was the recognition that any improvement in state benefits could temper the growth of the private pension provision and, in consequence, the facility for investment created by funded schemes. So, an ingenious system of 'contracting out' was made available to schemes (but not then to individual pension policies) meeting certain conditions. Members of such schemes could forego earnings-related benefits in return for reduced National Insurance contributions. Employers could thereby escape the troublesome (mostly weekly) calculations implicit in graduated contributions. To the extent that it was financially advantageous to contract-out employees earning above a certain level, the momentum of private pension scheme development was not retarded overall; if anything, it increased.

State and private pensions – further turmoil (1965–78)

The mid-1960s to the mid-1970s was a period of much frustration for offices operating in the field of group pensions. Three successive Governments developed elaborate plans for the extension of state pensions, albeit with facilities for 'contracting-out' (or, more realistically, abatement from part of the state benefits). On each occasion offices had to prepare the ground for much detailed change in the administration and documentation of schemes; yet because of changes of Government it was not until the third round of upheaval that the proposed legislation passed beyond the Bill stage and was enacted.

The Prudential was in the forefront of life office discussions with the political parties and Government departments. There was a dilemma stemming from the conflicting interests. This may be sensed from an extract from some reminiscences by Frank Redington about national pensions and concern that an unfair burden on future generations might in effect be implicit in the pension promises.

The Labour Party was in office 1964–1970 and Crossman's words saw the light of day in a Government paper in 1969. It was a fully fledged scheme of universal wage-related pensions. It was essentially pay-as-you-go although a small fund was to accumulate in the early years. ... We, on the Committee, had no mandate to countenance any kind of pay-as-you-go scheme and we knew very well that our superiors (the Directors and Management) would be overwhelmingly opposed to a comprehensive state pay-as-you-go scheme. So we steered clear of ideology and confined ourselves to practical problems of making the scheme work. Our relations with Crossman were, however, undoubtedly eased by the fact that opinion on the Committee itself was being forced gradually towards pay-as-you-go, not by desire or by ideology but by the sheer realities of the arithmetic. It is hard for the layman to appreciate fully how very slow any funded scheme is to come to fruition.

In the meantime, however, Frank and his colleagues had been approached in confidence by Sir Keith Joseph on behalf of the Conservative party, who had prepared a full-scale, but slowly maturing, scheme on a funded, pay-in-advance basis. This would have relied heavily on the private sector with fall-back facilities through the state system. Frank records:

On the grounds of self-interest we should have been overjoyed. But we were not because we knew that no funded scheme could provide a satisfactory answer to the country's pension needs. We explained our reasons of course but it seemed to me that they never took them to heart. ... They did not seem to translate the figures into the realities of food and clothing for the elderly.

When Labour lost the 1970 election and the Conservatives returned to office, the Keith Joseph plan was presented to Parliament in 1971. The Prudential then proceeded to prepare and later to launch new forms of with-profits pension plans on a 'money-purchase' basis with what were then many advanced 'indexation' features – such as bonus additions on pensions in course of payment and on paid-up benefits for members leaving service before retirement, thereby potentially offering some offset to erosion of benefits through inflation. The contracts were designed in particular to appeal to small businesses; and the field staff quickly seized the opportunity – helped by tax reliefs – to cultivate the new market. But the potential expansion was nipped in the bud by the oil crisis of 1973–74, another election and yet another change of Government.

This time the Labour Government was quick to act. Aided by more political consensus than had previously been the case, Mrs Barbara Castle introduced 'Better Pensions', which was mainly an updating of the Crossman scheme. The plan was enacted in 1975 and became operative in 1978.

So again the Prudential, and the other offices, had to scrap existing plans and proceed with intensive changes in administrative systems. But at least a more settled environment was at last in prospect. Moreover, although some employers and employees had been deterred from extending group pension provision by the political uncertainties, they had in the process acquired a keener interest in, and understanding of, pension matters, and remarkable growth for the Prudential's pension business ensued.

Somewhat perversely, when pressures from Government legislation later eased, other pressures took their place; and the relative advantage achieved by the Prudential on the group pensions front proved to be only temporary. The momentum began to be generated elsewhere.

Prudential Pensions Limited (1970)

In the midst of the lengthy debate on state and private pensions, other developments were taking place. One of these had significant implications, namely the decision to form a subsidiary, Prudential Pensions Limited, to write group index-linked schemes (commonly known as 'managed funds' and run on unit trust lines) for the largest schemes.

Unlike the introduction of with-profits deferred annuities, the Prudential was not the first to introduce the new index-linked plans. The Scottish Widows – a mutual office – had done so in 1968 and other offices then began to follow suit. Such moves were to some extent a defensive measure in an attempt to head off competition on another front. This was arising because the trend in industrial companies, through amalgamation and take-over, towards larger organisations was tending to bring 'self-administration' for pension plans more into the picture. In the process companies no longer necessarily looked to a life office to provide investment and other services. In any event, many employers, using better focused control techniques, began to demand contracts under which investment results and expense charges could be identified and quantified more precisely than in the broad framework of a with-profits system.

In due course the Prudential too took steps to get into the group index-linked market. At first, in an attempt to retain as much as possible in the existing with-profits format (and in parallel with an approach adopted for individual business), index-linking was offered by way of 'top-up' in an equity fund only; but this was not well received by employers and it was accepted later that it would also be necessary to offer separate fixed interest, property, cash and managed funds. For certain tax and other reasons the operation was financed by the shareholders; but the implications for shareholders' profits were relatively less favourable than under the with-profits deferred annuity business.

At first there was little switching of existing schemes to the index-linked basis, but it gradually became the fashion for large schemes to move into the new format. In the process specialist pension brokers and consulting actuary firms began to offer their own administration and actuarial services separately from the investment service; and competition for the latter began to intensify too as pension fund trustees focused on comparative investment returns achieved by different managers. In common with other life offices, the Prudential often found itself fighting a rearguard action over its most important schemes with each element of service coming under scrutiny. In the process, although investment services were usually retained (through the switching of uplifted values of deferred annuities contingent upon the money being transferred into the Prudential's own index-linked funds), administration and actuarial work began to be lost, and links with employers were inevitably weakened.

In some of the largest cases it became necessary to offer a completely segregated investment fund under which the investments were in the name of the employers, and were simply managed for a fee by the Prudential's Investment Department.

Fluctuating fortunes

By 1980 the annual revenue premium income of the Group Pensions area in the UK was some £250,000,000. This was about the same as the revenue premiums for individual UK Ordinary Branch business and likewise for the Industrial Branch. With nearly 10% of the 'insured' market in the UK, the Prudential came close to eliminating the gap that had existed between it and the long-standing leader in the UK Group Pensions market, the Legal & General. But the 1980s would see a number of changes to the traditional and unique character of the Group Pensions area. These would stem from the increasing competition for fragmented pension services which spread down from the largest schemes and began to emerge more strongly for groups of more modest size. Moreover, employers took a sharper interest in investment performance. Whereas the Prudential's investment results had been extremely good during the 1970s, with the assets being substantially in equities and property through a period of high inflation, the somewhat overweight position in property relative to other offices resulted in a disappointing investment performance overall in the 1980s when property investment began to lose its sparkle. The result was a loss to the Group of some substantial blocks of premium income from a few large schemes, though some were retained in the segregated form mentioned above. Later in the decade, the trend towards personal pensions gained ground encouraged by legislation; and in the process Group Pensions and other Prudential business became more intertwined. But that is a story for the final chapter.

Postscript

It was my good fortune to work on the Group through periods of much fascinating change and development. Partly because of the competitive pressures, not least for the large schemes, but also because of the pace of change from time to time, the Group needed, and was allowed, greater freedom in decision-making than was generally the case in the Prudential. This gave the Group a distinctive

improved technology; and the moves to encourage greater stock market investment among private individuals have all played their part in shaping the Prudential of today. In seeking to exploit these opportunities the Prudential's management has looked for new activities which either supported its existing business or were logical developments of it, rather than seeking to diversify for diversification's sake. There has been a continuing debate about the Company's core businesses as changing circumstances have forced the management to rethink aspects of their development plans, and even to retrace their steps from one expensive cul-de-sac. But although the Prudential is now active in areas far beyond the aims of its founders or even of those who created the Corporation, one fundamental principle has supplied the unifying thread through its 150-year existence: its business is to supply security, in the form of savings and protection products to the general public.

How the Prudential is organised

While the decision to establish the Prudential Corporation may have been taken with exemplary speed, it took rather longer for the new structure to settle. When in 1979 Sir Ronald Owen retired after five years as Chairman of the Prudential Assurance Company and also, in the last year, of the Prudential Corporation, he was succeeded by Lord Carr of Hadley, a former Home Secretary and Secretary of Employment, while Geoff Haslam became Deputy Chairman. At this point, the Board was still meeting twice a week.

Lord Carr was accustomed to work differently, and he recognised that it was necessary to have fewer meetings. Gradually this was achieved, and the Prudential moved to 12 or 13 board meetings a year. In 1983 Brian Corby, then Group Chief Executive, became the first executive to join the Corporation's Board. This development was consistent with the new Group structure and the role of the Corporation Board within the Group.

In 1984 a new management structure was established which organised the Group into five operating divisions: UK Individual (split into the UK Individual Life and General Insurance divisions and Vanbrugh); UK Group Pensions; International; Mercantile & General Reinsurance and Prudential Portfolio Managers. Prudential Property Services was launched in January 1986. Organisational structures are not cast in stone, however, and more modifications have been made over the years. Both Prudential Property Services and the M&GRe have been sold, and in 1991 a new division, Prudential Financial Services, responsible for the selling and marketing of all life and savings products outside Home Service, was established. Within this division Prudential Corporate Pensions and Prudential Holborn were reorganised into two distinct units. The International division headed by Brian Medhurst was restructured in 1993 to reflect the growing importance of Asian markets.

Lord Hunt of Tanworth succeeded Lord Carr as Chairman of the Prudential

Corporation in 1985, and he was followed in the chair by Sir Brian Corby, who was knighted in the 1989 Birthday Honours list, in May 1990. Mick Newmarch, who had joined the Company and worked his way up through the Investment channel, was appointed Group Chief Executive in his place. In 1995 Sir Brian Corby retired after 43 years with the Prudential and was succeeded by Sir Martin Jacomb. In the same year Peter (now Sir Peter) Davis became Group Chief Executive, following the resignation of Mick Newmarch.

In 1998, the Prudential's corporate structure consisted of Prudential UK, with its two subsidiaries Prudential Assurance and Prudential Banking; Jackson National Life; Prudential Asia; Prudential Portfolio Managers; and the international operations in Australia and New Zealand.

The general insurance businesses

At the time the new corporate structure was adopted in the late 1970s, the Prudential was operating against a background of deepening recession. Annual price inflation in the UK was still high and energy costs had soared as a result of the oil producers' cartel. Two years later the country was in the grip of a recession that led to riots and prompted calls for financial institutions to play their part in programmes designed to fight decay in inner city areas. The Prudential responded by taking an active role on the bodies working in areas of particular concern and by seconding staff to work on some of the projects.

The recession affected the Company's general insurance businesses particularly badly. In the 1980s high levels of inflation and over-capacity in the market contributed to difficult underwriting conditions for all general insurance companies. The bad situation was made worse by extreme weather conditions. The underwriting losses on general insurance during the early 1980s prompted the Prudential to pay more attention to this side of its business, and to take a fresh look at operating practices, particularly with regard to premium ratings and expense levels. There was a major review of the General Branch office structure in 1980 and during 1982 a three-year change in organisational and business strategy for general insurance operations was initiated. The aim was to extend computerisation and streamline working processes in order to reduce expense levels, which remained an objective for the rest of the 1980s. By 1991 the home service general insurance operation had been restructured, and the number of regional centres trimmed from 22 to 5. By that time, however, management had decided to focus on long-term business – life assurance, pensions, savings and investment – and to reduce exposure to unreliable sources of earnings such as commercial general insurance, where businesses were too small to compete. It was decided to withdraw from all general insurance except household and personal motor business, where the customer base provided a potential source of sales for life assurance and investment products. A series of radical measures was put into effect. By the end of 1992 Prudential had transferred its remaining general business to Provincial Insurance plc, sold its Canadian operation to General Accident, withdrawn from general insurance in Ireland and Italy, and closed down the marine and aviation business that it owned jointly with the Pearl. It was also decided to withdraw from the UK general insurance broker market. This involved closing the commercial lines business at a financial cost of £53,000,000 and a human cost of 400 jobs.

For a company with the traditions and attitudes of the Prudential this was a painful process. The measures taken produced scaled-down, more tightly focused and controlled general businesses and eradicated much of the volatility associated with the business in the past. In 1993 profits from the personal lines business from the field staff service nearly doubled as a result of good claims experience and improved efficiency. Indeed, the improvement in general efficiency meant that in 1994 the Company was able to absorb the newly introduced 2.5% Insurance Premium Tax, rather than pass it on to customers through premium increases. Today, in line with the Prudential's strategic decision to concentrate on core businesses, the household and motor insurance sold through the direct sales force is regarded as an integral part of the service and a useful prospecting tool, but as complementary to the provision of core savings, investment and protection products.

One further move was needed to rationalise the Prudential's insurance interests. At the time that the Prudential purchased the M&GRe there was commercial logic in the acquisition. Sterling was a weak currency and there were restrictions on overseas portfolio investment. The M&GRe offered exposure to overseas investment markets and to a stream of foreign currency. There was also the feeling already referred to, that the company should not pass into foreign ownership. It was active in both the life and non-life markets and the Prudential management felt that there was considerable value in the life reinsurance business. Too little attention, however, had been paid to the non-life reinsurance side. This market suffered badly in the economic recession of the 1980s and there were nearly six years of catastrophic losses, beginning in 1987. In 1989, a year of natural and man-made disasters included the Piper Alpha explosion (at the time the biggest individual marine insurance claim in history), Hurricane Hugo, the Texas oilfield explosion and the San Francisco earthquake. In early 1990 storms ravaged northern Europe while in 1991 the M&GRe was hit by claims arising from the Japanese typhoons, a fire at the London Underwriting Centre and the Calgary hailstorm.

The effect of these losses was exacerbated by some self-inflicted wounds. Originally the Prudential had run the M&GRe at arm's length, not least because many of its customers were the Prudential's competitors. Unfortunately, however, arm's length management was accompanied by inadequate integration with overall corporate strategy, a problem which was not properly addressed until the 1980s. In 1990, after an abortive attempt to sell the reinsurer at a realistic price, a senior Prudential team began to work closely with the management of the M&GRe to improve management systems and enhance operational efficiency. International reinsurance no longer fitted the Prudential's strategy. The core businesses, according to this, were of retail financial services and fund management. In 1992 a new management team was installed to deal rigorously with the loss-making general accounts. John Engestrom, Managing Director, and Hans-Erik Andersson, Director in charge of general business, were recruited from Skandia Re and Richard Brewster was transferred from Prudential Portfolio Managers as Finance Director. By the end of 1993, helped by the absence of severe catastrophe claims, the previous year's £143,000,000 loss on general business had been turned into a profit of £6,000,000. In 1994 the M&GRe was chosen as 'Reinsurance Company of the Year' by a panel of reinsurance professionals. The exposure to single catastrophes had been so lessened that even the 1995 Kobe earthquakes had very little impact on results. In August 1996 the M&GRe was sold back to Swiss Re for nearly £1,750,000,000, neatly rounding the circle. The sale has considerably reduced the Prudential's exposure to risk. It has also provided resources to develop mainstream activities, and to further the strategic ambition to expand the Prudential's retail financial services businesses in the United Kingdom, the United States and Asia.

The field force and other distribution channels
The Prudential is possibly the only insurance company whose name is as familiar to the general public as Woolworths, Marks & Spencer and the Co-op. In the past, this was thanks in no small part to the ubiquitous presence and the sterling reputation of 'the Man from the Prudential', who had provided the link between the Company and generations of its customers for more than a hundred years. The problem by 1979 was that the direct sales force was operating in a limited part of the market. The aim of the pilot schemes and project areas introduced during the 1960s and 1970s was to explore ways of keeping the Industrial Branch business going while at the same time expanding the Ordinary Branch or direct debit business. Many of the field staff who operated the system were reluctant to implement changes and inevitably friction arose between management and field staff. (Sir Brian Corby recalls that when he addressed the Superintendents' Conference at the Grand Hotel in Eastbourne in 1978, a small number of life inspectors left the hall in protest; some were reported to have climbed onto the hotel's grand piano and sung 'the Red Flag', which reveals that even in difficulties they retained a sense of humour.)

In 1979, the year after the Prudential Corporation was set up, the Company began a major consultative exercise with staff and unions over field staff reorganisation. During 1981 the functions of field staff management, marketing and sales and office staff administration were rationalised. This brought together the management and administration of the field, sales and office staff of the

Prudential Assurance Company for the first time. In the following year the traditional sales force was augmented by an increase in the number of specialist salesmen, and a widened product range. In 1986 there was a break with tradition when Keith Bedell-Pearce, Prudential Portfolio Manager's marketing director and former Prudential company lawyer, was appointed General Manager, sales and marketing, with responsibility for the field staff and reporting to Tony Freeman, Managing Director of the UK Individual Division. Both men were 'outsiders' without long experience of field staff activities.

The concept of home service had always been the hallmark of the Prudential's mainstream business. While other sales outlets had to be developed (not least stronger relationships with the Independent Financial Adviser (IFA) market, about which more will be said later), it was recognised that the direct sales force would remain central to the Prudential's sales strategy. Few of its competitors offered the same degree of direct contact with their customers in their homes and workplaces. Technological developments had nonetheless rendered the field staff structure old-fashioned, and by April 1988 Prudential had invested more than £6,000,000 in staff training, new computer systems and redesigned product literature. This investment in a higher standard of professionalism in both selling and customer service coincided with the implementation of the Financial Services Act (FSA) 1986 on 29 April 1988. The FSA provided legislation for many of the recommendations that had been put forward by Professor Gower in his 'Review of Investor Protection', which was published in February 1984. The Prudential was later to engage in some acrimonious, public debate about the details of the regulatory system created by the FSA, and the cost of enforcement. But initially the Company welcomed the Act's thrust towards achieving higher standards in financial services. Sir Brian Corby, a member of the Governor's Advisory Group (one of the bodies that led to the legislation), believed that the central tenets of the FSA were already enshrined in the business conduct of the Prudential and a number of other major companies.

One consequence of the FSA was that it put a premium on distribution power within the life insurance industry. A well-organised direct sales force such as the Prudential's gave an immediate competitive advantage. As Sir Brian Corby reminded shareholders in the Company's 1988 annual report:

Knowing the customer was the guiding principle on which the Prudential founded its business 140 years ago. We came to know our customers by providing a unique personal service to them in their own homes and responded to their changing financial needs with a range of insurance-related services. Our philosophy was simple. We believed that if we produced satisfied customers our business would flourish. Today we like to think that the eight million customers we serve in the UK alone bear testimony to the soundness of that policy.

M.G. (Mick) Newmarch
(*left*), and Sir Brian Corby.

The new FSA 1986 enshrined this principle, albeit requiring more stringent standards in the conduct of business than had hitherto been the case.

The financial services industry was changing rapidly, and the field force could not stand still. The management of the Prudential had long been aware that the Company was losing both customers and market share because of its continuing reliance on the Industrial Branch. As a result, the Prudential had benefited less than some of its competitors from the endowment mortgage boom that had followed the introduction of the MIRAS (Mortgage Interest Relief at Source) scheme in 1983. Four options (known internally as 'scenarios') were devised in an attempt to make the field force more competitive in the new environment. What was needed was a structure that would continue to provide existing customers with high quality products and services, while the Company's share of the mass middle market was expanded by attracting new customers. 'Scenario 3' was selected as the way forward. Its aims were to boost the productivity of the direct sales operation; to expand the Prudential's market share; to reassert its leadership position; and to place an increased emphasis on the use of information technology.

The subsequent reorganisation was highly complex, and inevitably there were some hitches; indeed there was some limited industrial action, but in the end Scenario 3 was recommended for acceptance by the field staff's union and the ballot resulted in an overwhelming majority in favour of change. By 1991 the agent's traditional role had been split between 6,000 Company service representatives (now equipped with electronic collecting books rather than manual ledgers!), who attended to the day-to-day needs of policyholders, and 3,000 financial consultants able to provide comprehensive financial advice focused on selling and new business. The restructuring resulted in a more efficient and effective direct sales operation and by the end of 1991 the Prudential was able to report that during the year 60,000 working days had been devoted to instruction and training. By 1993 the team of financial consultants had been enlarged to 4,500; there were 2,000 financial advisers providing advice and selling products to existing customers, and 1,800 customer account representatives who devoted their time to collecting cash premiums. A special facility – the Prudential Private Planning Service – was designed to develop relationships with higher income households.

During the modernisation of the direct sales force much thought had been devoted to strengthening Prudential Financial Services, the Prudential's IFA-orientated organisation which sold products through Prudential Holborn. For many years the Prudential had recognised that it needed to expand its distribution into the intermediary market, but this had been difficult to do without alienating the field staff. It had been hoped that Vanbrugh Life would provide the vehicle needed to enter the IFA market. This had not proved successful, however, and Vanbrugh was eventually absorbed into Prudential Financial Services. Thought continued to be given to broadening the range of products designed for IFAs, and the first significant breakthrough was the launch of the Prudence Bond in May 1991. The Prudence Bond, a whole life unitised with-profits bond, combined a strong brand name with good product features, and IFAs were eager to sell it. By the end of 1992 the popularity of the Prudence Bond had helped to treble the number of IFAs dealing with the Prudential. Seven years after its launch, sales totalled just under £5,000,000,000. In 1993 the Prudential ranked as the third most important supplier of products to IFAs, with more than a third of its total new UK business, on an annualised basis, coming from this source. In 1997 the acquisition of Scottish Amicable, the mutual life insurer, further strengthened Prudential's position. The last piece of the distribution jigsaw in the 1990s was the launch of Prudential Direct, first developed in 1993, which has increased Prudential's distribution through the use of direct marketing and telephone access techniques.

Farewell to the Industrial Branch

By the 1980s, the increased popularity of bank accounts and the growth of direct debits had made the personal collection of cash payments an expensive anachronism. With inflation and salaries increasing faster than the increase in premium income, the expense ratio was again giving cause for concern. Despite the convenience to the customer, industrial life policies were generally felt to offer poor value. At a time of growing consumer choice this made them awkward to promote. One of the central aims of reorganising the Prudential's direct sales operation, therefore, had been to accelerate the move from cash collection to direct debit business. Sir Brian Corby was anxious that this should be done without creating huge staffing problems. But while changes were made in the frequency of collections and the minimum premium required, the pressure on expenses continued.

In the late 1980s the Prudential came to an agreement with the Department of Trade and Industry to merge the assets of the Industrial Branch and the Ordinary Branch funds; and, since the pooling of assets facilitated more efficient use of free reserves overall as well as carrying more favourable tax implications, a competitive disadvantage – as against offices with pooled assets – was removed. One of the safeguards naturally agreed between the Prudential and the DTI was that Industrial Branch bonuses in the future be related to those declared in the Ordinary Branch. This ensured that Industrial Branch policyholders were not treated unfairly in the interests of new business acquisition in the Ordinary Branch. By 1994, Industrial Branch business accounted for only 2% of the Prudential's direct sales (it had been 55% ten years earlier) and on 1 January 1995 the Board took the difficult and emotional decision to cease selling new Industrial Branch business altogether. By coincidence the Industrial Branch shutters were put up 140 years (to within three days) after the Company had paid out its first claim – the sum of £30 6s to the family of a railway accident victim. The Prudential continues to service its existing Industrial Branch customers, however, and thanks to the long-term nature of life insurance, the last Industrial Branch payment is scheduled to be collected in the year 2045!

The estate agency venture

The perceived need to provide further points of contact with its customers was one factor behind what was, with hindsight, a badly misconceived new business venture. The move into estate agency was to prove a costly mistake, and it was small comfort that the Company was not alone among financial institutions in having taken this wrong turning.

In the summer of 1985 the Prudential acquired Ekins Dilley and Handley, a long-established and highly successful firm of estate agents in Huntingdon. The purchase was described as a first step towards building up a national chain of estate agents and establishing the Prudential as a leader in the estate agency field. At the time, the arguments in favour of this were highly plausible. It was originally initiated by the UK Individual Division, whose research suggested that the sale and purchase of residential property offered an important opportunity to sell insurance and savings products. It was argued that an estate agency chain would give the Prudential a presence in the High Street that would make it easier for potential customers to make contact with the Company. This in turn would promote its growth as a major supplier of a wide range of retail financial services.

On 2 January 1986 Prudential Property Services was launched as a separate operating division, and by the end of 1987 it had become the largest estate agency chain in Europe. There were 622 residential branches, the acquired businesses having all been rebranded. The Prudential's declared aim was to have complete coverage of the UK and a network of some 1,000 branches by the end of 1989. By 1989, however, the panorama had changed dramatically. Prices for estate agency businesses had spiralled out of control, as more and more financial institutions entered the market in the wake of the Prudential. At the same time, the branches of Prudential Property Services were failing significantly to enhance either the Company's distribution capability or its ability to cross-sell to a customer base deriving from an estate agency. With the collapse of the main UK housing market the Division lost £48,900,000 over the year.

Within the Company the strategy quickly changed. Mick Newmarch, the new Group Chief Executive appointed in 1990, commissioned a detailed review from accountants Coopers & Lybrand, and following this the Board concluded that estate agencies were not a business in which the Prudential should remain. In July 1990 the Corporation announced that 175 branches were to close, and in November the decision was taken to sell the remaining ones. Mick Newmarch described this as 'an unpalatable but necessary decision' that would allow the Company to focus its energies on its successful mainstream activities. 'Cross-selling wasn't working,' he said later. 'The estate agents wanted to sell houses. They were interested in commission but not in our products.' In short it had been a marriage of two conflicting cultures, and divorce had become inevitable. The majority of the estate agents were locally based entrepreneurial businesses – one admitted that when times were hard he tided himself over by selling flowers – and they were unsuited to centralised corporate control. Total losses from this injudicious venture amounted to some £340,000,000, though they fell on shareholders' funds rather than on those reserved for policyholders.

Coming out of Europe

By the time the Corporation was established the Prudential was active in 34 countries. Since then its overseas activities have been both expanded and rationalised, as key markets have been identified and the policy of concentrating the group's activities on core retail financial services and fund management has evolved. As a result, a number of overseas businesses have been sold, either because they no longer matched the Company's strategic ambitions, or because they were too small to enable the Prudential to be a significant player in that particular market.

In the early 1970s it had seemed as though a presence in each country of the European Community would be necessary, given the insurance legislation then prevailing. By the late 1980s, however, legislation had developed to the point where a company could, if licensed in one country, operate in all the others. This allowed the Prudential the flexibility to let go of some earlier acquisitions. L'Escaut, for example, by 1990 no longer fitted into the scheme which the management of the Prudential believed necessary to meet the challenges of the coming decade, and the decision was taken to sell it. Similarly, as we have seen, a series of measures in 1992 (which included withdrawing from the Irish and Italian markets) further reduced the Prudential's exposure to overseas general insurance markets. By early 1997 all of the Prudential's remaining European interests had been sold. Although the Company has not turned its back irrevocably on Europe, the management believes that it would now have the advantage of being able to come in as a new entrant, and a reassessment of the European markets is currently taking place.

And going into the USA ...

On the other hand, by the early 1980s there was also a feeling that too great a proportion of the Prudential's profits came from the UK, and it became a key objective to enter the United States, the world's largest life assurance market. Because of name agreements with The Prudential Insurance Company of America, the Prudential could not trade in the US under its own name. In November 1986 it bought an exceptionally successful, family-managed, American life company called Jackson National Life, founded in 1961 by the dynamic Tony Pasant, who remained as Chairman and Chief Executive. At the time of the acquisition the Company was licensed in 45 states and Washington DC, and sold its individual life and annuity products through some 50,000 independent agents. Jackson National Life was one of the first companies in the US to promote the virtues of term insurance, and in 1975 it had developed an early form of 'universal' life assurance, eight years before any competitor offered a similar type of protection.

The total consideration for Jackson National Life was approximately £405,000,000. In June 1986 Prudential had raised £357,000,000 for its expansion plans through a 1 for 5 rights issue, but the capital demands of other activities within the group (including the acquisition costs of the ill-fated UK estate agencies) meant that further funds were required. From 1986 to 1988, therefore, a total of £400,000,000 of long-term debt was raised in various currencies. The borrowings were rated AAA by Standard & Poors, the US credit-rating agency. Jackson National Life has proved to be one of the most significant acquisitions that the Prudential has ever made, and it is now its most important long-term business operation outside the UK. It has successfully expanded its products and enlarged its distribution channels to include broker dealers and banks. The Company is now registered to operate in 48 states, including New York state, the largest insurance market in the US. In 1996 its operating profits grew to $512,000,000, while single premium sales reached $3,800,000,000; total premium income has grown from $2,000,000,000 in 1986 to $27,000,000,000 in 1996.

... and in Asia

Throughout its history the Prudential has followed its customers, which has often meant following the British flag and even the military garrisons. As a result the Company has had a presence in Asia for more than 70 years, although since the loss of its businesses in India, Pakistan and Sri Lanka, this has been very subdued. Asian markets, however, again became a focus for development when Mick Newmarch became Group Chief Executive and planned the expansion of the Prudential's business in the Pacific Rim. Mark Tucker was sent to the Far East, with a brief to develop the whole region. Recent performance has been highly encouraging, if not yet measurably profitable. The Prudential has steadily expanded in Asia and now has operations in six countries: Singapore, Hong Kong, Malaysia, Thailand, Indonesia and the Philippines. It also has representative offices in China and Vietnam and is in the process of re-establishing a base in India. In 1996 sales of Prudential's regular premium products in Asia passed £100,000,000 and the Company further demonstrated its commitment to this part of the world with the launch of a US$1,000,000,000 fund designed to make direct investments in the growing Asian economies.

A global investment house

During the past 20 years the extension and rationalisation of the Prudential's presence overseas has been accompanied by its growth as a global investment house. A catalyst for this growth was the abolition of official exchange controls in October 1979. For the first time in 40 years UK residents and fund managers had the freedom to invest freely anywhere in the world. The Prudential had been investing in global markets for half a century by then, and its international department had recently been considerably enlarged, in part to reflect the growth of funds managed for external clients who wanted exposure to other markets. Following the abolition of exchange controls, the decision was taken to increase the overseas weighting of the Prudential's ordinary share portfolios to an initial level of 10%. This was achieved within a year, entirely by investing new money. In 1997 £13,000,000,000 of the £47,000,000,000 of equities managed by Prudential Portfolio Managers were invested in overseas markets.

The development of Prudential Portfolio Managers (PPM) has been central to the establishment of the Prudential as a leading global investment manager. Its success owes much to the successive leadership of Ron Artus, Mick Newmarch, Hugh Jenkins and, latterly, Derek Higgs. It will be recalled that PPM was originally established to manage the Prudential Unit Trust, a fund set up in 1968 more than 16 years before the range of Holborn unit trusts was launched. By 1980 PPM had been given the twin roles of providing investment services to that part of the Group where there was no separate investment capacity and building up fee-based management services. The aim, through the 1980s, was to create a quality investment management operation, able to operate efficiently in all world markets. In 1982 the Prudential Corporation launched a company in New York, Holborn International Portfolio Managers, to provide a global investment strategy segregated for US pension funds. This subsidiary of PPM was headed by Mick Newmarch, subsequently Chief Executive of PPM.

The 1984 Budget contained an unwelcome measure for the life insurance companies in the form of the abolition of Life Assurance Premium Relief (LAPR), one of the strongest selling aids for savings-related life insurance products. Mick Newmarch, convinced of the need to establish a unit trust business, was the prime mover in the launch of a new PPM subsidiary, Prudential Unit Trust Managers (PUTM), in 1988. Three mainstream trusts were launched initially, followed later in the year by five specialist funds, which were designed to appeal to more experienced investors and their professional advisers. The Prudential's presence in the unit trust marketplace was a natural development, and in the wake of the abolition of LAPR, a necessary one. Unit trusts were becoming important to all financial services companies, and the Prudential had the considerable advantage of being able to offer both the proven skills of its investment managers and a powerful sales force. There had nevertheless been some nervousness within the Company which echoed that felt 20 years earlier when unit-linked insurance had just been introduced. Given that the basis of the Prudential's business was life assurance in its various forms, there were fears that the field staff would switch all too enthusiastically to the new products, which were easier to sell now that LAPR had gone. There were also concerns about whether the sales force had sufficient training to understand and to explain the volatility and risk inherent in equity investments. The Prudential met these problems by restricting unit trust sales to Life Inspector grade, and by paying smaller commission on unit trusts than on conventional life policies.

Unit trusts also prompted some misgivings among the investment managers. They were long-term investors, accustomed to being judged by their results over time. They were understandably uneasy about the short-term character of the unit trust industry, where it was common practice to publish six-monthly and 12-monthly returns. In the event, Prudential's entry into unit trusts, which was backed by a powerful marketing campaign, proved to be a triumph. The debut of PUTM's funds was the single largest launch the unit trust industry had yet seen. By the end of 1985 PUTM was selling more unit trusts than any other manager and had attracted 30,000 new investors. Currently it has some £2,400,000,000 of unit trust funds under management. The original Holborn brand name has been dropped.

Events in 1986 marked a further important stage in the development of PPM. This was the year of the Big Bang, or the deregulation of the London Stock Exchange, an event strongly supported by PPM. Its policyholders, pension fund managers and unit trust investors were expected to benefit from the introduction of competition into the workings of the Stock Exchange. But the Big Bang was more than just a domestic incident. It was also associated with the modernisation of the London securities market. The degree to which the world's markets were becoming more international was accelerating. The changes in the London market marked a significant first step in the process of developing PPM as a global investment management organisation. The separate UK and foreign units were done away with and the investment management resource was reorganised into global units concerned with investment and currency policies, equities and bonds.

By 1986, too, investment management for external clients was becoming increasingly important and PPM made further significant progress in the UK pension fund market, winning two keenly contested opportunities to manage significant portions of the British Rail and Unilever pension funds. The Company also sided with the optimists – and they were not that numerous at the time – about the future of Personal Equity Plans (PEPs), which had been introduced in the Finance Act 1987. On 1 January 1987 PPM launched a range of PEPs, thus securing an early presence in what is now a £30,000,000,000 market.

The Prudential's long-established and experienced investment teams stood the Company in good stead in the increasingly complex international investment markets. The Company quickly recognised that it must capitalise on this strength. By the late 1980s Prudential Portfolio Managers were leaders in the use of information technology systems, and one of the major players in the financial futures and options markets. In March 1990 Mick Newmarch moved from being Chief Executive of Prudential Portfolio Managers to become Group Chief Executive of the Prudential Corporation. His place at PPM was taken by Hugh Jenkins, formerly Group Investment Director of Allied Dunbar Assurance plc.

'Think globally, act locally' neatly describes PPM's investment philosophy today. The usual practice has been to establish regional investment centres, managing funds invested in local markets, while the strategic allocation between asset classes, markets and currencies is controlled from London. By the end of 1994 PPM had established investment management operations in its main markets around the world. Its overseas offices in Cape Town, Chicago, Hong Kong, New York, Singapore, Sydney and Toronto now provide a global information network, feeding economic and market data back to London 24 hours a day and managing funds both for Prudential's own customers and for external clients.

By the end of 1997 the Prudential had over £110,000,000,000 of assets

PRUDENTIAL
SAVINGS

PRUDENTIAL
PLAIN SPEAKING HOME INSURANCE

under management, making it the largest UK-based institutional investor and one of the world's leading investment management companies. The largest of its funds is the £41,000,000,000 with-profits fund, which contains the savings and investments of most of its UK customers. Inevitably the sheer size of the Prudential as an institutional investor has implications. Its investments represent some 3.5% of the UK equity market and in any takeover or merger the Prudential is likely to be a substantial shareholder in one or both of the companies concerned. PPM therefore lays much emphasis on the need for corporate research and on maintaining close contact with all the companies in which it is a major investor. This ensures that it exercises its voting rights in the best interests of both its own investors and of the companies. Its preference is to support existing managements in good standing, if these wish to remain independent. There may, however, be a price at which a bid is too attractive for the Prudential – which must act in the interests of its customers – properly to reject.

Shareholders' funds

One guiding business principle for any life company is that it should still be around, 50 years on, to pay claims. If it is a proprietary company, another guiding

The Prudential's 'I Want To Be ...' campaign delighted the public in the late 1980s with its combination of good sense and humour.

principle is that it should try to be fair to both policyholders and shareholders. It was against this background, in the mid-1980s, that the Prudential began to reconsider its approach to the level of profits transferred out of the long-term fund of the Prudential Assurance Company into shareholders' funds. The PAC's Articles of Association allowed up to 10% of the profits each year to be transferred. Since 1952, however, partly in reaction to the competitive position of the mutual life insurance companies, the shareholder proportion had been gradually reduced to about 6%, leaving 94% of the profits to be distributed to policyholders.

By the late 1980s the pattern of the business had changed; moreover, these proportions had become a potential hazard. The fact that the Company was distributing only 6%, instead of the maximum 10%, to shareholders was seen as an attraction to possible predators. The Company also considered its mutual responsibilities to shareholders and policyholders. Sir Brian Corby recommended, and the Board agreed, that the shareholders' proportion be increased, and it was gradually adjusted upwards. By 1989 the Company was able to give formal notice, as it was required to do for other than marginal increases under the Insurance Companies Act 1982, that the shareholders' proportion should once again move to the maximum level of 10%.

Bonus trends

The arrival of unit-linked insurance in the UK, and its spectacular growth during the 1970s, had demonstrated to the traditional with-profits companies that there was a different and attractive way of packaging and selling life insurance policies.

One consequence of this was that the main competition facing Prudential shifted away from the mutual companies, and there was pressure on with-profits companies to increase their bonus rates to combat the threat of the unit-linked parvenus. The dramatic stockmarket collapse in 1974 had induced a sense of caution at the Prudential, and as a result the Company had been somewhat too restrained in its bonus distributions throughout the 1970s. By the mid-1980s, however, it appeared that the pendulum had swung too far, and bonus rate levels became a major issue for the Prudential's management. The Company began to warn policyholders that the life insurance industry's current rates of bonus were not sustainable. It was a difficult message to convey because insurance companies had never been markedly successful in explaining their products, let alone the reversionary bonus system.

As a prelude to cutting bonus rates, the Prudential improved its bonus illustrations, to explain better the connection between investment returns and inflation, and the implications of this connection for future profits and policy proceeds. The only question within the life insurance industry was 'which company would cut bonus rates first?'. In the end the Prudential, since it was in a strong position to do so, helped to lead the way and introduced the first of a series of bonus rate reductions in the early 1990s.

The pensions revolution

Two decades of radical legislation have changed the shape of the state pension scheme and of private pension arrangements. Little wonder, then, that during the past 20 years few subjects have attracted more comment within the financial services industry. The debate continues to rage. Demographic changes and an ageing population are forcing the UK, like other countries in the developed world, to rethink the cost of state pension provision and long-term care. There is pressure to develop new vehicles to help people to assume more personal responsibility and to invest for their own retirement and future financial security.

As will be recalled from the previous chapter, the changes in the legislation governing pensions began on 6 April 1978. Provisions in the Social Security Pensions Act 1975 replaced the old State Graduated Scheme with SERPS, an earnings-related additional pension. In the next ten years personal portable pensions, the facility to contract out of part of the state scheme and improvements in company pensions were to follow, reinforcing the position of pensions as one of the Prudential's core products.

As an established market leader in both group and individual pension products, the Prudential's approach assumed that pensions would be a growth area over the coming decades. It was particularly well placed to meet the needs of the new market, and to offer a lead on the direction this market should take. In 1984 the Company published a booklet 'Let's Get It Right', giving its views on portable pensions, and later contributed to the White Paper on pensions reform, published in December 1985. It welcomed the revised approach to modify SERPS, rather than to phase it out, and to encourage private sector provision on a voluntary basis, rather than imposing a compulsory system for private pensions as was originally envisaged. The Social Security Act 1986 encouraged private sector pension provision through the personal pension concept, which embraced both individual personal pensions and easily run group money purchase plans. In February 1987 the Prudential set the pace for new industry-wide group pension arrangements by setting up a pension scheme for the printing industry, together with the British Printing Industries Federation and the industry's two main unions, the NGA and SOGAT 82.

The new personal pensions went on sale on 1 July 1988. Although these were very similar to the old retirement annuity contracts there were fundamental differences. In particular, there was a facility to use a personal pension to contract out of the earnings-related portion of the state pension scheme. At the time of the launch of personal pensions the Prudential had about a quarter of the UK retirement annuity market. The new arrangements therefore presented the Company with a unique opportunity to persuade those who were not in company pension schemes of the benefits of having a personal pension. A new computer system was brought into operation, and because it was a lengthy business to explain the benefits of personal pensions and the pros and cons of contracting out of SERPS, the campaign to identify potential customers was started during 1987. This preparation paid off. In 1988 the Prudential's new annual premiums for individual pensions had risen from £51,000,000 to £105,400,000, while single premium sales reached £134,500,000, against £23,700,000 in the previous year. By 5 April 1989, which was the deadline for securing the maximum benefit from contracting out of SERPS, the Prudential had sold 434,000 personal pensions and won 12% of the new annual premium market. Particularly encouraging was the fact that many of the customers were new to the Company. Their age profile had also achieved a substantial shift in the Prudential's customer base towards younger age groups.

Personal pensions had been launched with such exaggerated publicity by both the Government and the financial services industry that realists might well have forecast the sorry saga of mis-selling that later emerged. The Prudential was one of the few companies that warned of the dangers in the initial marketing phase, and of the need for proper advice for consumers. As a result the Company received some complaints from members of the Government that it was undermining its pensions policy. Before personal pensions went on sale, the Prudential produced a 'Guide to the Social Security Act' in which it was reiterated that:

> *We cannot over-emphasise how important it is that you thoroughly understand just how your retirement benefits would be affected should you decide to opt out and go for a personal pension. If you are already a member of a company pension scheme or will soon be eligible to join one, you will probably feel it best to stay with your company scheme. If you have any doubts at all, do discuss them with either your employer or the trustees of your company scheme.*

Later, in the furore over mis-selling that first captured the headlines in the early 1990s, Prudential undoubtedly made a mistake in relying too heavily on published policy and claiming that the Company had never mis-sold a personal pension. Given the size of the Prudential's sales force and the demand for the product, such a proclamation was too sweeping to be verifiable. In fact, with the largest share of the personal pensions market Prudential has in recent years borne the brunt of the adverse media coverage which the mis-selling saga has generated.

Investor protection

The Financial Services Act 1986, which came into force in April 1988, introduced a system of regulation for investment businesses in the UK, comprising one central regulator – the Securities and Investments Board (SIB) – and a number of self-regulating organisations. The Prudential had endorsed the aims of this legislation but it had always argued that there should be a single regulator and it soon became uneasy with what it felt to be over-detailed and bureaucratic regulation.

There were many disagreements with Sir Kenneth Berrill, the first chairman of the new SIB, whose approach the Company felt to be overly legalistic.

Initial compliance with the rules of LAUTRO (the Life Assurance and Unit Trust Regulatory Organisation) had cost the Prudential £7,000,000. Mick Newmarch, by now Group Chief Executive of the Prudential, began to speak publicly on what the Board considered the shortcomings of the new regulatory system. The Directors believed that there was a distortion of the basic objective of the legislation, which was to prevent the reasonable citizen, who had taken reasonable precautions, from being defrauded. Instead, Newmarch argued, there was a presumption that the regulators were consumer champions, whose job was to do battle on behalf of the public against the practitioners. 'Regulation was not producing the right result for the consumer or for the industry,' he said later. 'The regulators were unable to distinguish between the people who were doing the job well, and those who were doing it badly.'

In 1993 there was further upheaval in the regulatory world when a new body, the Personal Investment Authority (PIA), took over the functions of LAUTRO. The Prudential Board did not feel that the central concept of the FSA – 'self-regulation within a statutory framework' – had worked, and it did not believe the PIA's approach to regulation was suited to the provision of adequate and cost effective protection. Mick Newmarch described it as 'an expensive irrelevance', and in March 1994, after much internal deliberation, the Prudential decided to opt for direct regulation by the SIB rather than by the new PIA. In making the announcement Newmarch emphasised: 'We believe that the only adequate basis for regulation of retail savings is a single-tier regulator with full accountability through Government to Parliament.' As Sir Brian Corby recalls: 'For the first time in the Prudential's recent history we were out of the mainstream. It was not a comfortable position to be in.' The Prudential's dissatisfaction with the manner in which the objectives of the Financial Services Act had been implemented came to a head in January 1995. Mick Newmarch felt that his relationship, at the helm of the Prudential, with the UK retail financial service regulators, had become untenable. To the Board's regret, after a meeting lasting many hours, he resigned.

In May of that year Peter Davis, a non-executive Board member and the former Chairman of publishing and information group Reed Elsevier plc, was chosen to replace Newmarch as Group Chief Executive, the first industry 'outsider' to hold the position.

New corporate identity
With the introduction of two major and far-reaching pieces of legislation, 1986 was a significant year for the financial services industry and its customers. For the Prudential it marked another milestone as it introduced a new corporate identity and logo. Since the formation of the Prudential Corporation eight years

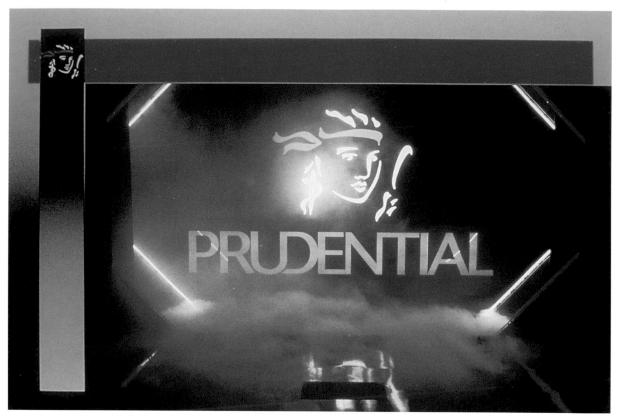

The Prudential's new logo, launched in 1986 with sound, light and dry ice.

earlier, the group had been steadily diversifying from its traditional life assurance base to provide a range of related financial services. Some visual expression of what had become a modern and forward-looking financial institution was wanted, but one which would retain the associations with the past upon which the Company's identity rested. The figure of Prudence, the cardinal virtue of 'wisdom in action' that had given the Company its name, was updated by the design firm Wolff Olins to provide the centrepiece of a new corporate identity.

A third of the staff was brought to the Royalty Theatre in London for the launch of the new identity, for what became known as the 'Star Wars laser and dry ice show' produced by Corporate Affairs Manager David Vevers. The staff loved it. The new logo showed a stylised female head with a gentle yet resolute expression, in the new corporate colours of vermilion and grey. As the Company's then Chairman, Lord Hunt of Tanworth, explained: 'It seeks to express us as we are – innovative, competitive and expanding in a fast-changing financial services market but retaining all the principles of wise conduct and integrity represented by Prudence, who has been our symbol for so long.'

Scottish Amicable

A significant part of the Prudential's expansion since 1970, both in the UK and overseas, has been by acquisition. The most recent strategic purchase was the

Company's successful bid, after a contested auction, for Scottish Amicable, a medium-sized mutual life company. The combined Prudential–Scottish Amicable group has some £110,000,000,000 of assets and more than 7,000,000 policyholders. The acquisition has strengthened the Prudential's position in the IFA market, extended its customer base and expanded its product range. It has also consolidated the Company's position as one of the UK's leading fund managers.

Prudential Banking

The move into banking has been another important step towards focusing the Group on those markets where it has particular expertise. Prudential Banking was launched on 1 October 1996, as a direct and branchless bank, linked to the field force. In product terms, the operation was started like a conventional building society, offering only deposits and mortgages. The intention is to operate a fully fledged bank in the course of time. Prudential's banking operation is an interesting hybrid. It is one of the new breed of banks accessed by telephone and post from a state-of-the-art centre at Dudley, West Midlands. But the banking operation, headed by Mike Harris, the former Chief Executive of First Direct, is also supported by the Prudential's direct sales force, which is an integral part of the initiative.

The establishment of the banking service involved a £70,000,000 investment in equipment, office space and training, but the Prudential will not have the costs of a traditional branch network and this saving will be passed on to customers. Sir Peter Davis says: 'We built it as a highly technology-driven, low-cost operation. It has a totally different culture from the Prudential.' Banking

Sir Martin Jacomb,
Chairman of the Prudential
Corporation since 1995.

has enabled the Prudential to widen the range of products it can offer to both new and existing customers and it has provided the Company with another facility to present to investors whose Prudential life policies have matured. Each year the Prudential pays out more than £1,000,000,000 in maturing policies, and at the time of the launch of Prudential Banking, research indicated that 54% of this money was still sitting in bank and building society accounts 12 months after it was paid out. By the end of 1997 35% of Prudential customers were investing their maturities in a Prudential Deposit account.

The founders, who first invested the modest sum of £5,280 in 'The Prudential Investment, Loan, and Assurance Association' in 1848, would not recognise the original Prudential in the market position and business of today's leviathan. From its small beginnings as a life insurance business firmly rooted in the industrial working classes of Victorian Britain, Prudential has now developed into an international financial services giant, with operations in ten countries offering a broad range of products not just via the traditional man from the Pru but also through Independent Financial Advisers, over the telephone and now even via the Internet. Today Prudential is a company with a broader scope, a wider geographic spread and greater investment power than could ever have been imagined in 1848.

Sir Peter Davis, Group Chief Executive of the Prudential Corporation since 1995.

The Man from the Pru may no longer be a physical presence on all doorsteps but the Company remains an influential and dynamic force within the financial services sector and it is a fact that as society changes, so too must the companies that serve it.

Notes and References to the Text

SECTION ONE

Chapter One: A Background Sketch

1. Phyllis Deane and W.A. Cole, *British Economic Growth 1688–1959* (1962), pp.308–09. In three or four decades, beginning in the 1830s, the money value of national income roughly trebled while that of national capital increased fivefold.
2. G.F.A. Best, *Mid-Victorian Britain* (1971), pp.20–21.
3. F.C. Mather, *Chartism and Society. An Anthology of Documents* (1980), pp.15–16.
4. Henry Mayhew, writing slightly later, calculated that of a working population of 'between four and five million in number' subject to seasonal employment and replacement by machines, 'there is barely sufficient work for the regular employment of half our labourers ...'. *London Labour and the London Poor* (1861), II, pp.364–65.
5. E.P. Thompson, *The Making of the English Working Class* (1963), pp.458–59. But Thompson asserts that while some societies were devoted to their ostensible purpose, others were almost certainly 'fronts for trades union activity or Jacobinism', and that therefore magistrates often assumed political activity even when there was none.
6. P.H.J.H. Gosden, *The Friendly Societies in England* (1967), p.11.
7. Gosden, *op. cit.*, p.33.
8. Gosden, *op. cit.*, pp.52–54. Benevolent individuals did sometimes succeed in organising – and running, on behalf of local workers – savings societies that Gosden calls 'County' societies, but these were not really a working-class phenomenon and were confined to the south of England.
9. Edwin Chadwick estimated the cost of funerals in 1839 as 13s per head for London pauper funerals, £5 for artisans and up to £50 for tradesmen.
10. Charles Hardwick, *Insolvent Sick and Burial Clubs* (1863), pp.13–14.
11. Friendly Societies Act, 13 & 14 Vict. c.115 s.2.
12. Barry Supple, *The Royal Exchange Assurance. A History of British Assurance 1720–1970* (1970), p.113.
13. Supple, *op. cit.*, p.119.
14. The *Morning Chronicle* of 1 January 1853 described the *Post Magazine* as 'a small but spirited and able, weekly publication which for several years has continued, almost single-handed and with amazing courage and perseverance, to attack bubble insurance schemes as they appeared. It has been successful in suppressing some worse than doubtful projects; and it has rendered valuable service to the really solid and respectable insurance offices'.

15. John Francis, referring to a work called 'Assurance Company Accounts' in his own *Annals, Anecdotes and Legends: A Chronicle of Life Assurance* (1853), pp.261–62.

16. Francis, *op. cit.*, pp.259–60.

17. *Post Magazine*, Vol. XIV, 13 August 1853.

18. Gosden, *op. cit.*, pp.96–97.

19. *Ibid.*

20. Edwin Chadwick, 'An Essay on the Means of Insurance', *Westminster Review*, No. XVIII, April 1828.

21. *Ibid.*

22. Hardwick, *op. cit.*, pp.16–17.

23. At the time Hardwick was writing he would point out the disparity in actuaries' estimates of duration of sickness. Henry Ratcliffe calculated 20 weeks annually at age 80, Neison 27 weeks, and Finlaison 14 weeks.

24. Gosden, *op. cit.*, p.12.

25. Hardwick, *loc. cit.*

26. R.C. Simmonds, *The Institute of Actuaries 1848–1948* (1948), pp.16–17, 23. The word 'actuary' is derived from the Latin *actuarius*, who was the man who kept the *acta* or minutes of the Roman Senate or of the Courts of Law.

27. The variation in life expectancy at birth in different localities was very marked. The middle-class child born in Bath had a predicted lifespan of 55 years; if born in Manchester, only 38 years. The labourer's child born in Bath had a life expectancy of 25 years; if born in Liverpool, 15! The most shocking statistics of all are those which reveal the enormous disparity between the classes: Derby middle-class children might live to 48; Derby labourers' children to only 21. Liverpool had the lowest life expectancy in the realm for all classes. See also F.B. Smith, *The People's Health 1830–1910* (1970), pp.320–23.

Chapter Two: In an Office in Hatton Garden

1. Prudential Archives. Documents relating to the formation of the General Investment, Loan, and Endowment Association, the Prudential Investment, Loan, and Assurance Association, and the Prudential Mutual Assurance, Investment, and Loan Association. The Prudential Investment, Loan and Assurance Association. Minute Book 1, 1847–52.

2. Prudential Archives. General Investment, Loan, and Endowment Association. Prospectus. The company was still only provisionally registered; the prospectus probably dates from June 1847.

3. David Morier Evans, *The Commercial Crisis of 1847* (1867), p.66.

4. Prudential Archives. General Investment, Loan, and Endowment Association. Minute Book 1, 21 April 1847. See also Morier Evans, *op. cit.*, pp.72–73. Larpent is thought to have been the subject of remarks delivered in the House of Commons by Disraeli on 30 August 1848, when he reflected on the financial distress of the past year: 'Day after day, gentlemen whom we had lived with in this house, and whom we respected and regarded, merchants of the highest European reputation, were during that crisis rudely torn, I may say, from these benches, if not with disgrace and dishonour, yet with circumstances of pitiable vicissitude seldom equalled.'

5. Prudential Archives. General Investment, Loan, and Endowment Association. Minute Book 1, 28 April 1847.

6. Prudential Archives. Prudential Mutual Assurance, Investment, and Loan Association. Prospectus.

7. Prudential Archives. Prudential Mutual Assurance, Investment, and Loan Association. Minute Book 1, 19 September 1848.

8. Prudential Archives. Prudential Mutual Assurance, Investment, and Loan Association. Prospectus.

Chapter Three: Tentative Beginnings

1. Prudential Archives. Prudential Mutual Assurance, Investment, and Loan Association. Minute Book 1, 2 November 1849.

2. R.W. Barnard, *A Century of Service. A History of the Prudential 1848–1948* (1948), p.5.

3. *Post Magazine*, Vol. XV, No. 15.

4. His three initial introductions, attending the meeting on 5 April, were John Webster, George Clark and a Mr Brocklebank, who all subscribed for 20 shares and were made Directors. Reemt Schenk, another Worthington contact, did likewise and was made a Director on 19 April, and Worthington himself, together with a further acquaintance, John Lutwyche, became Directors on 30 April. The Reverend Robert Lovelace Hill, who joined the Board in May, was probably another connection of Worthington. The Vestry Minutes of St Sepulchre, Newgate Street, where Worthington was curate from 1825 to 1830, show that John Lutwyche was Overseer of the Poor at the same time. Robert Lovelace Hill was incumbent of St Barnabas, King's Square, Goswell Road, from 1843, by which time Worthington was nearby at Holy Trinity, Gray's Inn Road.

5. Prudential Archives. Prudential Mutual Assurance, Investment, and Loan Association. Minute Book 1, 10 May 1849.

6. His letter of application for the Royal Geographical Society post, dated 16 January 1849, ran to seven foolscap pages and outlined his own qualifications as well as the reforms he saw as necessary for the running of the RGS. As to Worthington's finances, he seems always to have needed other income: as a young curate at St Sepulchre's in 1828 we find him offering to copy the parish registers and receiving a succession of 10-guinea fees for so doing. At the time of his death in 1879, having held various posts (including that of President) at Sion College since 1857, his estate was worth less than £300.

7. For an account of the cholera epidemic, see the *Annual Register*, 1849, pp.448–54. The unfortunate Croggan lived at Newington in south London, where the number of cholera deaths was four times the metropolitan average. The number of deaths from all causes for the summer quarter of 1848 was 13,645; the number for the same period in 1849, 27,109. Virtually the whole of the difference was due to the epidemic.

8. Prudential Archives. Prudential Mutual Assurance, Investment, and Loan Association. Minute Book 1, 6 September 1849.

9. Prudential Archives. Prudential Mutual Assurance, Investment, and Loan Association. Minute Book 1. Report of the Finance Committee, submitted 4 October 1849 and accepted 18 October 1849. A minute of 25 October records 'That upon the late treasurer rendering a statement of the account he admits to be due to the association and paying the balance over to the secretary, the voucher for the Tavern bill £24 10s, be admitted a payment by the association' and another of 14 November notes that Hanslip is to arrange with Harrison payment of the balance due as Treasurer. A further entry for 22 November details Hanslip and Manning to 'arrange accounts with the late treasurer'.

10. Prudential Archives. Prudential Mutual Assurance, Investment, and Loan Association.

Minute Book 1, 27 December 1849. Harrison's words of resignation carry an injured tone: 'Gentlemen, feeling that I can no longer in justice to myself occupy a seat at your board I beg to tender my resignation in the hope that it will be accepted.' It is interesting to find Dr George Steet on the Board of the Kent Mutual in 1855; unfortunately the records of the Kent Mutual do not survive to clarify how this came about. The company was one of the many assimilated by the Albert life office, whose crash in 1867 was the worst of the century.

11. Prudential Archives. Prudential Mutual Assurance, Investment, and Loan Association. Report and Accounts, 1849.

12. Queen Anne's Bounty was intended to augment the livings of the poorer clergy and was administered by commissioners known as the Governors of the Bounty of Queen Anne, who decided cases on the basis of a kind of means test. Those clergy who were considered insufficiently needy were left with no recourse but to borrow if, for instance, they were allocated to a living with no dwelling, or one in need of major repairs.

13. Prudential Archives. Prudential Mutual Assurance, Investment, and Loan Association. Minute Book 1, October–November 1850. There was evidently a little: the minutes record discussions with a Mr Scott about establishing 'penny banks in conjunction with life assurance under the direction of the Company directors', but the idea was never put into effect.

14. Prudential Archives. Prudential Mutual Assurance, Investment, and Loan Association. Report and Accounts, 1850.

15. One such instance came on 27 April 1850, when the Directors had to meet a bill for £300 falling due that day, and put up the money themselves. A fortnight earlier, an unhappy little minute had directed that 'the income and property tax paper be filled up with the words "no profit made"'.

16. Prudential Archives. Prudential Mutual Assurance, Investment, and Loan Association. Report and Accounts, 1850.

17. Timb's *Curiosities of London* (rev. ed. 1877?) calls it 'a specimen of the players' innyard from before our regular theatres were built', dating from the reign of Henry VI. Grinling Gibbons had lived in Belle Sauvage Yard, 'where he carved a pot of flowers which shook surprisingly with the motion of the coaches that passed by', according to Horace Walpole (p.452). The yard was occupied by Cassell's printworks when the Prudential moved to No. 35 Ludgate Hill.

18. The re-establishment of the Catholic hierarchy aroused strong public feeling and a high degree of resentment among many Church of England clergy, but the whole tone of Worthington's piece is deplorably undignified: at the end, he commands the Cardinal to 'be gone, to your home on the Flaminian Way, and trusting you will wend your way thither at your earliest convenience ...'.

19. Prudential Archives. Prudential Mutual Assurance, Investment, and Loan Association. Minute Book 1, 12 and 19 February, 9 September 1852.

20. Prudential Archives. Prudential Mutual Assurance, Investment, and Loan Association. Minute Book 1, 11 March 1853.

21. The name of 'T. Crawter' (possibly Thomas Crawter, brother, son or nephew of Henry; all the Crawters seem to have been called Thomas or Henry) appears as that of witness on the certificate of Henry Harben's first marriage, 1 August 1846. Another branch of the Crawter practice was located at Cobham, Surrey. Harben, then living at Isleworth, may have been employed by, or articled to, one of the Crawters. Guy Philip Harben wrote in a personal reminiscence in the Prudential Archives that his grandfather had

stopped for a cup of tea at the house of a Highgate friend and had there met Gillman, who told him that the Prudential was seeking a Secretary.

22. Anonymous (but known to have been written by Henry Harben), *History of the Prudential Assurance Company*, 1880. Harben himself is unfortunately the only source for this story, apart from the minutes. Nothing whatever is known of Henry Barfoot, Secretary to the Company during four of its formative years, beyond the information in the minutes regarding actions carried out by him.

23. According to the *Oxford Dictionary of the Law*, *capias* was the general name of several types of writs formerly used in English law. They were addressed to the sheriff and directed him to arrest a named person. Shillinglaw ended up spending six months in the Queen's Prison, which had replaced the Marshalsea, before finally emigrating to Australia. His eldest son, John Joseph, achieved a degree of fame as a historian in the new country, and is commemorated by entries in the *Australian Dictionary of Biography* and in J.H. Heaton, *The Australian Dictionary of Dates and Men of the Time* (1879).

24. Edward Ryley, formerly Actuary to the Australasian Assurance Company and founder member of the Institute of Actuaries, formed in 1848, had by now become a consultant and attended several companies. His testimony before the Select Committee on Assurance Associations of 1853 advocated *laissez-faire* with regard to assurance companies and friendly societies.

Chapter Four: Firmer Ground

1. Prudential Archives. Prudential Mutual Assurance, Investment, and Loan Association. Minute Book 1, 10 June 1852. Ryley also said he 'could introduce a person who could materially assist us in that business'. Whom this might have been is unknown, but if the account written by 'J.M., a Lancashire Artisan' were true, Ryley may have had the writer in mind. See Chapter Nine: The Field Staff Phenomenon, pp.125–146.

2. Sir Arnold Wilson and Hermann Levy, *Industrial Assurance* (1937), p.34.

3. See Barry Supple, *The Royal Exchange Assurance. A History of British Insurance 1720–1970* (1970), pp.139–41. The crux of the controversy was the assertion by some representatives of the older insurance offices that the high ratio of expenses to premiums that characterised the younger offices was evidence of unsound practice.

4. *Hansard's Parliamentary Debates*, 3rd series, CXXIV (1853), col's 1320–28.

5. Quoted in Wilson and Levy, *op. cit.*, pp.34–35.

6. Select Committee on Assurance Associations; Report and Evidence, Parliamentary Papers, 1853, Vol. XXI.

7. Prudential Archives. The British Industry Life Assurance Company and Family Friendly Society. Prospectus, 1853.

8. *Ibid.*

9. Henry Harben, *A History of the Prudential Assurance Company* (1880), p.5.

10. *Ibid.* Harben mentions another company called the Age Assurance Company which had also begun to do industrial business, but, as an extract from its Annual Report for 1854 makes apparent, found the going hard:
    In the early part of the year large expectations were also formed with respect to the Industrial Branch of Assurance, a business which is unquestionably susceptible of cultivation to an infinite degree, if the Directors were disposed to permit losses to run parallel with successes; but the experience of a few months proved it to be absolutely necessary to confine that department within very narrow limits. The Directors, however, are gradually raising the standard of assurance in this branch of business, so as to make it equally safe and profitable with the ordinary class.

11. As its Consulting Actuary Ryley defended it at length in the pages of the *Post Magazine* on 15 October 1853, in a rebuttal to the paper's running attack on the Company which began in July 1853 and went on until November.

12. Premium income was slightly down from the previous year at £3,018.

13. Prudential Archives. Prudential Mutual Assurance, Investment, and Loan Association. Sundries Minute Book. Thomas Clark allegedly helped to build up the British Industry in the north of England through his Chartist connections, but was forced out of the company after a dispute with *Reynolds' News* damaged its business.

14. Prudential Archives. Prudential Mutual Assurance, Investment, and Loan Association. Industrial Department Tables, 1854. British Industry Life Assurance Company and Family Friendly Society. Prospectus, 1853. See also H. Plaisted, *Prudential Past and Present* (1918), pp.5–7.

15. Prudential Archives. 'Address and Instructions to the Agents of the British Industry Life Assurance Company and Family Friendly Society', 1853–54.

16. *Post Magazine* Vol. XIX, No. 48, supplied statistics for miners' mortality that were truly horrifying: in 1851, 984 deaths; in 1857, 1,119, and a total for the seven years reviewed of 7,080. 'The duration of the lives of the pitmen is short,' it stated, 'and the great per centage of what are called accidental deaths shows the necessity of provision for families ....'

17. Prudential Archives. Prudential Mutual Assurance, Investment, and Loan Association. 'Rules or By-Laws of the Association Respecting Assurances Upon Lives and Upon Events Connected With the Duration of Life', 1854.

18. This allegation was repeatedly the subject of public attention throughout the century, and Charles Hardwick, Grand Master of the Manchester Odd-Fellows and a prolific writer on Friendly Societies, dismissed it with the comment that if a mother could kill an infant for the £5 burial money, why not her husband for his £100 insurance policy? *The History, Present Position and Social Importance of Friendly Societies* (1859), pp.247–48. Sidney Webb (Lord Passfield) still thought it necessary to refute the charge as late as 1915 in his *Report* on Industrial Insurance. 'Draft of the Report of the Sub-Committee of the Fabian Research Department', *New Statesman*, Special Supplement on Industrial Insurance, Vol. IV, No. 101, 13 March 1915, pp.26–27.

19. *Post Magazine*, Vol. XIV, No. 39, 24 September 1853. 'Monster Tea Meeting at Birmingham'. The British Industry's early life was not all plain sailing: the vast public meeting referred to ended in uproar with a paid organist attempting to drown out protesters after questions were raised about the directors' antecedents (some were said to be '*ci-devant* Chartists') and salaries, the amount of the company's paid-up capital, and the claim that its industrial policies were 'indisputable'.

20. F.G.P. Neison's letter to the *Morning Chronicle*, quoted in the *Post Magazine*, Vol. XIII, No. 37, 11 September 1852.

21. *Post Magazine*, Vol. XIX, No. 7, p.52.

22. According to the *Post Magazine*, there were 300 accredited agents in Manchester in January 1855; there were 417 by October 1857, 'some offices being represented by at least a dozen agents'. Quoted in J. Treble, 'The Standard and Life Assurance' in Oliver Westall, *The Historian and the Business of Life Assurance* (1984), p.109.

23. Charles Hardwick thought that agents and the direct approach were the only means of overcoming this, for 'Mankind in general feels much the same repugnance to sign the proposal form of a Life Insurance Company as they do to the making of a will or the taking of nauseous physic'. *The Present Insurance Crisis* (1870), pp.17–18.

24. Harben, *op. cit.*, pp.8–9, and Plaisted, *op. cit.*, p.10.

25. Prudential Archives. Prudential Mutual Assurance, Investment, and Loan Association. Minute Book 1, 28 February 1855.

26. Harben, *op. cit.*, p.11.

27. Presumably, since premium income exceeded £2,000 in 1855, Barfoot would have received the £50 due to him in this eventuality. As he was to receive an additional £50 for every further £1,000 of premium income, the more successful the Association became, the more expensive Barfoot would become.

28. Thanks are due to Mr John Harben, grandson of Henry Harben's brother Benjamin, for much of the information that appears here and elsewhere on the Harben family.

29. Chamberlain Papers, University of Birmingham Archives. Austen Chamberlain's notes on his family, AC1/3/60.

30. Harben married Ann Such in 1846; his daughter Mary was born in 1847 and his son Henry Andrade in 1849.

31. Plaisted, *op. cit.*, p.13, relates that at one time Harben had to take his salary in shares instead of cash, and that 'he had more than once to plead with his fellow shareholders not to shut up the business as a failure'. The origin of this story is not known.

32. Harben, *op. cit.*, pp.15–16.

33. Prudential Archives. Prudential Mutual Assurance, Investment, and Loan Association. Minute Book 3, 18 December 1856.

34. Harben, *op. cit.*, pp.13–16.

35. James Gillman's tribute to Harben at the Annual General Meeting in 1858 is worth quoting: '... if I were looking round the world for a Secretary, I should like first of all ... as a necessary qualification, perfect honesty and honourableness and uprightness in every respect. When I think of what is necessary in carrying out the affairs of this Association – of the enormous number of letters that must be written, and when to this I add good temper, which we have in our present Secretary, I should feel it very difficult to replace him were any accident to remove him from us.'

36. Prudential Archives. Table entitled 'Last No's of Policies Issued in the Following Years'. This table compares industrial policy figures in each year from 1854 to 1871 for the Prudential and 1852 to 1861 for the British Industry. A comparison reveals that the number of Prudential policies was actually increasing at a faster rate than that of the British Industry; the years of real British Industry growth were 1852 and 1853 when, from a standing start, it sold 11,980 and 68,961 policies respectively.

37. *Post Magazine*, Vol. XIX, No. 9, 27 February 1858.

38. Prudential Archives. Prudential Mutual Assurance, Investment, and Loan Association. Chairman's Speech, Annual General Meeting, 1 May 1859.

39. Little is known of R.T. Pugh, the career of his son William, who entered the Prudential as a junior when his father joined the Board, being the better recorded. Thomas Bulman Cole is an equally vague figure; his daughter Mary would become the second Mrs Henry Harben in 1890. Thomas Reid's profession is noted in various sources as auditor and as East India merchantman. Like a number of the other Directors, he lived in Camberwell.

40. Prudential Archives. Prudential Mutual Assurance, Investment, and Loan Association. Chairman's Speech, Annual General Meeting, 1 May 1859. William Chambers, William Sers and John Lutwyche had died by the late 1850s, and Alan Chambre had resigned. So had Reemt Schenk, who had gone to live in Budapest.

41. Harben, *op. cit.*, pp.19–20.

42. Prudential Archives. Prudential Mutual Assurance, Investment, and Loan Association. Minute Book 3, various entries between November 1860 and January 1861.

43. Prudential Archives. Letter to the Shareholders. Prudential Assurance Association [*sic*], 19 November 1860, signed by Henry Harben as Secretary.

44. Prudential Archives. Prudential Mutual Assurance, Investment, and Loan Association. Accounts Book 1.

SECTION TWO

Chapter Five: Confronting Mr Gladstone

1. *The Biographical Magazine*. New series. Vol. IX, No. XVII (May 1888), pp.331–36.

2. Patent No.2372, 27 August 1862. 'Improvements in the Manufacture of Paper and other Productions in which Fibrous Material is Employed'. Patent No.64, 7 January 1863. 'Improvements in the Manufacture of Fibrous Material for Cleansing Machinery and Other Purposes'.

3. As will be discussed in the following chapter, the Company's business continued to grow through acquisition. The Prudential also sought to venture into new areas at about this time: in 1859 it set up the Provident Assurance Company to transact sickness insurance, but because of fraud it proved so unprofitable that it was dismantled three years later. The Prince Fire Insurance Company was founded in 1862 but was similarly short-lived, and was wound up in 1866.

4. 'The British Prudential Assurance Company's Office, Ludgate Hill'. *Building News and Engineering Journal*, 27 March 1863, pp.238–41. Ludgate Hill had now been renumbered, so that No. 35 became No. 62.

5. Prudential Archives. Prudential Mutual Assurance, Investment, and Loan Association. The *Annual Report* for 1860 mentions the establishment and workings of the Finance Committee ('the Committee investigate the whole of the cash transactions item by item every week, and make a written report of the same to the Board') and the Directors' opinion that one reason for the Company's popularity was 'the prompt and cheerful payment of every claim'.

6. Although the facility existed, it was apparently never used, as the people for whom it supposedly catered did not want annuities, but ready burial expenses. Dermot Morrah, *A History of Industrial Life Assurance* (1955), p.30.

7. *Hansard's Parliamentary Debates*, 3rd series, CLXXIII (1864), col's 478–80.

8. *Hansard's Parliamentary Debates*, 3rd series, CLXXIII (1864), col. 1555.

9. Prudential Archives, 'Press Reports, Gladstone 1864' boxfile. Harben to Gladstone, 13 February 1864. It is clear that this was not the first time the two had entered into correspondence. Harben refers to Gladstone's reduction of the stamp duty a few years earlier as having greatly assisted the growth of the company: '... a few years ago I wrote to you drawing attention to the oppressive nature of the 6d. stamp and you kindly caused a clause to be inserted in a Stamp Act reducing the duty to 3d ... since that time (the fiscal impediment having been removed) the progress of the Company has been entirely uninterrupted.'

10. *Ibid*.

11. Prudential Archives, 'Press Reports, Gladstone 1864' boxfile. Harben to Gladstone, 16 February 1864. Finally, Harben ventured to suggest that the friendly societies could be put to rights if their activities were confined by law to the geographical areas in which they were founded, and if they were forbidden to use agents! This last was

a canny suggestion which – in the light of the subsequent history of government insurance – would have killed off a large part of the Prudential's competition for industrial business in short order had it ever been adopted.

12. Prudential Archives. British Prudential Assurance Company. Minute Book 1, 15 February 1864.
13. *Post Magazine*, 20 February 1864. p.67.
14. The *Post Magazine* carried a full Report of the Deputation's visit in 'What the Chancellor of the Exchequer's Bill is Likely to Lead to', 27 February 1864, pp.69–71.
15. John Stuart Mill, quoted by John Morley in *The Life of Gladstone* (1903), Vol. 2, p.123.
16. *Hansard's Parliamentary Debates*, 3rd series, CLXXIII (1864), col. 1565.
17. *Hansard's Parliamentary Debates*, 3rd series, CLXXIII (1864), col's 1569–70.
18. *Hansard's Parliamentary Debates*, 3rd series, CLXXIII (1864), col's 1571–73.
19. *Hansard's Parliamentary Debates*, 3rd series, CLXXIII (1864), col's 1576–81.
20. Prudential Archives, 'Press Reports, Gladstone 1864' boxfile. Harben to Gladstone, 17 March 1864.
21. *Hansard's Parliamentary Debates*, 3rd series, CLXXIV (1864), col's 248–49.
22. Prudential Archives, 'Press Reports, Gladstone 1864' boxfile. Harben to T.B. Sprague, 21 March 1864.
23. Prudential Archives, 'Press Reports, Gladstone 1864' boxfile. 'Case for the Opinion of Mr. Sprague', 8 April 1864.
24. *Ibid.*
25. Prudential Archives, 'Press Reports, Gladstone 1864' boxfile. 'Case for the Opinion of Mr. S.L. Laundy', 11 April 1864.
26. *Hansard's Parliamentary Debates*, 3rd series, CLXXIV (1864), col. 803.

Chapter Six: Acquisitions and Foundations

1. See Harben, *History of the Prudential Assurance Company* (1880), p.37:
   For a long time the Directors were appealed to to start a Fire Insurance Company, and eventually a Company, called the Prince Fire Insurance Company *was incorporated in July 1862. The influx of business was very slow, and the Directors considered that it would require a very large expenditure of time and money to make it a success. They therefore determined to concentrate their attention to the development of a good Life business, and in the year 1866 decided upon winding-up the Prince Fire Company, transferring the risks to another Institution, and returning the shareholders' capital in full, with five per cent interest.*
   Harben went on to add, with reference to the Prudential's forays into fire insurance and sickness insurance, 'The discontinuance of the Sickness and Fire insurance businesses had no effect whatever upon the Prudential, and the fears entertained that without these inducements the Life business would materially suffer, were proved to be groundless.'
2. Prudential Archives. Boxfile 1866–70. '*Report* made by Mr. A.H. Bailey to the Consolidated Assurance Company on the Position of the British Prudential'. See also Consolidated Assurance Company. Minute Book 8, 30 October 1865, 'Agreement between the Consolidated Assurance Company and the British Prudential Assurance Company'. 'General' here refers to ordinary business.
3. Prudential Archives. Consolidated Assurance Company. Minute Book 8, 30 October 1865, 'Agreement between the Consolidated Assurance Company and the British Prudential Assurance Company'.
4. Prudential tradition, as recorded by R.W. Barnard in *A Century of Service. A History of the Prudential 1848–1948* (1948), p.57, says that it was Charles Willis, one of a

numerous family which was associated with the Company as agents from 1861 when the first of them arrived with the British Industry, who was responsible for the suggestion that the Company's name be simplified.

5. Prudential Archives. British Prudential and Consolidated Assurance Company. Minute Book 2, 14 December 1865. Although not specified as such, it is reasonable to suppose that 'income' in this context meant New Premium Income. The note went on to say that the agreement would be reconsidered when this income reached £110,000, at which point Harben's annual salary would reach £1,500. In 1865 the Company's new premium income was £57,644, which included £4,322 from the Consolidated. It is thus interesting to note, in a minute of 4 January 1866, the formation of a Standing Committee composed of James Gillman, Edgar Horne and Thomas Reid 'to negotiate with any company desirous of selling its business to the Prudential'.

6. Prudential Archives. British Mutual Assurance Company. Minute Book 1, 29 September 1868. The first meeting, at which the draft agreement was discussed, took place on 2 October, barely three days after H.B. Sheridan, a Member of Parliament, had introduced the two companies. An open letter to shareholders from Charles Thicke, the British Mutual's Secretary, dated 17 October 1868, in Boxfile 1866–70, advised them unreservedly to accept the Prudential's offer. At a Special General Meeting on 30 October, the purchase was confirmed. Harben was paid a further £1,500.

7. The British Mutual Investment Company Limited was in turn dissolved in 1874 and a new company, eventually called the British Mutual Banking Company, formed in 1875. This became the repository for the security, first of £25, later of £50, which the Prudential required of each of its agents, to be set against any money that might be owed by the agent to the Company.

8. Prudential Archives. Boxfile 1866–70. 'The Government Actuary on the Position of the Prudential Assurance Company. Being a Report made to the British Mutual Life Assurance Society on the advisability of transferring its Business and Assets to the Prudential Assurance Company, of Ludgate Hill, London'. In common with every other industrial assurer at this point, whether company or friendly society, the British Prudential's rates of lapse and expense were very high. Industrial policies assuring £249,057 had lapsed during 1864, but as their average duration was less than two years and no surrender value was paid on them, this was not to the Company's disadvantage in the strictly financial sense. But high rates of expense and lapse were ammunition to the critics of industrial assurance, and therefore in the long run gravely detrimental to what, if expense and lapse rates could be forced downwards, was a socially useful and highly profitable business.

9. In Chancery. In the Matter of 'The Companies' Acts 1862 and 1867' and of The Hercules Insurance Company (Limited). Report of William Joseph White, the Official Liquidator of the Said Company. 13 July 1869.

10. In Chancery. In the Matter of 'The Companies' Acts 1862 and 1867' and of the International Life Assurance Society. Report of Frederick Maynard, the Official Liquidator of the Said Society. 13 April 1869.

11. Prudential Archives. Boxfile 1866–70. Henry Harben's open letters 'To the Policyholders and Annuitants of the International Life Assurance Society', 8 June 1869 and 3 February 1870.

12. Prudential Archives. Tin box 'A': Hercules and International Companies. Affidavits bundle.

13. Harben, *op. cit.*, p.30.

14. H. Plaisted, *Prudential Past and Present* (1918), p.38.

15. Harben, *op. cit.*, p.41.

16. *Post Magazine*, 'The Life Department', 13 February 1858, p.53. 'The more extended practice of Life Insurance amongst all classes of the community' was also judged to be the gauge of the country's 'progress as a nation'.

17. F.B. Smith, *The People's Health 1830–1910* (1990), p.209.

18. Harben, *op. cit.*, p.43. By 1880 the Prudential had nearly 2,000,000 children's policies. Some years later, James Moon in an address to the Insurance Institute quoted figures from the 1891 Census, showing that of 6,948,668 children under ten in England and Wales the Prudential assured 2,361,455. Half of the remainder were uninsured and half insured by other institutions. 'A Paper on Child Insurance', a meeting of the Insurance Institute, 12 March 1895.

19. Harben, *op. cit.*, p.43.

20. An extract from *Commercial World*, April 1873, entitled 'Some Wonderful Figures', reported that in addition to this number of new policies, 500 claims were being paid weekly, 1,400 changes of residence registered, and 2,500 agents' accounts received, entered and audited.

21. 'The Prudential. Visit to the Office – Description of its Organisation'. *Insurance Guardian*, January 1874.

22. Harben, *op. cit.*, p.44.

23. Harben, *op. cit.*, p.47.

24. Prudential Archives. British Prudential Assurance Company. Annual Report 1860. The Finance Committee, it will be remembered, had been meeting weekly since 1852. Its review of each seven-day period was presented in a Report to the Board and was judged by the latter to be 'a more efficient and searching system of checks' than any general public audit.

25. Barnard, *op. cit.*, p.26.

26. A wonderful vignette from the early 1860s at Ludgate Hill portrays Mrs Jobbins, the cockney housekeeper, sorting the mail by first emptying the bags on the floor; she came early to perform this task, handing over the sorted bags to the correct department as staff arrived. *Ibis Magazine*, Vol. 51, p.47.

27. Barnard, *op. cit.*, pp.4–5.

28. Prudential Archives. Prudential Assurance Company. Minute Book 3, 14 December 1871, *re* Miss Wood and others; 14 April 1870, *re* Charles Hanslip's resignation. Minute Book 4, 10 October 1872, contains the resolution that all women engaged by the Company be the daughters of professional men.

29. See Janetta Manners, 'The Employment of Women in the Public Service'. *Quarterly Review*, Vol. 151 (1881); Susanne Dohrn, 'Pioneers in a Dead-End Profession: the first women clerks in banks and insurance companies' in Gregory Anderson, ed., *The White Blouse Revolution* (1988); Ellen Jordan, *The Lady Clerks at the Prudential: the beginning of vertical segregation by gender in clerical work*, a thesis submitted to the University of Newcastle, New South Wales, Australia, 1992.

30. Gloria C. Clifton, *Professionalism, Patronage and Public Service in Victorian London. The Staff of the Metropolitan Board of Works 1856–1889* (1992).

31. Prudential Archives. Prudential Assurance Company. Salary lists for each year appear in Minute Books 3, 4 and 5. Staff regulations are also recorded in the minutes.

32. Prudential Archives. Abstract Ledger 1, 22 June 1865. Further to this, it was resolved on 21 March 1872 that 'all future candidates be required to produce a letter of

introduction from a well-known banker, army agent or gentleman known to the Directors in addition to the ordinary references'.

33. Barnard, *op. cit.*, p.24.

34. Prudential Archives. Harben to Dewey, 30 January and 6 February 1880.

35 *Ibis Magazine*, Vol. LI (Feb 1928), 'Early Reflections by an Old Hand', pp.48–50.

36. *Ibis Magazine*, Vol. 1 (1878), p.7. The Prudential Clerks' Society came into being 'upon an intimation from the Directors ... of their intention to present the Clerks of the Company with an annual grant which was ... to be expended entirely for their benefit, and to be devoted to some purpose they might select', and with the object of 'promoting cricket, rowing and similar outdoor exercises generally, and ... to encourage any scheme ... likely to benefit its members'. The Society also received the fines for late attendance. The rest of its income consisted of entrance and subscription fees – both nominal. All Prudential clerks were eligible to join as many clubs as they chose. The Managing Committee consisted of the Secretary, the Managers of the Industrial and Ordinary Branches, and ten members chosen by ballot.

37. Apparently the clerks, one of whom was Thomas Dewey, used to play cricket in Battersea Park in the late 1850s and the 1860s. From 1871, the year in which the Directors decided that the clerks had become too numerous to attend the annual Company dinner *en masse*, the Cricket Club benefited from half the donation – the Rowing Club got the other half – representing the cost of the meal for those clerks not invited. In the 1870s the Cricket Club led a peripatetic existence, and its lack of visible status sometimes meant that its challenges to City clubs were refused. Harben, a keen cricket supporter, apparently pleaded the case to the Board and got a loan, then a grant, for a ground owned by Dulwich College. Frederick Schooling was Captain in the momentous year 1882, when the club made its first tour, to the Isle of Wight. Membership by then was about 400, each man paying a subscription of 10s 6d a year. Numbers were severely depleted during valuations. T. Watson, *Ibis Cricket 1870–1949*. Privately printed, 1950.

38. Prudential Archives. Prudential Assurance Company. Minute Book 4, 7 March 1872. Also Abstract Ledger 1 under 'Miscellaneous'.

39. *Ibis Magazine*, Vol. 1 (1878), p.61.

40. Prudential Archives. British Prudential Assurance Company. Minute Book 1, 19 March 1863. Minute Book 3, 28 April 1870.

41. There may have been a certain degree of reallocation of tasks for reasons of age and health at about this time; the Reverend James Gillman was by now 70 years old, and Edgar Horne may have begun to take on some of the responsibilities of chairmanship which he assumed completely on Gillman's death three years later.

42. Prudential Archives. Open letter from Henry Harben to the Staff of the Prudential Assurance Company, 1 May 1873.

43. Prudential Archives. 'Diary', October 1880. See *Prudential Bulletin*, Vol. 49 (1967), pp.151–52; also Frederick L. Hoffman, *History of the Prudential Insurance Company of America* (1900), Earl Chapin May and Will Oursler, *The Prudential* (1950).

Chapter Seven: Holborn Bars and the Prudential Style

1. *Insurance Guardian*, January 1874, p.2. *Ibis Magazine*, Vol. 2 (March 1879), p.99. Like so many town houses that were turned into offices, No. 62 probably had lavatories and a cesspit in the basement. Drains that backed up could also have given rise to foul smells. Another *Ibis* article in May 1879 describes the noise: at any moment of the

working day, '... baskets full of papers are being dragged noisily along the floor; clerks are "calling over" at the top of their voices; the numbering machines are banging; the arithmometers loudly clicking; electric bells and whistles add their shrill voices to the din'.

2. Prudential Archives. Prudential Assurance Company. Minute Book 5, 4 November 1875.

3. Prudential Archives. Prudential Assurance Company. Minute Book 5, 18 February 1875, makes it clear that they were not satisfied:

   The Resident Director brought forward the question of the employment of an architect in place of Mr Moseley at whose hands he considered the interests of the company had not been so carefully attended to as he considered they might have been. Resolved: that no additional supervision be placed in the hands of Mr Moseley when the present alterations are complete.

   Clarke took over where Moseley left off and attended the board meeting of 25 November 1875 with plans for No. 64 Ludgate Hill. The Board 'approved the general plans of the building as proposed by him but suggested he should rearrange the elevations upon a less ornate and more economical principle, which he promised to do and retired'. But by March 1876 the Board had given the Holborn commission to Waterhouse.

4. Prudential Archives. Prudential Assurance Company. Minute Book 5, 4 November 1875.

5. Prudential Archives. Prudential Assurance Company. Minute Book 5, 9 March 1876.

6. Colin Cunningham and Prudence Waterhouse, *Alfred Waterhouse 1830–1905. Biography of a Practice* (1992), p.111.

7. More will be said in the next chapter about early automation. Harben claimed at a meeting of the Society of Telegraph Engineers in 1872 that the Prudential had been using six of Thomas de Colmar's calculating machines 'for a number of years'. The Company bought its first typewriter in 1875 and automatic dating machines arrived soon after.

8. See 'Sources, Styles and the Picturesque' in Sally Maltby, Sally MacDonald and Colin Cunningham, *Alfred Waterhouse, 1830–1905*, RIBA Exhibition Catalogue, 1983.

9. John Ruskin apparently thought that the Manchester Assize Courts were 'much beyond everything yet done in England on my principles'. Quoted by Sir Kenneth Clark in *The Gothic Revival* (1974), p.209.

10. Alastair Service, *The Architects of London* (1979), pp.143–44.

11. Colin Cunningham, *Prudential Building, Holborn Bars. A History and Appreciation* (privately printed by the Prudential Corporation), n.d., pp.8–10.

12. Maltby, MacDonald and Cunningham, *op. cit.*, p.8.

13. Cunningham, *op. cit.*, p.10, describes how

    Construction dragged on through 1877 and 1878 with a series of typical problems. The clerk of works was dismissed in January 1877 because portions of the Holborn building were not being carried out in a satisfactory manner. There were delays in the supply of terra-cotta from Gibbs and Canning of Tamworth – a common problem with this new material. There were also changes in the structure itself, involving the substitution of one material for another.

14. For the time being, the Ludgate Hill buildings were retained and let; eventually they were sold to the City of London Corporation. Concerning the move, there were men in the Company even in the 1920s who could recall it. Some said that the clerks conveyed office records from Ludgate Hill to Holborn Bars in wheelbarrows. Mr John Roy Lancaster, son of Sir William Lancaster and a Director of the Prudential from 1920 to 1948, was eight or nine years old at the time of the move to Holborn Bars,

and had a vivid memory of riding 'on the box seat of one of the four-wheeled cabs hired to move the books'. See R.W. Barnard *A Century of Service. A History of the Prudential 1848–1948* (1948), p.72.

15. See 'Materials' in Maltby, MacDonald and Cunningham, *op. cit.*, pp.44–45.
16. Cunningham, *op. cit.*, p.13.
17. *Illustrated Carpenter and Builder*, 8 October 1880, p.53.
18. *The Commercial World*, 2 June 1879, pp.144–46.
19. *Ibis Magazine*, 1879, pp.288–89.
20. Cunningham, *op. cit.*, p.34, note 21, quotes these figures.
21. Hitherto most investments had been in government stocks and in railway shares. A board minute of 26 October 1876 notes the resolution: 'That as the occasion may arise investments be made in Freehold property of adequate value in London'. From about this time there were a number of such purchases.
22. Cunningham and Waterhouse, *op. cit.*, p.115(f).
23. Cunningham and Waterhouse, *op. cit.*, pp.115–16.
24. Cunningham and Waterhouse, *op. cit.*, p.114. Employees at Nottingham, Birmingham and Leeds enjoyed these facilities; Portsmouth had the hotel, Leeds the art gallery and Bradford the Turkish bath.
25. Prudential Archives. Prudential Assurance Company. Minute Book 10, 10 October 1882, and other minutes, record the rentals of Brooke Street flats to the women clerks. In November 1886 Waterhouse attended a board meeting to present a sketch of his proposal for the restoration of Staple Inn. He had apparently received objections to the removal of the plaster facade from the Society for the Protection of Ancient Buildings, but the Prudential Board nonetheless approved his plan.
26. Cunningham, *op. cit.*, p.11.
27. It is interesting to hear today, in cities such as Nottingham or Bradford where the Prudential is no longer the occupier or even the owner of Waterhouse's unmistakeable buildings, how often they are still referred to as 'Prudential buildings'.
28. *Ibis Magazine*, 1879, p.226.

SECTION THREE

Chapter Eight: The Making of a Colossus

1. Prudential Archives. Figures are taken from the Annual Reports and Accounts and Quinquennial Reports and Accounts for the relevant years. See also returns submitted to the Board of Trade for the relevant years; and (Sir) Joseph Burn, 'Industrial Life Assurance', *Journal of the Federation of Insurance Institutes* (1902).
2. Prudential Archives. Prudential Assurance Company. Reports of the Quinquennial Valuations for 1881, 1886 and 1891, and thereafter the Valuation Reports for the relevant years. A few of the many available examples will suffice to illustrate this point. In a series of articles devoted to the Prudential under the title 'A Gigantic Concern', commencing with the issue of 7 December 1894, the *Sun* newspaper noted that only the Government had more people 'financially interested' in it than the Prudential, which in its annual income was 'only surpassed by four of our largest railway companies' and which, as 'far and away the largest institution in these islands' was 'emphatically the people's assurance company'. See also the *Post Magazine*, 10 April 1869; the debate

on the Friendly Societies Bill in *The Times* of 5 June 1875; and profiles including the *Insurance Guardian*'s of January 1874, 'The Prudential. Visit to the Office – Description of its Organisation', which outlined the Company's 'large and extraordinary operations', and of March 1870, on 'Industrial Assurance: Best Means of Improving the Condition of the Poor', the *Insurance and Financial Journal* of 5 March 1893, and one in the *Pitman Phonetic Journal* of 31 May 1902 entitled 'A Great Organisation and How It Works'.

3. *Hansard's Parliamentary Debates*, 3rd series, Vol. CCXXIV, col. 1410. In the House of Commons debate on the Friendly Societies Bill on 31 May 1875 it was mentioned that there were 32,000 friendly societies in the United Kingdom, with some 4,000,000 members. Most of these societies were of the village club variety, still unregistered and open to abuse.

4. Friendly and Benefit Building Societies. Report of the Assistant Commissioners. 1874, Vol. XII, part II.

5. Prudential Archives. Prudential Assurance Company. Minute Book 4, 23 July 1874.

6. *Op. cit.*, 30 July 1875.

7. Disraeli's biographers considered that the Act 'established the Friendly Societies, and with them the people's savings, on a satisfactory basis', whereas *The Times* viewed it as '… modest, if not timid, in its provisions'. It became evident fairly soon that some of its clauses were ambiguous, and that it did not go nearly far enough regarding the assurance of children. W.F. Moneypenny and G.E. Buckle, *The Life of Benjamin Disraeli* (1920), Vol. 5, pp.364–65. *The Times* was quoted in a piece of the Act which appeared in the *Annual Register* for 1875, 3rd series, 1875, p.47.

8. The Friendly Societies Act 1875, 38 & 39 Vict. (60); the Prudential Assurance Company Act 1875, 38 & 39 Vict. (lxxviii).

9. Namely, sections 111 to 114 inclusive, relating to 'the accountability of officers, as far as these sections relate to books, papers, writings, property, and effects'; 'The provisions with respect to the recovery of damages not specially provided for and penalties'; and section 3 relating to the interpretation of terms, defining the officers to whom the Act was to apply, viz., 'canvasser, agent, sub-agent, superintendent of agents, assistant superintendent of agents or inspector of agents'. A small amendment to section 111 removed the three days' grace which the agent had been hitherto allowed. 8 Vict. (16, 111–114).

10. Henry Harben, *A History of the Prudential Assurance Company* (1880), p.34. The Act covered England and Wales, but was amended to cover Scotland in 1876. Minute Book 5, 1 and 8 June 1875.

11. The Prudential Assurance Company Act 1875, 38 & 39 Vict. (lxxviii, 3). The reason given was that the Directors wished to create a new class of with-profits policyholders, and wished to remove any doubt about their power to do so. The Act also gave them the power to determine the amount of profit in the Branches and the division of all or some of this among the shareholders and policyholders, the allocation of receipts and expenses to the Branches and the debiting of the Company's share capital to the Industrial Branch.

12. F.W. Paish and G.L. Schwarz, *Insurance Funds and their Investments* (1934), p.56, gives a relatively simple definition of the valuation process. I am grateful to Mr Derek Fellows, formerly Chief Actuary of the Prudential Corporation, for this one.

13. Prudential Archives. Quinquennial Report for the period ending 31 December 1876, p.1. The Report says that the Directors 'thought it unadvisable [*sic*] to adopt a table of mortality that had not been made public'. The Prudential's *Mortality Experience* was

published in 1871, and was circulated to interested enquirers, but as Henry Harben wrote in his introduction to it, 'The Tables are merely nosological, and do not profess to give the rate of mortality; ...'.

14. *Ibid.*, p.3.

15. See 'The Prudential. Visit to the Office – Description of its Organisation'. *Insurance Guardian*, January 1874, p.5, for a description of how the cards were dated decimally so that the duration of a policy could be easily calculated. The article then goes on to explain:

    These cards having been filled up with the particulars on the policy are put away in pigeon holes on a system which makes them instantly accessible when required, and they are removed daily as they lapse or become claims, so that those remaining in the pigeon holes at any moment represent the risks of the Prudential *then actually current, and afford copious and invaluable materials for acturial* [sic] *and statistical purposes.*

16. Prudential Archives. Thomas Dewey's Report to the Directors of the Prudential Assurance Company in the Quinquennial Report for the period ending 31 December 1871, p.4.

17. Prudential Archives. Thomas Dewey's Report to the Directors of the Prudential Assurance Company in the Quinquennial Report for the period ending 31 December 1876, p.4.

18. Anon., 'The Prudential Annual Meeting', *Insurance Guardian*, 6 March 1877. For a description of the Colmar arithmometer and comments about it by Harben and others, see Thomas T.P. Bruce Warren, 'On the Application of the Calculating Machine of M. Thomas de Colmar to Electrical Computations', *Journal of the Society of Telegraph Engineers*, Vol. I, no. 2, 1872, pp.141–69.

19. Prudential Archives. Thomas Dewey's Report, in the Quinquennial Report for the period ending 31 December 1886, p.4.

20. William Lancaster wrote to *The Times* in 1879 about the Prudential's experience with the arithmometer, and described how the Company had offered a prize of £300 to any English manufacturer who could produce the machines free of defects. Two English machines were at that time being used by the Prudential, 'apparently perfect in every part ... but, unfortunately, they will not work accurately'. *The Times*, 30 October 1879, 10c.

21. Prudential Archives. Prudential Assurance Company. Minute Book 5, 29 July 1875.

22. 'The Prudential. Visit to the Office – Description of its Organisation'. *Insurance Guardian*, January 1874.

23. Prudential Archives. Prudential Assurance Company. Minute Book 6, 25 April 1878. But the Directors' interest was shortlived, and on 6 June the choice of the former system was minuted.

24. Going from the public office to the valuation or statistical departments a dozen times a day was calculated at one mile per clerk. If this mile a day took 20 minutes, each clerk would lose 13 working days a year covering his allotment of 313 miles. Multiplying this by 50 (10% of the clerical force of 500 being assumed to be in transit from one part of the building to another enough of the time to amount to a mile a day) produced the daunting assertion that 'In 12 months these 50 clerks would traverse 15,650 miles, wasting nearly 2 years of working time at 8 hrs [*sic*] per day ...'. *Commercial World*, 2 June 1879.

25. Martin Campbell-Kelly, 'Large-scale data processing in the Prudential, 1850–1930'. *Accounting, Business and Financial History*, Vol. 2, No. 2, 1992, p.125.

26. Prudential Archives. Prudential Assurance Company. A.H. Bailey's Report in the Quinquennial Report for the period ending 31 December 1891, p.2.

27. Prudential Archives. Prudential Assurance Company. Thomas Dewey's Report in the Quinquennial Report for the period ending 31 December 1891, p.3.
28. Prudential Archives. Prudential Assurance Company. Minute Book 5, 30 March 1876. Valuation hours were from 8.30 a.m. to 8.30 p.m. on four days of the week, and from 8.30 a.m. to 5.00 p.m. on the other two, Saturday half-day being unheard of during valuation time. From 1876, double salary was paid for overtime for the duration of the work.
29. Quoted in Campbell-Kelly, *op. cit.*, p.126.
30. Prudential Archives. Prudential Assurance Company. Quinquennial Report for the period ending 31 December 1871, p.1. The Directors proposed 'that this Contingency Fund shall be permanently maintained and increased, in addition to the amount required, for the liabilities under an ordinary valuation, so as to form a reserve, alike protective of the interests of the Share and Policyholders'.
31. See below; this average was for those holders of the recently issued 'Series B' policies. Those of the original 'Series A', by this time ended, were to be relatively larger.
32. Prudential Archives. Prudential Assurance Company. Quinquennial Report for the period ending 31 December 1891, p.1.
33. Prudential Archives. Numbers were hovering around the 1,000 mark by this time; by 1897 there were 1,298. Thomas Dewey, Memorandum Book.
34. Harben seems to have engaged in voluntary work all his life, having a strong interest in public health and social improvement. In his younger days he is said to have taught night classes to working men, and to have founded a school, though no details survive. From the 1860s he was active in his local vestry, St John's Hampstead. He had hardly taken his seat on the Metropolitan Board of Works in 1880 than he became a member of its Finance Committee, and for the next nine years sat on a varying number of committees that occupied him for 6 to 13 hours of meetings a week. See *Pall Mall Gazette*, January 31, 1889. 'What the County Council Has Got To Do. An Interview with One Who Knows' (just after Harben had been elected to the newly formed London County Council), which comments that 'no more useful member was returned in the whole metropolis'. Harben had other interests: besides the Institute of Actuaries he was by 1880 a Fellow of the Historical Society and of the Royal Institution. Through one of his uncles, Stanford Preston, clerk of the Carpenters' Company, Harben and his son Henry were both admitted to the livery in 1878 and Harben was Master in 1893–94. He was a Freemason from 1870, and was Worshipful Master of the Moira Lodge in 1873. He apparently founded Hampstead Lodge some time after that date.
35. Up to 1872, the number of shares issued of the potential 20,000 was 9,920 and the paid-up capital was £5,827. A few shares were paid up in full. In that year a call brought the paid-up capital to £10,052. In 1878 the amount paid up per share was raised to £2 10s, producing a paid-up capital of £24,920.
36. See the transcript of the Extraordinary General Meeting in the *Insurance Guardian*, 13 May 1881.
37. Fraser was made an Honorary Director in 1893 at the age of 88, having served as a Director and Medical Officer since the Prudential's formation.
38. A glance at the figures for 1891 is instructive. The shareholders' portion of the divisible surplus for that year (£1,700,000) was £340,000. As there were 100,000 shares issued, the earnings of each over the five-year period since the last valuation were roughly £3 8s. Anyone who owned, say, 1,000 shares, would on this occasion have made £3,400; a good salary for a surveyor (the profession in which Harben and Horne

must at one time have expected to spend their lives) at about this time was £500–700. See W.J. Reader, *Professional Men* (1966), p.202. 'At any time before 1914, £1,000 a year represented considerable worldly success ... and placed a man, economically speaking, well towards the top of the middle classes.'

39. 'Money Matters', *Sun*, 7–13 December 1894. During the 1890s, by virtue of almost annual scrip issues, the issued capital rose to £1,000,000 in fully paid shares of £5 each. These shares were split in 1912 into fully paid shares of £1 each.

40. Select Committee of the House of Commons on Friendly Societies. Report of the Evidence of Mr Thomas Dewey. First Day, Friday, 31 May 1889.

Chapter Nine: The Field Staff Phenomenon

1. The exact date in 1873 when the divisional structure was created is not known, nor is its originator. The way the country was divided bears a marked similarity to that used by Joseph Fletcher in his study of the geographical distribution of crime, published by the Statistical Society in 1849 under the title *Summary of the Moral Statistics of England and Wales*. The divisional structure was in place by January 1874, as it is clearly referred to in the *Insurance Guardian*'s article of that month, 'The Prudential. Visit to the Office – Description of its Organisation'.

2. Prudential Archives. Prudential Assurance Company. Figures for superintendents, assistant superintendents and agents are drawn from the annual reports and accounts for the relevant years.

3. Prudential Archives. Prudential Assurance Company. 'Special Instructions to Superintendents', 1874–94, pp.2–3.

4. *Ibid.*, p.7; see also 'Agents Instructions, 1887–1905', p.10.

5. *Ibid.*, p.11.

6. *Ibid.*, p.13.

7. Prudential Archives. Prudential Assurance Company. Memorandum Book, 1884. Holograph. n.d.; n.a.

8. Prudential Archives. Prudential Assurance Company. Thomas Dewey to all superintendents and assistant superintendents, August 1888.

9. Prudential Archives. Prudential Assurance Company. Minute Book 4, 5 June 1873. There were numerous cases brought against libellers. What to do about 'Knott's pamphlets', the 'libellous postcards' circulated by one Gathercole (who went to gaol rather than pay his fine and was then let out on promising to retract), and a host of similar instances provided many board minutes during the 1870s. On occasion the Directors had clearly been tipped off about verbal assaults on the Company: 'Mr Mills the Agency Superintendent of the Sceptre (a rival company) having at a meeting in Northwich spoken of the Prudential as insolvent and otherwise libelled the Company, was written to, requesting him to withdraw such expressions; and his letter in reply was read.'

10. Prudential Archives. Prudential Assurance Company. Special Instructions and Tables, 1887, p.21.

11. Prudential Archives. Prudential Assurance Company. Thomas Dewey and William Hughes to all superintendents, May 1892.

12. Prudential Archives. Prudential Assurance Company. Minute Book 3, 19 December 1870. See also the fulsome obituary of John Moon in *The Assurance Herald*, 16 July 1888, which claimed that he was often 'a mediator between office and agent, and the Directors of the Company he served relied largely upon his judgment, which was generally found to be good'. Moon's elder son John junior was suspended for a

fortnight in 1873 for printing and circulating derogatory newspaper comment about the Liverpool Legal Friendly Society.

13. Prudential Archives. Prudential Assurance Company. Minute Book 5, 18 March 1875.

14. Prudential Archives. Benjamin Botley, sheets headed 'Bradford Meeting', n.d.

15. Prudential Archives. Prudential Assurance Company. Minute Book 4, 26 January, 27 April 1873.

16. Prudential Archives. Griffiths Guardbook. Riley Lord was the first of a number of Prudential outdoor staff to enter local or municipal politics. He was elected Sheriff of Newcastle in 1892 and Mayor in 1895. The *Insurance Guardian*, 1 December 1892, and other press notices. Others who did so were the Willis brothers of Rochester, Aldermen and Freemen of the city of Rochester in Kent, and Edward Roberts, Mayor of Truro.

17. H. Plaisted, *Prudential Past and Present* (1918), pp.75–77. It is possible that John Moon was the author of a pamphlet called 'A Romance of Industrial Assurance, or The Scientists' Startling Blunder' signed by 'J.M. ("A Lancashire Artisan")', who claimed to have planted the idea of house-to-house collections in the mind of an actuary to a London company in 1851. He traces the course of the idea until the point where it took root in the Prudential, giving ample praise to Harben for having seen its potential. If Moon were the author, and his claim admitted, it might in part explain why he received such generous terms, although his exceptionally successful career was reason enough.

18. Prudential Archives. Prudential Assurance Company. Memorandum Book. Holograph. n.d.; n.a. Entries for 1883 and 1884. Also Register of Directors.

19. This deposit was still required of Prudential agents up to 1958. In the Prudential Archives is a personal account by James Moorfoot, an agent from 1925 to 1963, in which the author describes how he had to borrow the money from a friend in order to take up his appointment.

20. Prudential Archives. Prudential Assurance Company. Special Instructions and Tables, 1887.

21. The following letter to the Editor of the *London Standard* of 22 November 1888, whether genuine in the story it related or not, made the point:
    Sir,- Last night, about dusk, as my wife was walking along a quiet suburban road with our little girl, they were suddenly confronted and brought to a standstill by a tall man of forbidding aspect, who seemed to them to assume a threatening attitude. Nor were his first words reassuring, for, in a deep guttural tone, he demanded, "Is your life and the child's insured?"

    Now, it is not surprising that at a time when women's minds have been thrown into a state of nervous excitement by the East-end murders, this rencontre aroused horrible visions in my wife's mind of "Jack the Ripper"; but the man was not personating [sic] that fiend, he was only a local tout of the Prudential Assurance Company with more zeal than discretion. My object in narrating this incident is to suggest that the 'Prudential' should, for the present at least, induce its agents to adopt less startling modes of canvassing within the Metropolitan area.

    I am, Sir, your obedient servant,
    A suburban Resident

22. Critical agents from other companies claimed that the Prudential took unfair advantage of its pre-eminence to depress rates for the whole industry. There was also the matter of the 'stamp'. It was asserted in E.L. Stanley's Report to the Northcote Commission in 1874 that since the Prudential had to pay to have its policies stamped, as opposed to friendly societies, which did not, its agents impressed the ignorant among their proposals by telling them that the Prudential policy was the only 'official' one. The

Refuge Society was said to be prepared to lose its stamp exemption for the right to compete fairly with the Prudential on this point. *Friendly and Benefit Building Societies. Reports of the Assistant Commissioners ... with a Special Report on the Prudential Assurance Company by the Hon. E.L. Stanley.* Reports from Commissioners 1874. Vol. XII, part II, p.210.

23. Prudential Archives. Prudential Assurance Company. Figures are taken from the Quinquennial Valuation Reports for the relevant years.

24. Several classes of awards were given, the highest for weekly debits in excess of £7, the lowest for those of £2 10s or more. It would appear, since the average debit in the 1890s was still hovering around £5, that agencies may have been divided so as to keep them roughly at this level.

25. Prudential Archives. Prudential Assurance Company. Griffiths Guardbook 822. The insurance press carried, among the advertisements for calculators, celluloid collars and bicycles, advertisements for morale-boosting leaflets and the music to 'Stimulative [*sic*] Assurance Songs'.

26. Prudential Archives. Prudential Assurance Company. Instructions to Agents, 1868–1894. Up to 1868, the agent's remuneration was made up of commission on new business (the first four weeks' premiums), one of 2s in the £ on the premiums collected, and a special commission calculated as twice the amount by which the debit increased during each quarter of the year. These commissions were underpinned by another, which came to be called a salary, that began at 5s a week when the debit exceeded £3, and rose by sixpences to 7s for a £7 debit and on upwards, increasing by a shilling for every clear increase of £1 in the debit. The Company bore the cost of the agents' weekly postage for letters and parcels, and any charges for sending money.

27. While little can be made of the small evidence of the only two agents' Weekly Account Books that survive in the Company's archives, the figures they provide do fall into this category. One belonging to a H. Le Pla of Thornage in Norfolk shows earnings that varied widely from week to week during 1887 between 2s and 17s; the other, belonging to a W.G. Simmonds of Littlehampton, shows that his earnings during 1898 fell between 19s and £1 2s a week. Mr Le Pla was clearly starting from scratch with his agency and was probably a part-timer: his weekly debit began in March at 8d and by the end of August had been built up to 14s 1d. Simmonds, who came to the Prudential, according to a superintendent's letter tucked into the account book, 'with a reputation for obtaining results', took over an existing debit of £5 11s 3d in February 1898 and had enlarged it to £6 10s 10d by the end of the year.

28. The salaries of male clerks at Chief Office reached £50 a year only after three years. From then on much depended on a man's grade: fourth-, third-, second- or first-class clerks all had different scales of pay.

29. See the clauses relating to lapsed policies in the Agents' Instructions. See also *Friendly and Benefit Building Societies. Reports of the Assistant Commissioners, with a Special Report of the Prudential Assurance Company by the Hon. E.L. Stanley.* Reports from Commissioners 1874. Vol. XII, part II, p.211.

30. Prudential Archives. Prudential Assurance Company. Griffiths Guardbook. Thomas Dewey to Agents, 'Important Alteration in Favour of Policyholders'. As one directive put it, 'to advance the interests of the policy-holders will add to the popularity of the Company, and so augment materially the prosperity of the Agency Staff through the more rapid development of the business'.

31. Prudential Archives. Prudential Assurance Company. Thomas Dewey to agents, 7 March 1907. The qualifying age was reduced from 21 to 15 in 1907.

32. Prudential Archives. Prudential Assurance Company. Thomas Dewey, William Hughes and Frederick Fisher to agents, 2 March 1899.

33. See the *Reports of the Assistant Commissioners* cited above, and Quinquennial Valuation Reports.

34. Such as the National Union of Life Assurance Agents. See *Suggestions on Infantile Assurance and Plain Hard Facts on the Agents' Commission Question*, a submission from the Delegates of the North-East Lancashire Local Council of Life Assurance Agents to the Chairman and Members of the Select Committee on Friendly and Industrial Collecting Societies, 22 November 1888.

35. The text of this Memorial and the Prudential's reply to it was reprinted in *Commercial World*, 1 February 1890.

36. *Ibid.*

37. Prudential Archives. National Association of Prudential Assurance Agents. *First Annual Report*, March 1894.

38. Prudential Archives. See the circular addressed 'To the Agents and Collectors of Industrial Assurance Companies and Friendly Societies of the United Kingdom', 12 March 1899, which was highly critical of the Prudential's terms and the alleged effect its domination was having on agents at large.

39. Plaisted, *op. cit.*, p.89.

40. Prudential Archives. The Retirement Allowance Register dates from 1879 and lists all allowances made from that date to outdoor staff and their widows.

41. Prudential Archives. Copies of documents relating to the establishment of the Staff Provident Fund, the first of which is dated 25 February 1898, are contained in the Griffiths Guardbook.

42. Prudential Archives. Sundries Memo Book. 'Causes of Agents' Dismissals'.

43. Prudential Archives. Walmsley boxfile. *Prudential Assurance Agents' Review*, Supplement, August 31, 1896. '"Special Act" Edition. The Debit System of the Prudential Assurance Company under Transfiguration by the Rontgen Rays of Official Enquiry at the Blackburn Police Court, August 28th, 1896'. 'A Verbatim Report of the Action: Prudential Assurance Company Limited versus Walmsley heard in the High Court of Queen's Bench. January 25th, 26th, and 27th, 1898 before Lord Chief Justice Russell'. *The Insurance Record*, 4 February 1898.

44. One George Marchant was convicted in 1897 of having sent such threats, in the form of drawings and letters, to the Directors and their wives. One of the Directors (unnamed) paid him £253 to quieten him, but the threats began once more when Marchant had spent the money. A more bizarre case was that of a former agent, discharged for some infringement. Suffering from a religious mania and full of remorse, he hurled rocks through several windows of Chief Office with the intention of being arrested so that he could expiate the wrong he had done to the Company by going to gaol. At the Company's request he was sent, not to gaol, but for psychiatric treatment.

45. 'Money Matters', *Sun*, 7 December 1894.

Chapter Ten: Chief Office: More Than Just a Building

1. See C.J.C. Cunningham, *A History and Appreciation of the Prudential Chief Office Buildings in Holborn Bars* (1989). See p.12 for a visual depiction of how the site was gradually acquired; see also various ground and architectural plans in the Prudential Archives.

2. Purchase dates and prices for the main properties that made up the site were as follows: 11 Greville Street was bought for £840 on 7 October 1886 (Minute Book 13);

23 Greville Street was bought for £2,000 on 24 January 1889 (Minute Book 16); 24 Greville Street and 16 Brooke Street were bought for £11,500 and £1,250 respectively on 6 February 1890 (Minute Book 17); a Mr Whalley's interest in Wood's Hotel and adjacent houses was bought for £37,500 on 5 April 1894 (Minute Book 22); on 28 June 1894 Sir Henry Peto accepted £28,500 for his interest in the same (Minute Book 22). He accepted £65,000 on 16 April 1896 for his interest in Furnival's Inn. Ridler's Hotel was bought for £37,500 on 28 April 1898 (Minute Book 25).

3. Caroline Barron, *The Parish of St Andrew, Holborn* (1979), pp.16–17, 26–29, 124–25. The visit to Dickens' quarters in Furnival's Inn made by John Macrone, the publisher, and William Thackeray, the novelist, suggests that the Inn was anything but luxurious: '... standing in the most crowded part of Holborn' it was 'a large building used for lawyers' chambers'. Dickens resided on an upper storey, in 'an uncarpeted and bleak-looking room with a deal table, two or three chairs and a few books ...'.

4. Cunningham, *op. cit.*, p.11.

5. Cunningham, *op. cit.*, p.20, describes the East Court as a space having 'something of the quality of an afterthought', but which in compensation enjoyed 'a richer architectural treatment, one round and one square turret and its own statue of Prudence in a niche'.

6. See furniture drawings in the Prudential Archives.

7. Gloria Clifton, *Professionalism, Patronage and Public Service in Victorian England. The Staff of the Metropolitan Board of Works 1856–1889* (1992). See especially chapter 9 on salaries and promotion. The system of classification used in the Prudential was similar to the MBW's in the number of levels, and the annual review, but for a time around 1887 the Prudential had six classes of clerks, not four, and at that time there was no first-class for women. But the salaries were generally lower, especially in the fourth-class, than the MBW's. As well as being automatic and of an agreed sum, the amount of each clerk's yearly increment depended on the discretion of his principal, though the interview was held with the Manager of the Branch and later with the General Manager. The 'upper' third- and second-class clerks of certain departments were apparently not eligible for full increments, possibly because they worked through valuations and earned overtime payments.

8. See the drawings held by the Prudential Archives. Far more numerous are those donated by the Company to the Royal Institute of British Architects, London.

9. The writer of Waterhouse's obituary in *The Builder*, 26 August 1905, pp.221–22, claimed that the 'defect of his work' 'consisted in a lack of simplicity and reserve in outline and detail' and generally implied that Waterhouse's virtuosity was somehow in bad taste ('... he seems to have been dissatisfied unless he had covered a building with detail and had broken up the outline and the surfaces with clever and unsuspected manoeuvres').

10. See the photographs of the building in the process of refurbishment in 1992 in the Prudential Archives.

11. Prudential Archives. 'The Chief Office of the Prudential Assurance Company Limited. A Description of its Organisation and the Working Methods employed by the various departments in their relations with each other, the Outdoor Staff and the Public'. Internal document, 1911, p.69.

12. This room was first used for the Union's Annual Meeting in April 1903. *Ibis Magazine*, Vol. XXVI (1903), p.152.

13. Prudential Archives. Prudential Clerks' Society. Minute Books 1871–1969. But see T. Watson, *Ibis Cricket 1870–1949* (1950), pp. 26–28, which cites a meeting held in

1872 at which it was decided that the name 'Prudential' was not the best for a sports club, and one T.H. Richardson's suggestion of 'Ibis' for no particular reason. Watson however thinks that an 'association of ideas' with the 'IBs' was at work, and quotes E. Williams' memories of the Ludgate Hill meeting in support.

14. See Lancaster's verse on moving to Holborn Bars, 1879. Reprinted at the end of Chapter Seven: Holborn Bars and the Prudential Style.

15. Prudential Archives. 'Notes on Prudential and Ibis History' (n.d.), p.113.

16. *Ibis Magazine*, Vol. XXIX (1906), p.132.

17. *Op. cit.*, Vol. IX (1886), p.189.

18. *Op. cit.*, Vol. XII (1889), p.155.

19. *Op. cit.*, Vol. XXVI (1903), p.445.

20. *Op. cit.*, Vol. XI (1886), p.351.

21. *Op. cit.*, Vol. XXVII (1904), p.39.

22. *Op. cit.*, Vol. XXXI (1909), p.90.

23. See the *Ibis Appendix*.

24. A tribute to Henry Harben in 1886 called him 'one of the foremost leaders in a great movement which, in little more than a decade, had gone far to change the manner of living of young men by offering them increased facilities for an athletic education, and who had been so largely instrumental in placing within the reach of every member of the Society the attainment of that muscular Christianity of which Kingsley had been the prophet rather than the apostle'. Watson, *op. cit.*, p.70; *Ibis Magazine*, Vol. XI (1886), p.349.

25. There is a delightful vignette concerning the elegant and persuasive Alfred Corderoy Thompson, much later to be Chairman of the Prudential, but to whom it fell, as a young Captain of the Ibis Rowing Club, to return the President's toast at the Ibis dinner. Harben had expressed the wish to see the Ibis rowers compete at Henley, and Thompson 'in a masterful speech, stated the necessary requirements. ... These included the purchase of a boat-house, racing boats, and the engagement of a professional coach'. The request was promptly granted.

26. Watson, *op. cit.*, pp.101–102, where it is also stated that W.G. Grace expressed to Ernest Dewey the wish to play for the Ibis, using his position as a Prudential medical referee to qualify, but the rules of the Cricket Club did not allow this. It was nonetheless 'flattering to think that the greatest of all cricketers found Ibis and Penge sufficiently attractive to ask for selection'.

27. Watson, *op. cit.*, p.96. '... judging by an eye-witness account the cricket was secondary to the hospitality of the host, whose food and good ale were consumed in great quantity'.

28. Watson, *op. cit.*, p.154.

29. *The Times*, 4 December 1911; *Sussex Daily News*, 4 December 1911; *Insurance Record*, 8 December 1911; *Post Magazine*, 9 December 1911.

30. Watson, *op. cit.*, p.83.

31. *Sussex Daily News*, 4 December 1911. Harben also did this at the Prudential, where there was a squad of in-house firefighters.

32. When Harben was very old and had to use a Bath chair, he insisted on being positioned directly behind the batsman's wicket, for the best view of the bowling. Fender was a very fast bowler and the balls used on occasion to damage the wickerwork of Harben's chair – but true to form, the old man would not be moved!

33. Prudential Archives. Guy Philip Harben, Personal reminiscences. Typed pages and covering letter, 1947. The author in later life recalled the tone of Warnham Sundays

as stultifyingly formal. On one such sabbath he was locked in his room for the day for whistling as he ran downstairs. To keep his grandchildren's table manners up to the mark, Harben is said to have positioned tacks under the tablecloth at Sunday lunch, just where juvenile elbows were wont to rest. Such stories suggest that as a parent and grandparent Harben was a strict disciplinarian, though photographs of him with his grandchildren also show great affection on his part.

34. *Ibid.*

35. Henry Andrade Harben married Mary Frances James, daughter of C.F. James, in 1873.

36. R.T. Pugh died in 1885, Thomas Reid in 1886, James Allanson in 1890, Dr Robert Cross in 1893, and Dr Patrick Fraser in 1896.

37. Prudential Archives. Correspondence between Henry Harben and the British Institute of Public Health regarding establishment of the Harben Lectures and the Harben Gold Medal.

38. *Sussex Daily News*, 4 December 1911, p.8. The obituary carried by the *Hampstead and Highgate Express* of 9 December 1911 reported that Rustington cost Harben a total of £170,000. What the total of his giving to all causes amounted to is as yet uncalculated. For some of the gifts to his local communities, whether at Warnham or in Hampstead, the details are scanty. He founded Webster Lodge, a hostel for young women who had come to London to work, on the edge of Hampstead Heath. He is said to have founded a school (details unknown) and to have contributed to a school for the blind of which he was also vice-president. He is known to have given money to various churches other than St Saviour's in the Hampstead area, the Congregational Church in Haverstock Hill for one, and to have built the City Temple a Hampstead base.

39. Prudential Archives. 'Rustington Convalescent Home'. Information sheet supplied by the Carpenters' Company, which today administers the Home under the conditions outlined in Harben's bequest. See B.W. Alford and T.C. Barker, *A History of the Carpenters' Company* (1968), pp.160–61.

40. Until 1980 the Prudential could nominate convalescent members of staff and pensioners to five free places each year. Under a revised arrangement the Company may still take advantage of a preferential rate.

41. When the bidding exceeded this figure, Thomas Barratt, one of the guarantors and Chairman of the A. & F. Pears soap company, continued bidding on his own account and secured the property for £38,000, reselling it immediately at the same price to the Council.

42. *The Times*, 8 July 1898, p.7e; see also p.2f; 20 July, p.13f; 22 July, p.11e. A garden party held at Golders Hill on 21 July was attended by 10,000 people ranging in rank from the Duke and Duchess of Westminster and various MPs to local residents and people from all over London.

43. Prudential Archives. '1st Cadet Battalion Royal Fusiliers (City of London Regiment). Opening Ceremony of New Headquarters by the Prince of Wales, 15 May 1905'. Document on loan from the Royal Fusiliers. With regard to the Drill Hall in Pond Street, Harben had first offered £2,000 for the purchase of the land, then arranged for his daughter Mary Wharrie to donate the £6,000 needed to erect the hall. This consisted of a drill hall, gymnasium, shooting range and meeting rooms, comprising what was probably the best training facility in the country, rent-free for as long as the battalion occupied it.

44. *Sussex Daily News*, 4 December 1911. 'It is perhaps no secret that at the time of Mr Horne's appointment, Sir Henry stood aside in favour of his old friend'. There is no documentary evidence to substantiate this assertion regarding the manner of Horne's

succession to Gillman in 1877, but it is open to doubt on logical grounds. In view of the Board's resistance a few years earlier to concentrating too much influence in Harben's hands – or anyone's – it is difficult to imagine it being willing to make Harben Chairman while he retained the position of Resident Director. Conversely, if he gave up the latter, his talents would have been less well employed, resulting in a situation that was on balance less advantageous to the Company. He could have performed the Chairman's task, but not the Chairman his.

45. The New Year 1907 found Harben still unwell and he was given a six months' leave of absence from his duties as Chairman, renewed on 3 July. Guy Philip Harben in his Reminiscences reports his grandfather as having used a Bath chair from about this point, which may suggest that he had had another stroke.

46. Prudential Archives. Note entitled 'The President'. Harben Family boxfile. Also Prudential Assurance Company, Minute Book 33, 25 June 1907.

47. Prudential Archives. Harben Family boxfile 'Minutes of the Proceedings at an Extraordinary General Meeting of the Prudential Assurance Company Limited held at 142 Holborn Bars London on the 12 July 1907', p.4.

48. Prudential Archives. Griffiths Guardbook 822. Lancaster was knighted on 5 November 1906 on the occasion of a royal visit to King's Lynn, when Edward VII opened the grammar school.

49. Prudential Archives. Henry Andrade Harben file in Harben Family boxfile. Quoted in a letter to the author from the Curator of the Medical School Archives, St Mary's Hospital, Paddington, 17 February 1995, discussing Henry Andrade Harben's relationship with that institution.

50. See *The Times*, 19 August 1910; *Daily Telegraph*, 19 August 1910. Two examples which will be discussed in the next chapter are the Prudential's interpretation of the Assurance Act 1909, and the subsequent visit to Holborn Bars on 28 April 1910 of a deputation of agents to discuss grievances arising from the application of the Act.

51. Whether Sir Henry was troubled by misgivings about his grandsons Henry Devenish Harben (born 1874) and Guy Philip Harben (born 1881) must remain a matter for speculation. At the time of their grandfather's death they were 37 and 30 respectively, and had as yet shown no interest in the Company from which their wealth derived. As a young man Henry Devenish studied for the Bar, then abandoned law for a political career. He began as a Conservative, in the tradition of his father and grandfather, but soon took up reforming causes. He stood (unsuccessfully) as a Liberal candidate for the city of Worcester in 1906 and Portsmouth in 1910, but was moving steadily leftwards and was active in the Fabian Society from at least 1906. Both he and his wife Agnes were prominent campaigners for women's suffrage and helped to finance the movement. He helped to establish the London School of Economics and was one of the backers of the *New Statesman*; he was also interested in theosophy and was chairman of the London Vedanta Society. The political tracts that comprise his mature writings suggest that he sought to distance himself from the Prudential in every way. The feeling was mutual: his political views made a place on the Board impossible, and it was filled, from 1918, by his younger brother Guy Philip. In 1919, he left his wife and five children penniless to live with a Miss Mulock (always known as 'Baby'). Their relationship was portrayed in Aldous Huxley's short story 'Chawdron' in *Brief Candles* (1930). See Brian Harrison, *Prudent Revolutionaries* (1987).

Guy Philip Harben was more promising. He was a talented painter and became a successful society artist; he then entered the diplomatic service and spent the First World War as Board of Trade Commissioner for Italy and attaché at the British

Embassy in Rome, being awarded the OBE. He returned to join the Prudential Board after the war, and remained a Director until 1948, taking up some of his father's philanthropic causes, such as St Mary's Hospital, Paddington, and founding the Harben Trust for the staff of the Prudential. He became Deputy Chairman in 1936 and was Chairman of the Ibis. Guy Harben was a man of wide interests and extrovert personality; in 1928 he was photographed by the press while walking his pet cheetah along the Embankment. He also won many horticultural medals for his orchids.

52. See Sir Henry Harben's obituary. The fullest version appears in the *Sussex Daily News*, 4 December 1911.

SECTION FOUR

Chapter Eleven: A Turbulent Few Years

1. Association of Industrial Assurance Companies and Collecting Friendly Societies (AIACCFS). Minute Book 3, 5 October 1909. A circular of 5 October 1909 to Members of the House of Commons. Under the heading 'Ousting Pauperism', it held that the law was badly outmoded, and that saving for funeral benefits had done much to encourage respectability and elevate the working classes. The 80,000 agents employed by the Association's member companies were cited as having paid claims to some 3,000,000 families in the previous year.

2. *Hansard's Parliamentary Debates*, 5th series, XII (1909), col. 1951. During the debates on the Assurance Companies Act, Churchill referred to this figure – about a third of the total number of industrial assurance policies then in force – as the number technically illegal under 14 Geo.3, ch.48 which would be legitimised by the Act.

3. AIACCFS. Minute Book 3, 13 July 1909, cites the case of a certain 'Sophie Haberschitz of the East End of London', who at death was found to be insured with ten offices for a total of £300.

4. Prudential Archives. Prudential Assurance Company. *Report* of the Proceedings of the 61st Annual General Meeting, 3 March 1910, p.5.

5. Prudential Archives. Prudential Assurance Company. Industrial Branch. Instructions to Agents 1887–1905, section 35, p.10.

6. AIACCFS. Minute Book 3. This point was discussed on 13 July 1909. The Association recorded its disapproval of such policies, but also recognised that in exceptional cases they were legitimate. The Executive Council in turn accepted this position.

7. National Association of Prudential Assurance Agents (NAPAA). Report of the Deputation to Holborn Bars, London EC, April 28, 1910. This, of course, was a demand which the Company had consistently refused to grant. Another was the right to dispense with certain tables, the most objected to being the new Monthly Option Table, which the NAPAA feared would kill off small Ordinary Branch policies. (It was aimed at the more prosperous Ordinary Branch proposal, and carried a commission of 12½%, as opposed to other tables, which carried 20%.)

8. I am indebted to Mr Michael McLaughlin of the National Union of Insurance Workers for access to early numbers of the *Prudential Staff Gazette*.

9. Prudential Archives. Prudential Assurance Company. Minute Book 37, 19 October 1911.

10. *Ibid.*

11. As mentioned earlier, it had been founded in 1893. The radicalism of some of its leaders alarmed moderate agents. It never had a following among the upper echelons of the field staff, and the membership did not increase after 1910. *Daily News*, 1 July 1911; H. Plaisted, *Prudential Past and Present* (1918), p.89.

12. Prudential Archives. Field Staff and Unions boxfile. The Birmingham Handbill issued by the NAPAA.

13. Bottomley, who claimed to be the illegitimate son of the radical politician Charles Bradlaugh, began as a publisher and speculative company promoter. Since 1893, when he defended himself in the High Court against a charge of conspiring to obtain money for his own purposes from the shareholders of the Hansard Trust, he had become popularly admired for the bravado with which he exploited loopholes in the law. His personal extravagance, especially when it came to entertaining and horse-racing, gained him access to the best society and, inevitably, much gossip.

14. Bottomley's tactics did not alter much over the years. After the First World War, when the late Sir Nutcombe Hume was working on new issues alongside the legendary outside broker Sir Arthur Wheeler, he recalled the 'adman' from *John Bull* coming into his office with a poster in each hand. 'Take space in *John Bull* and it's this one,' the man would say, 'cut us out, and that's what you'll get.' The first poster would bear some slogan praising the company in question; the second would be a damning headline labelling it a swindle.

15. Prudential Archives. Bottomley boxfiles. Affidavit of Mr A.C. Thompson, 8 February 1912. In the Matter of Walter John Wenham, a Solicitor, and In the Matter of 'The Solicitors Act 1888'. Since the 1909 Act Wenham had been supplementing his income by seeking out policyholders whose assurances had become 'uneconomic': where, due to the longevity of the assured, total premiums paid amounted to more than the face value of the policy. This was a situation understandably resented. Wenham's method appears to have been to persuade such people to demand the return of their premiums by claiming to have been tricked by an agent into purchasing an 'illegal' policy. In instances when a refund was granted, he then absorbed the lion's share as 'costs' and returned a fraction to the policyholder.

16. Prudential Archives. Do Vey Case boxfile.

17. See the *Commercial World*, 1 April 1911 and 1 May 1911; the *Insurance Mail*, 1 and 8 April 1911, the *Agents' Journal*, 15 April 1911.

18. *Daily News*, 1 July 1911; *Prudential Staff Gazette*, Vol. 1, No. 10 (July 1911).

19. *John Bull*, 7 October 1911.

20. Prudential Archives. *John Bull* files. See Transcript of the Shorthand Notes of Mr Bottomley's Examination in Bankruptcy Taken on Behalf of the Prudential Assurance Company, Ltd., 1097–1107, pp.87–89. These deal with the Contempt proceedings and explain the very moderate penalty imposed: the judges saw no point in imprisoning or heavily fining Bottomley, as the only effect would be 'to hamper him in his duty towards his creditors, or injure them by taking from him money that could have been theirs'.

21. By the end of 1914, the annual premium income was back to £301,746, though some of the increase was due to policies taken out when war was declared.

22. Prudential Archives. Industrial Branch. Registers of Law Proceedings, Vols. 3 and 5; see also Instructions to Solicitors.

23. B.B. Gilbert, *The Evolution of National Insurance in Great Britain* (1967), p.326.

24. Quoted in Gilbert, *op. cit.*, p.328.

25. *Insurance Mail*, 14 January 1911.

26. Gilbert, *op. cit.*, p.338. Howard Kingsley Wood is better remembered as Chancellor of the Exchequer in Churchill's wartime Coalition Government, from 1940 until his own death in 1943.

27. *Insurance Mail*, 6 May 1911.

28. Prudential Archives. Prudential Assurance Company. *Report* of Annual General Meeting, 2 March 1911, p.7.

29. Lloyd George reported that well over 40,000,000 policyholders were already covered: 6,000,000 by friendly societies and 7,000,000 by the large collecting societies, and 30,000,000 by the industrial assurance companies. *Hansard's Parliamentary Debates*, 5th series, Vol. XXV, col's 609–610, 4 May 1911.

30. See *Hansard's Parliamentary Debates*, 5th series, Vol. XXVI; the discussion following the Bill's second reading on 29 May 1911 contains comment on the medical, friendly societies' and insurance companies' interests.

31. Edmond Browne and H. Kingsley Wood, *The Law of National Insurance* (1912), pp.xii–xiii.

32. *Insurance Mail*, 24 June 1911.

33. Gilbert, *op. cit.*, pp.381–82.

34. See Comyns Carr, Stuart Garnett and J.H. Taylor, *National Insurance* (1912), pp. 44–45. Prudential Archives. Prudential Assurance Company. *Report* of Annual General Meeting, 7 March 1912, p.7.

35. *Prudential Staff Gazette*, Vol. 4, No. 41 (5 January 1914).

Chapter Twelve: The Prudential in the Great War

1. Of the 1,183 male staff at this date, 896 belonged to the Rifle Club. The prominence given to the sport owed much to Harben, who viewed it as one that developed intelligence as well as physical coordination. Lord Roberts, on opening the rifle range, said that he hoped such facilities would become universal, and that 'Ladies should visit them and learn too'; Harben added, with reference to women, that shooting 'trained their eyes and brought them into the fresh air and was altogether beneficial'. *Ibis Magazine*, Vol. 29 (July 1906), pp.186–88. Prudential Archives. Prudential Assurance Company. *Report* of the Annual General Meeting, 5 March 1915, p.12. The Rifle Club was advanced the sum of £550 in 1913 to buy a clubhouse at Bisley.

2. Prudential Archives. Prudential Assurance Company. Minute Book 41, 13 August 1914.

3. One Prudential clerk, R. Davies, weighed only 7st 3lb, but succeeded in joining up on his third attempt. H.E. Boisseau, *The Prudential Staff and the Great War* (1938), p.8.

4. Prudential Archives. Prudential Assurance Company. Minute Book 41, 5 November 1914.

5. Prudential Archives. Prudential Assurance Company. *Report* of Annual General Meeting, 5 March 1915, pp.5–6. See also the statement entitled 'War Risks – 1914 Practice', together with correspondence between Joseph Burn and W.H. Aldcroft of the Refuge Assurance Company.

6. 4 & 5 Geo.5 Courts (Emergency Powers) Act, 1914 [Ch 78]. Prudential Archives. See *Reports* of Annual General Meetings of 5 March 1915, p.35, and 2 March 1916, pp.9–10.

7. *Ibis Magazine*, Vol. 37 (Nov 1914), p.431.

8. *Ibis Magazine*, Vol. 37 (Dec 1914), p.504.

9. W.H. Petty, quoted in Boisseau, *op. cit.*, p.17.

10. Boisseau, *op. cit.*, pp.25–26.

11. *Ibid.*

12. *Ibid.*, p.19.

13. *Ibid.*, p.18.

14. *Ibid.*, p.20.

15. *Ibid.*, p.39.

16. *Ibid.*, pp.48–50, 69–72. The account of Bedbrook's death was written by Hylton Cleaver, who became a successful novelist after the war but was at the time of writing employed by the Prudential.

17. E.T. Shilling had the weird experience of attending a dinner at the Portsmouth Guildhall, finding his own name on the list of the dead and hearing the 'Last Post' sounded for him.

18. Boisseau, *op. cit.*, p.33.

19. *Ibid.*, p.30.

20. *Ibid.*, p.33.

21. *Ibid.*, pp.80–81. This particular camp also produced a version of the pantomime *Aladdin*, written by F. Kenchington, mounted by the men of the Field Ambulance and featuring half a dozen ex-IDOS players. It was presented by the Guildhall School of Music for many years after the war.

22. Prudential Archives. Prudential Assurance Company. *Report* of Annual General Meeting, 2 March 1916, p.11.

23. Prudential Archives. Prudential Assurance Company. *Report* of Annual General Meeting, 6 March 1915, p.12.

24. Prudential Archives. Prudential Assurance Company. 'H' Division Memorandum Book, 19 May 1916.

25. This consignment of machinery, obtained through the Accounting & Tabulating Company of Great Britain, was apparently the largest punched card machine installation ordered by any organisation up to that time. Martin Campbell Kelly, 'Large-Scale Data Processing in the Prudential, 1850–1930', *Accounting Business and Financial History*, Vol. 2, No. 2, 1992. See also the following chapter for a discussion of the changeover to automated working.

26. Boisseau, *op. cit.*, pp.55–56.

27. These productions carried on until March 1919 and the number of men attending frequently exceeded 3,000. *Ibid.*, pp.50–51. The IDOS did carry on until 1916, with women for the first time taking women's roles in November 1914, in a revival of *Dr Wake's Patient. Ibis Magazine*, Vol. 38 (Jan 1915).

28. The Rifle Club raised the money to send its large spotting telescope to France at the request of a colleague in the Royal Field Artillery. It proved invaluable in identifying the precise location of the enemy, and travelled with the Prudential man for the rest of the war. Boisseau, *op. cit.* p.56.

29. Donations for each year appear in the board minutes. By the end of the war those listed amounted to £83,000,000.

30. Prudential Archives. Prudential Assurance Company. *Report* of Annual General Meeting, 8 March 1918, pp.6, 9–11.

31. Prudential Archives. Prudential Assurance Company. 'H' Division Memorandum Book, 1 July 1916.

32. Prudential Archives. Prudential Assurance Company. Minute Book 41, 29 July 1915, 12 August 1915; Minute Book 42, 19 August 1915, 14 October 1915. See also Max Aitken (Lord Beaverbrook), *Politicians and the War 1914–16*, quoted in W.L. Catchpole and E. Elverston, *BIA 50 1917–67 Fifty Years of the British Insurance Association* (1968), p.12.

33. Prudential Archives. Prudential Assurance Company. *Report* of Annual General Meeting, 2 March 1916, pp.7–8, 14.

34. Prudential Archives. Prudential Assurance Company. *Report* of Annual General Meeting, 5 March 1914, p.7.

35. Prudential Archives. Prudential Assurance Company. *Report* of Annual General Meeting, 2 March 1916, p.11.

36. Prudential Archives. Prudential Assurance Company. *Report* of Annual General Meeting, 7 March 1918, pp.13–14.

37. *Ibid.*, p.14.

38. *Ibid.*, p.11.

39. *Ibid.*, p.12. Five times as much was paid in claims on the lives of soldiers as on sailors: in 1916, for instance, the totals came to £627,750 and £113,336.

40. Prudential Archives. Prudential Assurance Company. *Reports* of Annual General Meetings, 5 March 1915, 2 March 1916, 1 March 1917, 7 March 1918 and 6 March 1919. Notable claims for civilian deaths included a total of £19,534 paid out on those who died when the *Lusitania* was torpedoed. Nearly £3,000 was paid on deaths in zeppelin raids.

41. *Ibis Magazine*, Vol. 41 (Dec 1918), p.391.

42. *Ibid.*, pp.393–94.

43. *Ibis Magazine*, Vol. 42 (Jan 1919), p.7.

44. Prudential Archives. Prudential Assurance Company. *Report* of Annual General Meeting, 4 March 1920, p.21.

45. Prudential Archives. Prudential Assurance Company. From an undated newspaper article entitled 'Men, Women and Memories' in Griffiths Guardbook 822. The Irish Parliamentarian and journalist T.P. O'Connor was one of several who commented on the contrast between Thompson's self-control and the inner anguish that marked his features '... never did I see a man in the chair more dignified, more efficient, more temperate. Not by domineering, but by sheer grasp of facts his word was law. ... But what fascinated and to a certain extent saddened me was the expression of his face ... there were deep lines in it, and above all there was a look in his eyes which haunted me for days after I had seen him'.

Chapter Thirteen: The Triumph of System

1. Sidney Webb, *Report on Industrial Assurance*. Supplement to the *New Statesman*, 13 March 1915. There may have been a connection between the origins of the *Report* and Henry Devenish Harben, who at this time was one of the early backers of the *New Statesman*.

2. S.G. Warner, 'Twenty Years' Changes in Life Assurance', *Journal of the Insurance Institute of Great Britain and Ireland*, XII (1909).

3. The other 11 were the Pearl, the Refuge, the Britannic, the London and Manchester, the British Legal and United Provident, and the Salvation Army (profit-making companies); the Royal London and the United Providence (mutuals); and the Royal Liver, the London Victoria and the Scottish Legal (collecting friendly societies). Passfield Report, p.3.

4. *Ibid.*, p.4.

5. *Ibid.*, p.16.

6. Although it is not specifically mentioned, Webb must have been aware that in 1915 the average duration of Prudential industrial assurances was almost 13 years, thanks to a series of measures introduced over the years to discourage lapsing.

7. *Ibid.*, p.9.

8. *Ibid.*, pp.30–31.

9. Sir Arnold Wilson and Hermann Levy, *Industrial Assurance. A Historical and Critical Study* (1937) p.107.

10. *Report of the Departmental Committee on the Business of Industrial Assurance Companies and Collecting Societies.* Cmd. 614. *Minutes of Evidence*, Cmd. 618, 1920. R.B. Walker and D.R. Woodgate, *Principles and Practice of Industrial Assurance* (1943), p.22, claimed that the Parmoor Committee was brought into being by 'the socialistic tendency of the period'. Its task was to look into the business carried on by industrial assurance companies and collecting societies, and into insurance as carried on under the National Insurance Act 1911, to determine whether the existing laws needed amendment.

11. Industrial Life Offices Association, *Jubilee Celebrations, 1901–1951*, p.32.

12. An interesting question later arose as to whether premiums paid on a child's endowment policy and returned on the death of the child had to be included in this total. The 1923 Act was considered ambiguous and the insurance offices succeeded in having the wording amended in 1929 to make it clear that such premiums were exempt from the total. See Dermot Morrah, *A History of Industrial Life Assurance* (1955), pp.104–105.

13. Prudential Archives. Prudential Assurance Company. *Report* of Annual General Meeting, 6 March 1924, p.4. As an aside, Thompson noted that conforming with the Act's demand that some of its conditions appear on each policy had involved the Prudential in hefty expense for new stationery: 394 tons of forms were printed at Holborn Bars and despatched to the agents in 60,000 parcels.

14. Prudential Archives. Prudential Assurance Company. Griffiths Guardbook, press cuttings on the Prudential 'B' shares. Initially there was a requirement that buyers take 250 shares before they could be registered, which was later rescinded when a Stock Exchange quotation was sought in 1924.

15. Prudential Archives. Prudential Assurance Company. General Branch boxfile; Griffiths Guardbook, cuttings; *Report* of Annual General Meeting, 2 March 1922, p.19.

16. *Prudential Bulletin*, March 1924, p.570.

17. Prudential Archives. Prudential Assurance Company. Griffiths Guardbook, Memorandum of November 1923.

18. Prudential Archives. Prudential Assurance Company. *Reports* of Annual General Meetings, 1923–29; General boxfile; Przezornosc Assurance Company of Warsaw boxfiles.

19. Joseph Burn in his series of lectures entitled *Vital Statistics Explained* (1914) noted the recent decline of tuberculosis and the microbic and childhood diseases. He claimed to have tested the theory that mortality was lessening by comparing the Prudential's experience, using its 20,000,000 industrial policyholders, with the findings of the 1911 census. The rate of mortality was found to be improved even between 1911 and 1913, confirming the theory and promising 'an enormous increase in the number of working years of life saved to the nation'.

20. See S.G.Warner, *op. cit.*, on the rise of endowments.

21. Prudential Archives. Prudential Assurance Company. *Report* of Annual General Meeting, 1921, pp.20–21.

22. Prudential Archives. Prudential Assurance Company. *Report* of Annual General Meeting, 6 March 1924, p.7. These included an increase in the sum assured, best illustrated by contrasting the amount secured by a premium of 1d a week in 1920, £10 5s, and in 1929, £14 12s.

23. Advertising posters in this series appeared as the inside back covers of issues of the *Prudential Bulletin* during the 1920s.

24. Prudential Archives. Prudential Assurance Company. *Report* of Annual General Meeting, 3 March 1921, pp.17–18.

25. One wishes the same could be said of his wife, Lady Burn, whose snobbery was notorious. See Sir Joseph Burn's biography, written by his daughter Kathleen and donated as a three-volume typescript to the Prudential Archives. This work reveals much about both her parents and contains many sidelights on the Prudential and on some of Sir Joseph's colleagues.

26. H. Plaisted, *Prudential Past and Present* (1918), p.124. *Prudential Bulletin*, July 1927, p.1210. The down-to-earth Burn came from a 'chapel' (as opposed to a 'church') family and disliked excessive fervour. The origin of this repugnance is said to have derived from an incident when Burn was a young clerk, learning to play the violin. Leaving Chief Office one evening, he was accosted at the corner of Grays Inn Road by a zealot brandishing tracts. 'Young man,' cried the zealot, 'you are fiddling your way to Hell.' That was the end of the future General Manager's formal religion. Prudential Archives. Transcript of an interview with H.A. Hurd.

27. Prudential Archives. Prudential Assurance Company. Unsigned typewritten report of a visit to the Prudential by representatives of the Metropolitan Life Assurance Company of New York (hereafter referred to as 'MLA document'), 1923, p.4.

28. *Prudential Bulletin*. Accounts of Burn's tours of the divisions as General Manager in Volumes 1–10 covering 1920–29.

29. Prudential Archives. Prudential Assurance Company. MLA document, p.7.

30. *Ibid*. Block System boxfiles.

31. Prudential Archives. Prudential Assurance Company. *Report* of Annual General Meeting, 4 March 1926, p.16.

32. *Ibid*. Thompson said on this occasion that 'the results achieved to date are so striking that in view of the criticisms that have from time to time been made with reference to the high rate of expense at which Industrial Assurance has been conducted it is astonishing that few outside those responsible for the change appear to realise its significance'.

33. This came into effect in March 1924. Policies of less than 15 years' duration were to continue to receive interim bonuses as they had up to that time.

34. Prudential Archives. Prudential Assurance Company. *Report* of Annual General Meeting, 6 March 1924, p.17.

35. See Martin Campbell-Kelly, 'Large-scale data processing in the Prudential, 1850–1930', *Accounting Business and Financial History*, Vol. 2, No. 2 (1992), pp.128–29.

36. Joseph Burn, *Vital Statistics Explained* (1914), pp.11–17.

37. Prudential Archives. Prudential Assurance Company. MLA document, p.2. The first payment relating to the machines was made to the 'Acc & Tab' on 3 February 1916, for £3996 6s 4d. The option to purchase the control of the British company ('for the purpose of safeguarding the future position of the Company with regard to the use of the Powers Tabulating Machines') was obtained from the Accounting and Tabulating Corporation of New York in April 1918 and exercised in the following year. Minute Book 44, 25 April 1918.

38. Campbell-Kelly, *op. cit.*, p.131. Prudential Archives. Prudential Assurance Company. MLA document, pp.3, 12.

39. Prudential Archives. Prudential Assurance Company. MLA document, p.8. See also the *Evening News* of 23 January 1926 for Sir Joseph Burn's comments about 'Far Too Many Clerks'.

40. Prudential Archives. Prudential Assurance Company. MLA document pp. 9, 12. This report was not entirely uncritical of the way the transfer of information had been done. The Americans could not see the point of duplicating the life and lapse registers at district office level and having no copy at Chief Office. The tracing of transfers had to be done at the district offices since no record of within-district transfers was kept elsewhere. The visitors suggested printing the agent's copy in duplicate and eliminating one district office copy.

41. *Prudential Bulletin*, July 1927, p.1210.

42. See Chapter Eight: The Making of a Colossus for a description of a valuation in earlier years: each of the several million cards passed through 16 pairs of hands and the whole process took months.

43. *Prudential Bulletin*, October 1927, p.1054.

44. *Prudential Bulletin*, August 1926, p.1031.

45. See *Prudential Bulletin* articles on the General Strike and on concessions from May 1926 to February 1927.

46. Prudential Archives. Prudential Assurance Company. 'Notes on the general consideration of Life Assurance outside the United Kingdom'. Unsigned, but understood to be by Sir Joseph Burn. Undated, but internal evidence suggests 1925.

47. Burn as Actuary and General Manager was not on the Board.

48. Prudential Archives. Prudential Assurance Company. 'Notes on the general consideration of Life Assurance outside the United Kingdom', p.2.

49. Prudential Archives. Prudential Assurance Company. Circular Memorandum about the Extraordinary General Meeting held on 21 November 1929.

50. The MLA document describes Burn's conversations with the visitors on a variety of subjects, including pensions. The employee's contribution was $3\frac{1}{2}\%$ of salary, while the Company's was a sum equal to nine-sevenths of the employee's contribution. Most prominent among those who developed the Staff and Group pensions areas during the 1920s were E.J.W. Borrajo and Frank Symmons.

51. Prudential Archives. Prudential Assurance Company. The Griffiths Guardbook contains assorted cuttings on many figures in the Prudential. There are also individual files on Dewey and Lancaster, and other Directors and office holders.

Chapter Fourteen: The Prudential Overseas

1. Prudential Archives. Overseas Branch History: India, p.5.

2. R.W. Barnard, *A Century of Service. A History of the Prudential 1848–1948* (1948), p.104, says that the Superintendent was Sardul Singh Jaaj, a Sikh, whose staff consisted of a Muslim Inspector and two agents, respectively Sikh and Hindu. The population of the territory was said to have been 60% Muslim, 20% Hindu and 10% Sikh.

3. Prudential Archives. Overseas Branch History: India, p.26. By 1937, agents for India, Burma and Ceylon numbered 1,058.

4. *Ibid.*

5. The disasters naturally affected the field staff as well. Barnard, *op. cit.*, p.104, mentions an agent called Seth Munshi Ram who, having survived the Quetta earthquake and the loss of his house and possessions, wrote asking for new proposal forms so that he could recommence canvassing.

6. See note 46 of Chapter Thirteen: The Triumph of System. Sir Joseph Burn certainly conceived of overseas expansion as part of a defence against nationalisation.

7. Prudential Archives. Overseas Branch History: Canada I and II. Also an unattributed unpublished ms entitled 'With Splendid Assurance'.

8. The Canadian per capita income in 1930 was about $3,000, depending on the area. There was a telling ambiguity in the approximate sums assured per head of population in the two countries: in 1931, £137 in Canada and £53 in Australia. See J.G. Parker, 'Financial Conditions in Canada as Affecting Life Insurance', *Journal of the Institute of Actuaries*, Vol. LX (1929).

9. Parker, *op. cit.*, pp.329–31.

10. Prudential Archives. Overseas Branch History: Canada I and II. Also, transcripts of taped interviews with Messrs. Jack, Desjeans, McNeill, Evans, Rowan and Mair.

11. Prudential Archives. Overseas Branch History: Canada I, B–7.

12. Hartley McNairn, a KC and Superintendent of Insurance for the Province of Ontario since 1935, was the first to unify the two sides of the business, bringing the Canadian Branch into line with the practice by then adopted by the Prudential in other countries.

13. During the 1920s the assisted migrant scheme was gradually populating a land mass four-fifths the size of Europe. The wealth of Australia was as yet barely tapped; per capita income, which at £440 per annum was substantially less than Canada's, nonetheless suggested that there was ordinary business to be had. Labour problems were reportedly more prevalent than in Canada. Robert Thoday, 'Life Assurance in Australia', *Journal of the Institute of Actuaries*, Vol. LX (1929), pp.24–82.

14. Prudential Archives. Transcript of a taped interview with E.D. Smout.

15. E.D. Smout, aged 93 at the time of the author's meeting with him, related these anecdotes in the short conversation preceding the formal interview.

16. Prudential Archives. *A Solid Foundation: A History of the Prudential in New Zealand 1922–1995*, pp.10–12.

17. *Ibid.*, pp.18, 22.

18. Prudential Archives. Overseas Branch History: South Africa.

19. Prudential Archives. 'South Africa Fifty Years Hence. Sir Edgar Horne Foresees Great Developments'. Unidentified newspaper article on Horne's trip to South Africa. N.d. but assumed to be 1934.

20. *Prudential African Gazette*, June 1929. The piece goes on: 'With the Editor's permission, we might publish the Doctor's remarks on this occasion. He, a dour Scotsman, said, "Why trouble to bring the lady across? Just ask her to undress on the opposite bank and I will examine her through my field-glasses." We need scarcely add that the Prospect preferred to risk the swirling waters.'

21. Prudential Archives. Report of the Financial Position of the Southern and East African Branch. Overseas/Africa boxfile 3, 1934–1948. Report for 1937, General Conclusions.

22. Prudential Archives. Overseas Branch History: Malaya, p.1.

23. Prudential Archives. Overseas Branch History: Near East. All figures shown here are taken from this account.

24. Prudential Archives. Transcript of a taped interview with Edward Goddard.

25. Prudential Archives. Prudential Assurance Company. *Report* of Annual General Meeting, 9 March 1939, p.4.

Chapter Fifteen: 'Strong roots, strong tree...'

1. He was the model laird to the tenants of his Sutherland estate, where his improvements brought full employment. See Lesley Ketteringham, *A History of Lairg* (1997).

2. Prudential Archives. Diary. N.a., n.d. Handwritten chronicle of Prudential events. The new wing was formally opened on 17 March 1933, and all the departments that had been relocated during the move were back by September.

3. Jonathan Goodman, *The Killing of Julia Wallace* (1969), p.7.

4. *Prudential Staff Gazette*, April 1931, p.1. To determine the degree of support for Wallace among the membership, the novel method was adopted of summoning the union's representatives from all over the country to attend a mock trial at Holborn Hall, its headquarters in Grays Inn Road. At the end of the trial the votes were unanimously in Wallace's favour. The Executive Council of the Union then guaranteed the whole cost of his defence. See Goodman, *op. cit.*, pp.153–57.

5. A change in the law in 1927 removed the limit of 15 weeks on unemployment benefit to permit the unlimited drawing of benefit.

6. There are innumerable studies of these events. For biographical information on May, see the *Dictionary of Business Biography*, edited by David Jeremy, Vol. 4 (1985), pp.203–06. An unflattering interpretation of May's role appears in Claude Cockburn, *The Devil's Decade* (1973), pp.40–49. May's semi-blindness was not a bar to his holding these positions of responsibility. Nor, apparently, did it lead him to moderate his driving. He was fined for speeding in 1939, as on several earlier occasions; specifically on this one, for having outraced a police car through Twickenham.

7. Prudential Assurance Company. Chairman's Speech, *Report* of Annual General Meeting, 5 March 1931, p.8.

8. Prudential Archives. Committee on the Industrial Assurance and Assurance on the Lives of Children Under Ten Years of Age. *Report*. Cmnd.43 76, London 1933. Minutes of Evidence of the Prudential Assurance Company, 11 and 12 November 1931 and 30 March 1933.

9. Prudential Archives. *Memorandum of Evidence submitted by Sir Joseph Burn KBE FIA On Behalf of the Prudential Assurance Company Limited to the Departmental Committee Appointed by the Treasury*. October 1931 (XII, 12). During the Cohen Committee's hearing of evidence, W.E. Mashford resurfaced as a critic of industrial assurance. His testimony proved unconvincing, however. See Dermot Morrah, *A History of Industrial Assurance* (1955), pp. 121–22; Sir Arnold Wilson and Dr Hermann Levy, who in their *Industrial Assurance* express admiration for Mashford, probably did not know of his chequered past as an agent.

10. Prudential Archives. Burn, Memorandum (XVIII, 21).

11. The expense ratio first fell below 30% in 1923, when it reached 29.7%. As recently as 1920 it had been 40.5%. Perhaps the Cohen Committee assumed that once the system was in place economies would be seen very quickly.

12. Apart from the fall in the market value of securities, there were other negative factors at work between 1931 and 1934, cited as default on foreign investments, currency depreciation, and the conversion of War Loan from 5% to 3½%.

13. G.E. May, 'The Investment of Life Assurance Funds', *Journal of the Institute of Actuaries*, Vol. XLVI (1912), pp.134–68; Prudential Archives, Prudential Assurance Company, Chairman's Speech, *Report* of Annual General Meeting, 3 March 1927.

14. Prudential Archives. Prudential Assurance Company. Balance sheets for 1911 and 1912.

15. Prudential Archives. Investment records relating to Marks & Spencer. Rees, Goronwy, *St Michael. A History of Marks & Spencer* (1969), pp.70–78. Paul Bookbinder, *Simon Marks, Retail Revolutionary* (1983), pp.93–96.

16. Prudential Assurance Company. Minute Book 63, 2 November 1933; one example was the development of the store in Oxford Street known as the 'Pantheon': Minute Book 69, 8 July 1937.

17. Prudential Assurance Company. *Reports* of Annual General Meetings, 11 March 1937 and 9 March 1939.
18. Prudential Archives. Prudential Assurance Company. London Films boxfiles.
19. Prudential Archives. London Films boxfile I. 'Report of Montagu Marks', July 1934.
20. Martin Stockham, *The Korda Collection* (1992), p.30.
21. Prudential Archives. London Films boxfile 1. P.C. Crump, Memorandum entitled 'Films', 2 August 1938.
22. Assistant Secretary C. Allan Ray was also much involved with monitoring the affairs of London Films; among those deputised to go to Denham were Leslie Brown and Trevor Eldrid; the latter recorded his impressions in an article called 'When the Shooting Had to Stop' for the *Prudential Bulletin*.
23. Prudential Archives. British Widows' Guardbook containing policies and agents' literature. British Widows, founded in 1902, offered industrial assurance through the medium of the weekly purchase from its agents of tea and cocoa, a portion of the price of these necessities being the premium.
24. Prudential Archives. Ireland boxfile. Memoranda and other documents relating to the establishment of the Amalgamated Company. Prudential Assurance Company. Extra-ordinary General Meeting, 29 June 1939.
25. Prudential Archives. These details are taken from transcripts of a number of recorded interviews with retired Prudential staff.
26. The Prudential restored Staple Inn in 1937, inserting steel reinforcements to support the timbered Holborn frontage.

Chapter Sixteen: The Prudential 'Family' and the Second World War

1. Peter Calvocoressi and Guy Wint, *Total War* (1974), p.136.
2. F.W. Morgan said that this amounted to 'never a penny less' than £600,000 a year. Time in the forces also counted for promotion and pensions purposes.
3. Prudential Archives. Prudential Assurance Company. Minute Book 72, 7 September 1939.
4. This applied to all policies taken out before 1 September 1939 on which at least two years' premiums had been paid and which assured sums under £50. Special concessions were available for policies assuring more than that. On new policies (those issued after 1 September 1939) restrictions were imposed: the benefit payable on death was limited, but an optional extra premium would assure full benefit.
5. In the course of the war some 640,000 policies would be issued and more than £3,000,000 collected on the Government's behalf.
6. Prudential Archives. Prudential Assurance Company. WWII boxfile. 'ARP. Staff Arrangements'. April 1940.
7. Prudential Archives. File on K.A. Usherwood; G.L. Hosking, *Salute to Service*, privately published by Prudential Assurance Company (1947), pp.9–10.
8. Prudential Archives. Prudential Assurance Company. Chairman's Speech, *Report* of Annual General Meeting, 2 April 1943.
9. See Chapter Fifteen: 'Strong roots, strong tree ...' for the creation of the Irish Amalgamation Company.
10. Prudential Archives. Prudential Assurance Company. Kennet Committee file. Letter from F.W. Morgan to C.B. Crabbe, Industrial Commissioner's Office, 30 July 1942.
11. Prudential Archives. Prudential Assurance Company. Kennet Committee file. 'The 1st Report of the Prudential (Kennet) Committee No. 1', signed by Sir George Barstow, 5 April 1943.

12. Hosking, *op. cit.*, p.43.

13. M. Broady, 'The Growth of the Residential Area' in *A Survey of Southampton and Its Region*, ed. F.S. Monkhouse (1964), pp.246–55.

14. Prudential Archives. Written account by Miss Elizabeth Rudd of Dundee, 1994, to whom thanks are due.

15. Hosking, *op. cit.*, p.48.

16. Calvocoressi and Wint, *op. cit.*, p.136.

17. *Ibis Magazine*, Vol.67 (Nov 1944), p.1.

18. Prudential Archives. Prudential Assurance Company. F.W. Morgan's Christmas letter to Prudential men in the forces and prison camps, 1942.

19. Hosking, *op. cit.*, pp.77–78. *Prudential Bulletin* (1947), Overseas Number.

20. *Ibis Magazine*, Vol. 65 (March 1942), p.29.

21. Hosking, *op. cit.*, p.76.

22. Prudential Archives. Transcript of an interview with Sid Proudley and Stan Le Cornu.

23. Prudential Archives. Prudential Assurance Company. Chairman's Speech, *Report* of Annual General Meeting, 3 March 1942, gives a figure of £392,921; the same for 1946 gives one of £571,821. See also *Prudential Bulletin*, Vol. 29 (January 1947), p.24.

24. *Prudential Bulletin* (1947), Overseas Number.

25. Prudential Archives. Transcript of an interview with Edward Goddard, then a member of the Overseas Life Department at Chief Office.

26. Prudential Archives. See *Annual Report and Accounts* for the relevant years; also *Prudential Bulletin* (1947), Overseas Number.

27. Prudential Archives. Prudential Assurance Company. *Report* of Annual General Meeting, 4 April 1946.

28. Prudential Archives. Prudential Assurance Company. *Report* of Annual General Meeting, 4 April 1945.

29. Prudential Archives. Prudential Assurance Company. WWII boxfile. F.W. Morgan's Christmas letter to Prudential men in the forces and prison camps, 1942.

30. Prudential Archives. Prudential Assurance Company. *Report* of Annual General Meeting, 2 April 1942, p.6.

31. Papers relating to Cockington Forge are lodged with Lovell White Durrant of Holborn Viaduct, London.

32. Several men (including John Maxted and Geoff Haslam, who make their appearance farther on) had the experience of being made Lieut.-Colonel or Major in their respective military roles, and of receiving soon after letters from the Prudential informing them of promotion to second-class clerks! Transcripts of interviews with the above, and notes contributed by Ronald Skerman.

33. Prudential Archives. Transcript of an interview with Wyn Cunnah.

34. *Prudential Bulletin* (1947), Overseas Number.

SECTION FIVE

Chapter Seventeen: Into a New Era

1. As early as 1 July 1940 an editorial in *The Times* declared that the problem of a new order after victory was 'social as well as international', and could not be 'based on privilege whether the privilege be that of a country, of a class or of an individual'. Churchill himself, in a Prime Ministerial broadcast in 1943, said, 'We must establish

on broad and solid foundations a National Health Service ...' and spoke of 'national compulsory insurance for all classes for all purposes from the cradle to the grave'. Quoted in Martin Gilbert, *Winston S. Churchill*, Vol. VII: *Road to Victory 1941–1945* (1986), p.367.

2. Over 100,000 copies of the Report were sold in the first month, and some 635,000 overall, with a paperback edition for the armed forces.

3. The Act begins with the declaration that; 'Every person who, on and after the appointed day, being over school-leaving age and under pensionable age, is in Great Britain and fulfils such conditions as may be prescribed as to residence in Great Britain, shall become insured under this Act and thereafter continue to be insured throughout his life under this Act.' The school-leaving age was 16 and pensionable age 60 for women and 65 for men.

4. *Report on Social Assurance and Allied Services*. Cmnd. 6404 (The 'Beveridge Report'). See 'Memorandum of the Evidence by the National Conference of Industrial Assurance Approved Societies', p.50.

5. *Ibid.*, pp.250–51. The earnings of the 'average' Prudential agent were said to be £3 15s 3d as Fixed Salary, 11s 11d for Approved Society work, 4s 8d as Ordinary Branch commission, 5s 4d as General Branch commission, and 16s 2d as bonus from the profit-sharing scheme, making a total of £5 13s 4d.

6. *Prudential Bulletin*, September 1948 (Supplement).

7. Three other pieces of legislation – the Family Allowance Act 1945, the National Insurance (Industrial Injuries) Act 1947 (which affected general insurance business by taking over workmen's compensation insurance), and the National Assistance Act 1948 (which provided a safety net against destitution for the inevitable few not included under other Acts) – are usually classed with these two major Acts. The Assurance Companies Act 1946 was a separate attempt to protect policyholders from hastily formed and unsound companies, and to prevent insolvency. As the Prudential already conformed to its standards, it is not included in this discussion of legislation.

8. Beveridge Report, pp.273–76. In 1942 the life offices (including the Prudential) that had given evidence to the Beveridge Commission formed a Committee to keep abreast of matters likely to affect them, with Frank Morgan of the Prudential as Chairman.

9. *Prudential Bulletin*, July 1949, p.62.

10. *Prudential Bulletin*, 3 May 1949 (Supplement).

11. Further to this assertion, in an address to the staff in September 1949 Morgan cited a meeting he had attended with the general managers of five of the other offices and six Labour MPs. On that occasion it was asserted that the funds were necessary to a planned economy, and that the conservative investment policy of the life offices kept them from investing in enterprises that they did not consider sound (p.7). On asking how the policyholders could be said to be better off if their funds were in future diverted into riskier state-approved investments, the life office representatives were told that their position would be improved 'because the State would guarantee their contracts'. Prudential Archives. See 'Nationalisation and the Staff'.

12. A lasting record of it was the book compiled by R.W. Barnard of the Chief Office Publicity Department and privately printed. *A Century of Service. A History of the Prudential 1848–1948* (1948).

13. *Prudential Bulletin*, July 1947, pp.14, 64.

14. 'Nationalisation and the Staff', September 1947, p.12. The Prudential's campaign was orchestrated by Kenneth Usherwood. The young Desmond Craigen (a future

Deputy Chairman) had his 'Circus' (advanced training scheme) condensed so that he could be seconded to the ILOA as Liaison Officer for the South Central Region. Prudential Archives. Transcript of an interview with Desmond Craigen.

15. Prudential Archives. Prudential Assurance Company. *Report* of Annual General Meeting, 11 May 1950, p.12.

16. *Industrial Assurance. A Reasoned Reply by the Industrial Life Offices to the Labour Party's Proposals*, February 1950, p.5.

17. The ILOA was not the only body that put up a fight. Tate and Lyle's 'Mr Cube' campaign on behalf of the threatened sugar-refining industry put a drawing on every packet and took the nationalisation issue into virtually every household in the country.

18. Prudential Archives. Prudential Assurance Company. *Report* of Annual General Meeting, 10 May 1951, p.14.

19. There are numerous entries about mass meetings, negotiations and alterations to pay and conditions. See the volumes of the *Prudential Staff Gazette* for the years 1951 to 1956. (For the march to Chief Office, see the edition of 20 October 1952.) See also the *Prudential Bulletin* for the same years.

20. Prudential Archives. Transcript of an interview with W.G. Haslam.

21. F.M. Redington, 'Review of the Principles of Life Office Valuations', *Journal of the Institute of Actuaries*, April 1952.

22. F.M. Redington, 'The Rebirth of Terminal Bonus – A Historical Note' in *Rambles Through the Actuarial Countryside* (1986), p.507. See also 'New Departures in Bonus Policy' in the same volume.

23. Papers relating to the sequestration and the settlement of the Prudential's affairs in Egypt are in unsorted boxfiles in the Prudential Archives.

24. Papers relating to the nationalisation of the Prudential's interests in India are in unsorted boxfiles in the Prudential Archives.

25. When L.A. Williams died in 1957 he was succeeded as Manager for Malaya by R.A. Blyth, who had formerly been in India. In the 1950s and 1960s the system evolved in which 'Inspectors' supervised teams or 'syndicates' of agents, with outstanding success. See transcripts of interviews with Messrs Wee Swee Cheng, Tan Kok Sun, Khoo Teng Hooi and Ma Kee Meng in the Prudential Archives.

26. Papers relating to the cessation of business in Ceylon are in unsorted boxfiles in the Prudential Archives.

27. Prudential Archives. Prudential Assurance Company. Annual General Meeting, 31 December 1961, p.5. Two brief quotations from Chairman's Speeches are interesting. Regarding the Ordinary Branch's Family Income and Mortgage Protection policies, it was noted that 'The emphasis in these policies is on death cover rather than on investment and the growth in their popularity has been an outstanding feature of the last decade' (12 May 1960). Of the Industrial Branch in the same year it was said that 'Although the provision of death cover is still a basic purpose of industrial assurance ... the public are increasingly attracted to policies which combine saving with death cover' (31 December 1960).

28. Prudential Archives. Transcript of an interview with the late John Maxted.

29. G. Clayton and W.T. Osborn, *Insurance Company Investment* (1965), pp.105–06.

30. Clayton and Osborn, *op. cit.*, p.177.

31. Prudential Archives. Transcript of a recorded interview with Leslie Brown. Anthony Sampson, *The Anatomy of Britain* (1965), p.11. Page 462 offers a sketch of Leslie Brown, 'sometimes talked of as the most powerful man in the City'. Transcript of an

interview with Peter Macey. Mr Macey, who worked under him, recalls with awe how he could reconcile whole series of figures called out by three clerks from statements two feet long, and unfailingly identify where a column was £2 or £3 out.

32. Sampson, *op. cit.*, pp.463–64.

33. Prudential Archives. Ronald E. Artus, 'A Case Study prepared at the Prudential Assurance Company Limited for the Committee to Review the Functioning of Financial Institutions under the Chairmanship of The Rt Hon Sir Harold Wilson, KG, OBE, MP', November 1978, pp.12–13.

34. Moracrest, which the Prudential established in 1976 together with the Midland Bank and the Gas Corporation Pension Fund, had a similar aim. In 1976, the Prudential would become one of several hundred institutions to establish Equity Capital for Industry in the wake of the 1974 Stock Market collapse.

35. Artus, *op. cit.*, p.18; Clayton and Osborn, *op. cit.*, pp.184–85; Prudential Assurance Company, Report and Accounts for the years 1954 to 1960. Later, in 1972, together with other insurance companies, the Prudential exchanged some of these interests for shares in the Throgmorton Trust, which specialised in small and medium-sized companies.

36. Artus, *op. cit.*, p.15.

37. Radcliffe Committee on the Working of the Monetary System (Cmnd. 827) and Minutes of Evidence (2 Vols.), 1958.

38. In only two companies did the Prudential hold a controlling interest. One was the wholly owned subsidiary Prudential Nominees, which held trustee investments and those of the staff pension funds. The other was the North Central Wagon and Finance Company, the interest in which was sold in 1959.

39. Prudential Archives. Transcript of a recorded interview with Leslie Brown.

40. See *The Times*, 2 August 1956, pp.8–9. Sampson, *op. cit.* pp.409–10 relates the Docker story; see also newspaper comment in the Prudential Archives, Griffiths Guardbook.

41. The Prudential was viewed as 'the absolutely dominant force in institutional investment' in the 1950s and 'Alan [sic] Ray – high principled, calm, sensible, much-respected – seemed to encapsulate that institution's very best qualities'. David Kynaston, *Casenove & Co. A History* (1991), p.250.

42. Some might see the Prudential's action as the catalyst in paving the way, following the retirement of Sir Leslie Gamage, for the rise of Arnold Weinstock and the renaissance of GEC as an electronics colossus.

Chapter Eighteen: Against a Backdrop of Change

1. *Prudential Bulletin*, January and February 1952.

2. *Prudential Bulletin*, March 1953.

3. *Ibid.*

4. *Prudential Bulletin* (1952), Overseas Number.

5. *Prudential Bulletin,* February 1955.

6. Prudential Archives. Prudential Assurance Company. 'Report of the Committee set up to examine the Chief Actuary's proposals relating to the introduction of an intermediate class of Industrial Branch business', October 1964.

7. Prudential Archives. Prudential Assurance Company. 'Report of the Working Committee appointed in December 1957 to discuss Field Staff Remuneration'.

8. Prudential Archives. Prudential Assurance Company. 'Report of the Committee set up to examine Yardstick and debit expansion rate', November 1966.

9. Prudential Archives. Prudential Assurance Company. 'Report of a Study undertaken by Dr Robert Rosenfeld of the Centre for Corporate Strategy and Change, as part of a three-year research project on the Management of Strategy and Operational Change' ('CCSC Report'), 1989, p.17.

10. Prudential Archives. Prudential Assurance Company. 'Report of the Committee set up to review the Company's existing Field Staff Organisation', November 1965.

11. Sir John Mellor represented the second generation of his family to serve on the Prudential Board. He took a great interest in Ibis doings. He was a keen gardener and each spring invited the Ibis Horticultural Society to view the breathtaking display of daffodils at his Andover estate. He sometimes wrote on gardening for the *Ibis Magazine* as 'J.S.P.M.'.

12. Prudential Archives. Prudential Assurance Company. Training and management reports.

13. Prudential Archives. *Ibid.* See also transcripts of interviews with Peter Macey, Arthur Metcalf, Jack Smartt, and notes of an interview with Jill Fowler.

14. Prudential Archives. Prudential Assurance Company. Chairman's Statement, *Report of Annual General Meeting*, 15 April 1970. It was estimated that the cost of field staff training and the conversion of millions of policies cost the Company about £1,500,000.

15. Clive Jenkins, *All Against the Collar* (1990), pp.113–16.

16. Prudential Archives. Transcript of interviews with Peter Macey, Jack Smartt and others. See also CCSC Report, pp.26–27. The productivity scheme '… gave the staff some reward for accepting change' – the change in question being the introduction of the first major computer systems for life insurance. But the scheme did not distinguish between productivity derived from changing work practices and that resulting from an increase in overall insurance business. By the end of the 1970s, with a revived economy and business on the rise, the Prudential's pay levels were also ascending to unforeseen heights. An end to the scheme was sought but it was not until 1986 that it was finally done away with.

17. With nearly 5,000 people employed there, Holborn Bars was virtually a town in terms of its self-sufficiency and the facilities it contained. The Estate Department of Chief Office still employed over 300 people, mainly skilled tradesmen, to service and decorate Holborn Bars, the regional offices and the host of other Prudential properties. Many of these were residential flats, some of which were let to members of the staff. The standard of workmanship was extremely high, the Company preferring to maintain and administer its own properties to ensure the best relations with its tenants. See also the transcript of an interview with Dennis Martin in the Prudential Archives.

18. Prudential Archives. Transcript of an interview with Jack Smartt.

19. Prudential Archives. Notes of an interview with Jill Fowler.

20. *Ibis Magazine*, Vol. XC, January 1967.

21. Prudential Archives. Transcript of an interview with Barry Serjent.

22. F.B. Corby, 'The UK Insurance Company Market – Now and in the Future'. Speech to the 10th Annual Insurance Conference of the Association of Insurance and Financial Analysts, p.2.

23. Prudential Archives. Notes of an interview with Sir Brian Corby.

24. Prudential Archives. 'The Mercantile and General Reinsurance Company 1907–1967'. Unpublished history, n.d.

25. The neo-Gothic Minster Court, designed by GMW Partnership, is one of the City's more dramatic office developments. It has been widely photographed and recently

provided the setting for the character Cruella de Ville in the new version of the film *101 Dalmatians*.

26. Prudential Archives. Prudential Assurance Company. Chairman's Statement, *Report of Annual General Meeting*, 12 April 1973.

27. The FLQ kidnappings and murders in 1970 shocked all Canada, but it was the stated intentions of the Parti Québecois which gave foreign companies, including the Prudential, considerable unease. Many abandoned Montreal for Toronto and other centres. The Manager of Prudential operations in Canada at this time was Arthur Boddiley, sent from London to take over on the retirement of the Canadian Hartley McNairn in 1964. It was assumed that the Prudential's British links made it a potential terrorist target. To safeguard the records of the life business, this was moved to Kitchener, Ontario, in 1974. Prudential Archives. Transcript of interviews with Arthur Boddiley, Iain Mair, John Rowan and Michael Beck.

28. Prudential Archives. Prudential Assurance Company. Chairman's Statement, *Report of Annual General Meeting*, 13 April 1972.

29. Prudential Archives. File on the Compagnie d'Assurance L'Escaut.

30. Prudential Archives. Prudential Assurance Company. Chairman's Statements, *Reports of Annual General Meetings*, 15 April 1971 and 10 April 1974.

31. Prudential Corporation. Group Secretarial department 'Black Books'. Sir Brian Corby recalls that the Prudential was criticised for purchasing Vavasseur, the critics claiming that the acquisition was 'opportunistic'.

32. Prudential Archives. Prudential Assurance Company. Chairman's Statement, *Report of Annual General Meeting*, 10 April 1975.

33. *Ibid.*

34. Prudential Archives. Ron Artus to Edward Hatchett, 31 March 1982; Edward Hatchett's Memorandum as dictated to Ron Artus, 15 April 1982. See also *Investors' Chronicle*, 31 January 1975. Mr Hatchett and Mr Artus, however, are agreed that the Bank of England neither initiated nor oversaw the institutional investors' action (Ron Artus to the author, 4 September 1997).

35. Prudential Archives. Transcript of an interview with Alex Davis.

36. From about this time the Company started to commission surveys on a regular basis to track the perceptions of the public and to conduct market research generally. Several firms were used, chosen for their expertise in specific fields, i.e. MORI on opinion surveys.

37. Prudential Archives. Prudential Assurance Company. Chairman's Statement, *Report of Annual General Meeting*, 13 May 1977.

38. Prudential Archives. Transcript of an interview with Geoffrey Haslam. Notes of an interview with Sir Brian Corby.

39. Prudential Archives. Transcript of an interview with Geoffrey Haslam.

Appendix One
Tables

COST OF LIVING INDEX, 1919–1994

Year	Cost of Living Index December (1918 = 100)	Change % In Year	Change % Five-year Average	Year	Cost of Living Index December	Change % In Year	Change % Five-year Average
1919	102.3	2.3	–	1958	156.0	1.8	3.9
1920	122.3	19.6	–	1959	156.0	0.0	3.1
1921	90.5	–26.0	–	1960	158.9	1.8	2.3
1922	81.8	–9.5	–	1961	165.8	4.4	2.5
1923	80.5	–1.7	–4.3	1962	170.2	2.6	2.1
1924	82.3	2.3	–4.3	1963	173.3	1.9	2.1
1925	80.5	–2.2	–8.0	1964	181.7	4.8	3.1
1926	81.4	1.1	–2.1	1965	189.8	4.5	3.6
1927	76.8	–5.6	–1.3	1966	196.8	3.7	3.5
1928	76.4	–0.6	–1.0	1967	201.6	2.5	3.4
1929	75.9	–0.6	–1.6	1968	213.6	5.9	4.3
1930	70.5	–7.2	–2.6	1969	223.6	4.7	4.2
1931	67.3	–4.5	–3.7	1970	241.2	7.9	4.9
1932	65.0	–3.4	–3.3	1971	263.0	9.0	6.0
1933	65.0	0.0	–3.2	1972	283.1	7.7	7.0
1934	65.5	0.7	–2.9	1973	313.1	10.6	7.9
1935	66.8	2.1	–1.1	1974	373.0	19.1	10.8
1936	68.6	2.7	0.4	1975	465.8	24.9	14.1
1937	72.7	6.0	2.3	1976	536.0	15.1	15.3
1938	70.9	–2.5	1.8	1977	601.1	12.1	16.3
1939	78.6	10.9	3.7	1978	651.5	8.4	15.8
1940	88.6	12.7	5.8	1979	763.9	17.2	15.4
1941	91.4	3.1	5.9	1980	879.4	15.1	13.5
1942	90.9	–0.5	4.6	1981	985.3	12.0	12.9
1943	90.5	–0.5	5.0	1982	1038.6	5.4	11.6
1944	91.4	1.0	3.0	1983	1093.8	5.3	10.9
1945	92.3	1.0	0.8	1984	1143.9	4.6	8.4
1946	92.7	0.5	0.3	1985	1209.0	5.7	6.6
1947	95.7	3.2	1.0	1986	1253.9	3.7	4.8
1948	100.4	4.9	2.1	1987	1300.3	3.7	4.6
1949	103.9	3.5	2.6	1988	1388.4	6.8	4.9
1950	107.2	3.2	3.0	1989	1495.4	7.7	5.5
1951	120.1	12.0	5.3	1990	1635.1	9.3	6.2
1952	127.8	6.3	6.0	1991	1708.1	4.5	6.4
1953	129.1	1.1	5.2	1992	1752.1	2.6	6.1
1954	134.2	4.0	5.3	1993	1785.4	1.9	5.2
1955	142.1	5.8	5.8	1994	1837.0	2.9	4.2
1956	146.4	3.0	4.0	1995	1896.2	3.2	3.0
1957	153.2	4.6	3.7	1996	1945.2*	2.6	2.6

* estimated

UK ANNUAL PREMIUM NEW BUSINESS STATISTICS, 1946–1997

Year	OB Individual Non-linked Personal Pensions	OB Individual Non-linked Endt., etc.	Individual Total	Group	OB Total Non-linked	IB	UK Total Non-linked	OB Linked Individual	PPL	OB Total Linked	UK TOTAL
1946	–	–	2.8	0.1	2.9	6.1	9.0	–	–	–	9.0
1947	–	–	3.8	0.9	4.7	6.2	10.9	–	–	–	10.9
1948	–	–	3.2	0.7	3.9	5.1	9.0	–	–	–	9.0
1949	–	–	2.7	0.4	3.1	4.8	7.9	–	–	–	7.9
1950	–	–	2.6	0.4	3.0	4.8	7.8	–	–	–	7.8
1951	–	–	2.9	0.5	3.4	5.1	8.5	–	–	–	8.5
1952	–	–	2.7	0.8	3.5	5.2	8.7	–	–	–	8.7
1953	–	–	2.7	0.6	3.3	5.2	8.5	–	–	–	8.5
1954	–	–	3.1	0.4	3.5	5.3	8.8	–	–	–	8.8
1955	–	–	3.4	0.8	4.2	5.8	10.0	–	–	–	10.0
1956	–	–	3.6	1.7	5.3	6.3	11.6	–	–	–	11.6
1957	–	–	3.5	2.5	6.0	6.8	12.8	–	–	–	12.8
1958	–	–	3.8	3.0	6.8	7.3	14.1	–	–	–	14.1
1959	–	–	4.1	3.1	7.2	7.5	14.7	–	–	–	14.7
1960	–	–	4.7	3.0	7.7	7.6	15.3	–	–	–	15.3
1961	–	–	5.0	4.3	9.3	8.4	17.7	–	–	–	17.7
1962	–	–	5.0	4.2	9.2	9.2	18.4	–	–	–	18.4
1963	–	–	5.7	3.7	9.4	8.8	18.2	–	–	–	18.2
1964	–	–	6.5	4.4	10.9	9.3	20.2	–	–	–	20.2
1965	–	–	6.8	5.1	11.9	10.6	22.5	–	–	–	22.5
1966	–	–	7.7	4.9	12.6	11.4	24.0	–	–	–	24.0
1967	–	–	8.2	4.7	12.9	12.3	25.2	–	–	–	25.2
1968	–	–	8.3	4.6	12.9	12.7	25.6	0.7	–	0.7	26.3
1969	0.4	8.0	8.4	6.0	14.4	13.8	28.2	0.8	–	0.8	29.0
1970	0.4	9.0	9.4	6.8	16.2	14.8	31.0	–	–	0.0	31.0
1971	1.0	11.0	12.0	7.4	19.4	15.0	34.4	–	–	0.0	34.4
1972	2.4	12.1	14.5	8.6	23.1	17.8	40.9	–	0.3	0.3	41.2
1973	2.8	12.4	15.2	10.8	26.0	18.1	44.1	–	1.2	1.2	45.3
1974	3.7	13.6	17.3	16.1	33.4	22.1	55.5	–	5.9	5.9	61.4
1975	3.4	17.6	21.0	14.1	35.1	25.5	60.6	1.4	6.9	8.3	68.9
1976	4.4	19.7	24.1	23.6	47.7	30.0	77.7	5.3	2.4	7.7	85.4
1977	5.9	21.6	27.5	16.7	44.2	32.8	77.0	1.0	8.3	9.3	86.3
1978	11.7	27.7	39.4	16.9	56.3	35.5	91.8	1.6	18.9	20.5	112.3
1979	15.6	40.4	56.0	27.8	83.8	49.4	133.2	1.9	16.4	18.3	151.5
1980	17.8	44.5	62.3	24.2	86.5	61.6	148.1	2.0	19.9	21.9	170.0
1981	19.9	46.6	66.5	26.5	93.0	65.8	158.8	7.8	18.7	26.5	185.3
1982	23.8	55.1	78.9	25.6	104.5	75.7	180.2	2.2	11.6	13.8	194.0
1983	23.7	76.7	100.4	26.9	127.3	72.3	199.6	2.4	12.4	14.8	214.4
1984	38.0	68.3	106.3	22.0	128.3	72.0	200.3	2.4	15.3	17.7	218.0
1985	47.4	53.7	101.1	23.1	124.2	78.5	202.7	3.8	5.9	9.7	212.4
1986	37.3	64.1	101.4	24.5	125.9	78.3	204.2	4.5	0.9	5.4	209.6
1987	51.2	67.0	118.2	25.1	143.3	81.9	225.2	6.3	0.9	7.2	232.4
1988	105.4	80.2	185.6	26.7	212.3	66.0	278.3	10.1	–	10.1	288.4
1989	137.6	72.1	209.7	36.7	246.4	65.0	311.4	13.1	–	13.1	324.5
1990	136.0	95.0	231.0	32.0	263.0	67.0	330.0	9.0	–	9.0	339.0
1991	132.0	84.0	216.0	49.0	265.0	57.0	322.0	3.0	–	3.0	325.0
1992	134.0	79.0	213.0	62.0	275.0	49.0	324.0	3.0	–	3.0	327.0
1993	120.0	74.0	194.0	72.0	266.0	16.0	282.0	4.0	–	4.0	286.0
1994	108.0	80.0	188.0	71.0	259.0	10.0	269.0	7.0	–	7.0	276.0
1995	101.0	71.0	172.0	69.0	241.0	0.0	241.0	3.0	–	3.0	244.0
1996	91.0	61.0	152.0	91.0	243.0	0.0	243.0	3.0	–	3.0	246.0
1997	78.0	51.0	129.0	110.0	239.0	0.0	239.0	21.0	–	21.0	260.0

NOTES

1 In the early years the group numbers are estimates as the DTI returns gave no details of new annuity business until 1958.

2 Prutrust launched in 1968, but until 1987 new business was normally included under non-linked.

3 PPL launched in 1971.

4 In 1978 commission based on premiums instead of sum assured.

5 Vanbrugh loanback scheme enhanced linked business in 1981.

6 In 1984 removal of LAPR.

7 From 1988 all PPL new business has been reported as single premium.

8 Teachers AVC launched in 1989, this is a major contributor to group new business.

9 1997 includes last quarter contributions from Scottish Amicable.

ORDINARY BRANCH FUND – UK ASSET HISTORY 1942–1986

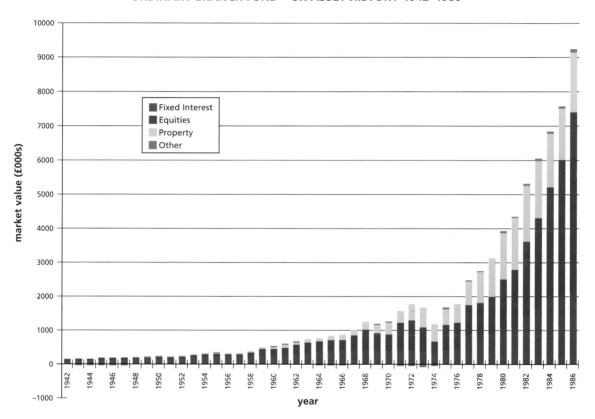

INDUSTRIAL BRANCH FUND – UK ASSET HISTORY 1942–1986

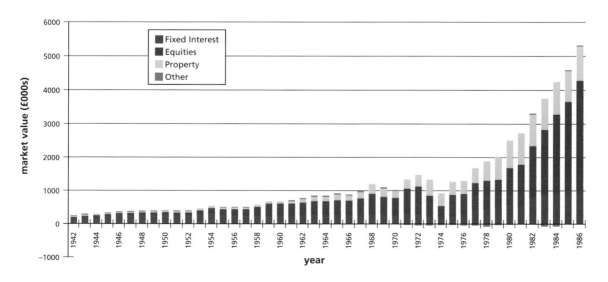

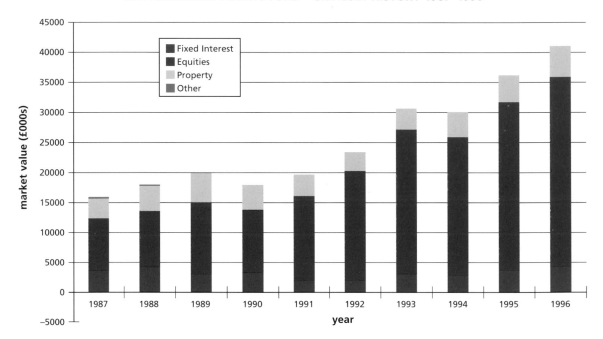

LIFE FUND/WITH-PROFITS FUND – UK ASSET HISTORY 1987–1996

Legend:
- Fixed Interest
- Equities
- Property
- Other

y-axis: market value (£000s) — 45000, 40000, 35000, 30000, 25000, 20000, 15000, 10000, 5000, 0, –5000

x-axis: year — 1987, 1988, 1989, 1990, 1991, 1992, 1993, 1994, 1995, 1996

NOTES

1   In 1989 the Life Fund was split into two (a) With-Profits Fund and (b) Non Profit Fund.

2   The above chart is in respect of the Life Fund prior to 1989 and the With-Profits Fund thereafter.

PRUDENTIAL ASSURANCE COMPANY
Market Value of Assets (Worldwide)

End of Year	Ordinary Life	Industrial Life	General Insurance	Total (£bn)
1961	0.70	0.68	0.03	1.41
1966	1.08	0.83	0.04	1.95
1971	2.05	1.31	0.12	3.48
1976	3.03	1.29	0.44	4.76

PRUDENTIAL PORTFOLIO MANAGERS
Total Funds under Management (Worldwide)

End of Year	Total (£bn)
1981	12
1986	28
1991	51
1996	91
1997 (Dec)	119

Appendix Two
Directors and Senior Management of the Prudential Assurance Company and the Prudential Corporation 1848–1998

Pres   President
Ch   Chairman
DCh   Deputy Chairman
Dir   Director

GCE   Group Chief Executive
CE   Chief Executive
CGM   Chief General Manager
GM   General Manager
JGM   Joint General Manager
DGM   Deputy General Manager
CAct   Chief Actuary
Act   Actuary
Sec   Secretary
JSec   Joint Secretary
MO   Medical Officer

PAC   Prudential Assurance Company
PC   Prudential Corporation
Note: PAC includes the earlier companies PILEA and PMAILA

Abrahams, Michael David, CBE
PC; Dir 1984– , DCh 1991–

Alger, Dr Owen Tickell
PAC; Dir 1850–51

Allanson, James
PAC; Dir 1848–50

Artus, Ronald Edward, FSIA, CBE
PC; Dir 1984–93

Ashworth, The Rev John Harvey
PAC; Dir 1849–50

Baker, Mary Elizabeth
PC; Dir 1988–94

Barnes, Dr Fancourt, MD
PAC; Dir 1884–1908

Barnes, Dr Robert, MD
PAC; Dir 1848–49, Auditor 1875, Dir 1884–1907

Barrand, Arthur Rhys, FIA
PAC; DGM 1920–23, Dir 1932–41

Barstow, John Anthony Tristram, DSO, TD, DL
PAC; Dir 1953–80
PC; Dir 1978–81

Barstow, Sir George Lewis, KCB
PAC; Dir 1928–53, DCh 1935–41, Ch 1941–53

Bedell-Pearce, Keith Leonard
PC; Dir 1992–

Bloomer, Jonathan William
PC; Dir 1995–

Borrajo, Edward Joseph William, MBE, AIA
PAC; DGM 1933–42, Dir 1942–60, DCh 1950–60

Boswell, John Irvine, JP, MD
PAC; Dir 1910–23

Brown, Leslie, FIA
PAC; Sec 1955–64, Dir 1965–77, DCh 1970–74

Burdus, Julia Ann
PC; Dir 1996–

Burn, Sir Joseph, KBE, FRICS, FIA
PAC; Act 1912–25, GM 1920–41, Dir 1941–50, Pres 1941–50

Butterfield, The Rt Hon Lord John William Hughes, OBE, FRCP
PC; Dir 1981–92

Caccia, The Rt Hon Lord, GCMG, GCVO
PAC; Dir 1965–80
PC; Dir 1978–80

Carr of Hadley, The Rt Hon Lord Leonard Robert, PC
PAC; Dir 1976–85
PC; Dir 1978–89, DCh 1979, Ch 1980–85

Chambers, William
PAC; Dir 1848–53

Chambre, Col Alan
PAC; Dir 1848

Clark, George
PAC; Dir 1849–65

Clarke, Harry Gordon, BSc, FIA
PAC; Dir 1973–84, DCh 1974–79
PC; Dir 1978–84, DCh 1978–79

Cole, Thomas B.
PAC; Dir 1856–73

Coleraine, The Rt Hon Lord Richard, PC
PAC; Dir 1961–74

Corby, Sir Frederick Brian, MA, FIA
PAC; DGM 1974–76, GM 1976–79, Dir 1980–95
PC; Dir 1983–95, GCE 1981–90, Ch 1990–95

Craigen, Desmond Seaward, BA
PAC; DGM 1968–69, GM 1969–78, CGM
1979–81, Dir 1980–89
PC; Dir 1982–89

Croggan, William Richard
PAC; Dir 1848–49

Cross, Lt Col Horatio Robert Odo
PAC; Dir 1911–15

Cross, Dr Robert, MD
PAC; MO 1849, Dir 1877–93

Crump, Percy Charles, OBE, FIA
PAC; JSec 1931–42, Dir 1942–53

Davidson, Sir Nigel George, CBE
PAC; Dir 1936–53

Davis, Sir Peter John
PC; Dir 1994– , GCE 1995–

Dearing, Sir Ronald Earnest, CB
PC; Dir 1987–91

Dewey, Ernest
PAC; DGM 1920–34, Dir 1935–50, DCh
1941–50

Dewey, Sir Thomas Charles, Bt, JP, FIA
PAC; GM 1904–07, Dir 1907–26, DCh 1907–10,
Ch 1910–20, Pres 1920–26

Donald, David M.C., WS
PC; Dir 1979–85

Fellows, Derek Edward, FIA, FPMI
PAC; CAct 1981–88
PC; Dir 1985–88

Fergusson, Sir John Donald Balfour, GCB
PAC; Dir 1952–63

FitzGerald, Niall William Arthur
PC; Dir 1993–

Fraser, Dr Patrick, MD
PAC; Dir 1852–93, Hon Dir 1893–96

Freeman, John Anthony, FCA, FCMA
PC; Dir 1985–94

Gallwey, Capt Henry John Windham Payne, RN
PAC; Dir 1848–50

Gardner, Walter Frank, CBE, FIA
PAC; Act 1945–50, GM 1950–60, Dir 1961–71,
DCh 1965–69

Garland, Sir Victor Ransley, KBE
PC; Dir 1984–93

Gay, Thomas Augustus
PAC; Dir 1848–49

Gibbins, Henry James
PAC; Dir 1865–77

Gillman, The Rev James, BCL
PAC; Dir 1850–77, Ch 1852–77

Gillmore, Lord David Howe, GCMG
PC; Dir 1995–

Goodman, Bruce Wilfred, CBE, FCA
PAC; Dir 1970–74

Gregory, Sir Philip Spencer
PAC; Dir 1908–18

Grigg, The Rt Hon Sir Percy James, KCB, KCSI
PAC; Dir 1948–64

Guillemard, Sir Laurence Nunns, GCMG, KCB
PAC; Dir 1929–46

Guthrie, Sir Giles Connop McEacharn, Bt, OBE,
DSC, JP
PAC; Dir 1962–64

Harben, Guy Philip, OBE
PAC; Dir 1918–48, DCh 1936–48

Harben, Sir Henry, FIA
PAC; Sec 1856–74, Dir 1873–1911, DCh
1878–1905, Ch 1905–07, Pres 1907–11

Harben, Henry Andrade
PAC; Dir 1879–1910, Ch 1907–10

Harrison, Charles Henry Rogers, FRCS
PAC; Dir 1848–49

Harrison, George Harrison Rogers
PAC; Dir 1848–49, Ch 1848–49, DCh 1849

Haslam, William Geoffrey, OBE, DFC
PAC; GM 1969, CGM 1974–78, CE 1979, DCh
1980–84
PC; Dir 1980–87, DCh 1980–84

Hatchett, Edward Preston, FIA
PC; Dir 1978–85

Haycraft, Frank
PAC; Dir 1929–32

Higgs, Derek Alan
PC; Dir 1996–

Hill, The Rev Robert Lovelace
PAC: Dir 1849–50

Hogg, Sir John Nicholson, TD
PAC; Dir 1964–85, DCh 1972–76

Holdsworth, Sir Trevor George
PC; Dir 1986–96, DCh 1988–92

Horne, Edgar
PAC; Dir 1848–1905, Ch 1877–1905

Horne, Sir William Edgar, Bt
PAC; Dir 1904–41, DCh 1917–28, Ch 1928–41

Horne, Major William Guy
PAC; Dir 1930–42

Hughes, William, FIA
PAC; Act 1872, GM 1873–98, JGM 1898–1903

Hunt of Tanworth, Lord John Joseph Benedict, GCB
PC; Dir 1980–92, DCh 1982–85, Ch 1985–90

Jacomb, Sir Martin Wakefield
PC; Dir 1994– , Ch 1995–

Jarratt, Sir Alexander Anthony
PC; Dir 1985–94, DCh 1987–92

Jenkins, Hugh Royston, FRICS, FPMI
PC; Dir 1989–95

Lancaster, John Roy, FRICS
PAC; Dir 1920–48

Lancaster, Sir William John, JP, FIA
PAC; Sec 1874–1900, Dir 1900–20, DCh 1910–17

Lane, Hubert Samuel, MC, Barrister-at-Law
PAC; DGM 1941–47, Dir 1948–62

Lawrence, Michael John
PC; Dir 1988–93

Lever, Ernest H., FIA
PAC; JSec 1931–40

Lock, John
PC; Dir 1988–92

Luscombe, Sir John Henry, JP
PAC; Dir 1906–37

Lutwyche, John
PAC; Dir 1849–55

Manning, William Thomas
PAC; Dir 1848–55

Maxwell, John Hunter, CA, CIM
PC; Dir 1994–96

May, George E., FIA
PAC; Sec 1915–31

Medhurst, Brian, FIA
PC; Dir 1985–94

Mellor, Sir John Paget, Bt, KCB
PAC; Dir 1923–29

Mellor, Sir John Serocold Paget, Bt, MP
PAC; Dir 1946–72, DCh 1959–65, Ch 1965–70,
Pres 1972–77

Montgomery, Reginald Edgar, ACII
PAC; DGM 1960, Dir 1965–75

Moody, Peter Edward, CBE, FIA
PC; Dir 1981–91, DCh 1984–88

Moon, James, JP, AIA
PAC; Dir 1915–30

Morgan, Sir Frank William, MC
PAC; GM 1941–49, Dir 1950–70, Ch 1953–65,
Pres 1965–70

Moseley, Herbert Harvey, MA, BCL
PAC; Dir 1935–50

Murray, Angus Fraser, CBE, FIA
PAC; JSec 1964–71, Dir 1972–83

Neave, Julius Arthur Sheffield, CBE, JP, DL
PC; Dir 1982–92

Newmarch, Michael George
PC; Dir 1985–95, GCE 1990–95

O'Brien of Lothbury, The Rt Hon Lord, GBE, PC
PAC; Dir 1973–80
PC; Dir 1978–83

Owen, Sir Ronald Hugh, FIA
PAC; DGM 1959, GM 1968–73, Dir 1974–85,
Ch 1975–80, Pres 1985–88

Petherick, Maurice, MA
PAC; Dir 1953–71, DCh 1965–67

Price, Rees
PAC; Dir 1854–56

Pugh, Richard Thomas
PAC; Dir 1855–85

Pugh, William Thomas
PAC; Dir 1885–1926

Ramsden, The Rt Hon James Edward, PC
PAC; Dir 1972–91, DCh 1976–82
PC; Dir 1978–91, DCh 1979–82

Ray, Charles William Allan, ALAA
PAC; JSec 1940–55, Dir 1955–70

Redington, Frank Mitchell, FIA
PAC; CAct 1950–68, Dir 1968–81

Reid, Desmond Arthur
PAC; Dir 1960–80, DCh 1968–72
PC; Dir 1978–83

Reid, Colonel Percy Lester, CBE
PAC; Dir 1926–59

Reid, Percy Thomas
PAC; Dir 1885–1908

Reid, Thomas
PAC; Dir 1858–85

Richardson of Duntisbourne, Lord G.W.H.,
KG, MBE, TD, PC, DC
PC; Dir 1984–88

Robertson, Sir George Stuart, KC, FSA
PAC, Dir 1937–52

Schenk, Reemt
PAC; Dir 1849–53

Schooling, Frederick, FIA
PAC; Act 1892–1912, JGM 1907–12, Dir
1912–36, DCh 1928–36

Sers, Peter
PAC; Dir 1851–71

Sers, William
PAC; Dir 1851–52

Shillinglaw, John
PAC; Sec 1848–52

Simmonds, John Whateley, JP
PAC; Dir 1893–1911

Skerman, Ronald Sidney, CBE, FIA
PAC; CAct 1968–79
PC; Dir 1980–87, DCh 1985–87

Smart, James
PAC; JSec 1907–14

Southgate, Sir Colin Grieve
PC; Dir 1989–93

Spens, The Rt Hon Lord William Patrick, KBE, PC
PAC; Dir 1948–60

Spurgeon, Ernest Frank, FIA
PAC; DGM 1925–41, Dir 1941––48

Stable, Daniel Wintringham JP, LLB
PAC; Sec 1900–07, JSec 1907–14, Sec 1914–15,
Dir 1915–29

Steet, George Carrick
PAC; Dir 1848–49

Stewart, Alexander Donald, DL, LLB, WS
PC; Dir 1997–

Strathalmond, The Rt Hon Lord, CMG, OBE, TD
PAC; Dir 1973–76

Sutcliffe, James Harry, FIA, ASA
PC; Dir 1994–97

Symmons, Frank P., FIA
PAC; Act 1925–35

Teare, Andrew Hubert
PC; Dir 1992–

Tennant, Sir Peter Frank Dalrymple, CMG, OBE
PAC; Dir 1973–80
PC; Dir 1978–86

Thompson, Alfred Corderoy
PAC; GM 1912–20, Dir 1917–28, Ch 1920–28

Thorp, Rupert Stanley
PAC; DGM 1945–60, Dir 1960–64

Tringham, Capt William, RN
PAC; Dir 1848–49

Tucker, Sir James Millard, QC
PAC; Dir 1955–63

Usherwood, Kenneth Ascough, CBE, FIA
PAC; GM 1961–67, Dir 1968–79, DCh 1969–70,
Ch 1970–75, Pres 1979–82
PC; Dir 1978

Webster, John
PAC; Dir 1849–50

Wharrie, Thomas
PAC; Dir 1893–1917

Wood, Francis Gordon, FIA, ACII
PC; Dir 1984–90

Worthington, The Rev James W., DD
PAC; Dir 1848–52, Ch 1849–52

Appendix Three
Select Bibliography

Bailey, A H, 'On the Principles on which the Funds of Life Assurance Societies should be Invested'. *Assurance Magazine*, vol X (1861).

Brown, W, 'Life Branch Work'. *Journal of the Federation of Insurance Institutes*, vol I (1898).

Burn, J, 'Industrial Assurance'. *Journal of the Federation of Insurance Institutes*, vol X (1907).

Burn, J, *Stock Exchange Investments in Theory and Practice* (1909).

Burn, J, *Vital Statistics Explained* (1914).

Campbell-Kelly, M, 'Large-scale Data Processing in the Prudential, 1850–1930'. *Accounting Business and Financial History*, vol II no 2 (1992).

Chadwick, E, *An Essay on the Means of Insurance Against the Casualties of Sickness, Decrepitude and Mortality* (1836).

Chapman, R, 'Insurance Field Work: Its Light and Shadows'. *Journal of the Chartered Insurance Institute,* vol XI (1903).

Chapman, R, 'The Agency System of Insurance Companies'. *Journal of the Federation of Insurance Institutes*, vol X (1907).

Chester, N, *The Nationalisation of British Industry 1945–1951* (1975).

Clarke, H G, 'A Broad Analysis of the Problem of the Investment of Life Funds'. *Journal of the Institute of Actuaries,* vol LXXX (1954).

Clayton, G, 'The Role of British Life Assurance Companies in the Capital Market'. *Economic Journal,* (1951).

Clayton, G, and Osborn, W J, *Insurance Company Investment: Principles and Policy* (1965).

Clifton, G, *Professionalism, Patronage and Public Service in Victorian London. The Staff of the Metropolitan Board of Works 1856–1889* (1992).

Cox, P R, and Storr-Best, R H, *Surplus in British Life Assurance. Actuarial Control over its Emergence and Distribution during 200 Years* (1962).

Deane, P, and Cole, W A, *British Economic Growth 1688–1959* (1962).

Deuchar, D, 'The Progress of Life Assurance Business in the United Kingdom during the last Fifty Years'. *Journal of the Institute of Actuaries*, vol VIII (1890).

Dohrn, S, 'Pioneers in a Dead-end Profession: the first women clerks in banks and insurance companies' in Anderson, G, *The White-Blouse Revolution* (1988).

Farr, W, *Vital Statistics, or the Statistics of Health, Sickness, Diseases and Death* (1837).

Garrett, R G, *A Century of Co-operative Insurance* (1968).

Gilbert, B B, *The Evolution of National Insurance in Great Britain* (1966).

Gosden, P, *The Friendly Societies in England* (1967).

Hardwick, C, *The Provident Institutions of the Working Classes; Friendly Societies, their History and Prospects, Progress and Utility* (1851).

Hardwick, C, *A Manual for Patrons and Members of Friendly Societies* (1859).

Hardwick, C, *Insolvent Sick and Burial Clubs* (1863).

Hardwick, C, *The Present Insurance Crisis: the Government Action and Mr Cave's Bill* (1870).

M'Candlish, J M, 'The Economics of Insurance'. *Journal of the Chartered Insurance Institute*, vol XXII (1919).

McKenzie, A G, 'On the Practice and Powers of Assurance Companies in Regard to the Investment of their Life Assurance Funds'. *Journal of the Institute of Actuaries*, vol XXIX (1891).

May, G E, 'The Investment of Life Assurance Funds'. *Journal of the Institute of Actuaries*, vol XLVI (1912).

Moon, J, 'Child Insurance'. A paper delivered at a meeting of the Insurance Institute, 12 March 1895.

Morrah, D, *A History of Industrial Life Assurance* (1953).

Nicholson, F, 'The Politics of Metropolitan Reform'. University of Toronto PhD thesis (1972).

Prudential Assurance Company, *Mortality Experience of the Prudential Assurance Company in the Industrial Branch for the Years 1867, 1868, 1869 and 1870*. With observations by Henry Harben, Secretary to the Company (1871).

Raynes, H, 'The Place of Ordinary Stocks and Shares (as distinct from Fixed Interest Bearing Securities) in the Investment of Life Assurance Funds'. *Journal of the Institute of Actuaries*, vol LIX (1928).

Redington, F, 'Review of the Principles of Life Office Valuation'. *Journal of the Institute of Actuaries*, vol LXXVIII (1952).

Robertson, B, 'Pension and Superannuation Funds. Their Formation and Administration Explained'. *Journal of the Institute of Actuaries*, vol LX (1929).

Sampson, A, *The Anatomy of Britain* (1962).

Schooling, F, and Rusher, E A, *The Mortality Experience of the Imperial Forces during the War in South Africa* (1903).

Smith, F B, *The People's Health 1830–1910* (1990).

Supple, B, *The Royal Exchange Assurance. A History of British Insurance 1720–1970* (1970).

Thomas, W A, *The Finance of British Industry 1918–1976* (1978).

Usherwood, K A, 'The Prudential Assurance Company Limited' in Milward, G E, *Large-scale Organisation* (1950).

Walker, R B, and Woodgate, D R, *Principles and Practice of Industrial Assurance* (1933).

Warner, S G, 'Twenty Years Changes in Life Assurance'. *Journal of the Insurance Institutes of Great Britain and Ireland*, vol XII (1909).

Westall, O, *The Historian and the Business of Life Insurance* (1984).

Wohl, A S, *Endangered Lives. Public Health in Victorian Britain* (1983).

Appendix Four
Picture Acknowledgements

The author and publishers are grateful to the following for permission to reproduce photographs and illustrations:

p.4 The Museum of Science and Industry in Manchester Trust; p.6 Mary Evans Picture Library; p.11 Tate Gallery, London; p.20 BMA Archive; pp.24, 42, 94 Guildhall Library, Corporation of London; pp.34, 143, 193 *Illustrated London News*; p.96 RIBA Photographs Collection; p.160 Getty Images; p.163 Patricia Neild; p.164 Lieselotte Clark; p.169 Camden Local Studies and Archives Centre; p.235 the *Daily Mail*; p.299 Association of British Insurers; p.305 Institute of Actuaries.

All other pictures were provided by the Prudential Corporation.

Every effort has been made to obtain permission for the reproduction of the illustrations and photographs in this book; apologies are offered to anyone whom it has not been possible to contact.

Index